Public Places and Spaces

Human Behavior and Environment

ADVANCES IN THEORY AND RESEARCH

Volume 1
Volume 2
Volume 3: Children and the Environment
Volume 4: Environment and Culture
Volume 5: Transportation and Behavior
Volume 6: Behavior and the Natural Environment
Volume 7: Elderly People and the Environment
Volume 8: Home Environments
Volume 9: Neighborhood and Community Environments
Volume 10: Public Places and Spaces

Public Places and Spaces

EDITED BY
IRWIN ALTMAN
University of Utah
Salt Lake City, Utah
AND
ERVIN H. ZUBE
University of Arizona
Tucson, Arizona

PLENUM PRESS • NEW YORK AND LONDON

Library of Congress Cataloging in Publication Data

Public places and spaces / edited by Irwin Altman and Ervin H. Zube.
    p.   cm.—(Human behavior and environment; v. 10)
  Includes bibliographies and index.
  ISBN 0-306-43079-7
  1. Urban ecology. 2. Plazas—Social aspects. 3. Open spaces—Social aspects. 4. Recreation areas. I. Altman, Irwin. II. Zube, Ervin H. III. Series.
BF353.H85   vol. 10
[HT241]
155.9s—dc19   89-30643
[307.3]   CIP

© 1989 Plenum Press, New York
A Division of Plenum Publishing Corporation
233 Spring Street, New York, N.Y. 10013

All rights reserved

No part of this book may be reproduced, stored in a retrieval system, or transmitted in any form or by any means, electronic, mechanical, photocopying, microfilming, recording, or otherwise, without written permission from the Publisher

Printed in the United States of America

This volume is dedicated to the memory of
Joachim F. Wolhwill
friend, colleague, and productive scholar

Contributors

MICHAEL BRILL • The Buffalo Organization for Social and Technological Innovation, Inc. (BOSTI), Buffalo, New York, and the School of Architecture, State University of New York at Buffalo, Buffalo, New York

MARK FRANCIS • Department of Environmental Design, University of California-Davis, Davis, California

KAREN A. FRANCK • School of Architecture, New Jersey Institute of Technology, Newark, New Jersey

JEFF HAYWARD • People, Places & Design Research, 4 Allen Place, Northampton, Massachusetts

GARY E. MACHLIS • Department of Forest Resources, College of Forestry, Wildlife, and Range Sciences, University of Idaho, Moscow, Idaho

JANAEA MARTIN • Program in Social Ecology, University of California-Irvine, Irvine, California

ROBIN C. MOORE • School of Design, North Carolina State University, Raleigh, North Carolina

JACK L. NASAR • Department of City and Regional Planning, The Ohio State University, Columbus, Ohio

JOSEPH O'REILLY • Mesa Public Schools, 545 North Stapley Drive, Mesa, Arizona

LYNN PAXSON • Environmental Psychology Program, City University of New York, Graduate Center, New York, New York

DAVID G. PITT • Landscape Architecture Program, University of Minnesota, St. Paul, Minnesota

ROBERT SOMMER • Department of Psychology, University of California-Davis, Davis, California

GEORGE H. STANKEY • Department of Leisure Studies, Kuring-gai College of Advanced Education, Lindfield, New South Wales, Australia

Preface

This tenth volume in the series addresses an important topic of research, design, and policy in the environment and behavior field. Public places and spaces include a sweeping array of settings, including urban streets, plazas and squares, malls, parks, and other locales, and natural settings such as aquatic environments, national parks and forests, and wilderness areas. The importance of public settings is highlighted by difficult questions of access, control, and management; unique needs and problems of different users (including women, the handicapped, and various ethnic groups); and the dramatic reshaping of our public environments that has occurred and will continue to occur in the foreseeable future.

The wide-ranging scope of the topic of public places and spaces demands the attention of many disciplines and researchers, designers, managers, and policymakers. As in previous volumes in the series, the authors in the present volume come from a variety of disciplinary backgrounds, research and design orientations, and affiliations. They have backgrounds in or are affiliated with such fields as architecture, geography, landscape architecture, natural resources, psychology, sociology, and urban design. Many more disciplines obviously contribute to our understanding and design of public places and spaces, so that the contributors to this volume reflect only a sample of the possibilities and present state of knowledge about public settings.

The present volume completes a trio of volumes that may be considered as a set. Volume 8 dealt with *Home Environments*; Volume 9 examined *Neighborhood and Community Environments*; this volume examines *Public Places and Spaces*. These three volumes address environments that are intimately linked with one another, with homes nested in neighborhoods and communities, which in turn are closely aligned with public places and spaces. The distinctions among these three types of settings are not always clear-cut, so that the 32 chapters in these three volumes offer readers a comprehensive overview of a variety of important environmental settings.

Volume 11 in the series, *Intellectual Histories of Environment and Behavior Researchers*, now in preparation, will offer insight into the environment and behavior field through the intellectual development of some of its most prominent participants. Kathleen Christensen, City University of New York, will join me in editing this next volume in the Human Behavior and Environment series.

This volume is dedicated to the memory of Joachim F. Wohlwill, who passed away suddenly in the summer of 1987. Jack Wohlwill was a close friend, excellent colleague, productive scholar, and coeditor of Volumes 1–7 in this series. He was a scholar and person whose loss will be deeply felt. Jack's interests were wide-ranging and ecumenical, and included a strong involvement in research and policy issues associated with esthetics and preservation of natural public environments. Ervin Zube and I are deeply saddened by the loss of our colleague and friend, and dedicate this volume to his memory.

IRWIN ALTMAN

Contents

INTRODUCTION 1

CHAPTER 1

TRANSFORMATION, NOSTALGIA, AND ILLUSION IN PUBLIC LIFE AND PUBLIC PLACE

MICHAEL BRILL

Introduction 7
Assumptions about Public Life and Public Environments 7
About Public Life 8
The Citizen of Affairs 10
The Citizen of Commerce and Pleasure 11
The Familiar Citizen 12
Public Life and Public Places: A Panoramic Mini-History 14
Loss of Categorical Distinctions between Public and Private
   Realms 20
Intrusions of the Public into the Private Realm 20
Loss of Life in the Street 21
Intrusions of the Private Realm into the Public One 22
   Public Environments Serving Private Wealth 22
   Erosion of Civil Liberties 23
Loss of Categorical Distinctions between Government and
   Business 24
   Loss of Categorical Distinctions between Public Services and
      Private Ones 24
   Nostalgia and Illusion 25
   Segmentation and Loss of Diversity 26
Future Directions of Research, Design, and Policy 26
References 28

Chapter 2

Perception, Cognition, and Evaluation of Urban Places

JACK L. NASAR

Introduction	31
Urban Public Places	31
Cognitive and Esthetic Quality	32
Urban Cognition	34
Urban Imageability	34
Building Recall	34
Relationship between Imageability and Perceived Quality	35
Urban Esthetics	36
A Framework	36
Urban Simulation	38
Salient Perceptual/Cognitive Dimensions	38
Salient Affective Dimensions	39
Esthetic Value	41
Design/Planning Recommendations	48
Future Directions of Research	49
Specifying the Full Lens Model	49
Movement	49
Change	49
Sociophysical Context	50
Public Policy	51
Conclusion	53
References	53

Chapter 3

Farmers' Markets as Community Events

ROBERT SOMMER

Introduction	57
Typology of Markets	58
History	59
Benefits	61
Civic Utility	61
Revitalizing Downtown	61
Assistance for Small Farmers	64
Consumer Benefits	64
Intergroup Contacts	66
Openness and Contact with Nature	68

Functional Requirements	69
Site	69
Shelter	69
Schedule	70
Customers	70
Vendors	71
Products	71
Tradition	72
Organization	72
Linkage to Other Open-Space Programs	73
The Future of Farmers' Markets	74
Desire for Fresh, Flavorful Local Produce	75
Desire for Festivity and Social Contact	75
Demonstrated Social Utility	75
Future Directions of Research	76
References	79

CHAPTER 4

PLAYGROUNDS AT THE CROSSROADS: POLICY AND ACTION RESEARCH NEEDED TO ENSURE A VIABLE FUTURE FOR PUBLIC PLAYGROUNDS IN THE UNITED STATES

ROBIN C. MOORE

Introduction	83
Children's Use of the Outdoors	84
The Child's Right to Play	85
Playground Research Findings	85
How Much Are Playgrounds Used?	86
How Safe Are Playgrounds?	87
Play Setting Studies	90
Play Value, Diversity, and Design	91
Site Planning: Patterns of Activity in Time and Space (PATS)	92
What Is the Play Value of Adventure Play?	93
What Types of Play Setting Support Social Integration?	99
Integration of Children with Disabilities	101
Future Directions for Research and Policy in the Planning, Design, and Management of Public Playgrounds	102
A National Action-Research Program	102
Play Leadership and Animation Training	103
Preventive Risk Management	105
New Media	105
Designer Awareness	106

Public/Private Partnership 106
The Choice 107
Appendix: Play Setting Research Recommendations 107
References 114

CHAPTER 5

WOMEN AND URBAN PUBLIC SPACE: RESEARCH, DESIGN, AND POLICY ISSUES

KAREN A. FRANCK AND LYNN PAXSON

Theoretical and Historical Overview 122
   Definition of "Public" and "Private" 123
   Separation of Sexes and Spaces 123
   Separation of Spheres in the 19th Century 124
   Nineteenth-Century Women in the Public Sphere 125
Contemporary Context for Women's Use of Public Space 126
   Socialization 127
   Household Work and Childcare 127
   Travel 127
   Crime and Fear of Crime 128
   Harassment 129
   Restricted Mobility and Necessary Activities 130
Conceptual Framework for Studying Women's Use of Public
Space 130
   Provision and Management of Public Spaces 131
   Location of Public Spaces 134
   Physical Design of Public Spaces 134
   Use and Users of Public Spaces 136
Future Directions for Education, Policy, and Design 137
   Directions for Education 138
   Directions for Policy 139
   Directions for Design 140
Epilogue 142
References 142

CHAPTER 6

CONTROL AS A DIMENSION OF PUBLIC-SPACE QUALITY

MARK FRANCIS

Introduction 147
Public Space and Urban Life 149

Contents

The Changing Face of Public Space	150
The Publics of Public Space	150
Users	152
Nonusers	152
Space Managers and Owners	152
Public Officials	153
Designers	154
Control as an Environmental Concept	154
Control as a Psychological Construct	156
Control as a Participation Concept	157
Control of Public Space: A Definition and Conceptual Framework	158
Control in the Public Landscape: The Example of Gardening	159
Some Control Issues with Respect to Public Space	161
Private Interests versus Public Needs	161
Public Space as Home	161
Personalization and Public Spaces	162
Accessibility	164
Ownership	164
Safety	165
Conflict	165
Some Design and Management Opportunities for Increasing Control in Public Space	166
Streets	167
Neighborhood Parks	167
Plazas and Downtown Public Spaces	167
Future Directions for Research and Design	168
Conclusions	169
References	169

CHAPTER 7

THE EMERGENCE OF ENVIRONMENT–BEHAVIOR RESEARCH IN ZOOLOGICAL PARKS

JANAEA MARTIN AND JOSEPH O'REILLY

Introduction	173
Historical Context of Zoological Park Development	173
The Contemporary Context of Zoological Parks	174
Design and Environment–Behavior Relationships	175
Animal–Environment Research	175
Visitor–Environment Research	177
Staff–Environment Research	185
Integrating Research on Animals, Visitors, and Staff	185

Future Directions of Research 185
    Methodological Issues 186
    Theoretical Issues 186
    Research Opportunities 187
References 188

Chapter 8

Urban Parks: Research, Planning, and Social Change

JEFF HAYWARD

Introduction 193
The Context for Change 194
Behavior-Based Trends in Park Planning 195
    Diversification 196
    Interpretation 197
    Cultural Programs 198
Case Study: A Large Multiuse Urban Park 198
    Rationale for a New Master Plan 199
    Planning Issues 201
    Research Strategy 202
    Research Results 203
    Applying Research Results to the Design Process 205
Case Study: Lowell, Massachusetts, Urban Historical Park 207
    The Need for Research 207
    Research Strategy 209
    Research Results 210
    Application to Planning and Management 212
Future Directions for Design Research 213
    User Analysis 214
    Design Review 214
    Evaluation 215
    Experimentation 215
    Education and Communication 215
References 215

Chapter 9

The Attractiveness and Use of Aquatic Environments as Outdoor Recreation Places

DAVID G. PITT

Introduction 217
    Significance of Water-Based Outdoor Recreation 217

Recreational Use of Aquatic Environments: A Transaction of
    People and Environment 218
  Outline of Chapter 219
Special Characteristics of Aquatic Environments That Frame the
  Transaction 219
  Physical Characteristics 219
  Institutional Characteristics 221
  Technological Adaptations to Extend Terrestrial Existence into
    Aquatic Environments 223
  The Attraction of Water 224
Characteristics of Participants Engaged in the Transaction 228
  Socioeconomic Characteristics 228
  Culture and Ethnicity 230
  Childhood Experiences 231
  Psychological Characteristics 231
Contextual Influences on Transactions 231
  Psychological Context of the Transaction 232
  Social Context of the Transaction 234
  Physical Context 238
  Managerial Context 239
Future Directions of Research 240
  Trends in Water-Based Recreation 240
  Research Needs 242
References 247

CHAPTER 10

MANAGING PARKS AS HUMAN ECOSYSTEMS

GARY E. MACHLIS

Introduction 255
Key Assumptions 256
The Roots of Human Ecology 258
The Human Ecological Perspective 258
The Human Ecology of Parks 260
People as a Dominant in Parks 262
Modeling Park Ecosystems to Include Humans 267
Future Directions in Research 271
Conclusion 272
References 273

Chapter 11

Solitude for the Multitudes: Managing Recreational Use in the Wilderness

GEORGE H. STANKEY

Introduction	277
Historical Evolution of the Wilderness Concept	278
The Dilemma of Wilderness Management	280
A Generalized Model of Privacy and Crowding	282
The Recreational Carrying Capacity Model	284
Appropriate Levels of Others	286
Appropriate Behavior of Others	287
Crowding as Evidence of Others	290
Future Directions for Practice, Policy, and Research	292
Managing Crowding in Wilderness Settings	292
Future Directions of Research	294
References	297

Index	301

Introduction

The title of this volume is composed of three somewhat slippery words—"public," "place," and "space." Collectively, these terms suggest an image of accessible urban, suburban, rural, and wilderness landscapes. The term "public" connotes the idea that these settings are accessible to everyone—people of a community, state, or nation, regardless of age, gender, ethnicity, physical handicap, or other characteristics. In this context, however, "public" does not necessarily relate to ownership, but rather to use. Some privately owned places and spaces are accessible to the public and some publicly owned areas are not.

About one-third of the land in the United States is publicly owned, and most of it is owned by the federal government (Pyles, 1970). However, these lands are not uniformly distributed. Comparatively little public land is urban; the vast majority of it is in areas best described as rural or wild. Furthermore, the geographic distribution of these public lands is sharply skewed to the twelve western states including Alaska (but not Hawaii). And Alaska accounts for nearly one-half of the public lands in the United States and 90% of the remainder is found in the other eleven western states. The situation is somewhat different in other regions of the world. Long-established and highly technologically developed countries, for example, in western Europe, probably have a relatively low proportion of their land mass available as public places. Or, if large areas of land are in the public domain, such as in Australia, they are often inaccessible or not readily habitable.

Public lands are not always accessible to citizens and users. Historically, much of the public land in rural areas has been either allocated to or usurped by special interest groups such as farmers, loggers, and miners—and frequently it was not accessible to members of the public who sought recreation or outdoor experiences.

The most obvious public lands in cities are streets, squares, playgrounds, and parks. But these settings have often been taken over by groups such as neighborhood organizations, teenage gangs, or street people, with the result that many segments of the public have been effectively excluded from gaining access to urban public settings. And, in some instances, these urban public places and spaces are lacking necessary facilities or are designed so that they are inaccessible to the handicapped or different age groups, thereby denying the broadest possible concept of "public." There are also privately owned areas in both urban and rural environments that function as public places and spaces, such as conservation areas owned and managed by nonprofit organizations and urban and suburban shopping malls.

"Space" and "place" are related terms, with "space" becoming "place" as it gains psychological or symbolic meaning. In Tuan's (1977) words, "what begins as undifferentiated space becomes place as we get to know it better and endow it with value" (p. 6). Thus "space" refers to the abstract geographical qualities of environments, which become transformed into meaningful places as people use, modify, or attribute symbolic value to specific settings.

Expanding on the concept of place and space, Sime (1986), in a comprehensive review, stated

> The term "place," as opposed to space, implies a strong emotional tie, temporary or more long lasting, between a person and a particular physical location. (p. 50)

In a related vein, Canter (1977) stated

> we have not yet fully identified the place until we know (a) what behavior is associated with, or it is anticipated will be housed in, a given locus, (b) what the physical parameters of that setting are, and (c) the descriptions, or conception which people hold of that behavior in that physical environment. (pp. 158-159)

And Dovey (1985) stated that place encompasses ideas of

> the interaction between people and a physical setting together with a set of meanings that both emerge from and inform this experience and interaction. (p. 94)

In some situations, we refer to an open-space "plan" and an individual site within the plan as a "place." Open space is the abstract concept that encompasses places and the undifferentiated areas that link places together. Thus a public place can be a particular portion of public space, a portion that has a specific identity, such as Times Square in New York City or Tuolumne Meadows in Yosemite National Park. To others, mid-Manhattan and Yosemite National Park may also be public places within the larger context of New York City and the national park system, respectively. Thus public places and spaces are found in wilderness areas as well as in urban settings.

Research, design, and policy issues associated with public places and spaces are so wide ranging that, following the pattern of previous volumes in this series, we invited contributors from a variety of disciplines to participate in the present project. As a result, authors have backgrounds in or are affiliated with a variety of disciplines, including architecture, geography, landscape architecture, natural resources, psychology, sociology, and urban design.

The issues addressed in the chapters of this volume cover a broad array of themes, research topics, and design issues. For example, they encompass a variety of public places and spaces, including urban, suburban, rural, and wilderness settings. Thus the first cluster of chapters focus on urban and, in some cases, urban-suburban places and spaces. In Chapter 1 Brill, an architect, pre-

Introduction 3

sents a broad-ranging essay on historical and contemporary issues of urban public places and spaces. Nasar (Chapter 2), a psychologist, considers perceptions and esthetics of urban streets and their associated buildings and homes. In Chapter 3, by Sommer, a psychologist, and Chapter 4, by Moore, an architect, specific urban settings are examined. These include farmers' markets and playgrounds, respectively. In Chapter 5, Franck and Paxson, psychologists, and in Chapter 6, Francis, a landscape architect, treat a variety of urban settings, such as malls, plazas, squares, streets, etc., in terms of access and control by specific users.

The next two chapters consider public places and spaces that have qualities of both urban–suburban and natural environments. Martin and O'Reilly, psychologists, analyze zoos and animal parks in Chapter 7. Hayward, an architect and psychologist, examines research and policy issues associated with urban parks in Chapter 8.

The last set of chapters reflects changes in both type and scale of settings, as the authors examine a variety of natural environments. For example, in Chapter 9, Pitt, a landscape architect, considers the use and management of natural aquatic spaces. Machlis, a sociologist, adopts an ecological approach to natural parks in Chapter 10, and Stankey, a geographer, examines wilderness areas and their use in terms of the concept of privacy regulation in Chapter 11.

Chapters in the volume also vary in the meanings and activities associated with different public places and spaces. Brill views public space as a setting for public life, a theme reiterated—albeit in a different context—by both Sommer and Francis. As might be expected in a collection of papers on public places and spaces, play and recreation are central to a number of chapters, including Moore's review of playgrounds, Hayward's and Martin and O'Reilly's analyses of parks and zoos, respectively, Pitt's discussion of aquatic spaces, Machlis's consideration of national parks, and Stankey's perspective on wilderness.

There are several other themes that run through these chapters. For example, Brill, Sommer, Martin and O'Reilly, Franck and Paxson, and Stankey provide provocative historical reviews of their respective topics. A common thread in these reviews is that of the changing values, meanings, and human relationships associated with public places and spaces over time. For example, Machlis applies a dynamic human ecological perspective in his discussion of national park management, and Pitt uses a transactional framework to explain human–aquatic environment relationships. From these and other chapters, it is clear that researchers and designers must attend to shifting social, political, economic, and cultural factors that bear on the use, control, and design of public spaces and places.

Another recurring theme that appears in the chapters by Moore, Hayward, Nasar, Martin and O'Reilly, Franck and Paxton, Francis, and Stankey is that of research applications to the design, planning, and management of public places and spaces. Many of these authors have multidisciplinary backgrounds, with roots in a design or management field and in behavioral research. Hence, they call for research that relates physical and behavioral dimensions of public settings and for the application of research knowledge to improve the quality of the design and management of public settings.

The chapters in the volume also address an interesting array of environment-behavior concepts, including environmental perception and esthetics (Nasar), privacy (Pitt, Franck and Paxton, and Stankey), accessibility (Moore, Hayward, Franck and Paxton, and Stankey), control (Frank and Paxton, and Francis), and safety (Moore, Hayward, and Franck and Paxton). Frequently, these concepts are related to the needs of specific users of public places and spaces. Access and safety are of particular concern for children in their use of playgrounds (Moore) and for women in their use of urban public places (Franck and Paxton). Hayward points out that safety is also a concern in the design and management of urban parks, and he notes the potential conflicts between different user groups. Stankey discusses the paradox of solitude or privacy and crowding in wilderness areas, a theme that is also addressed by Pitt in his review of aquatic spaces.

There are many ways in which the chapters in this volume can be organized. We elected to arrange them in terms of their focus on urban or natural environments and combinations thereof. The first several chapters deal with urban and suburban settings, such as streets, playgrounds, farmers' markets, plazas, squares, and malls. The last set of chapters focuses on natural environments of aquatic settings, natural parks, and wilderness areas. Of course, several chapters, most notably those dealing with zoos and animal parks, and urban parks, have features of both urban and natural environments. Paralleling this urban/natural environment organization the chapters move from smaller-scale urban places and spaces to larger-scale recreational and wilderness settings.

Our goal in developing this volume was to highlight the importance of public places and spaces in everyday life, illustrate the enormous opportunities for research, open up the possibility of linking knowledge from a variety of public settings, and emphasize the need for sensitivity to environmental design and the application of research knowledge to the design process. The study of public places and spaces is exciting and important and deserves the attention and energy of researchers and practitioners from many disciplines.

IRWIN ALTMAN
ERVIN H. ZUBE

REFERENCES

Canter, D. (1977). *The psychology of place*. London: Architectural Press.
Dovey, K. (1985). An ecology of place and place making: Structures, processes, knots of meaning. In K. Dovey, P. Downton, & G. Missingham (Eds.), *Place and placemaking: Proceedings of the PAPER 85 Conference* (pp. 93–110). Melbourne, Australia.

Pyles, H. K. (1970). *What's ahead for our public lands*. Washington, DC: Natural Resources Council of America.
Sime, J. (1986). Creating places or designing spaces. *Journal of Environmental Psychology, 6,* 49–63.
Tuan, Yi-Fu (1977). *Space and place: The perspective of experience.* Minneapolis: University of Minnesota Press.

1

Transformation, Nostalgia, and Illusion in Public Life and Public Place

MICHAEL BRILL

INTRODUCTION

When this chapter was first requested, it surfaced a set of assumptions I then held about public life and public place. These assumptions probably came from my lifelong experience as a big-city dweller and intense city user, from being an architect, and from the teaching of architecture and urban design.

This chapter is the physical trace of my examination of these assumptions, an examination held in a discourse with colleagues and friends, from much reading, and from analysis of both.

From this examination, I come away with more excitement about this discourse, with some assumptions substantially revised, and with a sense of the long-term transformation of our public life. As well, I see real problems for both public life and public place caused by some of our widely held and often simplistic assumptions and by our common nostalgia for a public life that may have been, at least partly, an illusion.

ASSUMPTIONS ABOUT PUBLIC LIFE AND PUBLIC ENVIRONMENTS

My assumptions at the beginning were:

- That public environments are a category of environments quite distinct

---

MICHAEL BRILL • The Buffalo Organization for Social and Technological Innovation, Inc. (BOSTI), 1479 Hertel Avenue, Buffalo, NY 14216, and the School of Architecture, State University of New York at Buffalo, Buffalo, NY. This chapter grew out of a keynote address given at the 18th annual meeting of the Environment Design Research Association (EDRA) in Ottawa, Canada, June 1987.

from private ones; that government has a special mandate regarding public environments; and that government could induce the private sector to successfully carry out part of this mandate.
- That the term "public environment" includes, as well as physical places: (1) the *public's interest* that *all* environments protect people's health, safety, and welfare, including people of limited and diverse capabilities; (2) the way in which the *public is involved in decisions* about all our environments; and (3) the *delivery of services to the public*, no matter how they're paid for.
- That public environments are places that profoundly affect *public life* and are (1) used for the common good, and for affecting it; (2) accessible to and shared by a diversity of people and open to general observation; and (3) an arena for a social life that can be apart from friends or family.
- That public life is most richly played out in our large urban centers and diminishes in quality and richness as city size decreases.
- That public life is distinct from private life and performs important functions: (1) It is a *forum* . . . where the individual's private pursuit of happiness gets constantly balanced by the rules of fairness and reason directed to the common good; (2) it is *group action* where people come together both to be power, and to symbolize their power; (3) it is a *school for social learning*, where the range of permissible behaviors gets explored; and (4) it is where the Stranger is met on *Common Ground*.
- And, given our penchant for intereweaving and integration, public life is also about learning of all kinds, about work, markets and commerce and, very largely, pleasure.

Because *public life* is what the public environment must support, much of my time was spent exploring the relationships between public life and public environments. Thus, my first thinking and set of readings, scholarly, popular and persuasive, were more about public life than public environments. When looked at as a set, these readings seem to embody a set of coherent ideas and attitudes.

ABOUT PUBLIC LIFE

- The literature of public life is a *literature of loss*—it contains a widespread acceptance of the idea that there has been substantial loss of public life—and although some think it is recent, the idea that we have *already* lost public life was in good currency over 100 years ago. Phrases abound such as "the crisis of the public realm" and "impoverishment of public life" (Sitte, 1889; Arendt, 1958; Sennett, 1978; Bellah, Madsen, Sullivan, Swidler, & Tipton, 1985).
- There is widespread *mourning* for this public life and much *nostalgia* for it, and many schemes have been offered, often by architects and urban designers, to retrieve it. These schemes generally involve the repedes-

Transformations in Public Life and Public Place

trianization of streets, banning the car from the city core, a nostalgic return to the preautomobile age (Tyrwhitt, Sert, & Rogers, 1952; Brambilla & Longo, 1976a,b,c).
- It is suggested that this loss of public life has already had substantial *negative consequences* for our society, and we should guard carefully against further loss if we wish the proper maturation of individuals and the proper functioning of society. Some, but little evidence is offered that this is actually the case (Goodman & Goodman, 1947; Levitas, 1986).
- Most discussion about public life is embedded in the larger *discourse about cities*, reflects our continuing ambivalence toward the city, and is especially hard on its streets. It tends not to recognize that there is substantial public life elsewhere than in the city.
- There is often a *condescending attitude*—the idea that if we Americans want to see how public life and public place is done really well, we must go to Europe's historic urban centers—always, it seems, to the Piazza Di San Marco or Milan's Galleria—and that, if we recreate these, we might be able to have that kind of public life here. I will call this attitude "Euro-Urbanist." Euro-Urbanists, here and abroad, recognize public life as that which happens in urban streets, squares, and parks and tend not to recognize it in other places (Rudofsky, 1969; Tyrwhitt et al., 1952).
- I note that although a rich public life is always considered desirable, it is *seldom described* clearly. The literature generally takes for granted that we know what public life is.
- As well, some of these readings suggest a parallel diminishment of *private life*, and many suggest loss of *neighborhood* life. And there may even be some *mistaking* the loss of neighborhood life for that of public life, increasing the mourning and nostalgia.

What could these ideas possibly mean? Do we not now have public life? Do we not have it here? What has been lost? It is seldom articulated, and then not clearly. The most pervasive and, frankly, appealing image of public life is the one our Euro-Urbanists tend to offer. But I think that image is an illusion now, and moreover, it was already an illusion a long, long time ago—and I think that sustaining this illusion prevents us from seeing our real public life more clearly, and this, in turn, prevents us from using our public resources more wisely.

I suggest this illusion comes from the movies, from historic and romantic fiction, from travel books, from trips to Europe, and photographs in *National Geographic* and coffee-table travel books. We've put together, in a romanticized jumble, a set of images of many forms of public life from many different times: a Platonic ideal of peripatetic discourse on the esthetics of justice in the Greek stoa—combined with movie images of romantically hurly-burly urban street scenes set in a timeless "anytime" from the Middle Ages to the Renaissance—combined with Parisian Boulevardiers, elegantly and daringly dressed, witty sophisticated cosmopolitans, holding court in cafes—combined with Citizen Tom Paine leading a crowd of citizens to the correct action of sacking the Governor's mansion. And this image of a wildly diverse public life comes packaged in a picturesque (and, I think, composite) physical setting, and, of course, with the filth and squalor romanticized or removed.

The public life that has, supposedly, been lost is imagined and longed for as if it were all one thing, when it may well have been several separate strands of a public life, less interconnected than in our popular image of it. In trying to disaggregate this image of lost public life, I see three separate strands, interwoven in our longing into one dreamt composite.

Let me personify these three strands of public life as the *"Citizen of Affairs,"* the *"Citizen of Commerce and Pleasure,"* and the *"Familiar Citizen."*

THE CITIZEN OF AFFAIRS

Richard Sennett (1978) best models the *Citizen of Affairs* for us in his vision of a public life based on *civility*, the activity that protects people from one another and yet allows them to enjoy one another's company and makes it possible for people to act together as citizens in the political and social affairs of the city. At civility's base was the right to talk to strangers while not burdening them with the cabinet-of-horrors of your own inner life, all citizens thus protected by the convention of The Mask of Civility. Civility among citizens helps people to learn to act impersonally, to join with other persons in social and political action, but *without* the modern compulsion to know them as persons.

Starting with DeTocqueville 150 years ago, and more recently Arendt (1958), Sennett (1978), Bellah *et al.* (1985), and others, each and all trace the several-hundred-year transformation of the public portion of life, with most seeing it as a *decline* (or "fall" or "loss"). Sennett traces the complex transformation, emphasizing a loss of civility, in the modern quest for "personality" and an articulatable inner life. Because people started to worry that their inner cabinet-of-horrors would spill out uncontrollably in their interactions with strangers, *silence in public* became the rule, where strangers have no right to speak to each other, where each person has the right to be left alone, a fairly recent right. Thus, public behavior has today become more about observation, passive participation, voyeurism, spectating—and thus knowledge gained in public becomes more visual, a matter of observation, rather than through social intercourse—giving us the modern paradox of visibility *and* isolation, a special kind of Space of Appearance.

But, even with this loss of civility, with the rise of spectating and the decline of verbal expressiveness in public, we are clearly still Citizens of Affairs, for we have not lost the power to come together and to act together. For ill or good, we do act—in neighborhood associations, parent teacher associations, boards of local institutions, stockholders' meetings, town meetings, political rallies, common council meetings, protest or support marches and campaigns, special interest groups—and we routinely challenge public servants, and we often toss the rascals out. But the testing and forming of opinion and the taking of action does not, as it once often did, rest on civility, nor does it happen primarily in the street or square. It now happens in a wider variety of places, which become, for that moment, our public environments, and some of these are not "physical" places at all, but channels for communication.

THE CITIZEN OF COMMERCE AND PLEASURE

The second strand of our image of public life, *the Citizen of Commerce and Pleasure*, remains very vigorous in this nation dedicated, largely, to Consumption as Spectacle. The new "festival markets" and the more temporary "greenmarkets" are doing well in many cities, as are the many new indoor public rooms. But there is, for many, a hollowness, a sense that something is missing. The Rouse Company's festival markets cater to a nostalgia for our images of the bazaars, souks, and open marketplaces of other places—but lack the expressive "theater" of these, for salespersons come and go, prices are fixed, and without the public spectacle of haggling and its entertaining discussion of personal traits, questionable ancestry, prices and values, workmanship, and freshness, buyer and seller are not joined for more than a moment, no one wins or loses, and no interest is aroused for spectators. Thus, there is no chance to build either the satisfying social relationships or the living theater of markets of the past or of more exotic places.

This commerce-and-pleasure strand of public life is carried in an image that comes in a bright, romanticized version we like and a darker one we conveniently forget. The bright vision is of the hurly-burly highly populated street, from one of our period movies, a wild urban street scene. The scene mixes spectacle, entertainment, eating, drinking, and amorous pleasure—with marketing, commerce, and work—with passionate religious and political activity—with exchanging news and information—and being expressive and aggressive in encounters with strangers—Life as Theater.

The scene is teeming, lusty, exhilarating, and wildly diverse. It bombards participants with a surfeit of information, makes demands on all the senses, forces close physical contact, engages you in full-body movement, and has frequent and highly personal verbal and gestural interchange. This image of public life is irresistibly exciting and adventurous. But this image of public life was, of course, only partly true, and then not for everybody.

Streets of the more affluent were far less interesting than this image, and the streets of the poor, often monstrous. And the middle classes rode through the streets in closed carriages to avoid harassment, for there was not yet a police.

Social critics and writers of those times, showing us the horrible reality of the streets of the poor, make it quite clear that part of that public life could not possibly be what we want.

Frederich Engels, in *The Condition of the Working Class in England in 1845*, described this life in the streets and says that his description was "far from black enough to convey a true impression of the filth, ruin and uninhabitableness, the defiance of all considerations of cleanliness, ventilation, and health. . . ."

Charles Kingsley, writing in *Alton Locke, Tailor and Poet*, in 1850, elaborates this for us:

> It was a foul, chilly, foggy Saturday night. From the butchers' and greengrocers' shops, the gas lights flickered and flared, wild and ghastly, over haggard groups of slip shod dirty women bargaining for scraps of stale meat. . . . Fish shops and fruit stalls lined the edge of the greasy pavement, sending up odors as foul as the language of sellers and buyers. Blood and sewer water crawled from under doors and out of spouts, and reeked down the gutters among offal, animal and vegetable, in every stage of putrefaction . . . while above, hanging like cliffs over the streets—those narrow, brawling torrents of filth, and poverty, and sin—the houses with their teeming load of life were piled up into the dingy, choking night.

Clearly not descriptions of a street life of commerce and pleasure, these horrible realities fueled several social movements—pro-public health, pro-reform, and antistreet. Taken together, they fueled an existing anticity movement that White and White (1960) have traced from Jefferson on. Writing earlier than Engels or Kingsley, Jefferson said, simply, "cities are pestilential to the morals, the health and the liberties of man." The social movements' supporters, reasonably, wanted to bring countryside to the masses and promoted environments with less crowding, more light and air, and more contact with nature. In this century, this has been often manifested in a visionary architecture of tall housing towers set in a green and sunny park, and often without streets at all. And we've built lots of these, called everywhere "the projects."

Few chose to protect the street from the reformer's anger directed against it. It has had few advocates, other than for its traffic function, which has grown in importance. And so there is less of a public life focused on commerce and pleasure in our cities' streets and they are used now more as conduits for movement than as public places. They do get used as places when special attempts are made to do so, where local events are planned, like parades, block parties, block-long garage sales, and local arts festivals, but, except for our "urban villagers," there is less use of street-as-public-place and less activity density, much of which has been transferred to our new indoor streets, skyways, and malls.

THE FAMILIAR CITIZEN

The third strand of our image of lost public life I call the *Familiar Citizen*. It is not really about a loss of public life but about loss of a familiar, local, social life, where people are *not* really strangers to each other. It is outside family life but family life is its model. I suspect that much of what we mourn is not really public life at all, not Sennett's civility, not a life of the city, but this—*small-*

scale neighborhood life. And it has eroded because economic principles of organization have, largely, replaced social ones.

These two principles act as polar opposites. A social mode of organization relates and unites people with personal ties whereas an economic mode of organization separates people and things into distinct commodities. Each social relation is unique, personal, irreplaceable; each economic relation is a commodity: impersonal, impartially selected and interchangeable with all others, separating us from other people—Alienation (Diesing, 1962). And every time we go to the supermarket to save a dollar, rather than to our corner grocer, we reinforce economic principles at the expense of social ones.

Except in the small town, some older suburbs, and for our "urban villagers," these social principles of organization have largely given way to economic principles of organization, a world of impersonal market situations. And so, many have lost, or never actually knew, and yet still long for this social mode of organizing life, and may confuse this loss with that of public life.

Further, there are many who feel the loss of, or nostalgia for, an actual, traditional *family life.* The facts are that the traditional family is now a statistical oddity, because family structure and family life have undergone massive transformation. Industrial captialism, along with other forces, altered the family profoundly. Young people leave it earlier; wives and mothers become independent economically; the family is scattered in space, in experiences, and in interests; and as these family-unifying forces are dissipated, its members are more isolated.

In parallel, Karl Marx's notion of "privatization" suggests that people in capitalist societies try to invest more feeling in their private realm of family and close friends because they invest less feeling in their work and its products, which under capitalism are impersonal commodities. But when family life and neighborhood life are both felt as diminished, and in a climate of Marxian "privatization" that seeks exactly those as places to invest feelings, there must be a hollowness indeed. The mourning for neighborhood life *and* for some of family life must reinforce, and may even be mistaken for, the supposed loss of public life—an intermixing, in one strand, of many forms of social relations.

In examining these three strands of our image and reality of public life, the Citizen of Affairs, of Commerce and Pleasure, and the Familiar Citizen, I'd conclude that

- Some of this public life has not been "lost," because we never had it to begin with. Its presence in our minds feels almost archetypal, a happy memory of a public life of wholeness triggered now by experiences of parts of it. (Our festival market image makers seem to be artists of the collective unconscious in the service of commerce.)
- Some of this public life has, indeed, been lost and we can't get it back, because we've changed, and now can't have it, or don't want it. (Much more of public life is now about spectating than about participating.)
- Some of this public life has been lost because it was squalid, dangerous, and unhealthy, and its loss is a good thing. (Engels was right about a lot of things.)

- Much of this public life has been transformed, yet many mourn it as a loss because they don't recognize it in its new forms, or in its new places. (Are expressively punk teenagers hanging out in the shopping mall arguing with the people in the church booth not engaged in public life?) And some of it is not place-based. (Are radio call-in shows discussing dreaded diseases or the Latin-American situation not public life?)
- Much of this public life is still quite with us, and in forms that any person from medieval times on would recognize instantly. (Gorging on fried chicken with strangers at a trestle table at a county fair is archetypal public festive gluttony.)
- Dire predictions about the negative psychosocial and cultural consequences of the loss of our public life have been made for generations, yet is there much evidence that we are actually worse off now than when public life flourished in its, say, 17th-century forms? (Dare anyone suggest we might even be better off?)

I argue that public life here and in Europe has gone through a transformation, not necessarily a decline, and that this has not been recent, but has taken, so far, 300 years. Of course, there will be continued transformation, with public life and environments of a different character than before.

I argue that the public life that many mourn as if it had been lost was never actually here in the first place and thus is an illusion, that many of the public places we've built were conceived of and designed for that illusion of public life, for a diverse, democratic, and classless public, and thus these places don't always fit the public life that we actually do have in our more segmented, pluralistic, and stratified society.

I argue that government has not been successful in shifting the responsibility for providing good places for public life to private enterprise, nor has it been successful in providing for good public places through incentive formulas in either private or public construction, that many of the newly made places for public life either don't recognize sufficiently that we are a stratified, segmented, and pluralistic public, or worse, do recognize it and support only the needs of that public with substantial disposable income.

I argue that we do not recognize much of our public life that really is here, nor do we recognize how much of it has moved into "virtual" space, the space of electronic media, and lastly, that we do not think often, systemically, comprehensively, or well about public life.

There may be a crisis, but it is not about the loss of public life, but about the problems of not paying enough critical attention to its long-term transformation.

PUBLIC LIFE AND PUBLIC PLACES: A PANORAMIC MINI-HISTORY

The public life Americans have now is richer and more diverse than the Euro-Urbanists see or will acknowledge. But it is not much like the high density,

Transformations in Public Life and Public Place

socially diverse one the Euro-Urbanists want or our romantic visions of one, for that public life was not wholly transplanted here, and that which was, often took uniquely North American forms. We've not had the *density* to obtain it, the *physical forms* to contain it, or the *socioeconomic structure* to sustain it.

Early on, our European forebears *did* have a highly interactive and vigorous public life based in the Common Ground of the street and the square, and later, in the park. But by the 1600s, public life starts to be transformed by powerful and pervasive psychosocial and economic phenomena, and the street and the square begin to loosen their hold on some of public life. (Arendt, 1958; Sennett, 1978).

After the great fires in London and Paris, around 1670, these cities were rebuilt by developers given special incentives and authorities. Houses built for the bourgeoisie around open squares became the preferred layout, and for the first time, developers, some of them royalty, were able to have most public activities strictly forbidden from the new squares.

By the early 1700s, the largest European cities were all growing from swift in-migration, developing networks of sociability, money, and power, much of it outside of royal control, and becoming Cities of Strangers. And, by this time, walking in the streets, seeing and being seen by strangers, became a major social activity.

The streets could not always comfortably support this activity, with their wooden sidewalks, often in disrepair, and the violence that often erupted in the absence of a police force, and so large urban public parks were built for these promenades.

Characteristic behaviors in the parks were observation of strangers passing by and the fleeting verbal encounter, much different from previous public behavior where strangers had easily approached one another and had engaged in more sustained discussions, in verbal posturing, and much more political and social interchange in the streets, squares, coffeehouses, and cafes.

By the mid-1800s, the street, losing its attraction for the well-to-do, and always the place of public life for the poor, is seen as an *urban pathology* to be excised—by social critics, reformers, and visionaries, and by those who thought to control the peculiar affinity of the poor for revolution.

America's founders and waves of subsequent settlers came, then, from this background, of a public life already in transformation and with changing ideas about public space. The transported norms were already changing, and the new land presented—demanded, really—more change.

In this new and endless wilderness, the mode of psychospatial expression most natural and native to Americans is the singular identity of free and independent equals. As rebellious colonies, our architecture was freed from spatial dependence on old-world models. The spatial language of even our dense settlements, early on, is mostly about free-standing buildings, with the "interval" or distance between them as our characteristic motif of urbanism, an interval that resonates with the sacredness of our beliefs in private property and free enterprise (Smithson, 1981).

The interval is manifested today by America's zoning envelopes, seldom used in Europe, which strictly mandate that there be front, rear, and side yards and fixes their sizes, making of most structures objects in space. And though we did make and designate squares and commons for public use, much of the open space in our cities is that which is *left over* from the process of building—diffusing any sense that they are outdoor "rooms," especially made to be especially used.

This physical form is in strong contrast to the older European cities, where *public* open spaces were defined first and the city fabric built around them. Camillo Sitte, writing in 1889, offers an image of these older cities as a relatively undifferentiated solid mass with public spaces "carved" out, a set of designed voids connected by streets, providing a rhythmic choreographic sequence, a continuity of spaces, where the street and square are three-dimensional rooms for public life, and public space is the starting point for city design.

In Sitte's European cities, the facades of buildings both *enclose* the outdoor public space and *signify* private space. The facade becomes willing *background* for public space and life, a gesture of civility. (What American architect today readily consents to producing a "background" building?) In most of America, facades do not enclose public space, but only signify private space, and wrap, to enclose buildings-as-objects situated in relatively unarticulated open space.

Robert Gutman (1986) reminds us that most North American interest in the *street* has always been *two* rather than three-dimensional, because speculators, bankers, developers, politicians, and engineers conceive of the street primarily in terms of its capacity to stimulate the market in land values by providing access to each and every land parcel through transportation. This grid of streets, within a larger grid of land, is a way of creating a very large number of small holdings and thus establishing an individual's identity using the land as a sign, making place and identity congruent.

J. B. Jackson (1985) continues to point out the peculiar quirk in our national character that causes us to *over*-celebrate individuality, and to thus minimize the role played by cities, towns, and work communities in the formation of American character, life, and landscape. He says "we forget that Jamestown and Plymouth came before the pioneer farm or the log cabin in the forest, and that *inter*-dependence in America came before Independence."

With others, he points out that there has always been substantial and satisfying public life in the small town and suburb, in its public places and public groups—the churches, fraternal associations, service sororities, public schools, fire companies, and political groups—and he even suggests that there is public life on the franchise strip (Zube, 1970). And, in these places, this life is also served by the bowling team, the softball league, the Little League, and takes place in privately owned places, in the hardware store, and the drugstore that also serves as the post office and bus depot. It is no longer a public life centered on the small town's courthouse square with its historic cannon and large boulder made commemorative with its bronze plaque.

The back-to-the-small-town movement has brought it some renewed attention by designers (Barker, Fazio, & Hildebrandt, 1975), who frequently apply a Euro-Urbanist perspective even to analysis of these small towns and

Transformations in Public Life and Public Place

whose romantic historicism overlooks the changes in the ecology of the small town over time as it has overlooked it in analyses of the large city, where they still suggest that it is only the creation of the great outdoor rooms and indoor gallerias that would make public life more possible.

We will probably build very few more Piazza Di San Marcos or Rockefeller Centers or Toronto City Hall Squares, the great, outdoor public rooms for their success depends on great local density, and we're experiencing a population redistribution that decreases density in many urban centers. Conversely, in those cities where daytime density remains high, the land is often too precious to be aggregated to form any new grand spaces. (Even New York City has been unable to use its formidable powers of incentive zoning to make tradeoffs so as to aggregate small spaces into one large public space.)

We should recognize that, in general, American affluence has spatially dispersed, stratified, and segmented its population, reducing both the density and diversity in any one place, a necessary ingredient for a public life based in the street, square, and park. Our land may have been a melting pot, but, clearly, it seems not to have been a mixing chamber.

As well, the information and communication portion of public life has migrated, largely, into the private realm and has become more nonspatial in character. Our information and communication lives today are substantially augmented by an extraordinary array of information available through many media, by swift and increasingly interactive electronic communications, and by easier access to near and distant places. All these are currently the subjects of explorations to make them more interactive, in networks, and to use them in new ways, in commercial, political, and social action. And many are *not* place-based forms of public life—that is, either these communications and interactions are in the "virtual" space of the airwaves or hard-wired networks or the places in which they take place do not powerfully affect the nature or quality of the interaction.

At the same time, we still have much place-based public life in our small towns, some neighborhoods, and in many suburbs, but we may not see it, for it is not in the Euro-Urbanist tradition of a *high-density* public life lived primarily in the street, the square, and the park.

The fact is we've chosen *not* to live at the high densities that support a Euro-Urbanist public life. Comparing U.S. density with that of countries whose public life is vastly admired, the French have 4 *times* more people per square mile, the Italians *8*, the English *10*, and Holland *15* times as many.

But wherever and however public life occurs, it still maintains its primary goals of spectacle, entertainment, and pleasure; marketing, commerce, and work; shaping public concepts of governance, religion, and social structure; exchanging information; and a great deal of learning from face-to-face encounters with or observation of strangers. Some few examples of new forms of public life, or old forms in nontraditional places, or in virtual place, are

- Many successful newspapers now publish several localized editions, each one targeted to a county or community in its market area, so in addition to carrying national and state news, they can have news and announcements *specific to that community*. Thus, these newspapers take on a more extensive role in local public life. In contrast, colonial newspapers, often read aloud in public gatherings, didn't carry *local* news because it was *assumed* you got that in the street, square, tavern, and marketplace. Those newspapers focused on colonial and European events and on trade and shipping.

- Print and electronic media, once only operating in the one-way broadcast mode, have become fairly interactive. Some currently available examples are "man-in-the-street" interview sections and letters-to-the-editor columns in newspapers and magazines, radio call-in shows, TV interview and talk shows, and now some forms of anyone-can-broadcast cable television. All these extend the numbers of people a single individual may reach and are real forms of public expression.

- The network of airlines and telecommunications devices supports the communal life of special-interest groups of all kinds. The explosive growth of conferences and meetings discussing an enormous range of issues brings together people from substantial distances with relative ease. Attendees self-select based on many criteria such as issues, social strata, job category, or aspiration. The networks developed around these have many aspects of community and often have important public purposes and substantial longevity.

- There is emerging the possibility of a nationwide television-linked, event-based public life. Examples are the 1986 July 4th Liberty extravaganza and its multimedia blitz, with analysis and interpretation before, during, and after; the Live-Aid and Farm-Aid rock concerts with their links of call-in, be there, local parties, and internationalization of spirit; entertainment as politics or real politics in public, like the Tower Commission on the Iranian–Contra issue, actually working in public on TV. (There is, however, substantial danger that this social production of images could be, or become, large-scale manipulation by the media, providing another illusion, one that we are all participating in national life when we are only consumers of images.)

- Theatre groups, publicly funded—through local arts councils, or civic cultural institutions, or sometimes more directly through pass-the-hat—are seen performing more and more in the park, in the street, in prisons, and in hospitals, and being more interactive and interpretive. As well, the tradition of public street entertainment is reemerging with jugglers, singing groups, mimes, comedians, and musicians working the street corners, parks, and waterfronts in many cities.

- There is still substantial individual expression in public—life as theater—witness Mardi Gras, the multi-hued chaos of Venice Beach, people acting out the Rocky Horror Picture Show every Saturday night for ten years, and the elaborate expressive public life centered on the skateboard, the car, and the motorcycle.

- As our shopping malls have aged, they've developed characteristics of community centers, with local groups, causes, and institutions setting up shop in the middle of the malls, with booths for bake sales, save-the-whales or let's-topple-Jane Fonda-and-Tip O'Neill booths, or raffles for the Little League, or a welcome wagon, neighbors proselytizing neighbors. And many malls, responding to other community needs and accepting an expanded communal role, do such things as open early, for groups of elderly who wish to stroll or jog the mall, and provide a place for meetings and public gatherings.

These are clearly public life, and are not only linked to large urban concentrations. The *capacity* for a public life for most tastes exists in many towns and most cities. A public life of substance can be available to everyone, often to each individual's taste, one that does not deny their development of personal style, but does not demand one either. Geographically mobile people try to select a place to live in for its quality-of-life, in which they try to achieve their particular ideal mix of the forms of public and private life.

Amos Rapoport (1969) gives this city-selection process useful physical images in his two settings for life. In one the *settlement* acts as the total setting for life, with the dwelling as part of a whole (as in Latino and Mediterranean towns), and in the other the *dwelling* is the total setting for life, with the settlement acting largely as connective tissue and waste space (as in Los Angeles). These are, of course, much simpler images than the places actually are themselves. And these don't necessarily correspond to the (somewhat simplistic) two physical forms of cities—the European "solid city" of the past, imaged as a solid mass with its public squares carved out, and the more modern new-world "tower city," which favors buildings over spaces. Only the staunchest advocates of architectural determinism would suggest that a public life can be had in one and not the other. Or some Euro-Urbanists might.

There seems, everywhere, the possibility of substantial public life both in old forms and in new ones. Although all our activities are, obviously, place linked, some of the new forms of public life are not really as place based as before—and some of them are very place-based, but in places some Euro-Urbanists disdain (the shopping mall, the atrium) because they're not the street, the square, and the park. And even these three classic forms seem somewhat threatened, and for many reasons—because we have not paid sufficient attention to changes in the demographics that effect public life; because we have retained, doggedly, some assumptions that need reexamination; because the widely held intellectual distinctions between categories (such as public realm versus private realm or business versus government) are not, any longer, so distinct from each other. Some of the loss of distinction is due to intrusions of one category into another, and some seem a kind of blurring, of a lens hazy with nostalgia for situations long gone, and this nostalgia sustains illusions that prevent us from seeing much of the public life there really is.

These are not merely intellectual problems, for loss of distinctions and sustaining of illusions have real-world consequences. We see actions taken by public bodies that impoverish public life, actions that backfire, where the opposite happens of what we wanted because we're not seeing things clearly or don't understand them. These unintended consequences continue to let us know just how counterintuitive the complex system of public environments can be—and how careful we must be of simple solutions in complex systems.

Let me offer some examples of what I mean by loss of categorical distinctions, and nostalgia and illusions.

LOSS OF CATEGORICAL DISTINCTIONS BETWEEN PUBLIC AND PRIVATE REALMS

The two fundamental forms of social relations are those of public life and private life. They are distinct, traditionally, in that private life is personal, controlled by the dweller, sequestered, a sheltered region of life, one with family and friends. In contrast, public life always combined three characteristics: a common-wealth for the common good or benefit, open to general observation by strangers, and involving a diversity of people and thus engendering tolerance of diverse interests and behaviors. With public concerns intruding massively into private life and private interests profoundly altering public life and environment, these distinctions are blurring.

INTRUSIONS OF THE PUBLIC INTO THE PRIVATE REALM

Michael Foucault, in his great studies of medicine (1973), the history of sexuality (1978), and of delinquency (1977) and of madness (1965), explored how power came to be exercised. He wrote about a detailed technology of intrusions into the private realm by the public realm, all developed for some sort of curative policy, to somehow better *know* humanity. These intrusions, by public bodies, gather and organize all kinds of information about people and then control private acts and decisions: what we eat and drink; the stimulants we may use; the noises we can make; how we may keep our lawn; what constitutes legitimate sex; how children are to be educated; what cures are legitimate; how many people may live in a house; what kinds of pets we may have; what houses are built of and how; their plans, shapes, and esthetics; how we take care of them; methods for their protection; and how they may be inherited. All these exceedingly private acts are now framed so as to provide for a public gaze, supporting public control over them.

The word "intrusions" can be used in a neutral sense, where some are beneficial, some not, and sometimes it depends on other factors. As well, there are other public intrusions into private life, some welcomed and some not, but which were once centered in public life. Information pours into your home through public means, through the mails, under your door, through the TV, radio, and telephone, and strangers intrude at your door or by phone, proselytizing, selling something, or seeking aid. These public intrusions, over sev-

Transformations in Public Life and Public Place

eral hundred years of their history, have tended to erase the early, seemingly clearer distinctions between private and public.

Human settlement is now seen as a public enterprise, so every holder of private place must build it and run it so as not to interfere with the public good. All *building and zoning codes*, at their core, do this. These codes are often based on public health concepts that have analyzed the spatial component of disease and wellness. Public health bodies have developed ideas about the systemic relationships among human density, sanitation, light and sunlight, air movement, and air quality. These have become part of public policy, operationalized in codes and thus reflected in every built place, public and private.

The concept that *hazards to private individuals have public consequences* has brought public attention and support to the lives of vulnerable publics—the disabled, children, and the elderly—attempting to ensure that their rights, especially of physical access and use, are not denied through place design that excludes. This concept of hazard reduction, as well, has been used in *life safety and property-safety ordinances*, strongly guiding the design of private place.

The use of homes for purposes in addition to dwelling, such as home day care or home-based work, are often constrained by public standards controlling the doing of work and the offering of services in a home. As new issues surrounding home-based work emerge, they cause the criterion for appropriateness of the home for work to fluctuate. The government earlier permitted and then forbade work at home to prevent exploitation of women and children and is now under pressure to modify that stance to once again permit work at home. We don't know yet how much "gaze" the public will choose to maintain over the homes where home-based work is done.

LOSS OF LIFE IN THE STREET

Based on ideas developed within public health, zoning and code officials and reformers, in the laudable desire to prevent harm to the public, particularly those thought vulnerable, intruded first into the *location* of buildings (through zoning) and then their *design* (through codes). These intrusions took control of the most private realm, the dwelling. Some of these intrusions have unwittingly reduced possibilities for public life. *Zoning-by-use* segmented the city by function and building type, reducing localized diversity and disaggregating community life that had formerly mixed residential, work, commerce, and entertainment in a more random fashion. More recent ordinances welcomed the tower-in-the-green-park super-block concept, and wherever they were built they literally abolished both through streets and their street life.

The street, a traditional locus of public life for the less-well-to-do, and for the cosmopolitan, has been attacked ever since its horrors in English industrial towns were exposed by Engels and others. Changes were made, generally for the better. But the concept of the street as an *urban pathology* still lingers, and much new, publicly sponsored action further empties the street of public life—

public action impoverishing public life in one area in an attempt to bring it to another. Two modern examples of this tradeoff are the *indoor mall* and the downtown *skyway* system. Both were conceived of as ways to revitalize downtown life and have had, in many cases, the opposite effect.

The *indoor malls* built downtown and often as parts of larger building complexes act as a destination, not a naturally occurring passage. When successful, they tend to impoverish street life in their area by vacuuming the street of its normal commercial and service life and reconstituting it in a building's interior, thus privatizing public life and robbing the street of it.

The *skyway* system is a set of bridges connecting private buildings one level above the street. It creates, as it has in at least ten major American cities, downtown's response to being competitive with the suburban mall, "assembling" an urban mall by adding second-level circulation connecting several buildings.

Most of these passageways connect private places to each other, although the passages are, to varying degree, public places. They create a second-level city, a "bourgeois boutiquesville," abandoning the first-level streets to the automobile and the nonshopping, probably poor, pedestrian. This further removes the citizen from the city (Rowe, 1985).

INTRUSIONS OF THE PRIVATE REALM INTO THE PUBLIC ONE

Public Environments Serving Private Wealth

The concept of government permitting, or even encouraging, the private sector to provide public places is not a new one. Over time, methods have been developed linking the public and private sectors in development activities that have as their public goal the provision of more public environments with less expenditure of public money. The older, classical relationship was one where our public environments provided our primary image of place. The new relationship between public and private sectors has tended to reverse that relationship, and one of the results of these joint ventures are many newer public environments that feel subservient to, or seem appendages to private place—a loss of an important physical image about the importance of public life.

Many spaces intended as public environments are now generated through *incentive formulas embedded in zoning laws*. These law permit the private developer a substantial increase in allowable rentable floor area if a public indoor or outdoor space is provided. Thus, public environments are created simply as a "byproduct" of normal development. Because the developers have substantial control over how these incentive formulas will be manipulated, many of these spaces are designed to be used as antechambers, passages, or forecourts to private development, enhancing private value more purposefully than providing public place. Their size, purpose, location, and design are outcomes of other decisions, ones not necessarily made for the public good. They are creatures of economics rather than civic good. They are an automatic by-product of any development that chooses to take advantage of the incentive schemes, and in New York City, after the 1961 zoning law provided these incentives, every development that could take advantage of them did.

Erosion of Civil Liberties

A new phenomenon is the fact that environments made privately but for use by the public are increasingly permitted to restrain public use or access. Since the mid 70s, there has been an erosion of civil liberties when space, used as public space, is owned privately. Early on, in 1946 and again in 1968, the Supreme Court extended free speech to private property if the owners of the place were assuming public roles and functions. At that time, the court reasoned that the new indoor shopping malls were the *functional equivalent* of the old downtown business district and should be treated as a public space.

The Supreme Court's balance then tilted toward conservatism, and in 1975 these laws were reversed, forbidding free speech in such places, and that law has stood when tested, although a few liberal states have used state constitutions to protect free speech on private property used as public space, in shopping malls, corporate office parks, and private university campuses (Warner Jr., 1985).

Erosion of civil liberties also comes in a more insidious form, delivered through the powerful *visual language of design*. For example, private developers in large cities have been offered incentives to provide indoor public rooms. The publicly approved zoning ordinances permit building volume to go beyond that allowable on the site, reasoning that these enclosed public rooms are the developer's "payment" to the surrounding neighborhood for the light and space denied the neighborhood by the building's increased bulk.

Some of these are truly public space and some are privately owned, built for public use with bonuses and tax incentives. In both, the "spirit" of publicness is an issue. Many of these spaces have designs whose cues suggest denial of access to the homeless, those wishing to spend a lot of time there, those not well dressed, or those behaving differently from others. These denial cues include: the simple fact of having doors to a public place, as well as obviously lockable ones; the use of ornate private-sector materials; the social filter of the presence of "hosts," often armed private guards at the entrances; expensive shops rimming the public space; elegant furniture; and sometimes location of the public space in ways that limit public knowledge that there even is one. New York City, responding to complaints about design cues that clearly limit access, now requires signs to be prominently placed stating that here *is* a "public space." But the signs are often bronze plaques or incised into the marble walls, becoming part of the forbidding elegance, not easily noticed, further reducing civil liberties.

LOSS OF CATEGORICAL DISTINCTIONS BETWEEN GOVERNMENT AND BUSINESS

There is a blurring of the distinctions between government and business. Although private enterprise has been made, or agreed willingly to be, a collaborator with public bodies in the provision of public environments, its representatives still have as their primary objective the enhancement of private wealth rather than the provision of common-wealth. Goals become blurred in these situations. And because the provision of quality public environment often seems not a very high priority for government, business interests are often more served in these places than is public interest.

And, increasingly, government uses the same "economic calculus" to make decisions as does business—cost justification, benefit–cost analysis, return-on-investment—all the paraphernalia of an organization that emphasizes economic more than social goals. That, quite simply, *denies* what government is for—as Lincoln said, to do what the people cannot do at all, or as well—primarily actions in relationship to wrongs or that which requires combined actions. Economic calculus guarantees that injustice will be done, for it does not value all people equally and, further, never places a very high value on enhancement of public life. And the government does not even use this economic calculus evenhandedly, invoking it as it does in some situations and not others, acting capriciously, as if a private body. Thus, many former, clearer distinctions between business and government are questioned.

Loss of Categorical Distinctions between Public Services and Private Ones

I assumed, early on, a clear distinction about what public *services* are as contrasted with private ones. But a review of their history shows that to be a false distinction, for the seeming only "naturally public" service has been to service the need for gathering. From the archaic Dancing Ground to its successors, our public squares and plazas, we've always provided public open space for people to come together. (Ancient Spanish law required one of every 15 leagues of land to be set aside for public use.) Yet, the notion of which services should be provided to the public, and by whom, has from its origin varied widely. Some services we now take for granted as being publicly provided are only recently so.

Police, fire, education, sanitation, and transportation all started as *private enterprises* and were given over to public bodies to run when they became less viable economically. New York City's IRT and BMT subway lines were the initials of the names of the private companies that were taken over by the Transit Authority. Universities started as placeless groups of students who hired master scholars to teach them. And now it appears that where these services again might be turned to profit, we're seeing them become, again, privatized, such as private garbage pickup and firefighting services in many towns.

Nostalgia and Illusion

Nostalgia seems a harmless indulgence, and illusions can offer solace in a harsh world, but when both become major factors in public discourse and public action, priorities can be easily skewed. The nostalgia for a lost public life seems often to include nostalgia for something very different—*neighborhood or community social life*—different from public life. Mistaking public life for neighborhood life can create problems, for public life is largely with strangers, and is much about spectating and observation, and neighborhood life, where people are not strangers, is more about verbal interaction. Appropriate design for each of them would be somewhat different, and so mistaking one for the other has consequences.

We have images of a public life that are idealized, that perhaps were never really true, and with the several-hundred-year transformation, may have become illusions for which we have great nostalgia.

The nostalgia for these idealized and older forms of public life prevents us from seeing the trans-forms or new forms of public life in new or old locations, and not seeing them reduces our desire and capacity to support them and sustain them.

Private enterprises, often with the support of public funds, now cater brilliantly to this nostalgia and market illusions of public life, such as in festival markets. These may be fun the first and even second time, but they can be hollow experiences for those who seek a more adventuresome and authentic public life, who don't thrill to two-dollar chocolate chip cookies or T-shirts saying Harborplace, Quincy Market, or South Street Seaport, and who, looking around, must wonder, "Is this all it was?"—and this gives public life a bad name. The inauthenticness of this form of marketed public life stems from corporate sponsorship and control over an entire experience . . . a control that sanitizes and limits surprise, whose economic structure precludes participation by the marginal, experimental, and untested enterprise, and whose corporate dedication to inoffensiveness carefully filters out less desirable people with their less desirable behaviors.

The nostalgia for the Euro-Urbanist public life of the square and plaza has had many of us convinced that more of these are what we should build. The result is zoning incentives and planning concepts that automatically builds an indoor and outdoor square in every development. In New York City, one outcome of the 1961 zoning ordinance was to litter Manhattan's Avenue of the Americas with a startling array of poorly shaped, poorly placed, underused plazas, piazzas, piazzettas, and piazzettinas.

And this nostalgia continues now as design ideology. Architects' recent emphasis on the search for and reuse of historic prototypes for public space quite overlooks the different social and economic conditions in which they came into existence and the different public life they served. Making public spaces just like the old ones can't bring back the old public life for which we have such nostalgia. They were part of a different ecology, one that has changed and we need to look at the new ecology that surrounds public life in our towns and cities, in search for new, appropriate forms. In discussing the pitfalls of historicism in design for today's streets, Gutman (1986) asks the critical question "What does one do to compensate for the possibility that radical new forms of social life are constantly developing, perhaps so radical that no reasonable adaptations and adjustments in the stock of typologies will be adequate for dealing with them?"

SEGMENTATION AND LOSS OF DIVERSITY

There are many forces in American life that lead to increased socioeconomic stratification, segmentation, and loss of localized diversity. As a people Americans are still quite diverse but we are more and more organized in spatial patterns that are socially segmented, reducing diversity in any locality and limiting social learniing. And, now, it is not only elite groups that support this. Some minority groups, who originally had assimilation as their goal, who wanted to be more "American," have reversed their stance and are receiving much support in their new quest for positive identity based on nonassimilation and on the uniqueness of their ethnicity or race.

They now often choose to exclude others, to live together, even when there is choice, furthering segmentation. An example is the tightly knit Italian community in Boston's North End, which has used public policy as an expression of their choice *not* to assimilate. Five successive down-zonings have finally brought the permissible building envelope to be equal to the *actual* envelope, reducing development pressure by reducing the value of the land. Essentially, this guarantees no new outsiders, and a Boston community in which the preferred language in the home, street, and workplace is a foreign tongue.

This aggressive exclusion of "foreigners" is mirrored by the suburban no-growth movement, the youth-excluding communities for the elderly, the Yuppie condos, and the "private, gated communities" advertised in rapidly developing areas, which all exclude by age or class, and often, by race. All are exclusionary actions played out within a framework of public life, further reducing localized diversity and access of people to one another, taking away Common Ground.

FUTURE DIRECTIONS OF RESEARCH, DESIGN, AND POLICY

There is still much more to learn about the three enduring archetypal places for public life: the street, the square, and the park. Galen Cranz (1982) has done a wonderful social history of the park and is extending that study in new directions. We need a parallel understanding of the square, perhaps like Korosec-Serfaty's (1982) study of the Main Square in Malmoe, Sweden. Stan Anderson (1986), Tony Vidler (1986), Bob Gutman (1986), Mark Francis (1987), and others have done excellent work on the street and we need that work extended and built upon. Many of our older public places are now becoming candidates for reuse and I worry that our knowledge to remake or make new ones is both insufficient and stale. We need to understand more about vernacular public places and public landscapes, as J. B. Jackson does (Zube, 1970) and as Bob Riley (1987) has started to do in his survey of vernacular landscapes.

We have few institutions whose mandate is to sensitively and properly look after or to work for public life. Both popular discussions and serious discourse regarding public life are uncommon. We don't often set overt goals for the support of public life before we design or redesign our public environments. Public life and its environments should be more emphasized as public issues—as should the socioeconomic and political mechanisms for bringing them into being and using them—for these delivery mechanisms powerfully affect what we get and how we use it. Within this framework of needs, some useful activities are described below:

- We might do more *systematic critiques* of the full range of public places in terms of how well they serve public life. This requires sustained discourse about many topics—such as a better understanding of the implications of segmentation and loss of localized diversity in public life, about methods for public legitimation of a much wider range of places seen as fit for public life, and a modernization of concepts of Common Ground to include those that are temporary, virtual, or ephemeral.
- We sorely need an economic calculus that more highly values public life. As Wolf (1986) suggests, we could work with zoning and legal groups to conceive of mechanisms that could capture the true economic value of the street and return it to the street—somehow making streets their own tax increment district, giving the street back some of the public power it once had, and in so doing, perhaps mitigate the century-old attack on the street as a public place.
- Most architectural and urban design competitions are, or include, public environments. The design-research community could be more proactive and aggressively offer human-environment-relations-based predesign programming and jurying services to every municipality considering design competitions that include public environments, and to the half a dozen active and recognized professional advisors to competitions in this country and the federal agencies that support design competitions.
- We should investigate new concepts of the *esthetics of public environments*, to confront the current norm of inoffensiveness. We need to explore ideas of what a true *public biography* might be as a basis for design of public place as opposed to what we normally get, which is the *designer's autobiography*. This public biography must include all users of public space and for all purposes, for we have seen how elite-group tastes in esthetics might be construed as a form of *social oppression* and recognize that those who feel oppressed fight back with what the elite call ugliness, as in wall-size graffiti, behaviors Jivan Tabibian (1972) once called "the politics of ugliness." A new esthetics for public places for new forms of public life may be radically different from the Euro-Urbanist histo-

ricism we've seen in design. I'd like to see the speculative production of images for such places.
- We could examine our town's and city's *inventory and system of public places*, in an ecological analysis, to suggest portions that need rethinking. Many cities have misused and underused public environments and have no system of using them. To legitimize this examination, we should attempt to establish civic bodies or commissions to understand, care for, develop, and manage public life and public place.
- The field of design research has something to offer the social-psychologists of public life, who, strangely, dwell very little on public environments. The establishment of a real dialogue could be very productive. The social-psychologists, in turn, have much to offer those who commission designs for public places and those who design them.

The idea of public environment can be *reconceived* to more include, and thus *legitimize*, the full range of places related to public life, both as it really it is and what it could be—extending our concepts far beyond the street, the square, and the park. These must include the strip, the suburb, the water's edge, the boardwalk, communal gardens, the electronic and print networks, portable public places, the indoor and outdoor mall, the skyway, the highway, the schoolyard, the parade and the Parade, the festival market, the vacant lot, the parking lot's Sunday life as a flea market, public building, public gardens, public landscapes, and public theater. And these must be examined as part of an ecology, freed from the overly simple Euro-Urbanist historicism that has snobbily hobbled discourse about public life and public place. Within such a frame of informed, passionate discourse, it seems possible to re-present our public life to us in ways that continue the 300 years' transformation, that prevent or redefine decline, and that seek more "authenticness," or at least better illusions for our use.

Acknowledgments

Because many of the ideas here came from or were sharpened in discussion, the following people must be treated as references and thanked publicly for their graciousness with their time and their wise counsel: Irwin Altman, John Archea, David Bryan, Kathleen Christensen, Galen Cranz, Daniel Friedman, Al Katz, Michael Kwartler, Magda McHale, Bonnie Ott, Michael Pittas, Robert Riley, Lynda Schneekloth, and Nancy Tobin.

REFERENCES

Anderson, S. (1986). People in the physical environment: The urban ecology of streets. In S. Anderson (Ed.), *On streets* (pp. 1–11). Cambridge, MA: M.I.T. Press.
Arendt, H. (1958). *The human condition*. Chicago: University of Chicago.

Barker, J. F., Fazio, M., & Hildebrandt, H. (1975). *The small town as an art object*. Mississippi State University.
Bellah, R., Madsen, R., Sullivan, W., Swidler, A., & Tipton, S. (1985). *Habits of the heart*. New York: Harper & Row.
Brambilla, R., & Longo, G. (1976a). *Banning the car downtown*. Washington, DC: U. S. Government Printing Office.
Brambilla, R., & Longo, G. (1976b). *A handbook for pedestrian action*. Washington, DC: U. S. Government Printing Office.
Brambilla, A., & Longo, G. (1976c). *The rediscovery of the pedestrian*. Washington, DC: U. S. Government Printing Office.
Cranz, G. (1982). *The politics of park design: A history of urban parks in America*. Cambridge, MA: M.I.T. Press.
Diesing, P. R. (1962). *Reason in society*. Urbana, IL: University of Illinois Press.
Francis, M. (1987). The making of democratic streets. In A. Vernez-Moudon (Ed.), *Public streets for public use* (pp. 23–39). New York: Van Nostrand Reinhold.
Goodman, P. & Goodman, P. (1947). *Communitas: Means of livelihood and ways of life*. New York: Vintage.
Gutman, R. (1986). The street generation. In S. Anderson (Ed.), *On streets* (pp. 249–264). Cambridge, MA: M.I.T. Press.
Jackson, J. B. (1985). Urban circumstances. In J. B. Jackson (Ed.), *Design Quarterly 128: Urban Circumstances*. Minneapolis: M.I.T. Press.
Korosec-Serfaty, P. (1982). *The main square*. Lund, Sweden: Aris.
Levitas, G. (1986). Anthropology and sociology of streets. In S. Anderson (Ed.), *On streets* (pp. 225–240). Cambridge, MA: M.I.T. Press.
Rapoport, A. (1969). *House form and culture*. Englewood Cliffs, NJ: Prentice-Hall.
Riley, R. B. (1987). Vernacular landscapes. In E. H. Zube & G. Moore (Eds.), *Advances in environment, behavior and design*. New York: Plenum Press.
Rowe, C. (1985). I stood in Venice on the Bridge of Sighs. In M. Friedman (Ed.), *Design Quarterly 129: Skyways* (pp. 8–15). Minneapolis: M.I.T. Press for Walker Art Center.
Rudofsky, B. (1969). *Streets for people: A primer for Americans*. Garden City, NY: Anchor Press/Doubleday.
Sennett, R. (1978). *The fall of public man*. New York: Vintage.
Sitte, C. (1965): *City planning according to artistic principles*. (G. Collins & C. Collins, Trans.). New York: Random House. (Original work published 1889)
Smithson, P. (1981). Space is the American mediator, or the blocks of Ithaca: A speculation. *Harvard Architectural Review*, 2, 107–114.
Tabibian, J. (1972). The politics of ugliness. In N. Polites (Ed.), *Design and the new esthetics* (pp. 33–39). Washington, DC: RC Publications.
Tyrwhitt, J., Sert, J. L., & Rogers, E. N. (Eds.). (1952). *C.I.A.M.8: The heart of the city*. New York: Pellegrini & Cudahy.
Vidler, A. (1986). The scenes of the street: Transformations in ideal and reality, 1750–1871. In S. Anderson (Ed.), *On streets* (pp. 29–110). Cambridge, MA: M.I.T. Press.
Warner, S. B., Jr. (1985). The liberal city. In M. Friedman (Ed.), *Design Quarterly 129: Skyways*. Minneapolis: M.I.T. Press for the Walker Art Center.
White, M., & White, L. (1960). *The intellectual versus the city*. Cambridge, MA: Harvard University Press and M.I.T. Press.
Wolf, P. (1986). Rethinking the urban street: Its economic context. In S. Anderson (Ed.), *On streets* (pp. 377–383). Cambridge, MA: M.I.T. Press.
Zube, E. H. (Ed.). (1970). *Landscapes: Selected writings of J. B. Jackson*. Amherst, MA: University of Massachusetts Press.

2

Perception, Cognition, and Evaluation of Urban Places

JACK L. NASAR

INTRODUCTION

> Just walking through the vast main concourse of Grand Central Terminal in New York . . . almost always triggers in me a spontaneous and quiet change in perception. . . . The change—one that is reasonably well known to all of us . . . — lets me gently refocus my attention and allows a more general awareness of a great many things at once: sights, sounds, smells and sensations of touch and balance as well as thoughts and feelings. When this general kind of awareness occurs, I feel relaxed and alert at the same time. (Hiss, 1987, p. 45)

Clearly, our physical environment can evoke strong emotional responses, such as the esthetic experience described above—an awareness both relaxed and alert at the same time. It can also evoke less pronounced but nevertheless, important feelings and thoughts. This chapter discusses these reactions as they relate to urban outdoor public places. Rather than providing a comprehensive review, I intend to summarize important empirical findings and directions. First, however, let me describe the kinds of places and reactions to be discussed.

URBAN PUBLIC PLACES

In common usage, the word "urban" may imply city concerns, but in practice it includes other public places. Urban designers deal with many different large-scale public environments—cities, neighborhood, suburbs, commercial strips—all of which fall among the concerns of architects, landscape

---

JACK L. NASAR • Department of City and Regional Planning, The Ohio State University, Columbus, OH 43221.

31

architects, and city planners. In agreement with practice, this chapter considers not only the city but also these other kinds of large-scale urban places.

I choose an urban emphasis because most Americans live in urban areas. Occupying 16.2% of the U.S. land area in 1985, urban areas had 182.5 million residents or 76.5% of the population (Bureau of Census, 1987). The urban population has been increasing, up 10 million (5.9%) from 1980 and 29.7 million (16.3%) from 1970. The land occupied by metropolitan areas has also increased, up by almost 200,000 square miles (33%) from 1970.

Streets and the streetscape are particularly important in defining the character of urban areas (Nasar, 1979). Streets are public places. Most Americans live on streets and regularly pass through urban streets in their neighborhoods and on their way to work, shop, and recreation. In metropolitan areas alone, we drive over 4,000 billion daily vehicle miles per mile of road (Bureau of Census, 1987). Beyond that, we spend much time as pedestrians along the streets of central business districts, retail areas, and neighborhoods. So it is not surprising that the character of streets and their surroundings have been found to have major impacts on quality of life (Appleyard, 1981; Lansing, Marans, & Zehner, 1970). Accordingly, although this chapter discusses research at various scales in the urban environment, it emphasizes the street and the streetscape.

In the streetscape, buildings are prominent and costly objects, which have been rapidly changing the public face of urban areas. New construction in 1985 in the United States was valued in excess of 35 billion dollars (Bureau of Census, 1987), of which 19 billion dollars was spent on public buildings (often located in prominent locations) to produce 25 million square feet of space. Although much new construction is private (915 million square feet of commercial space, mostly office, and 2364 square feet of residential space), the exteriors of these buildings are public. Because of their public nature, the exteriors of public and private buildings should meet the visual needs of the public. This is "where issues of public policy meet questions of esthetics" (Goldberger, 1983, p. 3).

Homes and building along the road may occur as isolated objects in space, but they can be planned and designed to define and give character to space. With knowledge of empirical findings, decision makers can guide the design toward such desirable ends.

In summary, this chapter centers on urban places (the city, neighborhoods, suburbs, commercial districts). Particular emphasis is placed on the roadside environment, because of the impact of this environment on the public experience of urban areas.

COGNITIVE AND ESTHETIC QUALITY

Urban cognition and esthetics are crucial parts of that experience. By "urban cognition," I refer primarily to Lynch's (1960) concept of imageability. Among other things, imageability (clear identity and structure) gives us knowledge of where we are—orientation—and how to get to desired destinations—wayfinding. The importance of such environmental knowledge is self-evident. Being lost—not knowing where you are or not knowing how to get to where you want to go—can be distressing, particularly for a newcomer. So an imageable or legible city can make one feel more secure by providing cues for orientation and wayfinding (Lynch, 1960). In addition, through understanding imageability, practitioners can better predict patterns of use.

By "esthetics," I refer to urban affect or the perceived quality of the urban surroundings. Esthetic quality has been identified as a major dimension in the public's perception of their surroundings (Carp, Zawadsky, & Shokrin, 1976); variables such as pleasure or beauty represent the most influential dimension of environmental assessments (Hershberger & Cass, 1974; Horayangkura, 1978; Oostendorp & Berlyne, 1978; Ward & Russell, 1981); and esthetic factors have major influences on judgments of community satisfaction (Lansing et al., 1970).

Unfortunately, urban decision makers often gloss over these experiential factors as "subjective" and unquantifiable. They are neither. So, without overlooking the importance of other concerns in the design, planning, and management of urban areas, this chapter deals with the empirical findings on cognitive and esthetic quality. My intent is to inform those decisions where cognitive and esthetic considerations play a role.

Such a review might not be needed if design professionals and the public shared similar values, or if design professionals correctly gauged public needs. Unfortunately, this is not the case. Design professionals have been found consistently to differ from the public in their appraisals of the built environment (Devlin & Nasar, 1987; Groat, 1979; Purcell, 1986).

Two kind of information are relevant to making user-sensitive decisions about urban environmental quality. On the one hand, solutions at an urban scale for many people should fit public images. For this purpose, information on shared values among large numbers of the populace is needed to achieve the requisite community acceptance (Lynch, 1960, p. 7). On the other hand, solutions for distinct populations and places should fit the particular requirements of the sociocultural and physical context. Here, information on differences in response across various groups and settings is relevant. In light of the need for these two kinds of information, this review discusses both commonalities in response and differences in response across various sociodemographic and physical contexts.

In the following sections, I first briefly discuss urban cognition—imageability and building recall. Next, I discuss the linkage between imageability and affect. Then, I discuss urban esthetics—including a framework, environmental simulation, salient dimensions of perception, salient dimensions of affect, and the relation of various attributes to urban affect. The chapter concludes with discussion of five future directions of research. These include specifying the full model of esthetic experience, studying urban affect in relation to movement through the environment, studying changes (and development) of esthetic values, considering socioperceptually relevant categories of scenes, and integrating public policy questions into the research agenda.

URBAN COGNITION

URBAN IMAGEABILITY

What features of the urban surroundings contribute to orientation and wayfinding? This question has been dealt with extensively in edited texts and reviews of the research (cf. Evans, 1980; Moore, 1979). Briefly, the results support Lynch's (1960) contention that the identity and structure of a city is influenced by five physical elements: paths, edges, districts, nodes, and landmarks. The stability of these five elements has been confirmed in many studies employing diverse methodologies, populations, and locales including the United States, South America, the Netherlands, Italy, the Middle East, Paris, Mexico, and Spain.

Presumably, the use of these elements to reinforce one another can strengthen the urban image. For example, the identity of a district may be strengthened through internal unity, strong edges that also serve as major paths, and a hierarchy of landmarks (tied to nodes), which link to a related hierarchy of paths. Defining the ways in which these elements should be combined to best enhance imageability remains an interesting and relevant area for inquiry.

In a related matter, there is uncertainty about the relative importance of paths and landmarks in cognitive learning. What do people rely on when first learning their way around an unfamiliar place? Some studies find paths as more important (Appleyard, 1976; Devlin, 1976). Others find landmarks as more important (Evans, Marrero, & Butler, 1981; Heft, 1979). Aside from the effects of variations in the task and scale of environment, the differences probably result from differences in physical context. In areas lacking landmarks, paths take on greater importance, and in areas with poorly defined paths, landmarks take on greater importance. Because of real-estate speculation and the nature of development in big cities, landmarks may take on more importance to newcomers than paths in cities.

There is also evidence of individual differences in urban cognition (cf. Evans, 1980). Lower-income residents have been found to have less extensive maps than do higher-income people; children proceed through a developmental stages from route knowledge to a Euclidian coordinate system; and males have sometimes been found to have more developed mental maps than females. These differences probably result from differences in environmental experience. Interactive experience with the environment enhances the development and accuracy of internal representations of the environment.

BUILDING RECALL

What factors enhance the imageability of landmarks, paths, edges, districts, and nodes? In one study that considered all of these elements, an individual's selection of imageable elements was found to depend on appearance, location, and meaning (Harrison & Howard, 1972). Most other research on influences on imageability has centered on buildings, perhaps because of the importance of landmark buildings in urban orientation and wayfinding. Nevertheless, the results parallel those of Harrison and Howard (1972).

In a study of Ciudad, Venezuela, Appleyard (1969) found three factors related to building recall—form, visibility, and use. These factors are essentially the same as appearance, location, and meaning. Form included distinctive contour, height, shape complexity, maintenance quality, and movement around the building; visibility included visibility from roads, proximity to important decision points, and number of people passing a major viewpoint; and use included intensity, uniqueness of building function, and significance.

Furthermore, a study in Orange, California, confirmed the stability of these factors (Evans, Smith, & Pezdak, 1982). Building recall improved with movement around the base, clear contours, large relative size, shape complexity, maintenance quality, and use intensity. Building recall was also found to improve with building significance, accessibility from the street, uniqueness of architectural style, and naturalness. In a cross-cultural study between Japan and the United States, Nasar (1984a) confirmed the importance of form (clear contour) and visibility (time-in-view).

There is also evidence of individual differences in relation to building recall. Examination of these differences indicates that they probably result from variations in the sociophysical milieu. For example, Evans et al. (1982) found that the impact of symbolic significance was reduced in a city lacking historic buildings, the impact of singular function was reduced in a city lacking singular function buildings, the impact of signage was reduced for a less literate population, and the emphasis on *significance* and *building access* (important concerns to the elderly) was higher for elderly respondents than for others. Nasar (1984a) found memorability related to visibility more in U.S. scenes than in Japanese scenes (which had more vegetation and traffic).

In sum, building imageability is enhanced by exposure, use significance, and visual contrast, but the influence of these factors may vary with the sociophysical milieu. Although the research has not adequately addressed the factors that affect the imageability of paths, edges, nodes, and districts, it seems likely that their imageability may also depend on the same variables.

RELATIONSHIP BETWEEN IMAGEABILITY AND PERCEIVED QUALITY

Although Lynch (1960) chose not to examine meaning, it is often assumed that imageability has favorable meanings. In theory, imageability, like coherence (Kaplan & Kaplan, 1982), should enhance perceived quality by helping people make sense of their surroundings. In practice, however, the quality of imageable elements can vary: a landmark might be an obtrusive water tower, a path might be surrounded by billboards, an edge might be a polluted river, and a district might be identified by its blight. Such a city would be imageable but ugly. Because of their prominence, imageable elements define the evaluative image of a city, but the direction of that evaluation—pleasant or unpleasant—depends on the perceived quality of the elements.

In agreement with this view, Nasar (1979) found that imageable elements influenced both favorable and unfavorable images of the city. When residents and visitors were asked what areas they liked visually in Knoxville, their responses centered on paths, districts, edges, nodes, and landmarks. When asked about dislikes, participants again cited paths, districts, edges, nodes, and landmarks. Similarly, in Chattanooga, the shared evaluative image depended on the perceived quality of the imageable elements (Nasar, 1980a). If this is so, improvements in the perceived quality of the imageable elements should have significant impacts on the perceived quality of the whole urban area. The following sections discuss the specific kinds of changes that may help achieve the desired esthetic quality. Although much of the research considers buildings and the view from the road, the findings should be relevant to the design of landmarks, paths, and districts for visual quality.

URBAN ESTHETICS

A Framework

First, it may be useful to consider a framework for organizing the research on urban esthetics. My framework, an extension of Brunswik's lens model (discussed by Craik, 1983), is displayed in Figure 1. This framework includes five measures—physical, perceptual/cognitive, urban affect, well-being, and spatial behavior. According to Brunswik's model, these measures should have probabilistic relations to one another (Craik, 1983), and with experience humans adjust the probabilities to improve their functional accuracy. In light of the role of experience, the framework also includes two contextual variables: sociodemographic and environmental context. Correlates of esthetic value may vary with context.

Two of the measures in the framework refer primarily to the features of the physical surroundings. These are the physical and perceptual/cognitive measures. Features of the physical surroundings can be measured directly through *physical* measures (such as measurements of the size of an open space, the amount of vegetation in a scene, or the number of different colors in a scene). Such concrete physical measures, however, may lack relevance to perceived esthetic quality unless they are combined into a broader index (Wohlwill, 1976). Consensus judgments of attributes of a scene have been used as an alternative. These measures, called "perceptual/cognitive" measures (Ward & Russell, 1981), can often capture environmental dimensions of relevance to esthetic value that cannot be gleaned through direct physical measurement (Wohlwill, 1976). They might include ratings of such attributes as compatibility, complexity, order, and naturalness. According to the lens model (Craik, 1983), these measures should have probabilistic relations to environmental cues. The evidence of high interobserver reliability (Craik, 1983; Nasar, 1983; Oostendorp & Berlyne, 1978; Ward & Russell, 1981) supports this view.

Next, consider esthetic response. Although esthetic response might be

Perception, Cognition, and Evaluation of Urban Places

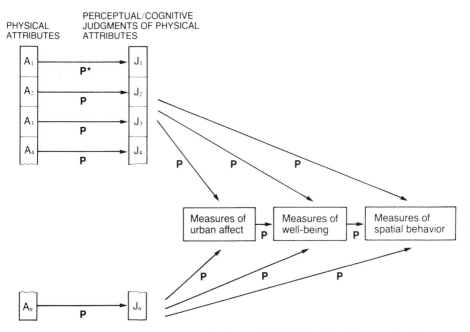

Figure 1. A framework for environmental esthetics. Probabilities (P) might vary for different sociophysical categories of scene. Physical attributes may also have direct effects on urban effect, well-being, and spatial behavior.

viewed as a mix of high pleasure, excitement, and relaxation, most urban design neither seeks nor achieves this state. Of more relevance to urban design is how the physical surroundings influence affective response. Therefore, I use a looser definition (cf. Wohlwill, 1976) in which urban esthetics refers to positive feelings in relation to the urban surroundings. This *urban affect* might include judgments of the pleasantness, excitement, or safety of an urban area. According to the lens model, measures of urban affect should have probabilistic relations to perceptual/cognitive measures and urban features.

Improvements in visual quality may also affect two other kinds of variables: psychological *well-being* and *spatial behavior*. Psychological well-being refers to an individual's internal state, and this might be assessed through psychophysical measures or questions aimed at uncovering mood. Spatial behavior refers to how people use the environment, which places they visit, avoid, how long they stay. This can be observed directly, measured indirectly through its traces, or estimated from verbal report of behavioral intent or how individuals expect to use an environment.

In sum, the lens model applied to urban esthetics suggests probabilistic relations between five kinds of variables: urban physical features, perceptual/cognitive measures of those features, affective appraisals of the scene, psychological well-being, and spatial behavior. Only a handful of studies has examined the relationship between esthetic attributes and psychological wellbeing or spatial behavior (Locasso, 1988; Mintz, 1956; Ulrich, 1973; Ulrich, 1984). Most of the research has concentrated on relationship of environmental features or perceptual/cognitive measures to affective appraisals of the environment. And this review reflects that emphasis.

For the research to have practical value, the chosen perceptual/cognitive and affective measures must have ecological validity. They must be salient in people's regular experience in their urban surroundings. So, this chapter first discusses findings with regard to salient perceptual/cognitive dimensions and salient affective dimensions in response to urban scenes. Because much of this research uses photograph or slides, I first discuss the ecological validity of these simulations to on-site experience.

URBAN SIMULATION

Human responses to color slides or photos of urban or architectural scenes have been consistently shown to accurately reflect on-site response (Craik, 1983; Hershberger & Cass, 1974; Oostendorp, 1978). This view is also supported by the evidence that visual cues dominate auditory cues in judgments of the pleasantness of environments (Gifford & Ng, 1982) and by the evidence that ambient sound has little effect on scene judgments (Esposito, 1984). There are, however, some caveats.

Sound and familiarity have some effects on environmental appraisals. The relative influence of visual and auditory cues has been found to vary in relation to arousal (Gifford & Ng, 1982). Noise, especially from traffic, has been found to produce major decrements in judgments of environmental quality (Appleyard, 1981; Craik, 1983; Esposito, 1984). Familiarity has been found to influence cognitive and evaluative response (Craik, 1983; Zube, Vining, Law, & Bechtel, 1985). As a result, when seeking information for specific settings, on-site response by familiar observers is preferable. Nevertheless, for identifying salient dimensions of environment response, color slides and photos are acceptable. In fact, Oostendorp (1978) found that color photos of scenes in two distinct neighborhoods yielded the same dimensions of response that were found onsite with familiar observers.

SALIENT PERCEPTUAL/COGNITIVE DIMENSIONS[1]

What are the salient visual attributes of urban scenes and buildings? The research indicates four dimensions as stable across various populations and

---

[1] Early attempts at finding these salient dimensions used factor analysis of semantic-differential ratings of scenes (Hershberger & Cass, 1974; Lowenthal & Riel, 1972; Osgood, Suci, & Tannenbaum, 1957). This approach has been criticized because semantics and the investigator's choice of variables may bias the outcome and because a failure to separate affective and perceptual/cognitive measures yields dimensions that do not accurately reflect either domain of response. Although the Osgood *et al.* (1957) dimensions of meaning—evaluation, potency, and activity—have been confirmed across a variety of situations, their relevance to environmental response was uncertain. My review centers on that research that uses nonverbal (comparative) ratings of scenes and tries to derive dimensions of perception or affect from the structure of those judgments.

environments: naturalness (vs. man-made or urban), complexity, clarity/order, and openness. Natural–man-made qualities (or related variables such as building prominence, urbanization, and greenery) have emerged as salient in the perception of a wide variety of molar environments (Ward & Russell, 1981), urban scenes (Geller, Cook, O'Connor, & Low, 1982), housing scenes (Nasar, 1988a; Horayangkura, 1978), and architecture (Oostendorp, 1978; Oostendorp & Berlyne, 1978). Complexity (or related variables such as visual richness, ornamentation, or information rate) has emerged as salient in the perception of a wide variety of molar environments (Ward & Russell, 1981), housing scenes (Nasar, 1988a), and architecture (Oostendorp, 1978; Oostendorp & Berlyne, 1978). Openness (or related variables such as density or spaciousness) has emerged as salient in the perception of a wide variety of molar environments (Ward & Russell, 1981), urban scenes, (Geller *et al.*, 1982), and housing scenes (Nasar, 1988a; Horayangkura, 1978). Openness may not have appeared in Oostendorp's studies because by emphasizing building exterior she eliminated variation in openness. Finally, clarity or order has emerged as salient in housing scenes (Horayangkura, 1978; Nasar, 1988a) and architecture (Oostendorp, 1978; Oostendorp & Berlyne, 1978.

For particular kinds of urban scenes or building types, however, other dimensions may emerge. For example, Oostendorp (1978) found some variance in the dimensions of perception of scenes in two physically distinct neighborhoods; Geller *et al.* (1982) found land use (commercial–residential) as a salient dimension of the urban scenes they examined; and Oostendorp and Berlyne (1978) found angularity/functional expression as a prominent dimensions in the perception of architecture. Because design/planning decisions often deal with specific sociophysical contexts, additional research is needed on the dimensions of perception within and across various land uses, districts, and sociocultural groups. In addition, identifying probabilistic relations between perceptual/ cognitive judgments and environmental cues has practical value. For example, judgments of the prominent dimensions or order, naturalness, or complexity may be influenced by nuisance factors, such as traffic, dilapidation, signs, wires, and poles.

SALIENT AFFECTIVE DIMENSIONS[2]

Now consider environmental affect. Along what affective dimensions does the public judge urban quality? Esthetic value has been treated as a mix of pleasure and interest (Wohlwill, 1976), but research suggests that emotional appraisals of the physical surroundings have some additional components.

In a major set of studies, Ward & Russell (1981) used a variety of methods and measures to derive the salient affective dimensions of response to a wide variety of molar environments. In contrast to many earlier studies, they also treated measures of affect as separate from other kinds of response. As can be seen in Figure 2, their results indicate that environmental affect consists of two

---

[2] See footnote 1.

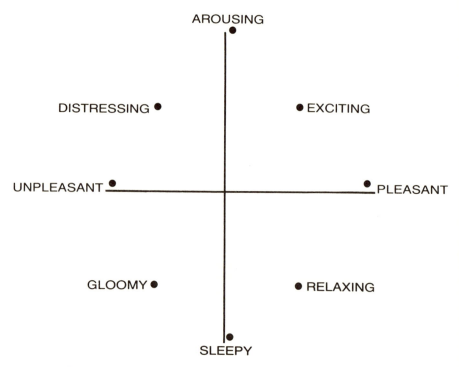

Figure 2. Dimensions of environmental affect (Ward & Russell, 1981).

primary orthogonal dimensions—pleasantness and arousal—and two combinations of these dimensions that yield the additional dimensions of excitingness and distress. A pleasant, arousing place feels exciting; an unpleasant, sleepy one feels gloomy. A pleasant, sleepy place feels relaxing; an unpleasant, arousing one feels distressing. Unlike arousal, which is orthogonal to evaluation, both excitingness and distress involve evaluation. Urban evaluation, then, has three interrelated parts—evaluation, excitingness, and distress.

The Ward and Russell (1981) dimensions show stability to urban and architectural scenes. Nasar (1988b, pp. 257–258) found that the adjectives selected by people as relevant to the assessment of urban scenes included descriptions along the dimensions of arousal, evaluation, excitement, and distress. Furthermore, factor analysis of responses to urban scenes on these selected adjectives yielded evaluation and arousal (tension and excitement) as the significant factors. In studies of urban buildings (Oostendorp, 1978) and of architecture from around the world (Oostendorp & Berlyne, 1978), the derived dimensions also involved evaluation and arousal. Interestingly, the two dimensions of evaluation and arousal are similar to two factors of Osgood *et al.* (1957)—evaluation and activity.

Esthetic Value

At this point, we have seen that *naturalness, complexity, order,* and *openness* are salient features of urban scenes and that evaluation, excitement, and clamness are salient evaluative dimensions of response to urban scenes. What is the relationship between environmental attributes and the perceived quality of urban areas? The evidence suggests that the salient perceptual/cognitive variables may have important influences on affect.

The esthetic value of the environment has been described as related to four classes of physical variables: collative, organizing, psychophysical, ecological/content, and spatial (Berlyne, 1971; Kaplan & Kaplan, 1982; Wohlwill, 1976). Collative variables involve comparison between stimulus elements, and they create uncertainty. Included among collative variables are *complexity* (a comparison of information), novelty and surprise (comparisons between the object and expectations for the object), and incongruity and ambiguity (comparisons of meanings).

Organizing variables provide structure and reduce uncertainty. They include such attributes as *order*, unity, coherence, *clarity*, and compatibility. Psychophysical variables involve intensity, such as size, brightness, color, or contrast. Ecological/content variables "belong to the content rather than the formal aspect of the work" (Berlyne, 1971, p. 138). They might include such variables as *naturalness*, architectural style, and environmental nuisances, such as traffic, poles, wires, and signs and nonconforming uses. Spatial variables include prospect (the *openness* of the view), refuge (the protection of the observation point), and mystery (the promise of additional information).

I discuss the collative and organizing variables first (and that discussion also includes some psychophysical variables of relevance to collative and organizing attributes). Next, I discuss the spatial variables and then the ecological/content variables.

Collative and Organizing Variables

Complexity and Order. For centuries, writers have speculated on the esthetic value of the combination of variables such as complexity, variety, or ornament that provide visual richness with variables such as order, unity, or harmony that structure the richness (cf. Oostendorp, 1978). Of course, these two kinds of variables—complexity and order/clarity—are two of the salient dimensions in urban perception. Berlyne (1971) theorized that these two kinds of variables affect uncertainty and arousal. According to him, complexity increases arousal, order decreases it, and esthetic value is highest at a moderate (or optimal) level of arousal. (Similarly, the intensity of psychophysical variables might affect arousal, and a moderate level of intensity may be desirable.) Kaplan and Kaplan (1982) also adopt a two-process model in which esthetic value depends on our need for *involvement* and *comprehension*. The environment must be involving to attract our attention, and it must make sense for us to find our way around. Complexity creates involvement, and coherence (order) aids comprehension. Again, moderate complexity and high order should be desired. What has the research found for complexity and order?

In agreement with theory, complexity has consistently been found to increase involvement or arousal (measured via interest, excitement, or looking time) (Berlyne, 1971; Wohlwill, 1976). With regard to evaluation, the results are inconsistent, but the inconsistencies may stem from methodological problems confounding the results (Kaplan & Kaplan, 1982; Wohlwill, 1976). For example, several studies failed to define complexity for the judges and overlooked nonlinear relationships (Wohlwill, 1976, p. 49). Studies of the environment have also been confounded by the uncontrolled covariance of complexity with such affect-loaded variables as upkeep, naturalness, visual nuisances, and land-use intensity and by the failure to include an adequate range of complexity for the expected decrement in evaluation to emerge. In the few studies that deal with these problems, the results have found the expected preference for moderate complexity over either low or high complexity (Nasar, 1987a; Wohlwill, 1976, pp. 47–48).

The findings for order have been consistent with theory. Increases in order (or related variables such as clarity, or unity) have been found to enhance the evaluative quality of cities (Nasar, 1979, 1980a), downtown scenes (Lowenthal & Riel, 1972; Nasar, 1984b, 1987b), housing scenes (Nasar, 1983), architecture (Oostendorp, 1978; Oostendorp & Berlyne, 1978), and buildings in natural settings (Wohlwill, 1982). In addition, compatibility has been found to influence perceived order (Nasar, 1987a); and preference has been found to increase with the compatibility of signs to their surroundings (Nasar, 1987a), the compatibility of buildings to nature (Wohlwill, 1982), and the compatibility of buildings to neighboring buildings (Groat, 1984). Furthermore, research has identified environmental cues for compatibility. For natural settings, judged compatibility has been found related inversely to contrast in color, texture, size, and shape of buildings relative to their natural surroundings (Wohlwill, 1982). For urban settings, judged compatibility of buildings resulted primarily from replication of surface features such as materials, style, rooflines, and overall shape (Groat, 1984).

Consider one set of studies on the combined effect of complexity and order (coherence) on evaluative response. A first study of photos of 30 retail scenes (Nasar, 1986) found complexity and coherence (low contrast) as salient dimensions of perception of retail scenes. A second study (Nasar, 1987a) tested the influence of these variables on evaluative response. The research used as stimuli color photographs (Figure 3) of a scale-model retail strip in nine different signscape configurations (three levels of complexity by three levels of contrast). First, the influence of physical contrast on judged coherence was examined. As expected, increases in contrast produced decreases in judged coherence. Then public ratings of each scene in terms of its pleasantness, excitement, relaxingness, and desirability as a place to visit, shop, linger, and spend time in were obtained.

The results support the two process model and suggest behavioral implications of environmental complexity and coherence. Complexity increased ex-

Figure 3. Black and white photographs of tested signscapes.

citement; and coherence decreased excitement. The moderately complex and most coherent signscape (i.e., the moderately exciting signscape) was rated as most pleasant and most desirable as a place to visit, shop, and spend time in. When merchants were asked which signscape they most wanted their strip to resemble, they most often selected the moderately complex and highly coherent signscape.

What about the other collative variables—ambiguity, incongruity, surprise, and novelty? We have already seen that people dislike environmental ambiguity and incongruity. They prefer environmental clarity, fittingness, and compatibility. Published research on environmental surprise is lacking, perhaps because of the difficulties in manipulating this variable because it requires movement through space. With regard to novelty, there has been extensive published research.

Novelty and Familiarity. Novelty can be defined as discrepancies from what is expected relative to an observer's previous experience. These discrepancies may include previously experienced elements organized in unique ways, unexperienced elements organized in familiar ways, or some mix of familiar elements. The findings on novelty seem contradictory.

On the one hand, some studies find that people prefer novelty. Studies of landscapes, churches, and homes (Purcell, 1986), central business scenes (Nasar, 1984b), and campus and contemporary buildings (Herzog, Kaplan, & Kaplan, 1976) have identified preferences for novelty. On the other hand, some studies find that people prefer familiarity. Studies of landscapes (Sonnenfeld, 1966), various land uses seen from the road (Craik, 1983), commercial scenes (Nasar, 1980b), cultural buildings, entertainment buildings, and commercial buildings (Herzog et al., 1976), and house types (Canter & Thorne, 1972) have identified preferences for the familiar. What is going on?

Purcell (1986) argues and demonstrates that affective response depends on the amount of discrepancy (novelty) between the object and a prototype for that kind of object. Interest increases with the discrepancy; and for the public, preference is highest for a moderate discrepancy. Does this sound familiar? It is an extension of the optimal-level-of-arousal theory (Berlyne, 1971; Wohlwill, 1976), and it may help explain inconsistencies in the results. If a moderate level of novelty is preferred, then studies examining "novel" or "familiar" scenes may get different results depending on the levels of novelty, familiarity, or typicality examined.

The inconsistencies may also result from other factors. Individuals differ in their preference for novelty. For example, young adults have been found to prefer novelty whereas older people favor familiarity (Sonnenfeld, 1966), and architects prefer interest and novelty more than the public does (Devlin & Nasar, 1987; Purcell, 1986). Expectations for novelty may also vary across settings. Furthermore, novelty has been shown to have interactive effects with complexity and initial affect. For complex stimuli, familiarity is preferred, but for less complex stimuli, novelty is preferred (Berlyne, 1971; Smith & Dorfman, 1975). When a stimuli is initially disliked, repeated exposure (familiarity) has been found to reduce pleasure (Mandler & Shebo, 1983).

Future study of familiarity/novelty is needed. This research might do well to consider separately the effects of different settings and populations and to use scenes that have been systematically scaled for various levels of familiarity/novelty, complexity, typicality, and first impressions. Now, let us consider the spatial dimensions of experience.

Spatial Variables

Appleton's (1975) theory on prospect (openness) and refuge (protection) has relevance to spatial variables. According to this theory, prospect and refuge are preferred because of their survival value. Prospect affords the opportunity to see threats in advance; and refuge affords protection. An extension of this framework includes two kinds of prospect and refuge—primary, where the view has prospect or refuge, and secondary, where the view looks toward a place with prospect or refuge (Woodcock, 1982).

With regard to prospect, research in a variety of urban contexts has consistently demonstrated that people prefer openness/spaciousness (Gärling, 1976; Horayangkura, 1978; Lansing et al., 1970; Nasar, 1983). For practical application, however, additional research should attempt to identify the desirable characteristics of openness and its enclosing elements.

With regard to urban refuge, the findings do not support the theory. Woodcock (1982) studied responses to three biomes and found primary prospect strongly related to preference, primary refuge inversely related to preference, and secondary prospect and refuge related to preference but only in the savanna biome. One study (Nasar, Julian, Buchman, Humphreys, & Mrohaly, 1983) had observers rate either an open or enclosed urban campus scene from either a protected or unprotected observation point. The open view was rated as safer than the enclosed one, but refuge had no main effects and reverse effects for males and females.

Another spatial variable is mystery, the anticipation of additional information through advancing into the scene (Kaplan & Kaplan, 1982). Scenes having a curving road have mystery. In theory, mystery should enhance esthetic value because it affords interest and progress toward coherence. Research has consistently found preference related to mystery in the expected direction (cf. Kaplan & Kaplan, 1982). Although much of that research is set in natural settings, Hesselgren (1976) found similar results for urban streets. Now, let us consider those features that are thought to influence affect through their content rather than form.

Ecological/Content Variables

Naturalness. Kaplan and Kaplan (1982) describe nature as a content variable with restorative and esthetic value; and an extensive empirical record has consistently demonstrated preferences for nature and preferences for natural over man-made elements (Appleyard & Lintell, 1972; Kaplan, Kaplan, &

Wendt, 1972; Nasar, 1979, 1980a, 1983, 1984b; Wohlwill, 1976). Water has also been found to enhance scenic quality (Ulrich, 1981). A closer look at the evidence raises some questions about naturalness.

First, the research does not necessarily demonstrate a preference for "nature" or "trees." Research on "nature" has consistently obtained responses to vegetation. We cannot conclude that the findings apply to trees and bushes without leaves. In fact, the preliminary results of a pilot study I am conducting suggest that scenes without trees may be preferred to scenes with leafless trees.

Second, preference for vegetation may result from form rather than content. Vegetation correlates with order, unity, upkeep, and openness, all of which increase preference (Nasar, 1983, 1984b), and analyses reveal that vegetation enhances unity (Nasar, 1987b). Wohlwill (1983, pp. 14, 15, 17) has suggested other structural properties of nature that may account for the preference for natural over man-made scenes. Natural scenes may have smoother, less intense, and less predictable irregularities, movement, and sounds than man-made scenes. Consider also one class of man-made urban scene that elicits favorable responses: nighttime views of a city skyline or highway in the distance, where the sounds are too distant to be heard. As with nature, the scene (in this case the lights of the city or vehicles) changes in an irregular, continuous, and orderly fashion.

Third, the restorative value of vegetation has not yet been demonstrated. In a rare study that tied esthetic variables to well-being, Ulrich (1984) found faster recoveries for patients having a natural view than for patients having a view of a brick wall. However, because of the extremity of the manipulation and the lack of control, other factors (such as complexity or simply esthetic value) may explain the differences.

Symbolic Meanings of Styles. Symbolic meanings of styles are central to esthetic response to architecture (Rapoport, 1982). Thus, when architects rejected Greek Revival for Gothic Revival, Gothic Revival for Queen Anne, Queen Anne for Modern, they described each replacement as more *honest* (Lynes, 1954, p. 244). The styles had not changed, their connotations had. Not until recently have empirical researchers turned their attention to the symbolic meanings of architectural styles.

In one of the first of these studies, Groat (1979) found that architects differed from an educated lay group (accountants) in the meanings inferred from Post-Modern architecture. The public favored recognizable historic styles. Devlin and Nasar (1987) extended the Groat study in two ways. We examined two broad style categories, "high" and "popular" architecture, and we used a more representative group of lay respondents. Again, style influenced architect and public ratings of the buildings. Both groups rated "high" architecture as more complex and novel than "popular" architecture, and this difference was more pronounced for the architects. More to the point, architects judged "high" styles as more meaningful, coherent, clear, and pleasant than "popular" architecture, whereas lay people judged "popular" styles as more meaningful, coherent, clear, and pleasant than "high" styles.

Researchers have also looked at the meanings inferred from particular popular styles. Lansing *et al.* (1970) reported that most residents of several planned communities preferred the Colonial style. A minority preferred Modern styles. In a study of eight popular home styles (presented in mechanically drawn elevations), Kinzy found that Buffalo suburbanites preferred Tudor and Farm to Modern (Langdon, 1982). Unfortunately, the results were confounded by other variations in the homes (such as their size, number of stories, presence and size of garage, and amount of windows). In another study of stylistic preferences, Tuttle (1983) found that Wisconsin residents favored Colonial and Tudor to Mediterranean and Contemporary styles.

Unlike these earlier studies, we went beyond preferences to examine other dimensions of home-style meaning and we compared responses of various sociodemographic groups (Nasar, Zaff, Dunworth, Duran, & Rezoski, 1987). In one question (evaluation), we asked respondents which home they would select if they had won the "dream house lottery." In another question (perceived friendliness of assumed resident), we asked them which home they would approach for help if they had a flat tire. And in another question (perceived status of assumed resident), we asked which home would most likely house the individual who would "take charge" or "lead" the group if they worked together. The results confirmed systematic differences in symbolic meanings across styles and across sociodemographic groups. Participants made snap judgments about the desirability of the homes and about the character of the assumed residents. As did Kinzy, we found favorable responses to Tudor and Farm, but we found some variation in responses across the scales. For example, Colonial was judged as fourth in desirability, first in leadership, and fifth in friendliness.

Interestingly, I have also found a similar pattern of response from people in Los Angeles. The research also identified significant differences that related to education, occupation, age, and gender. For example, decreases in education, occupational class, and increases in age related to increases in preference for Colonial and decreases in preference for Contemporary. A follow-up study of architects indicates that they evaluate the styles differently from the public and they misgauge the public responses.

Taken together, these studies suggest that cues in broad stylistic categories and in specific styles may organize and give meaning to buildings and that training or exposure influences those meanings. Furthermore, the findings indicate limitations in the continued study of formal attributes as if they were independent from the style in which they are imbedded. Through study of other building types and respondent groups, we can find ways in which stylistic elements can be applied to specific contexts to achieve meaningful and pleasant public surroundings.

Nuisances. Certain nuisances—dilapidation, poles, wires and signs, industrial uses, and vehicles—have been found to depress perceived environmental quality (Appleyard, 1981; Lansing *et al.*, 1970; Nasar, 1979, 1980a; Winkel, Maiek, & Thiel, 1970). In particular, dilapidation and traffic (and its sound) have significant negative effects on the perceived quality of residential streets, neighborhoods, and quality of life (Anderson, Mulligan, Goodman, & Rezen,

1983; Appleyard, 1981; Craik, 1983; Lansing et al., 1970). Interestingly, traffic sounds downtown have been found to be related to favorable responses (Anderson et al., 1983; Southworth, 1969). Context may have importance. Additional research is needed on the sonic quality of our surroundings.

DESIGN/PLANNING RECOMMENDATIONS

Street right-of-ways represent valuable urban resources that need not be the empty spaces they are in many American cities. With proper planning, they can become meaningful public places. This means planning streets as more than just efficient passageways for movement. We must plan the placement and character of objects along the street—the streetscape.

The empirical evidence reviewed in this chapter points to several guidelines for improving the streetscape and perceived urban quality. These are listed below. Of course, implementation of any change should be monitored to determine effects.

With regard to cognitive quality, it may be desirable to

1. Guide development toward an organized system of landmarks, paths, edges, nodes, and districts
2. Strengthen imageable elements through visibility, contrast, and use significance
3. Consider specific requirements for sociocultural and physical context
4. Focus esthetic improvement efforts on the imageable elements (not to the exclusion of other elements)

Because urban areas consist of a hierarchy of elements (from individual sites, to street, to district, and the full urban area), one set of esthetic criteria may not apply everywhere. Esthetic requirements may vary with the character of the area and the character of user activities and purposes. Consider two motivational states that may influence perceived environmental quality: *specific* and *diversive* exploration (Wohlwill, 1976). In the former, individuals prefer a reduction in uncertainty: they would desire more coherence and less complexity. In the latter, they prefer increases in uncertainty: they would prefer the excitement of high environmental complexity and contrast (such as that in Times Square or Las Vegas). Speed of movement may also affect visual needs. As speed increases, concentration (specific exploration) increases, peripheral vision decreases, and the scale of environment noticed changes (Lozano, 1974). Within those limitations, design for various settings, scales of environment, and speed of movement might enhance esthetic value by providing:

1. Moderate levels of complexity
2. High coherence and compatibility and low contrast
3. Familiar (and historical) elements
4. Moderate levels of novelty (discrepancies from the expected)

5. Vegetation
6. More open space
7. Mystery through streets and walkways that curve out of sight
8. Building styles that are perceived to fit building purposes
9. Reductions in the prominence of traffic, traffic noise, dilapidation, litter, poles, wires, signs, and intense industrial uses

FUTURE DIRECTIONS OF RESEARCH

This chapter points to several topics that represent promising new directions for inquiry. In particular, we need research that specifies the full lens model, that considers esthetics in relation to movement through space, that considers change, that considers socioperceptually relevant categories of scenes, and that addresses public policy questions.

SPECIFYING THE FULL LENS MODEL

Recall that the lens model posits probabilistic relationships between urban cues, perceptual/cognitive measures, urban affect, well-being, and spatial behavior. The research has focused on the relationship between perceptual/cognitive measures and urban affect. The consistently high reliabilities for the perceptual/cognitive measures suggest some objective basis, but research has only occasionally examined the relationship between environmental cues and perceptual/cognitive judgments. Similarly, the influences of affective quality and esthetic attributes on spatial behavior or sense of well-being has not been adequately documented. Effects of esthetic surroundings have been found in response to extreme manipulations. Study of the effects of less dramatic and more realistic changes is needed.

MOVEMENT

Movement through space and sequence of scenes is central to urban perception and preference (Lozano, 1974). Certainly, the collative variable "surprise" in the environment cannot be studied without consideration of movement through space. Similarly, speed of movement affects what people notice and how they react to their surroundings. Although findings for urban cognition depend on assumed or actual movement, the empirical study of urban perception and evaluation, with its reliance on static stimuli or observers, has not adequately examined this process.

CHANGE

What is valued esthetically may change with time—with experience and lifespan development, from day to night, and over generations. The research on cognition has addressed some relevant changes. For esthetics, the findings on familiarity/novelty, architect/lay differences and sociocultural differences indicate the importance of experience. But only one published study has examined developmental change: Zube, Pitt, and Evans (1983) applied a lifespan developmental perspective to the study of esthetic value. They demonstrated distinct lifespan developmental changes in preference. More work from a developmental perspective can illuminate the process through which people form esthetic values.

The empirical study of urban esthetics has also neglected the evening experience. Principles of esthetics that emerge in daylight may apply to evening experience, but the specific features for change may vary. Similarly, it may be useful to study esthetic needs as they relate to seasonal changes—such as changes in vegetation (leafless trees) or ground cover or extremes in temperature. Some of these conditions may affect motivational states, which in turn may alter esthetic preferences.

Finally, long-term (generational) changes are important to architectural meaning and change (Rapoport, 1982). For example, Lynes (1954) reported variations in architectural norms ("taste") over time in roughly 30-to-50-year periods. The continued study of esthetics as a static process (human responses to stimuli) cannot enhance our understanding of these dynamic processes. How can we empirically examine historical trends? Simonton's (1984) use of "historiometric" methods may be transferable to the analysis of long-term design trends. In a successful merging of the history of music with empirical observation, he quantified and compared melodic originality of 15,618 classical themes with thematic fame (measured relative to frequency of performance). In agreement with the optimal-level-of-arousal model, he found that the most famous themes tended to have a medium level of melodic originality. In addition, his findings support the concept of generational changes in esthetic norms. He found that melodic originality increased over the long term but it did so in cycles in which the most distinguished melodies of each generation departed from expectations of their era toward either more or less originality. Similar study of changes in design norms over time can uncover those principles of esthetics that are independent of location, period in time, or a particular designer. Such analysis can enhance our understanding of the nature of urban design masterpieces—those buildings and places that hold lasting appeal.

SOCIOPHYSICAL CONTEXT

As in language, where the same word takes on different meanings depending on context (how it is said, who is saying it, and what other words surround it), sociophysical context may influence the meanings of physical elements in the urban environment. Thus, for example, individuals from different-sized cities evaluate the same city differently (Wohlwill & Kohn, 1973).

Research has shown that sociodemographic factors such as life cycle, education, occupation, and gender influence environmental preferences (Carp &

Perception, Cognition, and Evaluation of Urban Places 51

Carp, 1982; Lyons, 1983; Nasar *et al.*, 1987; Zube *et al.*, 1983). At a minimum, these findings indicate major limitations in findings based on responses from the undergraduate subject pool. Beyond that, research on the specific needs of various sociodemographic groups has potential for application to environmental design. Planners/designers can easily find the sociodemographic characteristics of a city, neighborhood, or block in census data. It would be more difficult and time consuming for them to survey local populations for preferences. But, if research had already identified environmental preferences of the relevant sociodemographic groups, practioners could apply those findings to the local situation.

With regard to the environment, building types have been found to influence public response to buildings (Groat, 1979). In fact, research has found that people use different criteria in evaluating different housing types (Michelson, 1976). So, although research considering mixtures of building types or land uses may have value for identifying broader patterns of preference, we also need to understand the preferred features within particular categories of scene. Existing planning classifications by land use or building type can suggest some tentative categories of settings for study, but such categories may not reflect the categories used by the public. Information on the perceptually relevant categories of scenes is needed.

Taken together, the evidence on sociodemographic and environmental-category differences suggests a need to disaggregate populations into relevant sociodemographic groups, derive perceptually relevant categories of scenes for each group, and then identify the visual quality needs for each socioperceptually relevant entity. The concept here is similar to the ecological psychology concept of "behavior setting." Just as behavior settings consist of a population–environment mix and standing patterns of behavior, so particular categories of urban population–environments may have particular visual quality needs.

PUBLIC POLICY

Finally, research in urban esthetics can be informed by public policy concerns. At the national level, acts such as The National Environmental Policy Act (National Environmental Policy Act of 1969), require the federal government and its agencies to plan for esthetics and to give environmental amenities appropriate consideration in development. In addition, the Supreme Court has increasingly supported community efforts to control esthetics (Pearlman, 1988). The court has moved from accepting regulation of nuisances (for health and welfare), to agreeing that esthetics (as related to property) was a valid public purpose, to treating esthetics *per se* as a valid public purpose and arguing that communities have a right to regulate beauty. Many state courts have also moved to accepting esthetics as an adequate basis for decisions (Pearlman, 1988).

If challenged, however, the esthetic regulation must be based on a serious and comprehensive plan. Although the burden of proof rests with the plaintiff, the regulation is more likely to be upheld if it is based on solid applied research.

Presumably, such research should seek internal and ecological validity; it should consider both perceptually and policy-relevant attributes of the environment; it should consider the needs of various groups and places; it should identify limitations; and it should point to a comprehensive plan for control.

Through examination of the instruments of design control, one can identify relevant research questions. Consider the roadside environment. Its character results from public, private, and quasi-public actions. Public agencies own and control the design of public buildings and public rights-of-way. Of course, public development can be informed directly by research findings. Private individuals own and develop land adjacent to the rights-of-way, but that development must fit public controls. Cities and administrative bodies control the appearance of private development through such instruments as regulations (zoning, graphics, and building codes), incentives (revolving loans, tax credits, or other uses of city leverage), and design review. These all depend on guidelines, either formal (written standards and codes) or informal (judgments of experts) to control the design product. Research that considers the guidelines can have a substantial influence on urban form. By examining the breadth, depth, and enforcement procedures for local and national codes or design review, researchers may find questions of both practical and theoretical interest. For example, Wohlwill (1976) found fittingness and congruence as variables having practical and theoretical relevance. I chose to study complexity and contrast, because they were controlled in an existing graphics code and because of their potential theoretical relevance (Nasar, 1987a).

A recurring issue in environmental design research has been the gap between research and application. Why don't architects use design research? The public, not the architects, will be the main beneficiary of the research. As a result, we should gear research to the public (a natural and potentially powerful constituency) and elected officials. Through the vote, the public selects officials who shape policy about the built environment (how much money is allocated for building, what kinds of things get built, and what kinds of controls are appropriate). Consumer research on public policy questions can bring together the necessary coalitions to advocate certain policies. It can identify politically safe actions for elected officials, who have some interest in making popular decisions. The resulting public policy can set the guidelines within which designers and developers must operate.

Research that connects to public policy has had demonstrated success in changing our surroundings. Whyte's (1980) livable space findings, for example, were integrated into incentive zoning in New York and affected development in New York. Similar efforts could be undertaken for urban visual quality. For example, my research on the retail signscape (Nasar, 1987a) was motivated by a public policy question. A neighborhood planning agency had asked for recommendations for an overlay (special) code to regulate signs. The revised graphics code that was derived from the research findings received the support of the merchants association, the residents, and ultimately by a neighborhoodwide task force that adopted the code and passed it on to the Columbus City Council for approval. Public policy questions can inform research, and research can change public policy.

CONCLUSION

This chapter presented evidence of both systematic commonalities and sociodemographic differences in cognitive and evaluative response to attributes of the urban environment. For some attributes, clear policy directions are suggested. For others, additional research is needed.

In some ways, however, the research questions have been relatively safe. If we are concerned with improving the quality of our surroundings, and if our research is to guide planning decisions, then we may have to study some more risky questions, such as the symbolic meanings attributed to styles within various building types, the process through which esthetic norms change over generations, and esthetics in relation to the sequences of experiences when one move through space. We may also need to consider the specifics of preference within relevant sociophysical contexts. Finally, we should look to public policy questions facing courts, administrative bodies, and decision makers. With the solid grounding that has been developed in formal esthetics, we are at a crossroad; that is, we can continue to reexamine the same old questions or we can step into a new, and perhaps less controllable and less certain, research environment. Such a step is fitting to practical concerns in the environment and behavior field.

REFERENCES

Anderson, L. M., Mulligan, B. E., Goodman, L. S., & Rezen, H. Z. (1983). Effects of sounds on preferences for outdoor settings. *Environment and Behavior, 15,* 539–566.
Appleton, J. (1975). *The experience of landscape.* London: Wiley.
Appleyard, D. (1969). Why buildings are known. *Environment and Behavior, 1,* 131–156.
Appleyard, D. (1976). *Planning a pluralistic city.* Cambridge, MA: M.I.T. Press.
Appleyard, D. (1981). *Livable streets.* Berkely: University of California Press.
Appleyard, D., & Lintell, M. (1972). The environmental quality of city streets: The residents' viewpoint. *Journal of the American Institute of Planners, 38,* 84–101.
Berlyne, D. E. (1971). *Aesthetics and psychobiology.* New York: Appleton-Century-Crofts.
Bureau of Census (1987). *National data book and guide to sources: Statistical abstracts of the United States* (107th ed.). Washington, DC: U.S. Department of Commerce.
Canter, D., & Thorne, R. (1972). Attitudes to housing: A crosscultural comparison. *Environment and Behavior, 4,* 3–32.
Carp, F., & Carp, A. (1982). Perceived environmental quality of neighborhoods: Development of assessment scales and their relation to age and gender. *Journal of Environmental Psychology, 2,* 295–312.
Carp, F., Zawadsky, R., & Shokrin, H. (1976). Dimensions of urban quality. *Environment and Behavior, 8,* 239–265.
Craik, K. H. (1983). The psychology of the large scale environment. In N. R. Feimer & E. S. Geller (Eds.), *Environment psychology: Directions and perspectives* (pp. 67–105). New York: Praeger.
Devlin, A. (1976). The "Small Town" cognitive map: Adjusting to a new environment. In G. Moore & R. Golledge (Eds.), *Environmental knowing* (pp. 58–67). Stroudsburg, PA: Dowden, Hutchinson & Ross.
Devlin, K., & Nasar, J. (1987). *Beauty and the beast: Some preliminary comparisons of "popular" vs.*

"High" architecture and public vs. architect judgments of same (Department of City and Regional Planning working paper). Columbus, OH: Ohio State University.

Esposito, C. V. (1984). Methodological issues in the assessment of environmental sound perception: A strategy for empirical research. In D. Duerk & D. Campbell (Eds.), *EDRA 15: The challenge of diversity* (pp. 179–184). Washington, DC: Environmental Design Research Association.

Evans, G. (1980). Environmental cognition. *Psychological Bulletin, 88,* 259–287.

Evans, G., Marrero, D., & Butler, P. (1981). Environmental learning and cognitive mapping. *Environment and Behavior, 13,* 83–104.

Evans, G., Smith, C., & Pezdek, K. (1982). Cognitive maps and urban form. *Journal of the American Planning Association, 48,* 232–244.

Gärling, T. (1976). The structural analysis of environmental perception and cognition: A multidimensional scaling approach. *Environment and Behavior, 8,* 385–415.

Geller, D. M., Cook, J. B., O'Connor, M. A., & Low, S. K. (1982). Perceptions of urban scenes by small town and urban residents: A multidimensional scaling analysis. In P. Bart, A. Chen, & G. Francescato (Eds.), *Knowledge for design: Proceedings of the 13th International Conference of the Environmental Design Research Association* (pp. 128–141). College Park, MD: Environmental Design Research Association.

Gifford, R., & Ng, C. F. (1982). The relative contribution of visual and auditory cues to environmental perception. *Journal of Environmental Psychology, 2,* 275–284.

Goldberger, P. (1983). *On the rise: Architecture and design in a postmodern age.* New York: Times Books.

Groat, L. (1979). Does post-modernism communicate? *Progressive Architecture, 12,* 84–87.

Groat, L. (1984). Public opinions of contextual fit. *Architecture, 73,* 72–75.

Harrison, J. D., & Howard, W. A. (1972). The role of meaning in the urban image. *Environment and Behavior, 4,* 398–411.

Heft, H. (1979). The role of environmental features in route-learning: Two exploratory studies of way-finding. *Environmental Psychology and Nonverbal Behavior, 3,* 172–185.

Hershberger, R. G., & Cass, R. (1988). Predicting user responses to buildings. In J. L. Nasar (Ed.), *Environmental aesthetics: Theory, research and application* (pp. 195–211). New York: Cambridge University Press. (Original work published 1974)

Herzog, T. R., Kaplan, R., & Kaplan, S. (1976). The prediction of preference for familiar urban places. *Environment and Behavior, 8,* 627–645.

Hesselgren, S. (1976). *Man's perception of man-made environment.* Stroudsburg, PA: Dowden, Hutchinson & Ross.

Hiss, T. (1987, June 22). Reflections: Experiencing places—I. *New Yorker,* pp. 45–68.

Horayangkura, V. (1978). Semantic dimensional structures: A methodological approach. *Environment and Behavior, 10,* 555–584.

Kaplan, S., & Kaplan, R. (1982). *Cognition and environment: Functioning in an uncertain world.* New York: Praeger.

Kaplan, S., Kaplan, R., & Wendt, J. S. (1972). Rated preference and complexity for natural and urban visual material. *Perception and Psychophysics, 12,* 354–356.

Langdon, P. (1982, April 22). Suburbanites pick favorite home styles. *The New York Times,* p. C12.

Lansing, J. B., Marans, R. W., & Zehner, R. B. (1970). *Planned residential environments.* Ann Arbor: University of Michigan, Survey Research Center Institute for Social Research.

Locasso, R. (1988). The influence of a beautiful vs. an ugly interior on ratings of photographs of human faces: A replication of Maslow and Mintz. In J. Nasar (Ed.), *Environmental aesthetics: Theory, research, and applications* (pp. 135–142). New York: Cambridge University Press.

Lowenthal, D., & Riel, M. (1972). The nature of perceived and imagined environments. *Environment and Behavior, 4,* 189–204.

Perception, Cognition, and Evaluation of Urban Places 55

Lozano, E. (1974). Visual needs in the environment. *Town Planning Review, 43,* 351–374.
Lynch, K. (1960). *The image of the city.* Cambridge, MA: M.I.T. Press.
Lynes, R. (1954). *The tastemakers.* New York: Harper.
Lyons, E. (1983). Demographic correlates of landscape preference. *Environment and Behavior, 15,* 487–511.
Mandler, G., & Shebo, B. J. (1983). Knowing and liking. *Motivation and Emotion, 7,* 125–144.
Michelson, W. (1976). *Man and his urban environment: A sociological approach.* Reading, MA: Addison-Wesley.
Mintz, N. L. (1956). Effects of esthetic surroundings: II. Prolonged and repeated experience in a beautiful and an ugly room. *Journal of Psychology, 41,* 459–466.
Moore, G. T. (1979). Knowing about environmental knowing: The current state of theory and research on environmental cognition. *Environment and Behavior, 11*(2), 33–70.
Nasar, J. L. (1979). The evaluative image of the city. In A. D. Seidel & S. Danford (Eds.), *Environmental design: Research, theory, and application. Proceedings of the 10th Annual Conference of the Environmental Design Research Association* (pp. 38–45). Washington, DC: Environmental Design Research Association.
Nasar, J. L. (1980a). *Chattanooga preference survey and design recommendations.* Knoxville: University of Tennessee, School of Architecture.
Nasar, J. L. (1980b). Influence of familiarity on responses to visual quality of neighborhoods. *Perceptual & Motor Skills, 51,* 632–642.
Nasar, J. L. (1983). Adult viewer preferences in residential scenes. *Environment and Behavior, 15,* 589–614.
Nasar, J. L. (1984a). Cognition in relation to downtown street-scenes: A comparison between Japan and the United States. In D. Duerk & D. Campbell (Eds.), *EDRA 15 1984 proceedings: The challenge of diversity* (pp. 122–128). Washington, DC: Environmental Design Research Association.
Nasar, J. L. (1984b). Visual preferences in urban scenes: A cross-cultural comparison between Japan and the U.S. *Journal of Cross-Cultural Psychology, 1,* 79–93.
Nasar, J. L. (1986). *What the public notices and prefers in commercial signs.* Paper presented at the 94th Annual Convention of the American Psychological Association, Washington, DC, August.
Nasar, J. L. (1987a). Effect of sign complexity and coherence on the perceived quality of retail scenes. *Journal of the American Planning Association, 53,* 499–509.
Nasar, J. L. (1987b). Environmental correlates of evaluative appraisals of central business district scenes. *Landscape and Planning Research, 14,* 117–130.
Nasar, J. L. (1988a). Perception and evaluation of housing scenes. In J. L. Nasar (Ed.), *Environmental aesthetics: Research, theory and application* (pp. 275–289). New York: Cambridge University Press.
Nasar, J. L. (1988b). Urban scenes: Editor's introduction. In J. L. Nasar (Ed.), *Environmental aesthetics: Theory, research and applications* (pp. 257–259). New York : Cambridge University Press.
Nasar, J. L., Julian, D., Buchman, S., Humphreys, D., Mrohaly, M. (1983). The emotional quality of scenes and observation points: A look at prospect and refuge. *Landscape Planning, 10,* 355–361.
Nasar, J. L., Zaff, B., Dunworth, L. A., Duran, J., & Rezoski, A. (1987, August). *House style and meaning.* Paper presented at the 95th Annual Convention of the American Psychological Association, New York.
National Environmental Policy Act of 1969, 42 U.S.C. §4332 (1976).
Oostendorp, A. (1978). *The identification and interpretation of dimensions underlying aesthetic behavior in the daily urban environment.* Doctoral dissertation. University of Toronto. *Dissertation Abstracts International, 40*(028), 990.
Oostendorp, A., & Berlyne, D. E. (1978). Dimensions in the perception of architecture: Iden-

tification and interpretation of dimensions of similarity. *Scandinavian Journal of Psychology,* 19, 73–82.
Osgood, C. E., Suci, G., & Tannenbaum, P. (1957). *The measurement of meaning.* Urbana, IL: University of Illinois Press.
Pearlman, K. T. (1988). Aesthetic regulation and the courts. In J. L. Nasar (Ed.), *Environmental aesthetics: Theory, research and application* (pp. 476–492). New York: Cambridge University Press.
Purcell, A. T. (1986). Environmental perception and affect: A schema discrepancy model. *Environment and Behavior,* 18, 3–30.
Rapoport, A. (1982). *The meaning of the built environment.* Beverly Hills, CA: Sage.
Simonton, D. K. (1984). *Genius, creativity and leadership: Histiometric inquiries.* Cambridge: Harvard University Press.
Smith, G. F., & Dorfman, D. D. (1975). The effect of stimulus uncertainty on the relationship between frequency of exposure and liking. *Journal of Social and Personality Psychology,* 31, 150–155.
Sonnenfeld, J. (1966). Variable values in the space and landscape: An inquiry into the nature of environmental necessity. *Journal of Social Issues,* 4, 71–82.
Southworth, M. (1969). The sonic environment of cities. *Environment and Behavior,* 1, 49–70.
Tuttle, P. (1983). *Suburban fantasies.* Unpublished master's thesis, School of Architecture, University of Wisconsin, Milwaukee, WI.
Ulrich, R. (1973). *Scenery and the shopping trip: The roadside environment as a factor in route choice.* Doctoral dissertation, University of Michigan, Ann Arbor. *Dissertation Abstracts International,* 35(01A), 346.
Ulrich, R. (1981). Aesthetic and affective response to natural environment. In I. Altman & J. F. Wohlwill (Eds.), *Human behavior and environment: Advances in theory and research: Vol. 6. Behavior and the natural environment* (pp. 85–125). New York: Plenum Press.
Ulrich, R. (1984). View through a window influences recovery from surgery. *Science,* 224, 420–421.
Ward, L. M., & Russell, J. A. (1981). The psychological representation of molar physical environments. *Journal of Experimental Psychology: General,* 110, 121–152.
Whyte, W. (1980). *The social life of small urban spaces.* Washington, DC: Conservation Foundation.
Winkel, G., Malek, R., & Thiel, P. (1970). A study of human response to selected roadside environments. In H. Sanoff & S. Cohn (Eds.), *Proceedings of EDRA* (pp. 224–240). Raleigh, NC: North Carolina State University.
Wohlwill, J. F. (1976). Environmental aesthetics: The environment as a source of affect. In I. Altman & J. F. Wohlwill (Eds.), *Human behavior and environment: Advances in theory and research* (Vol. 1, pp. 37–86). New York: Plenum Press.
Wohlwill, J. F. (1982). The visual impact of development in coastal zone areas. *Coastal Zone Management Journal,* 9, 225–248.
Wohlwill, J. F. (1983). The concept of nature: A psychologist's view. In I. Altman & J. F. Wohlwill (Eds.), *Human behavior and the environment: Advances in theory and research: Vol. 6. Behavior and the natural environment* (pp. 5–37). New York: Plenum Press.
Wohlwill, J. F., & Kohn, I. (1973). The environment as experienced by the migrant: An adaptation-level view. *Respresentative Research in Social Psychology,* 4, 35–164.
Woodcock, D. M. (1982). *A functionalist approach to environmental preference.* Doctoral dissertation, University of Michigan, Ann Arbor, *Dissertation Abstracts International,* 43(028), 515.
Zube, E. H., Pitt, D. G., & Evans, S. W. (1983). A lifespan development study of landscape assessment. *Journal of Environmental Psychology,* 3, 115–128.
Zube, E. H., Vining, J., Law, C. S., & Bechtel, R. B. (1985). Perceived urban residential quality: A cross-cultural bimodal study. *Environment and Behavior,* 17, 327–350.

3

Farmers' Markets as Community Events

ROBERT SOMMER

INTRODUCTION

The design and management of many urban public spaces have been criticized for failing to serve the needs of residents (Hester, 1984; Jackson, 1981). Nonuse rather than overuse of parks and plazas is the problem (Gold, 1978). Francis (1987) traces the origins of open-space research to public awareness of the social failure of these settings. Some aspects of nonuse have been dealt with through redesign. Another approach to nonuse involves expanding the range of uses through innovative programs that attract larger numbers and broader categories of users. Special events such as concerts, exhibits, and festivals create secondary territories under the control of vendors, city agencies, etc., in contrast to anonymous public areas seemingly belonging to no one. One of the most successful means for bringing large numbers of people into urban open spaces on a regular and predictable basis is the farmers' market (FM).

This is an old institution being revived to fit new times. It is returning not out of nostalgia but because of the benefits it offers. All across the nation, FMs are springing up in city parks, plazas, pedestrian malls, parking lots, barricaded streets, county fairgrounds, and courthouse squares. Most are seasonal, conducted weekly throughout the summer months, but a few operate year-round selling stored, preserved, or nonseasonal items. Each takes its form from the community and region served.

Government has played an important role in encouraging the development of FMs. The Massachusetts Department of Food and Agriculture assisted in the establishment of more than 50 community markets around the state. West Virginia established seven permanent farmers' markets in different cities and

---

ROBERT SOMMER • Department of Psychology, University of California-Davis, Davis, CA 95616.

provided the staff to run them. The Pennsylvania Department of Agriculture assisted over a dozen tailgate markets for farmers selling directly to the public. The Honolulu City Government sponsored 20 markets on city-owned land. In the past five years, the Texas Department of Agriculture has helped to establish 80 farmers' markets across the state.

TYPOLOGY OF MARKETS

Buying and selling food are such basic human activities that many different market types have evolved. Some semantic clarification is required, although any typology must acknowledge that hybrids are more common than pure types. As Pyle (1971) indicates, to identify or define a farmers' market is "no easy task; for everything that is called a farmers' market may not be one, and other names are given to meetings that have the form and function of a farmers' market" (p. 167).

They are called by many names in the United States—Community Farm Markets in Illinois, Food Fairs in Alabama and Louisiana, Court Days in Wisconsin, where they follow the old route of the circuit court through the counties, Curb Markets and Trade Days in the Northeast, People's Open Markets in Honolulu, and Certified Farmers' Markets in California. The following list of definitions emphasizes retail activities rather than wholesale transactions, which warrant separate treatment.

The *public market* is a place where a variety of goods, invariably including produce and other foodstuffs, is sold on a periodic basis by numerous small, private vendors (Plattner, 1978).

The *farmers' market* as a pure type is a public market restricted to produce and other basic foodstuffs sold by growers to consumers. It is a form of direct marketing that prohibits participation of peddlars who purchase food for resale.

The *flea market* is a public market devoted to the retail sale and exchange of second-hand goods. Frequently flea markets include produce sellers who may or may not be farmers.

The *festival market* is specifically designed to combine retail sales with recreation and entertainment activities. Such markets are often constructed around a theme related to period, site, architecture, or previous functions, giving rise to the alternative term *theme market*.

The retail *produce market* is a private enclosure specializing in the sale of fresh produce. Typically, its operation is under a single owner or lessee. To the degree that a retail produce market accommodates multiple vendors selling directly to consumers, it is the private counterpart of a public market.

The *supermarket* is a one-stop retail outlet for food and other household items. It is the dominant retail outlet for basic foodstuffs in the United States and many other Western nations. The *supermarket chain* is a vertically and horizontally integrated institution, often with its own factory-farms, transportation, storage, processing, distribution, and retail facilities under corporate ownership and management.

Farmers' Markets as Community Events

The focus of this chapter is the farmers' market in the United States, although other types of markets and other regions will be mentioned occasionally for purposes of comparison. As indicated earlier, there are many hybrid forms, for example, festival markets allowing use of their facilities by flea markets, flea markets that include farmers selling their own wares, farmers' markets held in shopping malls. Every conceivable combination of market format can be found.

HISTORY

Early American FMs were copies of their European cousins. Farmers came into town in horse-drawn wagons to sell their crops to city dwellers. Most of the selling initially took place on open lots along a major thoroughfare, which became Market Street. Soon closed sheds protected temporary stalls, but these, in turn, gave way to large buildings on land donated by the city or by a wealthy citizen.

The first market on record in the English Colonies was established in 1634 in Boston in open space in the center of town. In 1655, a leading Boston merchant left a bequest to the City stipulating that a third of it was to be used for construction of a permanent marketplace and town hall. Completed three years later, the building became the focal point of civic activity. Although it was primarily a market, it also served as a courthouse, library, armory, and commercial center (Burke, 1977). Philadelphia had the distinction of having the best planned and regulated markets in the colonies. William Penn's plans for the city included a market along the main thoroughfare, High Street, later renamed Market Street. According to the original proclamation in 1693, the market was opened twice weekly by the ringing of a bell and no one was permitted to buy or sell on the way to the market (Burke, 1977).

Colonial markets guaranteed equal access to all producers. This was ensured by a "king's peace" and later by a "market peace" enforced by a market master or special market court. Pillories were constructed for those who violated its laws and were used for offenses such as *forestalling*, which meant attempting to privately purchase goods before they reached the market; *engrossing*, or attempting to create a monopoly in order to limit supply and control prices; and *regrating*, which way buying at a market for the purpose of reselling at the same market. The prohibition against regrating was largely a sanitary measure intended to minimize the amount of rehandling of perishable foods (Mund, 1948).

As an inducement to their formation, markets were protected in various ways. Some cities prohibited the sale of competitive products during the hours that the public market was open. Others prohibited stores from being established within a quarter mile of any public market or prohibited pushcart vendors from selling competitive products on the streets during market hours (Sweet, 1961).

The public market reached its peak during the 19th century and then declined swiftly. The growth of cities brought new health and sanitation regulations and architectural codes that many older buildings could not meet without enormous capital outlays. It often seemed more economical to tear down a building than to renovate it. Improved transportation and the development of refrigeration techniques made it possible to ship crops long distances. Suburban development began to chew up much of the land around the city previously cultivated by gardeners and farmers.

The creation of food chain stores was a heavy blow to small farmers who had sold at the public market or directly to small grocery stores. A regional warehouse was not interested in a load of near-ripe melons or cherries. The chains turned instead to factory farms at distant locations capable of delivering fruits and vegetables at specific times that could travel long distances and maintain their appearance through numerous loadings and unloadings. Neighborhood grocery stores coexisted with public markets, which were no longer expanding. These grocery stores offered personal service on a small scale and friendly setting, and they often became neighborhood social centers where customers came to exchange news as well as purchase merchandise (Beckman & Nolen, 1976). However, the local grocery stores did not offer the variety and social opportunities of a large public market building.

Small neighborhood stores and the public markets coexisted for several decades until the rise of the supermarket in the 1930s, when convenience became the byword in retailing. The supermarket did not come into being as a totally new, mature institution but evolved as a series of separate, distinct concepts including cash-and-carry merchandise, self-service, and convenience retailing (Markin, 1968). A supermarket contained under one roof everything the average household needed, readily available for quick inspection, purchase, and checkout. The trend undermined the local grocers, who were unable to compete with the supermarket in terms of price or variety, and undermined the public markets by reducing patronage and eliminating the small farmers who had previously sold at public markets.

The 20th century brought a rapid decline in the public market throughout the nation. Some of the best-loved buildings were torn down and the land sold to developers. The district commission in Washington, D.C., rented the Georgetown Farmers Market to an automotive parts company, even though the property had been deeded to the city in 1802 with the provision that it remain a public market "forever." Other buildings were preserved at the cost of conversion into boutiques and specialty shops with rents far beyond the means of small farmers.

Burke (1978) decries this trend: "Somewhere along the line it appears that a number of cities are missing the point. The public market's integrity is dependent on the simple fact that it is essentially an egalitarian setting where real people buy real and essential things" (p. 12). Implicit in Burke's comment is the fact that a public market is more than a building; it is an institution that encompasses a multiplicity of activities centered around, but not restricted to, retail food sales. Its roots can be found in the Greek agora, village markets in

Africa, the 15th-century Great Bazaar in Istanbul, medieval markets held in Western European cathedral squares, and the colonial markets in the United States (Kowinski, 1986).

BENEFITS

Civic Utility

Because farmers' markets fulfill many worthy social and economic objectives, there will be less resistance to a temporary appropriation of city open space by a farmers' market than for most other purposes. This is true even in regard to prominent, highly valued locations, such as a courthouse square, city hall plaza, or park. The widespread appeal of the farmers' markets has helped to overcome the resistance of many public agencies to the multiuse concept.

The popularity of farmers' markets has helped to overcome this type of bureaucratic single-mindedness and gain temporary occupation of valued public space at nominal or no cost. The latter consideration is important because a farmers' market has minimal surplus capital. In contrast to a concert held in a public park, where the promoters must have extensive insurance coverage and provide their own security patrols, these requirements are likely to be waived for a farmers' market where the risks of untoward incidents are extremely low. The density, demographics, and attitudes of participants and the presence of so many vendors with jurisdiction over secondary territories make the markets largely self-policing. Farmers' markets have been deliberately introduced into some city parks to dilute the presence of streetpeople.

The appeal of the FM cuts across ideological boundaries. Environmental activists link the markets to family farms, land preservation, organic farming, opposition to pollution, and a general antidevelopment, small-is-beautiful philosophy that leads some writers to classify the FM as part of a nostalgia movement (Meisner, 1984). It is common to find environmental organizations at FMs collecting signatures and conducting outreach. On the other end of the political spectrum, conservatives have no difficulty in supporting an institution so rooted in individualism, economic exchange, the family farm, and localism. More than 90 percent of Illinois FMs are sponsored by a Chamber of Commerce or downtown merchant's association (Archer, 1978).

Revitalizing Downtown

Markets scheduled in city plazas or parks attract shoppers who might otherwise not travel to the central city. Many of these shoppers will patronize nearby shops and thereby strengthen the downtown area (Tyburczy & Sommer, 1983). In 1973, the Syracuse (New York) Chamber of Commerce assisted in starting a downtown farmers' market as a means of urban revitalization. City officials agreed to close off a street block every Tuesday from late spring through fall. A traffic count one year after the market began showed more than 12,000

Figure 1. Madison, Wisconsin. Street in front of the State Capitol closed to traffic for a noontime farmers' market.

visitors on a typical summer Tuesday and downtown merchants reported sales increases of 8% to 14%. The presence of the FM had a snowball effect on improvement in the immediate area. The City offered a free bus tour of the downtown district that ended at the market and the Parks Department installed picnic tables on a small lawn adjoining the market for people to sit down and snack. At election time, political candidates set up tables because the market was a good place to meet potential voters (Hess, 1974).

Paramount among the reasons for starting the Eugene (Oregon) FM in 1970

Farmers' Markets as Community Events 63

Figure 2. The 59th Street Greenmarket in New York City started in a vacant lot. Photograph by Alan Elms.

was a dying downtown in need of revitalization. The principles for site selection as listed in the Market brochure are as follows:

1. Outdoors. The open-air quality of the market is an essential ingredient in its success. It makes it beautiful, free, and varied with the weather. It has encouraged the vendors to construct imaginative, weather-proof, individual booths which are a colorful and lively addition to the downtown area. Also, because there is no door to open and no building to enter, a hesitant first-time visitor is able to look the situation over before plunging in.

2. Downtown location. Larger and perhaps more beautiful locations might be available on the outskirts of town, but the Board has always felt it essential to be centrally located, both to enhance the downtown, and to enable people to use . . . means of transportation other than the car for getting to the market.

3. Public property. All three of the market's sites so far have been on public property and we hope to continue in this way. It is felt that the market is a public service, and the Oregon Constitution recognizes this fact by permitting counties to set up public markets and even to spend money for this purpose if necessary.

4. Aesthetics. The Saturday Market is beautiful to look at and this is not entirely by accident. We have consistently tried to find a site which has some trees and greenery, some shielding from traffic, some interesting design, etc.

5. Winter closure. The Market closes from the last Saturday before Christmas to the first Saturday in May. The weather is terrible during this period, and there are no fruits, vegetables, or flowers. . . . The re-opening of the Market in

the spring becomes a big event. Everyone looks forward to it and the media give it a lot of free publicity. (Streisinger, 1974)

These principles reflect the direct connection of the markets to region, season, downtown revitalization, and public open space. Organizers were as motivated by ecological considerations as by economic and social benefits.

Assistance for Small Farmers

Based on the belief that the family farm maintains important democratic values, government policy for the past century has been to support it through various legislative programs. The establishment of FMs is seen as one way of accomplishing this. Although few growers will use them as exclusive outlets, FM markets have become increasingly important as secondary or incremental outlets. In a comprehensive survey in six states, Henderson and Linstrom (1980) found that 15% of all farmers sold some products directly to consumers and these sales represented almost $260 million dollars or 2% of the total farm product sales in the six states.

Returns are higher to small farmers selling directly to the public than on the wholesale market. Moulton (1977) found that farmers selling vegetables through the wholesale market received only 40% of the retail price compared with an estimated 65% to 85% at a farmers' market. Pederson (1984) found that small growers received almost two-thirds more selling at a farmers' market than at a nearby wholesale market.

Declared sales of individual vendors tend to be relatively low. Two-thirds of the Louisiana farmers surveyed cited annual sales through the FM of less than $2,500 (Roy, Jordan, Law, & Leary, 1978). Texas producers selling at farmers' markets in 1986 averaged about $3,000 each in profits (Hightower, 1987). However, there is reason to suppose that these figures are underestimated. Researchers in Upstate New York abandoned any attempt to obtain information on sales with the comment "The informal atmosphere and sometimes intense activity with many small cash sales make accounting difficult. A special study of sales volume at FMs would be a challenging project" (Pease & Eiler, 1976, p. 6).

The farmers' markets cannot by themselves reverse the national decline among small family farms, but they provide an incremental retail outlet for small growers who depend on diversification as a means of economic survival. Few of the sellers use the market as an exclusive outlet; most use it in addition to a roadside stand, U-pick, or selling through the wholesale market. In many localities, the proliferation of farmers' markets has induced hobbyist gardeners to become part-time farmers and some part-time farmers to become full-time farmers. It is still too early to assay the economic impact of the farmers' markets' resurgence on the farming community.

Consumer Benefits

Surveys undertaken at farmers' markets in Illinois (Archer, 1978), Missouri (Brooker & Taylor, 1977), Louisiana (Roy, Leary, & Law, 1977), and California

(Sommer & Wing, 1980) have shown that the primary reason that customers shop at farmers' markets is food quality as signified by improved freshness and flavor. The second and third most important reasons respectively are lower prices and social atmosphere. Available research indicates that all these motives are realized at the markets. Nothing is free, of course, and these benefits carry a cost in convenience, travel time, and cosmetic appearance of food items. Here is the summary of some of the available research on the consumer benefits of farmers' markets.

Prices

Food prices at eight FMs in four Southeastern states were 28% lower than the supermarket prices for the same items (Virginia Polytechnic Institute, 1978). A study of food fairs in 22 Alabama and Tennessee towns showed a 50% average savings on produce over retail costs (Agricultural Marketing Project, 1977). Studies at Seattle's Pike Place Market showed an 8% to 15% saving relative to nearby supermarkets (Pike Place Merchant's Association, 1978). Prices at four of Philadelphia's FMs found prices 27% lower than in nearby supermarkets (Hanssens, 1978), and a study in Hartford, Connecticut, found supermarket prices 29% to 46% higher than FM prices for the same items (Taylor, 1979). Plattner (1979) estimated that there is a 55% price benefit to FM customers. A systematic price comparison in 17 California farmers' markets found that the overall unit cost at the farmers' market was 34% lower than at supermarkets in the same cities (Sommer, Wing, & Aitkens, 1980).

Freshness and Flavor

For fresh seasonal items, there is no comparison in freshness between farmers' markets and the wholesale food marketing system, where produce may be handled eight times prior to retail sale (Jumper, 1974). Double-blind flavor tests, in which neither the consumer nor the researcher knew the origin of the produce, showed that FM tomatoes, bell peppers, peaches, apricots, and watermelons were preferred over their supermarket counterparts (Sommer, Stumpf, & Bennett, 1982).

Social Atmosphere

Various writers have described the supermarket as one of the more alienating public settings (Burke, 1978; Cross, 1976; Lozar, 1975; Markin, 1968; Silverstein & Jacobson, 1978). In their look at marketplaces around the world, Isogai and Shanjiro (1972) maintain that the supermarket "takes away the social pleasures of shopping" and removes the vitality, excitement, and exchange of opinion and gossip characteristic of the traditional marketplace. A French visitor observed that American supermarkets "all look alike and you can do your entire shopping without exchanging a word with anybody" (Griswold-Minois,

1980). There are reports that the early supermarkets were not nearly as unfriendly as their present-day counterparts (*Progressive Grocer*, 1952). The loss of friendliness has been attributed both to the sociofugal layout of the stores and the faster tempo. According to Beckman and Nolen (1976), the tempo of the successful modern supermarket is too fast to permit extended social intercourse.

Lozar (1975) and Silverstein and Jacobson (1978) suggest dividing large supermarkets into smaller areas, each under the jursidiction of different employees, similar to the public market concept. This would increase autonomy and leadership of employees while giving them more direct responsibility for territories and at the same time increase contact with customers. Some supermarkets have experimented with singles nights, coffee bars, deli service, and salad bars (Dietrich, 1982; Higgins, 1983). These attempts are the exception and the generally sociofugal quality of the modern supermarket has created a niche for smaller, more sociopetal retail settings.

By contrast, consumer surveys, semantic differential ratings, and systematic counts of conversations have shown a livelier social atmosphere at farmers' markets than in nearby supermarkets (Sommer, Herrick, & Sommer, 1981).

Hours of Operation

It is typical of farmers' markets around the world to operate on a limited basis. This is partly due to the combination of a restricted occupation of public space, temporary shelters that do not provide adquate protection during inclement weather, and the dependence of the markets on regional and seasonal production. There are technical limitations on the types of items suitable for a farmers' market and statutory restrictions forbidding the sale of certain products. Unlike public markets in Third World countries where these restrictions do not apply, one-stop shopping is not feasible at most farmers' markets in the United States, where they are ancillary rather than primary retail centers.

Appearance of Fruits and Vegetables

Supermarkets cull their produce more closely than do small farmers at FMs. Double-blind consumer ratings show that the appearance of supermarket tomatoes was rated higher than that of farmers' market tomatoes (Sommer, Knight, & Sommer, 1979). This is probably true of other items, but the research has not been undertaken.

INTERGROUP CONTACTS

The markets provide settings in which diverse groups interact under conditions likely to engender positive attitudes. Burke (1978) describe the FM as "one of the few places in the city where economic and social distinctions tend to fade. The egalitarian social character of the market is one of the most frequent

Farmers' Markets as Community Events

Figure 3. The West Oakland (California) Farmers' Market is held in a downtown parking lot that is not used on Saturday mornings. The market is a social center for nearby residents.

themes struck in journalistic descriptions [as] places where rich and poor rub shoulders" (p. 11).

The markets also provide a setting for urban–rural contacts. As nations become more industrialized, city residents lose touch with the sources of their food supply. At the same time, urban problems encroach on the rural landscape in the form of tract development, rising land costs, and air and water pollution, which threaten the productivity of agricultural land. City dwellers who lack understanding of agriculture may be uninterested in pollution abatement or programs to protect the rural landscape, except as a recreational resource. Rural residents who form their images of city life from media may be unwilling to open recreational space to city residents or support programs through their legislative representatives that will be of primary benefit to cities. The FM is a mechanism for bridging the gulf between city and country.

Contacts also cut across traditional ethnic barriers, as in the case of the Asian-American truck farmers selling to Anglo customers at the San Francisco Farmers' Market or the white Protestant New Jersey farmers selling to Hispanic

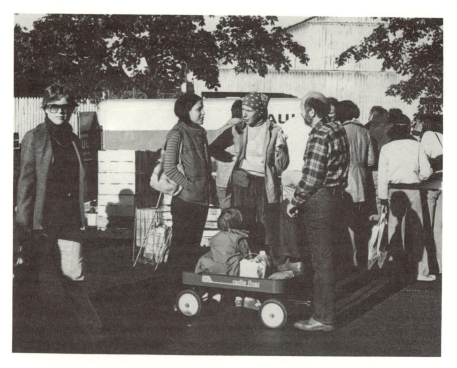

Figure 4. Evanston, Illinois. Unlike the supermarket with its narrow aisles, the open spaces and layout of the farmers' market encourage social encounters.

and black customers at New York City's Greenmarkets. The cultural diversity is illustrated by this description of the Stockton (California) farmers' market on a Saturday morning:

> For two hours every week, a piece of the downtown becomes anything but a modern California urban commercial district. It becomes the central market of a town in Mexico or Thailand or any city in any faraway land, a place of crowds, of smells, of noise, of haggling and bargaining . . . there were vegetables with no known English name, sold by vendors to customers in deals in which no English name was needed. (Wiley, 1987, p. B1)

Openness and Contact with Nature

A park or plaza is often chosen as the site of a farmers' market because it is available open space, with high symbolic value, good access, and public amenities. Incidental benefits include the available landscaping, which introduces natural elements to a degree difficult to replicate indoors. Many new shopping malls have replaceable plant displays, but these are not equivalent to the mature trees, birds, and squirrels of an outdoor setting. Seasonal changes in the landscape parallel changes in the types of produce available. The openness of the market has been considered a psychological benefit. Writing in 1913, Sullivan compared markets held indoors and outdoors and comes out firmly on the side of the *market ouvert*. He quotes promoters of open-air markets in the United Kingdom and on the Continent who maintain that the public "shows a preference for free open-air markets to closed-in market halls" (p. 311). Sullivan maintained that open-air markets are economical to the city, because they can be located or removed without cost to suit neighborhood changes, whereas fixed market halls are costly to establish and financial burdens when they fail.

FUNCTIONAL REQUIREMENTS

Requirements for a FM include a site, schedule, shelter, products, vendors, customers, social organization, and tradition. These requirements will be discussed primarily with reference to farmers' markets, but many of the points apply to other market types.

Site

Most often a farmers' market involves an alternative use of public open space, such as a park, plaza, lawn of a civic building, or municipal parking lot. This is an open region (Goffman, 1963) where people can enter and leave freely without, for example, meeting entrance requirements or paying a fee. The site may be closed off to other activities on market day or shared on a multiuse basis. Figure 1 shows a prototypic FM in a public park or plaza. The typical layout is linear, although modifications will be made to fit site characteristics. Three zones are recognizable without being formally marked. The *vendor delivery and preparation area* consists of those portions of the street abutting the park or plaza; *display and sales* occupy the area between the curb and the sidewalk; and the sidewalk represents the *customer transit area*, which includes social space and amenities.

Shelter

Protection against the elements is accomplished sometimes with permanent structures and at other times with makeshift arrangements. Well-established FMs may have some permanent buildings, although they may also use outdoor space. Soulard Market in St. Louis has been operating in its present city-owned building since 1927. The City rents out almost 300 stalls to vendors, who include both small farmers selling their own produce and hawkers who buy produce from a nearby commercial terminal for resale. The farmers' market in Terre Haute occupies a building owned and managed cooperatively by the farmers who sell there.

Markets that lack buildings must rely on temporary structures supplied either by vendors or the market. This arrangement is compatible with the multiple-use concept for public open space. An informal technology has arisen among vendors as to ways of mounting poles and canvas covers on pickup trucks for weather protection. Vendors supply these according to personal inclination, or a general theme may be required by market regulations; for example, awnings must be of the same color and material for visual consistency and market identification. Personalization of stalls is strongly encouraged, particularly when it derives from the product sold or otherwise reflects local culture.

Schedule

Because they are intended to satisfy basic food needs, markets operate according to schedules that allow customers to plan their shopping and farmers to plan their harvest and delivery to fit market days. Seasonal variation in crop production will influence the schedule. A pure farmers' market in cold-weather countries is likely to operate only during the summer months one or two days a week. In warmer areas with longer growing seasons, markets can operate on a year-round basis.

Market days can be coordinated with other events, as in the case of Wisconsin's historic "circuit markets" held on court day along the route of the circuit court through local counties. Some markets coordinate their schedules with complementary events, such as swap meets, craft shows, and concerts, which do not represent expanded functions, as when an FM sells nonfood items, but rather involves multiple events under separate management sharing the same public space and customers.

Temporal constraints are market derived in terms of product availability, customer expectations, and the vendor's desire to obtain a favorable location share by arriving early. The vendor will leave as soon as products are sold or when other commitments arise (as in the case of a vendor attending two markets serially on a single day) or customer traffic is light. Unlike supermarket employees who have scheduled hours, farmers as independent entrepreneurs can come and go as they want so long as they do not violate the informal choreography, or "place ballet," as Seamon and Nordin (1980) describe it.

Customers

Most FM shoppers are permanent local residents. Ninety-four percent of customers at seven Missouri FMs were year-round residents of the area who traveled less than four miles to the market (Collins, Munankami, & Breimyer, 1978). Approximately three-quarters arrived in groups, mostly all family units. This can be contrasted with the 75% single-person shopping at conventional supermarkets (Sommer, Herrick, & Sommer, 1981). The difference seems attributable to the sociopetal quality of the FM, which allows groups to remain

Sommer, R., Knight, H., & Sommer, B. A. (1979). Comparison of farmers' market and supermarket produce: Tomatoes and bell peppers. *Journal of Food Science, 44,* 1474–1477.
Sommer, R., & Nelson, S. A. (1985). Local use of survey data: Impact of research findings on farmers' markets. *Human Relations, 38,* 233–245.
Sommer, R., Stumpf, M., & Bennett, H. (1982). Quality of farmers' market produce. *Journal of Consumer Affairs, 16,* 130–136.
Sommer, R., & Wing, M. (1980). Farmers' markets please their customers. *California Agriculture, 34,* 11–12.
Sommer, R., Wing, M., & Aitkens, S. (1980). Price savings to consumers at farmers' markets. *Journal of Consumer Affairs, 14,* 452–462.
Streisinger, L. (1974). *Saturday market.* Lane County, OR: Saturday Market Association.
Sullivan, J. W. (1913). *Markets for the people.* New York: MacMillan.
Sweet, M. L. (1961). History of municipal markets. *Journal of Housing, 18,* 237–247.
Taylor, S. (1979, April 26). Food, home grown—how long? *The Hartford Courant,* p. A10.
Tyburczy, J., & Sommer, R. (1983). Farmers' markets are good for downtown. *California Agriculture, 37,* 30–32.
U.S. Department of Agriculture and Department of Health and Human Services. (1980). *Nutrition and your health: Dietary guidelines for Americans.* Washington, DC: U.S. Government Printing Office.
Virginia Polytechnic Institute. (1978). Planning a farmers' market (Publication No. 776). Blacksburg, VA: Virginia Polytechnic and State University, Extension Division.
Wann, John L., et al. (1948). *Farmers' produce markets in the United States: Part 1. History and description.* Washington, DC: U.S. Department of Agriculture.
Whyte, W. H. (1980). *The social life of small urban spaces.* New York: Conservation Foundation.
Wiley, W. (1987, April 10). Stockton farmers' mart: A taste for all palates. *Sacramento Bee,* p. B1.

4

Playgrounds at the Crossroads
POLICY AND ACTION RESEARCH NEEDED TO ENSURE A VIABLE
FUTURE FOR PUBLIC PLAYGROUNDS IN THE UNITED STATES

ROBIN C. MOORE

INTRODUCTION

Public playgrounds in the United States have entered a crisis stage in their evolution. They have been criticized as adults' attempts to control children's behavior (Wood 1977), damned as irrelevant to children's developmental needs (Frost & Klein, 1983), and described by children as boring, hurtful, and antisocial (Moore, 1989a). More often than not, these supposed spaces for healthy child development contain vast expanses of hot, hard asphalt, poorly maintained old metal equipment—oftentimes installed without adequate safety surfaces—water features that have not worked for years, pokey sandboxes without sand, and vegetation—if it exists at all—installed as an esthetic buffer rather than as a play setting (Bruya & Langendorfer, in press). And yet these spaces where children spend so much of their time could very well support educational principles and stimulate child development (Schools Council, 1974b; Sebba & Churchman, 1986).

Poor environmental quality goes hand in hand with a poor safety record. There has been a long history of concern extending back to 1909 when the first soft swing seat was introduced (Frost, 1986). But progress has been slow. Several massive suits in recent years (Sweeney, 1987) have made public officials apprehensive about what they should or should not be providing in the name of playgrounds and very cautious about accepting design innovations for fear they might be defined as "attractive nuisances" in a court of law.

ROBIN C. MOORE • School of Design, North Carolina State University, Raleigh, NC 27695.

The purpose of this chapter is to provide a perspective on the current state of public playgrounds in the United States and to propose research and policy directions to support their improvement as viable places for child development. A frame of reference drawn around children's use of the outdoors and children's right to play is briefly sketched. The main issues current in the field of practice and arising from a review of the empirical literature are discussed in depth. They include playground use, safety, the play value of different types of setting, adventure play, site planning, and the characteristics of settings that support social integration. A national action-research program is proposed. Emphases include play leadership and animation training, the implementation of risk-management models, the use of new media for public education, improvement of designer awareness, and the need for increased public–private partnership. Last, a detailed action-research agenda (Appendix) describes interventions required to solve specific problems associated with the design and development of particular play settings.

CHILDREN'S USE OF THE OUTDOORS

It is a clearly proven empirical fact that children are the major users of the outdoor environment in residential areas of the city (Björklid, 1982; Cooper Marcus, 1974; Moore & Young, 1978; U.K. Dept. of the Environment, 1973). It has been well documented that even in the most constraining environments children will wring the play potential from whatever is at hand: each other, street furniture, parked cars, vegetation, found objects, etc. (Moore, 1986a, 1987; Moore, 1989a). One may argue that developmentally this is the best of circumstances. It offers children a maximum opportunity to explore, to discover, to acquire knowledge of themselves and their surroundings through interactions with what van Vliet (1983) has called the "fourth environment," where they develop that sense of autonomy and self-esteem so critical to individual well-being (van Vliet, 1985).

The problem is that even though children are very resourceful in discovering free-play opportunities, often they are simply not available; or if they are, the perceived physical and social dangers are too great for parents to sanction their use. High-profile news stories about child molestations, attacks, and kidnappings (the large proportion of the latter perpetrated in custody battles) have made parents wary of allowing their children "free range." Social safety is a serious barrier to children's free play. "Fear of strangers" is deep-rooted among parents (Moore, 1986a). In a study of 8 to 12-year-olds' use of the San Francisco Bay Area landscape (Moore, 1980a), when asked the reasons why travel to certain places was prohibited, 27% of the children's replies covered social fears (fear of attack, assault, and kidnap; threats from other children; and nonspecific social apprehension, e.g., "There's a lot of strange people around here.").

We need to know (by analyzing police reports, for instance) how, and in what environments, children get attacked, and by whom. Until countered by more solid evidence, many parents and others directly or indirectly responsible for children will, with good reason, restrict their children's territory.

Physical safety is an equally important and more tangible issue (Wilkinson & Lockhart, 1980). In 1984, 34% of all pedestrians killed or injured in traffic accidents were children under the age of 15 (National Safety Council, 1986). In the Bay Area study referred to above, traffic danger accounted for 22% of the replies stating why travel to certain places was prohibited by parents (Moore, 1980a). In addition to traffic, other physical dangers (fear of water, getting wet, drowning; snakes, dogs, bugs, animals; and miscellaneous other things) accounted for a further 25% of the children's replies.

THE CHILD'S RIGHT TO PLAY

At the very time children are losing many traditional social supports (two-parent households, caregiver at home, proximity to extended family) and suffering restrictions on their free-range opportunities, public playgrounds are threatened with extinction. But children have a basic human right to play. The principle dates back to Jean-Jacques Rousseau's 1762 "charter of childhood" (Whitehead, 1922). In 1959, the right to play was built into the U.N. Declaration of the Rights of the Child, and in 1979, it was elaborated into a comprehensive mission statement (International Association for the Child's Right to Play, IPA, 1979). But implementation has been slow. At last count (Esbensen, 1979), only ten countries had some form of national standard for children's play spaces in the residential environment. The United States was not one of them.

Public playgrounds need to be as diverse, exciting, and accessible as the play opportunities elsewhere in the child's habitat. They must compensate for the restrictions of traffic dangers and parental apprehension and function as a valuable social asset in children's lives. The types of playground addressed here include small neighborhood facilities in residential districts, schoolgrounds, miniparks in new or redeveloped areas, and playgrounds sited in community parks.

PLAYGROUND RESEARCH FINDINGS

Of 34 empirical studies reviewed by Moore and Young (1978), only six related to play areas. Since then, a review by G. T. Moore (1985), focusing on the developmental impacts of play environments, appeared in a volume containing a number of new studies of playgrounds and manufactured equipment (Frost & Sunderlin, 1985). Several more studies have appeared in special issues of *Children's Environments Quarterly* (neighborhoods, 1984/1985; schoolyards, 1986; and safety in outdoor play, 1985). This new work represents a further addition to a knowledge base that is now substantial enough to both support together, as contrasted to the sociofugality of the supermarket with its narrow aisles and shopping carts, which make it difficult to interact during shopping. There is little point in having someone along in the supermarket without the possibility for interaction. Supermarket customers regard their shopping experience as less friendly and less personal than do FM shoppers (Sommer, Herrick, & Sommer, 1981).

The age distribution of FM customers is weighted toward seniors with an underrepresentation of young individuals. This seems due to the social atmosphere, the hand-to-hand commercial transactions, and the relationship of the markets to garden activities, which are also very popular among seniors.

Vendors

Vendors are necessary at an FM, unlike a supermarket, where merchandise is expected to sell itself. Through their appearance and behavior, vendors add color and vitality to the market. Because sellers are farmers in the pure FM (rather than jobbers or clerks), it is common to find rural costume and iconography, for example, plaid shirts, straw hats, red bandanas, overalls, and the like. During the peak harvest season, entire families will attend the market. Off-season, only a single individual will accompany the load to town.

Most of those selling at farmers' markets have relatively small holdings, that is, less than five acres in production (Collins *et al.*, 1978; Pederson, 1984; Roy *et al.*, 1978). Linkage to a specific market is particularly strong; 87% of the vendors at eight Louisiana farmers' markets sold only in the market in which they were interviewed (Roy *et al.*, 1978). Vendors at farmers' markets also tend to be in the senior age range. Of those willing to state age in the Louisiana survey, 41% were above 60 (Roy *et al.*, 1978), and at Seattle's Pike Place Market, the vendors' average age was 70 years (Pike Place Project, 1974).

Products

Unlike the traditional marketplace in developing nations, the American FM is relatively odorless. There are not likely to be pots of cooking food so characteristic of traditional markets or meat hanging on racks surrounded by clouds of flies. This is the result of stringent health regulations and the antiolfactory bias in the American food marketing system. Odors have been almost completely banished from American supermarkets, where everything is packaged or behind glass. Even cooking foods, such as hot barbecued chicken or ribs in a deli section, will be totally encased. Supermarket produce is regularly culled to remove anything before it becomes redolent, and a powerful air conditioning system sweeps away remaining odors.

The auditory environment of an FM is more lively than the supermarket, but not nearly as active as the traditional marketplace dominated by incessant hawking and bargaining. These are legitimate practices in an FM, albeit relatively uncommon. For the most part, the auditory environment is subdued, dominated more by conversations among customers or between customers and sellers, with an occasional guitar or fiddle player in the background rather than loud, inescapable hawking and bargaining. Sound amplification is rare at a farmers' market, because this is antithetical to the rural ambiance.

The dominant perceptual stimuli are visual and kinetic. The produce provides an amazing array of colors, textures, and shapes not only in the items on display but also as they are carried through the market after they are purchased. A floral display on the back of the pickup truck will be a riot of color, but the choreography of customers who have purchased flowers adds vibrancy to the sidewalk.

TRADITION

Markets are perceived as a return to an earlier, less complex time of direct exchange between producer and consumer, rather than the eight levels of wholesalers, jobbers, transporters, and retailers found today in the wholesale food marketing system (Jumper, 1974). There are those who argue that farmers' markets are "functional anachronisms" in a modern economy (Meisner, 1984; Pyle, 1971). Burke (1977) maintains that the markets have been appreciated more as symbols of conservative cultural values than as economic institutions. Among the reasons why major cities over the past decade have decided to maintain a public market are the architectural quality of the building, the place of the market in local history, the market as a physical and psychological point of interface between the natural world of the built environment, and the public ceremonial aspects.

In the American FM, food-related rituals will develop mostly in the form of festivals, tastings, and contests devoted to specific fruits or vegetables. Prizes are awarded for the largest, most unusual shape, best-tasting, or most interesting carved item. Vendors are likely to be costumed and special entertainment will enhance a festive atmosphere. Public space facilitates the holding of festivals. Market organizers will attempt to support this through the provision of benches, picnic tables, banners, and entertainment.

The range of products sold has changed little over the decades, except that health regulations prohibit the sale of many prepared or cooked foods. Anything requiring refrigeration is likely to be covered by chopped ice, a technology available a century ago. The main physical changes are in mode of transportation, where the pickup truck has replaced the horse-drawn wagon and customers arrive by car rather than on foot or by public transportation.

ORGANIZATION

Organization rests on a combination of written rules and informal understandings relating to health and sanitation, insurance, internal assignment of space, and who may sell at the market. This necessitates some type of formal structure with designated lines of authority and responsibility. The typical market has a board of directors, usually composed of growers with an occasional civic or public representative, which sets policy and appoints a part-time manager who handles day-to-day operations. This part-time manager, typically the only paid employee, has a salary derived from stall fees paid by vendors.

A major responsibility of the manager is to develop or implement space-assignment policies. This can be an emotion-charged issue in regard to location, size, and the presence of amenities. Vendors want to be in the main traffic flow and have sufficient space for unloading and display and access to whatever amenities and weather protection are available.

Smaller markets may operate without written space-assignment policies, leaving the matter on a first-come, first-serve basis. The situation becomes more critical when there are a large number of sellers offering equivalent items. When products are outwardly similar and prices adjusted to a general market level, differentiation among vendors will be made on other factors, including location, stall arrangement, attractiveness of the display, and sales approach.

Vendors' secondary territories will ordinarily be respected by other sellers and the locations learned by customers who can walk directly to a favorite stall rather than engaging in trial-and-error search. Secondary territories will also reduce the potential for conflicts for desirable spaces and provide opportunities for vendors to learn the specal characteristics of particular locations, for example, the degree of shade or rain protection, where to display signs or other promotional materials, and so on.

LINKAGE TO OTHER OPEN-SPACE PROGRAMS

Farmers' markets are of particular interest to environmental psychologists because of their regional and local emphasis. They express local culture through people, place, products, and iconography, creating a locus for cultural events and environmental outreach. Buying locally means keeping money in the community and thereby aiding one's neighbors, the community, and indirectly benefiting oneself.

Regional consumption (eating what is grown locally) is critical to current efforts being made to redirect and decentralize the American food production and marketing system in the hopes of reducing energy loss, soil erosion, and resource concentration (Rodale, 1980, 1981). Nonregional foods have an atemporal quality, because they are likely to be available year-round, whereas regional foods tend to be seasonal. Various types of food outlets, including supermarkets, have found that labeling items as local, such as "grown in New York State," increases sales (Goldstein, 1976). To encourage local consumption, many departments of agriculture distribute farmer-to-consumer directories and maps showing the location of direct marketing outlets.

Fjeld and Sommer (1982) compared the food purchase behavior of farmers' market and supermarket customers. The key factor that differentiated their consumption patterns was not the absolute amount of fruits and vegetables consumed, but rather the timing of consumption. Farmers' market customers were more likely to eat fresh fruits and vegetables during the growing season and less likely to eat them off-season. Lockeretz (1986) found a greater preference for local produce among FM customers in Massachusetts than among supermarket customers. In Vermont, Pelsue (1984) found a strong preference among FM customers for locally grown produce. Lockeretz (1986) recommends that promotion for farmers' markets should emphasize their local ties:

> Buying local produce and supporting local producers apply to every step in the marketing chain—where the produce is raised, how it gets from farm to market, and where and by whom it is sold. Farmers' markets embody this totally local orientation. (p. 88)

Organizations dedicated to environmental activism feel that the markets are excellent places for outreach and recruitment. This links the markets directly to programs for open-space acquisition, protection, and enhancement. The Project for Public Spaces, following the theories of Whyte (1980), is working with the League of American Cities to protect historic market buildings. Pressure from market enthusiasts in Seattle resulted in the passage of an initiative that established a seven-acre historic district and allocated urban renewal money to rebuilding and enhancing the Pike Place Market (Burke, 1977). FMs also serve as retail outlets for community gardens, another successful open-space program. The San Francisco Farmers' Market started in 1943 as an outlet for the surplus production from backyard "victory gardens." Both farmers' markets and community gardens attract a disproportionate number of senior participants.

The flexible space requirements of FMs make possible the temporary appropriation of areas not typically included among lists of accessible urban open space, such as parking lots, sidewalks, and streets. Some of the most successful farmers' markets are held on streets barricaded on market day. This expands the amount of urban open space usable by pedestrians through temporary appropriation. The breakdown of rigid conceptions of single function can open up new possibilities for multiple uses of other open space. Local residents who see a street closed for a farmers' market may want to know why this cannot be done for an art show, concert, or sporting event. When a street is not a street and the parking lot is not a parking lot, this can be an important lesson for all those concerned with expanding urban open-space opportunities.

THE FUTURE OF FARMERS' MARKETS

Farmers' markets occupy a marginal niche in the American food marketing system and this is not likely to change in the future. Estimates have been made that all types of direct marketing represent less than 2% of retail food sales (Henderson & Linstrom, 1980; Leveen & Gustafson, 1978). We should not underestimate the tangible economic benefits to consumers and small farmers, but the social and civic benefits seem equally or more significant in the long run. The social utilities provide justification for current and continued government programs to promote the markets and allow them to use public open space without charge.

There is an interesting cleavage in the views among consumers and producers as to the future of the markets. Shoppers interviewed at Missouri Farmers' Markets were extremely optimistic and positive about the future of the markets. More than 95% wanted to see the markets encouraged. Vendors' confidence in the future did not match the shoppers' enthusiasm. Only 22% of the vendors held attitudes that could be called positive or optimistic; 11% were clearly pessimistic about the future of the market or their continued presence there (Collins et al., 1978). To some extent, the pessimism reflects the precarious nature of the farm economy, but it also indicates that the markets are providing more social and economic benefits to consumers than to farmers. The future of the institution requires that this imbalance be redressed. Very few sellers are able to make a livelihood selling exclusively at farmers' markets. At best, the markets are an additional source of income for small growers. As farmers' markets increase in number, sales volume, and coordination, it is likely that farmers can rely more heavily on them as all-weather outlets throughout the growing season and year-round for stored, preserved, or prepared items.

The survival of farmers' markets in an increasingly urban society depends on their ability to satisfy important human needs and wants not being adequately addressed by the commercial food marketing system.

Desire for Fresh, Flavorful Local Produce

For items such as sweet corn and whole peas, where freshness is associated with desirable flavor, the FM is likely to maintain a niche indefinitely. It is very difficult for the wholesale system to deliver vine- or tree-ripened varieties. Numerous packings and repackings and long-distance haulage require tougher skins and durable varieties that are picked green and ripened artificially and can hold up to extended refrigeration. The markets also offer local varieties largely excluded from the wholesale system, which emphasizes product standardization. The FM is used to test sales opportunities for unusual items.

Desire for Festivity and Social Contact

The sociofugal spatial layout and organization of the supermarket discourages contact among customers and between customers and employees. A few supermarket chains attempt to counteract this by providing community notice boards and meeting space for local organizations, but there is little indication that this can be done to the same degree as at a public marketplace.

Demonstrated Social Utility

The temporary appropriation of valued public space represents an indirect subsidy to the markets. Continuation of this subsidy rests on the public perception that the markets provide important civic benefits. Not all writers are convinced that this is the case. Rogers (1979) discounts "the rosy visions of farmer-to-consumer sales offered by consumer advocates and agrarian reformers" (p. 2). Meisner (1984) questions the claimed benefits of the markets in such areas as price, quality, and support for small farmers. Researchers can address these issues by documenting the tangible and intangible effects of the markets. Research on price savings and social atmosphere in California markets was used to support existing markets and start markets in new locations (Sommer & Nelson, 1985).

History teaches us that the farmers' market is a cyclical phenomenon, waxing and waning in popularity with economic conditions and other factors. Its survival over the centuries indicates that it continues to provide valuable benefits to producers, consumers, and to cities. According to Pyle (1971),

> Over the years the market has been stoutly defended by those who see in it old-fashioned virtues of individuality and direct connection with Mother Earth, has been attacked by those who see in it an unwarranted subsidy of inefficiency in small-scale distribution, is fondly remembered by those who think it no longer exists, and is faithfully patronized by those who prefer the quality of freshness over quantity. . . . (p. 197)

FUTURE DIRECTIONS OF RESEARCH

Numerous factors combine to make the farmers' market an excellent research site. An interviewer's table or clipboard blends with those of other organizations engaged in solicitation or outreach. A market is an open region (Goffman, 1963), with high density and a heterogeneous population, providing many opportunities for unobtrusive observation by anonymous observers. Typically, no permission is needed to undertake nonintrusive observations in a public setting. The high density allows for multiple observers and reliability checks. There is also a wide range of serious and nonserious activities occurring at a single time, from bargaining for livelihood (vendors) and sustenance (customers) to play and entertainment. The multiplicity of markets within and across regions allows replication of studies and cross-cultural comparisons.

The festiveness and friendliness facilitate the use of research techniques requiring voluntary participation. We have a lower refusal rate in surveys undertaken at farmers' markets than at supermarkets in the same communities. People generally had time and the inclination to talk to an interviewer at a FM, whereas supermarket customers were in a hurry to get into the store, do their shopping, and depart.

Like other open space, the farmers' market frees the researcher from the constraining influence of walls and doors. Environmental psychology began as a self-conscious field under conditions of confinement—in mental hospitals, convalescent homes, submarines, classrooms, and Arctic stations. Even when the occupants were not prisoners in a literal sense, they were confined in boxes regulated by time clocks, meal schedules, and buzzers. By contrast, open space provides for voluntary association during discretionary time without the constraints of the box. This has significant methodological and epistemological implications for research and theory in environmental psychology. Choice becomes a more significant concept in open space than in most types of enclosures. In undertaking an environmental assessment of a mental hospital or office building, there was little point in asking the residents about their motives for entering the setting or remaining.

The public nature of the market allows the use of photography as a research tool. The celebratory ambiance makes it permissible to bring cameras into the setting. Most participants are open to being photographed. As a point of comparison, photography was more difficult to employ in supermarkets, where a camera had to be introduced and used surreptitiously.

The keen competition among vendors for the most desirable stall locations offers interesting possibilities for research on secondary territories (Altman, 1975). Virtually every form of space assignment can be found, from an absence of written policies to individually owned stalls in fixed locations. In new markets, it is possible to study the evolution of territorial systems and their formalization over time.

The boundaries of each vendor's territory extend beyond the stall itself to the area around the pickup truck. Together the vendors have a group territory vis-à-vis customers that symbolically blocks customer passage through the unloading and sales zones (Figure 1). There are interesting possibilities in studying the response of individual vendors to staged invasions by customers into the unloading area and other vendors into the sales area. Following the research paradigm developed by Knowles (1973), group defense of the loading and table zone can be experimentally tested.

Because most research on farmers' markets has concerned economic issues, many of the important social and behavioral questions have not been investigated. The effects of intergroup contact (interethic and rural–urban) have not been the subject of published research. According to Sherif and Sherif (1956), mere contact between groups is not likely to reduce negative stereotypes. If, however, the functional relationship between groups is positive, favorable attitude change is likely to occur. It is interesting to consider this theory in the context of a farmers' market. If the relationship between buyer and seller is construed as competitive or exploitive in the sense that only one side can gain in the encounter, the likely effect of market transactions on attitudes is likely to be negative. This may occur in developing nations where members of one ethnic group dominate a trading economy that is largely patronized by other ethnic groups, for example, East Indian vendors at market stalls in Fiji patronized by native Fijians. By contrast, the American farmers' market is an incremental outlet for self-selected customers and vendors who engage in a festival-like, mutually beneficial activity. Relative to other retail outlets, returns at the farmers' market are higher for vendors and prices lower and quality higher for customers. The voluntariness of the setting and the objective gains for both vendors and consumers suggest that this is a situation of "both sides win" (Milburn, 1961), which meets the Sherifs' criterion for conditions likely to result in favorable intergroup relations.

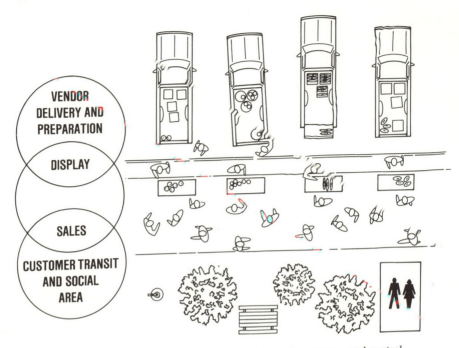

Figure 5. Spatial layout of FM showing zones of occupancy and control.

Lifestyle issues at the markets are a fruitful area of research. Fresh fruits and vegetables fit into the current emphasis on health and nutrition as expressed in the widely distributed USDA Dietary Guidelines (1980). Many of the organic growers began farming as part of the 1960s back-to-the-land movement. Aggregated case studies among individual growers can provide insights on adaptation of the urban counterculture to a rural context.

Gender role issues are another area of study. A sizable number of vendors are family units with shifting roles among husbands, wives, and children. Among the market types identified in the historical analysis by Wann *et al.* (1948) was the farm women's market in which farm wives sold fruits and vegetables, home-cooked items, dressed chickens, meats, handicrafts, and flowers. Most of these markets were organized during the Depression of the 1930s and disappeared or have been integrated into more heterogeneous markets.

Traditional gender roles are in evidence in farmers' markets in family units where the husband interacts directly with customers while the wife tends the cash box. At peak season, another traditional pattern is for women and children to do the selling while the men remain on the farms completing the harvest. Nontraditional sex roles are seen in the occasional instance of women farmers selling their own produce. Women farmers are still a definite minority but there is some indication that their percentage is increasing.

Interesting possibilities exist for comparing American farmers' markets with their European and Third World counterparts, some of which have been operating on the same site for centuries. There is an extensive literature on market history and geography in Europe and the Third World, including detailed spatial analyses of customer and vendor travel patterns (Davis, 1973; Polanyi et al., 1957). Nordin (1983) interviewed 917 traders and 446 customers at 19 French markets and mapped the spatial layout of each market and the travel patterns for vendors and customers. She found that these markets play an important role in the distribution of fresh produce, clothing, shoes, and household items.

Attitudes of residents and storekeepers living in the vicinity of farmers' markets need further investigation. One might suppose that local merchants would resent the presence of a farmers' market whose vendors paid no rent or overhead. However, available research indicates that local merchants are generally favorable toward farmers' markets. Karim (1981) and Tyburczy and Sommer (1983) found that most merchants believed that the markets were good for business and some linked special sales and product promotions to market day.

Some research questions involve institutional change rather than specific behavioral adaptations. Among the more important long-term effects of the markets is their role in raising environmental awareness. Besides teaching lessons of seasonality and region, the markets provide a defined locus for environmental activists to reach a sympathetic public. It is possible that the discrete behavioral measures favored by environmental psychologists are less satisfactory than the tools of sociology and cultural anthropology for understanding the market as a social institution.

A few disadvantages of the FM as a research site should be mentioned. Foremost among these is the lack of an accessible technical literature. As the reference list for this chapter indicates, most studies are available in limited distribution reports that are difficult to obtain and many of the data collection procedures are informal and not fully described. This will prove an impediment to longitudinal or cross-sectional comparison using archival sources.

Most markets are held on specified days for a limited number of hours during the main growing season, which reduces the times when observations can be made. Inclement weather reduces attendance and is an obstacle to interviews or naturalistic observation. The dense crowds in good weather make it difficult to track single individuals or observe from a distance. Market participants are not a random sample of the community; there are demographic and attitudinal differences, which have already been mentioned, that limit generalizability of findings. However, the disadvantages seem far outweighed by the research potential. The cooperativeness of the participants in an open setting is difficult to surpass elsewhere and my colleagues and I have used the FM frequently as a locus for student projects.

REFERENCES

Agricultural Marketing Project. (1977). *Cost benefit analysis for food fairs in Tennessee and Alabama.* Nashville, TN: Author.

Altman, I. (1975). *The environment and social behavior.* Monterey, CA: Brooks/Cole.

Archer, R. (1978). Community-farm markets in Illinois. In R. Archer (Ed.), *Proceedings of the 1978 Illinois Community Farm-Market Conference.* Villa Park, IL: Cooperative Extension Service.

Beckman, T. N., & Nolen, H. C. (1976). *The chain store problem.* New York: Arno Press.

Brooker, J. R., & Taylor, E. J. (1977). *Direct marketing of produce—The Shelby County Farmers' Market case* (Bulletin 569). Knoxville, TN: University of Tennessee, Agricultural Experiment Station.

Burke, P. (1977). Faneuil Hall Marketplace is making history again. *Historic Preservation, 29,* 32–38.

Burke, P. (1978). Reviving the public market, "Don't fix it up too much." *Nation's Cities, 16,* 9–12.

Collins, A. J., Munankami, R., & Breimyer, H. F. (1978). *Farmer to consumer food marketing in Missouri* (Extension Circular No. 932). Columbia, MO: University of Missouri.

Cross, J. (1976). *The supermarket trap* (rev. ed.). Bloomington, IN: Indiana University Press.

Davis, W. G. (1973). *Social relations in a Philippine market.* Berkeley, CA: University of California Press.

Dietrich, R. (1982). The rethinking of the supermarket. *Progressive Grocer, 12,* 48–67.

Fjeld, C. R., & Sommer, R. (1982). Regional-seasonal patterns in produce consumption at farmers' markets and supermarkets. *Ecology of Food and Nutrition, 12,* 109–115.

Francis, M. (1987). Urban open spaces. In E. Zube & G. Moore (Eds.), *Advances in environment, behavior and design* (pp. 71–106). New York: Plenum Press.

Goffman, E. (1963). *Behavior in public places.* New York: Free Press of Glencoe.

Gold, S. M. (1978). Neighborhood parks: The nonuse phenomenon. *California Parks and Recreation, 34,* 16–17.

Goldstein, J. (1976). New state ag program helps local markets. *Organic Gardening and Farming, 23,* 136–138.

Griswold-Minois, R. (1980, July 27). A French view of Sacramento. *Sacramento Bee,* Scene, p. 4.

Hanssens, C. (1978). Farmers come to Philadelphia. *Food Action,* 13–14.

Henderson, P. L., & Linstrom, H. R. (1980). *Farmer-to-consumer direct marketing in six states* (USDA, ESCS, Agriculture Information Bulletin No. 36). Washington, DC: U.S. Department of Agriculture.

Hess, J. L. (1974). Return of a farmers' market. *Organic Gardening and Farming, 21,* 64–67.

Hester, R. (1984). *Planning neighborhood space with people.* New York: Van Nostrand Reinhold.

Higgins, K. (1983). Safeway enters quest for supermarket of future. *Marketing News, 17,* 1–6.

Hightower, J. (1987, August 7). Here's how to help boost agriculture locally. *Davis Enterprise,* p. 9.

Isogai, H., & Shanjiro, M. (1972). *Marketplaces of the world.* Palo Alto, CA: Kodansha.

Jackson, J. B. (1981). The public park needs reappraisal. In L. Taylor (Ed.), *Urban open spaces* (pp. 34–35). New York: Rizzoli.

Jumper, S. R. (1974). Wholesale marketing of fresh vegetables. *Annals of the Association of American Geographers, 64,* 387–396.

Karim, M. B. (1981). *A farmers' market in America.* New York: Carlton Press.

Knowles, E. S. (1973). Boundaries around group interaction. *Journal of Personality and Social Psychology, 26,* 327–332.

Kowinski, W. S. (1986). Endless summer at the world's biggest shopping wonderland. *Smithsonian, 17,* 35–43.

Leveen, E. P., & Gustafson, M. R. (1978). *The potential impact of direct marketing policies on the economic viability of small fruit and vegetable farms in California* (Giannini Foundation Research Rep. No. 327). Berkeley, CA: University of California.

Lockeretz, W. (1986). Urban consumers' attitudes towards locally grown produce. *American Journal of Alternative Agriculture, 1,* 83–88.

Lozar, C. C. (1975). Application of behavior setting analysis and undermanning theory to supermarket design. In D. H. Carson (Ed.), *Man–environment interactions: Evaluations and application:* II (pp. 271–279). Stroudsburg, PA: Dowden, Hutchinson, & Ross.

Markin, R. J. (1968). *The supermarket: An analysis of growth, development, and change* (rev. ed.). Pullman, WA: Washington State University Press.

Meisner, F. (1984). Farmers' markets have merchandising image which is not supported by reality. *Marketing News*, October 26, p. 17.

Milburn, T. (1961). The concept of deterrence. *Journal of Social Issues*, 17, 3–11.

Moulton, C. J. (1977). *King County agricultural marketing study*. Seattle, WA: King County Office of Agriculture.

Mund, V. A. (1948). *Open markets*. New York: Harper & Brothers.

Nordin, C. (1983). *Markets, traders and customers: The periodic market trade in the Paris region*. (Publication No. B: 71). Goteborg, Sweden: Department of Human and Economic Geography.

Pease, R. L., & Eiler, D. A. (1976). *Farmers' markets return* (Bulletin Agricultural Economics Extension No. 76–14). Ithaca, NY: Cornell University, Department of Agricultural Economics.

Pederson, A. (1984). *Direct marketing in the Central Valley*. Unpublished master's thesis, California State University, Sacramento, CA.

Pelsue, N. H. (1984). *Consumers at farmers' markets and roadside stands in Vermont* (Research Rep. No. 41). Burlington, VT: University of Vermont, Agricultural Experiment Station.

Pike Place Merchants Association. (1978). *Food price survey*. Seattle, WA: Department of Community Development, August 21.

Plattner, S. (1978). Public markets: Functional anachronisms or functional necessities? *Ekistics*, 45, 444–446.

Plattner, S. (1979). Support your local farmers' market. *Christian Science Monitor*, August 17, 4–5.

Polanyi, K., et al. (Eds.). (1957). *Trade and market in the early empires*. Glencoe, IL: Free Press.

Progressive Grocer. 1952, October). Food retailing—A restless, ever-changing business. *Progressive Grocer*, p. 64.

Pyle, J. (1971). Farmers' markets in the United States: Functional anachronisms. *The Geographical Review*, 61, 167–197.

Rodale, R. (1980, September). The cornucopia project. *Organic Gardening*, pp. 22–24.

Rodale, R. (1981, August). *How agriculture hurts—and can help—the soil*. Paper presented at the World Botanical Congress, Sydney, Australia.

Rogers, H. T. (1979, October). Direct marketing's NONIMPACT in California. *Western Fruitgrower*, p. W2.

Roy, E. P., Jordan, E. J., Law, J. N., & Leary, D. (1978). *Sellers of produce at Louisiana farmers' markets* (Research Rep. No. 534). Baton Rouge, LA: Louisiana State University, Department of Agriculture Economics and Agribusiness.

Roy, E. P., Leary, D., & Law, J. (1977). *Customer evaluation of farmers' markets in Louisiana* (DAE Research Rep. No. 516). Baton Rouge, LA: Louisiana State University, Agricultural Experiment Station.

Seamon, D., & Nordin, C. (1980). Marketplace as place ballet: A Swedish example. *Landscape*, 24, 35–41.

Sherif, M., & Sherif, C. W. (1956). *An outline of social psychology*. (rev. ed.). New York: Harper & Row.

Silverstein, M., & Jacobson, M. (1978). Restructuring the hidden program: Toward an architecture of social change. In W. F. E. Preiser (Ed.), *Facility programming* (pp. 10–26). Stroudsburg, PA: Dowden, Hutchinson & Ross.

Sommer, R., Herrick, J., & Sommer, T. R. (1981). The behavioral ecology of supermarkets and farmers' markets. *Journal of Environmental Psychology*, 1, 13–19.

the development of comprehensive design guidelines and help identify gaps still needing research (Moore, Goltsman, & Iacofano, 1987).

How Much Are Playgrounds Used?

For years, the term "playground" was shunned by many experts in the field because they felt playgrounds were unused facilities—at best irrelevant, at worst detrimental to children's developmental needs. But playground use varies greatly, even in the same community. The Berkeley Park Use Study (Mason, Forrester, & Herman, 1975) compared the use of six minipark sites containing playgrounds and showed a wide variation in the pattern of use, depending on the content and location of individual sites and the socioeconomic characteristics of the user population (Figure 1). The influence of these factors was confirmed by a comprehensive study of playgrounds in Rotterdam (Derickx, 1985), which concluded that "Urban design has a direct influence on the use of playgrounds . . . play equipment only partially determines the use of the site. . . . Identical sites in different circumstances yielded very different data" (p. 28).

Previously reported neighborhood behavior mapping studies (Moore & Young, 1978) indicated anywhere from 2% to 42% of children's outdoor activity taking place on public playgrounds. Schoolyards and playgrounds were mentioned as favorite places to go to in only 9% of the replies by 8- to 12-year-olds interviewed in the San Francisco Bay Area (Moore, 1980a). In Holme and Massie's study (1970), only 5% of Stevenage New Town mothers reported that their children played in the recreation grounds (in contrast to the 64% who reported garden play and 21% who reported street play). A study by Becker (1976) showed an average of 15% for playground use, with high values of 36% to 40% in four lowrise, multifamily developments in New York State.

More recent behavior-mapping studies, by Francis (1984/1985) and Björklid (1982), confirm these variations. Francis' study of Village Homes indicated only 4% activity on a playground that had been developed with prolonged community participation—reflecting the many other play options available in this innovative Californian suburban development. In contrast, Björklid's study of two Stockholm housing estates showed high levels of use for playgrounds adjacent to the Tanto Estate blocks (29% to 39% for girls aged 0–15) and even higher use levels for the adjacent playpark (33% to 45% for boys aged 7–15). These results suggest that children are much more dependent on public playgrounds in built-up urban areas because neighborhood play opportunities are more limited or inaccessible.

A similar conclusion was reached in a study of British children's favorite places. Playgrounds and schoolyards were the second most frequently mentioned item in children's drawings (Moore, 1986a). Some of the public playgrounds were in fact highly valued and were particularly well used when alternative options were limited. In a district like central London, even poor-quality traditional playgrounds served as important gathering places. When easily accessible to children's homes, play facilities were well used if they offered a choice of settings. Playgrounds located in parks were especially popular because they were used in conjunction with other park settings: trees for climbing, water features, monuments, flower gardens, and wildlife (Moore, 1986a).

How Safe Are Playgrounds?

Several well-publicized cases of death and serious injury in playground accidents, massive awards to the plaintiffs, and an independently developing liability crisis, have brought the issue of playground safety to the forefront (Sweeney, 1987). City officials, staff, designers, manufacturers—all those involved in the provision and staffing of children's playgrounds—are apprehensive. But part of the apprehension has been bred from a lack of information describing both the general and detailed picture of playground safety.

A more accurate picture is needed of playground injuries compared with injuries in the child environment as a whole. In 1984 (National Safety Council, 1986), 4,300 accidental deaths occurred to 5- to 14-year-olds in the United States (a rate of 12.7/100,000 population). Of these, 2,300 (6.8/100,000) were motor-vehicle related (and of these, 1,070, or 3.2/100,000, involved pedestrians); 1,100 (3.2/100,000) occurred in the public environment but were not vehicle related; 800 (2.4/100,000) were home related; and 100 (0.3/100,000) were work related. In 1975, it was estimated that 23 children were killed on American playgrounds during a 15-month period (U.S. Consumer Product Safety Commission (hereafter USCPSC), 1975, cited in Sweeney, 1979), or approximately 18 per year. In other words, the chances of being killed at home or in the street as a pedestrian are roughly 45 to 60 times greater than the chance of being killed on a playground. Motor vehicles as a whole are about 125 times more lethal than playgrounds.

Narrowing the scope of the safety issue to school environments, where children spend the most amount of time, what is the comparative safety record of play settings? The National Safety Council (1985), reporting on 15,000 K–12 accidents for 8,600 school jurisdictions for the 1983–1984 school year, quoted rates per 100,000 K–6 student days as follows: equipment-related accidents, 0.42; ball playing, 0.18; running, 0.31; and miscellaneous accidents (including those on walls, fences, steps, and walks), 0.54. The rate for all school-related accidents for grades K–6 was 4.92. The rate for all building-related accidents was 1.40 while for physical-education-related accidents it was 1.04. In other words, equipment-related accidents accounted for about one-tenth of all accidents in the school environment and were less than one-third as frequent as accidents inside the school building (i.e., on stairs, with lockers, in classrooms, auditoriums, washrooms, and toilets). These data tell us that schoolyard play equipment is certainly a significant source of injury, but so are many other school settings.

What do we know about the characteristics of playground accidents? In Australia, they include impalment, laceration, fractures, amputation, crushing, suffocation, dental damage, blindness, ruptured spleens, and kidney damage. Many could be prevented through improved setting design and manage-

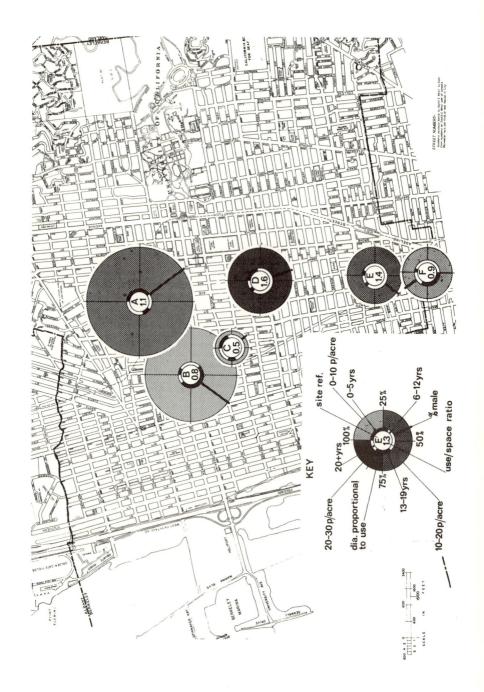

Figure 1. Variations of use profiles of miniparks in the same community. Behavior-mapping data were gathered over a 12-month period (1974–1975), for six mini-parks located in Berkeley, California (population, 100,000), in neighborhoods of similar population density and housing type but varied social characteristics. Although the sites were similar in size (0.15–0.43 acres), a variety of user groups and a wide range of use levels were indicated. In all the parks, use by children and adolescents predominated; in all but one (A) by more than 75%. In three of the parks (C, D, and E), 6- to 12-year-olds were dominant. Park A was fenced and had facilities specially designed for families with preschool children; hence the high proportion of 0–5 and 20+ age groups.

Three of the parks (A, C, and D) had more female than male users; in park A, this was because of the large number of mothers accompanying their children. In the other two cases, female dominance lay in the 6–12 age group, reflecting the value of close-to-home spaces to girls who, as shown in many research studies (Moore & Young, 1978), have a more restricted territorial range than boys. The male dominance in park F is explained by the presence of a basketball semicourt and its location in a predominantly black area of town.

The two smallest sites (D and E) were the most efficiently used, with the highest use density and use/space ratios (1.6 and 1.4 respectively). Effectiveness of the other sites varied considerably, with use/space ratios ranging from 0.5 to 1.1.

The analysis shows that each park has a distinct use profile, reflecting the physical content of the park and the characteristics of the surrounding population. These data give a standard of comparison for the diagnosis of each site, resulting in implications for site modifications and program changes, and acquisition criteria for new sites (source: Mason *et al.*, 1975).

ment (Root, 1983). The National Electronic Survey System 1978 figures used by USCPSC (Rutherford, 1979) highlighted the fact that 71% (66,000 of 93,000 reported cases) of public playground equipment-related injuries to under-10-year-olds resulted from falls, with half being head and neck injuries; 55,000, or almost 60% of the total, were direct falls to the surface.

The results of a two-year study in a large U.S. urban school district (Boyce, Sobolewski, Springer, & Schaefer, 1984), indicated that 23% of school injuries were related to play equipment, with about one-fourth being considered severe (concussion, crush wounds, fractures, and multiple injuries). Almost 60% occurred on climbing equipment. Rutherford (1979), citing injury estimates by type of equipment, showed climbers leading (42%), followd by swings (23%), slides (16%), merry-go-rounds (8%), seesaws (5%); with all others accounting for 6%. A New Zealand study (Langley, Silva, & Williams, 1981) indicated 21% of all *school* accidents (48% of these resulting in fractures) as falls from playground equipment, predominantly climbing structures. Even though these data are more than ten years old, and safety surface treatments have surely improved during this period, the figures still indicate that falls and safety surfacing are priority safety issues.

Until 1981, there were no acceptable national safety standards available to protect either the consumers or the designers and manufacturers of play equipment. After six years of work, the USCPSC (1981) published a two-volume report that has become the source of prevailing industry standards. However, the perspective of the reports is limited to a narrow range of issues, dealing only with play equipment design and installation. At this point, the guidelines are in need of revision and expansion, now based on several years of application. More detailed information is needed on playground accidents.

PLAY SETTING STUDIES

Investigations of play settings through observation, interview/questionnaires, and drawings or mental mapping are the most effective means of producing results that can be used to upgrade play-setting design guidelines to meet developmental objectives. Examples include a study of physical changes on a schoolyard (van Andel, 1986), a study comparing adventure playground behavior with neighborhood settings (Moore, G. T., 1985), and Hayward, Rothenberg, and Beasley's (1974) classic study comparing user responses to three different types of playground environment. These they termed "traditional" (typical schoolyard play equipment area with swings, slide, jungle gym, etc.), "contemporary" (professionally designed, supposedly with children's needs in mind), and "adventure" (no adult-provided permanent play structures, but instead loose materials and simple tools for children to build their own play settings).

The results clearly demonstrate differences in user–environment interaction between the three sites, especially differences between the adventure playground and the other two sites. Setting records show that the five most time-consuming activities on the adventure site were playing in clubhouses (31 minutes average duration per occurrence), followed by building and "fixing-up" the clubhouses, passive activity, and talking. On the contemporary site, top activities were play on multiple equipment (11 minutes per occurrence), followed by arts and crafts, water play, games, and sand play. On the traditional site, the top activity was swinging (8 minutes per occurrence), followed by water play, arts and crafts, connective play, seesawing, and general play. The authors conclude that "the opportunities and constraints of the physical environment may be seen to predict the majority of predominant activities" (p. 154).

PLAY VALUE, DIVERSITY, AND DESIGN

These results, pointing to the developmental benefits of setting diversity, are reinforced by a study by Campbell and Frost (1985), who coded behavior for developmental impact in a comparison of traditional and contemporary playgrounds. Three times the amount of constructive and solitary behavior occurred on the latter because of the presence of a wider diversity of equipment and materials.

A common argument against diversity equates it with chaos, or with placing the burden of an overwhelming number of choices on the child. But this concern is not reflected in research findings, and in any case overlooks the way in which children's play patterns in space and time are moderated by access. Diverse landscapes cannot be experienced all at once. They become progressively disclosed, over periods of time—years in some cases—at many levels of detail, through many seasons. Space–time sequences become gradually embedded in memory (Boulding, 1956; Moore, 1986a) as they are trodden on the ground. Diversity broadens the repertoire of possible behaviors as well as allowing for the simultaneous playing of individual children with different needs.

Besides expert opinion and practical site considerations, design decision making can be based on play value (measured by developmental objectives, user feedback, and preferences). Some work has been done using developmental objectives to guide the design of settings (Moore, Cohen, Oertel, & van Ryzin, 1979; Verkerk & Rijmpa, 1985), but we are far from being able to compare the developmental effects of a full range of settings. To be more effective, the developmental approach needs to be informed by children's *preferences* based on the results of empirical investigations of settings in use (Hayward et al., 1974; Moore, 1980b, 1986b, 1986c). Direct measures of play value derived from behavior mapping, questionnaires, and mental mapping can be applied in design programming decisions so that intelligent tradeoffs can be made between play value and the dollar costs of installation and projected maintenance, for example, trees and vegetation compared with manufactured equipment.

A behavior-mapping study of the Environmental Yard (Figure 2) (Moore, 1978a, 1986b) identified 58 individual behavior settings ("activity places"), grouped into 10 major types of settings ("behavior-environment ecosystems") and three primary zones. The results (Table 1) show a range of preference across

Figure 2. The Environmental Yard, Berkeley, California (founded 1971; photo by author, 1982), looking from the top of the school building across the central community play area to the natural resource area in the rear.

settings. The amount of use was not in direct proportion to size of settings, however; therefore the *density* of setting activity varied greatly (Figure 3), showing that it was not an accurate indicator of play value. Fixed play structures and manufactured equipment settings were the most densely used, whereas densely vegetated and asphalted settings were least used (Moore, 1986b).

Methods of assessing children's preferences include the use of questionnaires and so-called mental mapping (Moore, 1975, 1986b). The latter reveals the broadest range of setting impacts and is therefore the most useful in assessing the aggregate value of variables such as "nature" (biotic characteristics; Moore, 1986b).

SITE PLANNING: PATTERNS OF ACTIVITY IN TIME AND SPACE (PATS)

The spatial patttern of use can be misleading because it does not reflect the space-time dynamics of individual and small-group behavior. In an attempt to document this aspect, nine patterns of activity in time and space (PATS) were observed on the Lenox-Camden site and described along dimensions of territorial range and mobility (Moore, 1974). At one extreme were "concentrated foci" of intense activity in very limited spaces, for example, small-group social interaction, and play on single items of equipment. At the other extreme, were "expansive flowing" games of chase that occupied the whole site.

TABLE 1. USE/SITE RATIOS FOR THREE PRIMARY ZONES AND TEN PLAY SETTING TYPES FOR A RECONSTRUCTED SCHOOLYARD[a]

Percent use, percent site, ratio	Percent use, percent site, ratio	Percent use, percent site, ratio
	Primary zones	
Natural resource area	Main yard	Asphalt
38%, 33%, 1.2	33%, 23%, 1.4	29%, 44%, 0.7
	Play setting types	
Structures	Structures	Ball play areas
11%, 4%, 3.0	4%, 7%, 2.2	17%, 26%, 0.7
Aquatic	Edges	Circulation/games
9%, 6%, 1.7	12%, 13%, 0.8	12%, 20%, 0.6
Pathways	Traditional equipment	
6%, 5%, 1.1	7%, 3%, 1.9	
Densely vegetated areas		
6%, 8%, 0.7		
Meadows		
6%, 8%, 0.7		
100%, 100%, 1.0	100%, 100%, 1.0	100%, 100%, 1.0

[a] Based on behavior mapping data collected at the Environmental Yard, Spring 1977.

The validity of these patterns was further supported by tracking studies conducted at the Environmental Yard, showing a wide range of individual PATS (Figure 3). Some children confined themselves to an intensive involvement in very small areas; others ranged over the broad terrain during the same time segment.

The variety and complexity of these patterns of play calls to question the simple notions of play behavior that designers often apply to the physical form of playgrounds. This is one area of design where environmental determinism has no hope of succeeding. Functional, site-related issues (size, shape, orientation, drainage, existing vegetation, location of utilities, circulation, etc.) need to be considered, together with the predicted behavioral consequences of alternative setting configurations, so that the designer can make informed programming tradeoffs. Simplistic conventions used to "zone" playground sites into so-called "passive" and "active" or age-segregated areas are likely to fail. Indeed, the idea of zoning by age is unrealistic and unnecessary according to expert opinion (Moore et al., 1987), except *maybe* for preschool ages and certainly for infants and toddlers. Any public playground that rigidly segregates ages will run into problems because older siblings are responsible for younger sisters and brothers and "best friends" often play in mixed age groups (Moore, 1980a, 1986a).

WHAT IS THE PLAY VALUE OF ADVENTURE PLAY?

Considering how strongly adventure playgrounds have been promoted in the last 40 years, there is surprisingly little empirical research to complement

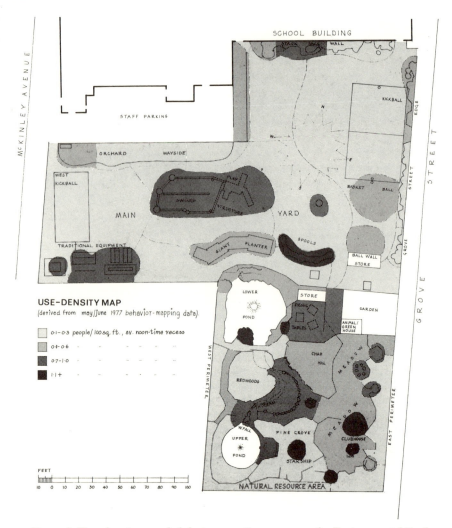

Figure 3. User density recorded during noontime recess on the Environmental Yard.

the substantial anecdotal literature (Balmforth & Nelson, 1978; Bengtsson, 1972; Benjamin, 1974; Lambert & Pearson, 1974; Petersen, 1985; Shier, 1984; Sutherland & Soames, 1984).

The empirical cupboard is not entirely bare, however. In addition to Hayward et al. (1974), G. T. Moore (1985) investigated the relationship between physical setting and developmental impact by comparing behaviors on an inner-city adventure playground with those occurring in the surrounding neighborhood. Twenty-six different behaviors were mapped in 31 different types of setting. A marked difference between the two environments was that

40% of cognitive play behaviors occurred on the adventure playground, compared with 10% in the neighborhood settings. Moreover, two to ten times the amount of fantasy, constructive, and cooperative play occurred on the adventure playground. On the other hand, there were more mixed-age and mixed-gender groups in the neighborhood settings who engaged in more social play. A further interesting observation was that adults in the adventure playground participated more by observing and interacting with the children (as Cooper, 1970, discovered), whereas in the neighborhood settings, adults exhibited more supervisory and controlling behavior.

Hayward *et al.* (1974) showed that adventure playground activity was quite different from the traditional and contemporary sites and focused to a large degree on building, fixing up, and playing in and around the clubhouses. Because the site could change and evolve over time according to the children's interests, it contrasted strongly with the permanence of the other two sites. Children who named the adventure playground as their favorite, said it allowed them freedom to do what they wanted.

The contrast in diversity of opportunity and experience is illustrated by differences in the children's conversations recorded at the three sites:

> The overwhelming majority of conversational excerpts and topics at the traditional and contemporary playgrounds focused on aspects of equipment use and mutual play activities. . . . At the adventure playground, in contrast, children's conversations did not reflect a narrow focus on the immediate setting. Rather, the conversations dealt with building materials, mothers, dreams, marriage, seasons, fighting, spelling, clothing, house cleaning, and a host of other topics. (p. 156)

These findings mirror those of an earlier action-research study of the Lenox-Camden Playground, Boston (Moore, 1966, 1974), using play setting records. Lenox-Camden was not an adventure playground in the European sense because it lacked properly trained leadership; neither did it support large-scale hut building. Nonetheless, a diversity of loose play materials and objects was provided to compare the effects of fixed and manipulable settings on children's play behavior.

Adventure play was defined as any activity using loose materials. The proportion of children engaged in such activity at any given moment varied between 3% and 66%, with an average for all observation periods of 27% (Moore, 1974). Typical durations of adventure play ranged from a half to one hour and sometimes several hours (compared with a few minutes for equipment play). One of the more elaborate examples was spread over three days (reported by Moore, 1974):

> On the first day, a small group of eight to 12-year-old boys spent an hour building two clubhouses and another couple of hours playing in and around them, adding to them, and just sitting inside talking—dreaming up imaginary situations, like being in the middle of a jungle. Finally, they smashed what they had built with energetic pleasure.
> The second day I arrived to find a "Pepsi cart" constructed on a large wooden pallet in the same vicinity. A "milk-truck" was under construction, suggested

by the milk crates. The constructions were done in beautiful detail, complete with "levers," "head lamps," "wheels," "seats," "steering wheels," etc. Group imagination was flowing the whole time, the group growing in size (mostly boys), the younger members following behind, taking "orders" from the older members. Then for a long, long time the kids "drove" the vehicles, delivering milk and Pepsi, chatting to the "store-keepers" and "housewives," negotiating hazards on the highway—encountering "lights," "cops," "steep hills"—acting-out spontaneously scripted episodes from their perceptions of every-day adult life.

The third day saw the addition of two "motor-bikes," a "car," and a "club-house," again involving large group fantasy play. During the complete three-day period one 12-year-old boy maintained leadership of the group (which continuously changed members) for much of the time, directing action and contributing ideas.

Construction activity died down during the next four days—then started up again, the same boy leading. This time two "battleships" were built (two hours). Then followed a long period (three hours) of fantasy play centered around the ships with the two "crews," two "captains" and a "commander," acting out their conception of life on board ship—"sailing orders" from the "bridge," "sea-battles," "eating," "going to sleep," etc. About an hour was spent with the captain "drilling the crew," giving orders, getting them lined up, being saluted. Much of this activity occupied the whole 30' × 40' area behind the playhouse. The kids still imagined they were "on board," although in reality they were standing several yards from their "ships." Later on, one of the ships was smashed in battle and became replaced with a "hide-out." The play turned to "soldiering" and finally ended with a game of "combat" taking in the whole playground. This final sequence of events lasted about eight hours—a rich flow of imagination and expressiveness, truly wonderful to witness. (p. 131)

These observations, along with those of G. T. Moore (1985) and Hayward et al. (1974), reflect the deeper meaning of the open-ended, child-managed setting of the adventure playground, and its close relation, the urban farm (Boehm, 1980), and support an interactional–ecological, environmentally based theory of play (Björklid, 1986; Moore, 1986a). This suggests that development through play results from the child's interaction with the total physical, social, and cultural environment and that different types of settings support different types and amounts of developmentally related behaviors. A major implication of this theory points to the importance of physical and social diversity in play settings (G. T. Moore, 1975). For Petersen (1985), Danish adventure playgrounds (Figure 5) best illustrate this concept of the play environment as a developmental setting for childhood and culture:

> To get the chance to discover oneself, not only as a biological being but as a cultural one and not only as an individual but also as a part of a totality bigger than oneself, is a fundamental right for every human being. Without this possibility, culture ceases to exist. For a child it is a question of discovering himself or herself by doing something with hands and imagination. The child has to gain . . . personal experiences, not by being taught by others, usually grownups. This is the challenge and the answer for the child. But the "classical playground" does not provide . . . for handling basic elements like fire, water and earth or for creating something of one's own out of raw materials such as wood, stone, clay and soil. It does not offer possibilities for contact with plants and animals,

Playgrounds at the Crossroads

a

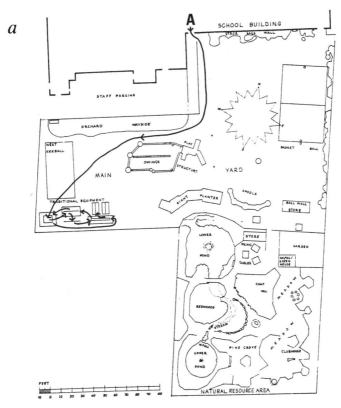

Figure 4. Individual differences in Patterns of Activity in Time and Space (PATS). Children were "tracked" during noontime recess (30 min) on the Environmental Yard (1977). Following are three contrasting examples illustrating the wide range of individual behavior of the 8-year-old users:

    a. Traditional Equipment. Child A goes to the monkey bars, hangs upside down. Goes to rings, hangs, holds on with two hands, talks to friends. Goes to pole, holds on and twirls around. Goes to bars, climbs up, hangs and swings. Drops to ground. Goes to other side, climbs up, swings while going across. Goes to rings, then to monkey bars. Does a trick. Puts hands on ground, leans over lowest bar. Stands up, looking at kids playing. Does trick again on other side. Joins friend on same bars. Climbs and talks to her. Swings on bars. Laughs and smiles. Goes to rings again. Goes across swinging. Comes over to me [observer], puts flower in my hair. Goes to low bars, swings. Leans on bar, watching kids on other bar. Turns upside down, staying there a second, then swinging over. Repeats it several times. Talks to a girl, swings some more. Watches a girl do a trick, going around with one leg. Tries it. Gets stuck. Watches girl run up to bars going round fast. Keeps going around. They play "monkey tag" (the person who is "it" is a monkey). Bell sounds.

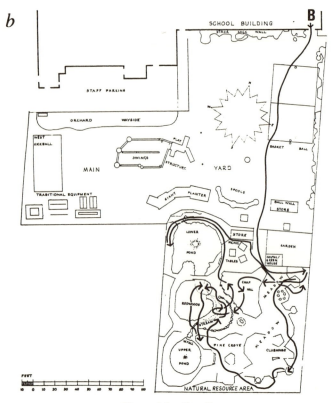

Figure 4 (*continued*)
b. Wandering, Vegetation Play. Child B walks to eucalyptus tree in NE corner of Natural Resource Area, plays with friend (another girl). They walk out of trees to fence by chaparral, stand by fence and talk, climb over fence and up chaparral hill. Walk to top, then down to beach. Jump over river together. B runs away, the other follows. They return to chaparral.

B picks a flower. Talks about how it looks like a tooth. Says "ow, that's my tooth!" Picks leaves off an acacia tree. Sits on fence with the same friend. Holds hand to mouth pretending to have toothache. Puts arm around friend. Holds up flower—says "an ant just crawled out—it's an ant house!"

They walk around lower pond. Stand on path. Walk back over rocks. Stand by dead tree. Walk back along path towards tables. Talk about how a witch lives on the island in the middle of the pond. Walk to picnic tables. Follow each other back to eucalyptus tree. They look at some playing cards together. Walk towards pine trees, return. Sit on branch of eucalyptus. Friend stands up, tries to clear ground of leaves with foot. Helps B off of branch. They wander to Corral #1, climb through fence.

B picks plants, shreds them. Walks toward clubhouse, past it to Corral #3 in corner. Fashions some grasses into a bouquet. Walks along fence edge toward sitting platform, picking plants along the way. Walks past railroad ties to trees by beach, making bouquet all the while. Picks pussy willows. Stands on ground while friend stands on fence trying to pick them. Adds pussy willows to bouquet. Stands on stepping stone. Picks more grasses. Walks toward upper pond, picks a flower. "Come over to me," she says, "we're going to give this [bouquet] to our teacher." Walks back to pussy willows. Comes over to me [observer], gives me a pussy willow. Picks more grasses. Walks back toward me, toward railroad ties, then back to the big rock. Picks more flowers. Bell sounds.

Playgrounds at the Crossroads

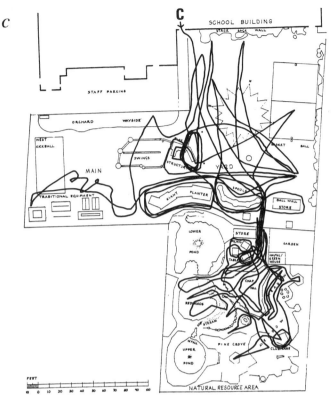

Figure 4 (*continued*)
c. Chase! Child C represents an extreme example of chase, tag, and hide-and-go-seek behavior ranging back-and-forth all over the space. There were many variations in the complex environment of the Yard.

not just in affectionate play but in situations demanding care and responsibility. And it does not provide many situations for building up a constructive comradeship where the desired goals are attained through cooperation, and life as a whole functions by virtue of mutual consideration. (p. 202)

WHAT TYPES OF PLAY SETTING SUPPORT SOCIAL INTEGRATION?

Socialization is an important function of children's play, and interaction between girls and boys is a critical aspect of socialization. Detailed behavior-mapping studies at the Environmental Yard (Moore, 1980b, 1986b) indicate that some types of settings tend to be segregated and others are integrated by sex (a conclusion also reached by Rijnen, 1985, in her study of Rotterdam playgrounds). Traditional equipment was almost exclusively used by girls; ball play on the asphalt was almost entirely engaged in by boys. Swings were dominated

Figure 5. Bispevangens Adventure Playground, Copenhagen, Denmark (photo by author), is an example of the classic adventure playground. It is an active social center for all ages, with meeting rooms, kitchen facilities, a childcare center, and youth club. Animals of many types are to be found there, cared for by the children. Opportunities for "building play" abound. There are fireplaces, water play areas, and permanent play structures. The whole facility is managed by a team of play leaders.

by girls, climbing structures by boys. Behavior-mapping data converted into sex/use ratios show the pattern of these differences and indicate more integration by sex in the natural resource area of woodland, meadows, and ponds (Moore, 1986b). Play-setting observations in this area indicated many examples of play in groups mixed not only by sex but by age and ethnic background as well (Moore & Wong, in press).

Children can create their own world in natural settings (Olweg, 1986). In so doing they in effect support their own development (Hart, 1987). In a study of the impact of environmental diversity on social/emotional behavior, primary-aged children were asked to compare their feelings about a traditional schoolyard playground with their feelings for the site after it was reconstructed (the Environmental Yard). The addition of natural resources to the new site received the most positive comments (Moore, 1989a).

Natural materials that are alive, ever changing and renewing themselves, have very high play value. They stimulate imagination and fine-muscle coordination through play with vegetation parts, sticks, and dirt. They engage children in problem solving when making clubhouses from natural materials. They support large-muscle activities though games like hide-and-go-seek played among bushes and weeds and in climbing rocks and trees.

The way children describe natural play settings as being alive (Moore, 1986b) illustrates something very deep and universal (Cobb, 1977), unavailable in other settings. Biotic settings powerfully impact children's untarnished senses, stimulating the creation of a world of fantasy and delight that knows no boundaries of mind or spirit (Moore, 1989b). Nature has this unique power because of its special content and process. Interactions with nature transport the child through her or his imagination to another state of being, where the world is presented as an open environment, one the child must understand and redefine for herself or himself. This life work provides a powerful opportunity to develop our humanity and sense of oneness with nature—it helps guarantee the future of our planet.

INTEGRATION OF CHILDREN WITH DISABILITIES

Passage in 1975 of Public Law 93-142, the Education of All Handicapped Children Act, which included recreation as a related service, paved the way for parents to demand integrated recreation facilities and programs for their children. The integration of children with disabilities into play settings allows them to gain the developmental stimulation of prolonged contact with able-bodied children instead of being segregated with other disabled children and special education staff. In integrated play settings, child-to-child interaction helps the able bodied discover that the disabled are basically children like themselves (Iacofano, Goltsman, McIntyre, & Moreland, 1985).

To what extent do children with disabilities have special environmental needs? This question has attracted a scatter of research interest (Duncan, Calasha, Mulholland, & Townsend, 1977; Schneekloth & Day, 1980; Shaw, 1987; Moore et al., 1987; G. T. Moore et al., 1979). The most promising broadening of this existing knowledge base will come from the three-year project conducted by Roger Hart and associates at the Playground for All Children, New York.[1] The main thrust of their work has been to consider the full range of disabilities in a public playground purposefully designed to meet the needs of all children and to encourage integration. Results have yet to be published.

Valuable development work has also been done, for example, by Adaptive Environments in Boston, the Playing and Learning in Adaptable Environments program in Berkeley, California, and the Handicapped Adventure Playground Association (1978) in England.[2] But their orientation is toward the higher priority of demonstration, advocacy, and training rather than empirical environmental design research.

---

[1] Children's Environments Research Group, Environmental Psychology Program, 33 West 42nd Street, New York, NY 10036.
[2] Adaptive Environments, Massachusetts College of Art, 612 Huntinton Avenue and Evans Way, Boston, MA 02115-5801. Playing and Learning in Adaptable Environments, 1824 A Fourth Street, Berkeley, CA 94710. Handicapped Adventure Playground Association, Fulham Palace, Bishops Avenue, London SW6 6EA, UK.

One of the reasons for a lack of research interest is the sheer complexity of the issue. The range of disabilities is vast. Many are rarely seen. A national seminar of design educators held in 1982 concluded that if designers cared enough about the needs of people in general, the special needs of people with disabilities would not need so much attention (Ostroff & Iacofano, 1982). There is a very real question concerning the extent to which physical settings can be permanently modified to accommodate the vast array of possible needs, versus relying on day-to-day management to make temporary modifications and adaptations as the need arises. The latter demands more staff understanding and involvement, and more staff effort, but it is an infinitely more feasible strategy. Hence there is a need to train staff (playleaders, teachers, parents) to also be environmental managers (Moore et al., 1987; Ostroff, 1978).

FUTURE DIRECTIONS FOR RESEARCH AND POLICY IN THE PLANNING, DESIGN, AND MANAGEMENT OF PUBLIC PLAYGROUNDS

Public playgrounds are at a crossroads in their evolution. Either they will become more and more irrelevant to the needs of contemporary childhood, less and less used, and finally abandoned altogether, or they will change radically to become significant child development sites and a vital aspect of local community life.

There is a growing literature supporting the idea that playgrounds can be an important factor in child development (Frost & Klein, 1983; G. T. Moore, 1985; Moore & Wong, in press). They are an important local resource where people can come together to share, reflect on, and create a common culture, to give their lives meaning and significance. Playgrounds have a respectable social history (Eriksen, 1985; Rainwater, 1922) and in a different form could be part of a new movement toward social integration and family support. To fulfill this promise, the physical quality of playgrounds must be improved through action-research-driven design. Safety issues must be counteracted through risk management and better information about accident prevention.

A NATIONAL ACTION-RESEARCH PROGRAM

A national program, Play For All, was launched in 1985 to establish a dialogue between the researchers, providers, designers, and manufacturers of children's environments. This culminated in 1986 in a working conference of more than 130 experts at Stanford University and in the publication of the *Play for All Guidelines* (Moore et al., 1987) targeted toward the practical needs of designers, manufacturers, and managers of public play environments.

The Stanford Conference identified a program of design action-research needed to improve the physical quality and play value of specific types of play settings (Appendix). Until some of this work is carried out and the results presented, decision makers will find it difficult to make innovative choices and will fall back on conventional wisdom with its overemphasis on fixed, manufactured equipment. Hopefully, the play equipment industry will expand its vision, realize that manufactured equipment is but one part of the picture, and become involved in developing other types of settings.

PLAY LEADERSHIP AND ANIMATION TRAINING

A new type of specially trained professional is needed in our nation's playgrounds. Free play provides children with the first essential steps of exploration and discovery—the building blocks of child development and culture. But to take the process further requires adult intervention, to remove inhibiting barriers and to extend the full developmental potential of the play process. The usual adults in this process are of course parents. But in many industrialized countries, because of factors such as both parents working and the increase in single-parent families, caretaking has been shifting to other professionals working in daycare centers, afterschool facilities, libraries, hospitals, playparks, and playgrounds. In her study of Stockholm housing estates, Björklid (1984/1985) concludes that the playparks with their playleaders and organized programs satisfied needs that could not be provided at unsupervised playgrounds.

Playleaders are different from teachers, parents, or conventional recreation leaders (Miller, 1987). In essence, they have the ability to interact with children at their own level in the most open "pure" spirit of play as an end in itself—whether at home (parents as playleaders) or in any other place where children gather. Play leadership covers the short-term organizing of activities by and with children. Nothing tangible need be produced except enjoyment for its own sake, the free movement of mind, body, and spirit. The principal measures of success are smiles and laughter. Results are indeterminate. On the other hand, productions (performances, artifacts, structures, stories) do occur because children like to have a sense of accomplishment, and it is healthy for their self-esteem.

Animation extends the spirit of play into a deliberately specified cultural frame, one created by playleaders or "animators" in response to particular circumstances of space, time, and culture. Animators use play as a tool to change behavior, perceptions, and attitudes. In this sense, animation can be considered an art form, using the movement, life, and vigor of play to achieve a social purpose, to create situations that children can take over themselves. As "enablers" or "facilitators," animators help children learn how to make their own decisions. Initially, they act as catalysts, but in the long run the idea is to make the animator redundant, as young people achieve decision-making skills and autonomy.

Animators assume play to be the raw material of education—helping children to express, apply, and assimilate experience in personal and community life, and to accommodate concepts about the world to their new experience. Themes range widely, from peace education to converting a playground into a temporary circus or making it into a living stage where child-scripted works can be presented. There are no limits to the possibilities (Westland & Knight, 1982).

Animation is a very international field.[3] Animators usually have backgrounds in theater, education, and design. They are able to draw the community into a political realm—not power politics, platforms, and speeches, but a more gentle, indirect rhetoric communicated through artistic expression. Important social products include development of solidarity and organization, which then helps the community work toward more explicit political ends (Fritid Stockholm, 1987).

Part of the job of an animator is to set up, manipulate, and modify the physical environment in order to facilitate creative, culturally relevant activity. Many times it is conducted on a temporary, short-term basis, day-to-day, often at lightning speed. It must be sure-footed to succeed. That is why designers sometimes make good play leaders and play leadership trainers. Designers must learn to design settings to support creative, effective leadership. Playleaders must learn to be environmental managers. Effective play leadership can be either greatly facilitated or greatly hampered by the form and content of the physical setting (Moore et al., 1987). Compensating for inadequacies in the physical environment is extremely demanding on leaders and takes too much of their time and energy.

A better understanding of the relationship between design and leadership will result from detailed action-research documentation of the day-to-day workings of animated settings. Children's play in the United States must move away from an overemphasis on physical setting, which in its most extreme form is a piece of equipment unloaded off the back of a truck and instantly installed, without any involvement or foreknowledge of the community. At the other extreme is the concept of the mobile play programs known as "playbuses" common in Europe, each of which has a team of playleaders and props on board and is able to serve virtually any space in the city (Westland & Knight, 1982).

Play leadership and animation have become or are becoming professionalized in several countries, including Sweden, Denmark, France, Japan, and the United Kingdom (Westland & Knight, 1982). In the United States, the approach is beginning to receive serious attention because of the recognition that, to solve the present crisis, playgrounds must be staffed, not with temporary, minimally trained staff with whistles around their necks, but with professional leaders able to organize and facilitate a wide range of creative, engaging activity for all children. Without this, children will find adventure elsewhere. However,

---

[3] In helping me understand this somewhat confused area, I am indebted to IPA colleagues Nick Balmforth, Ted Birch, Nilda Cosco, Susan Goltsman, Isami Kinoshita, Jane Knight, Karla Leonhardt-Zacharias, Wolfgang Leonhardt-Zacharias, Nic Nilsson, and Junzo Okada; and the animation groups where several of them work: Fritid Stockholm, Pädagogische Aktion, Munich; Inter-Action, London; Kinderfreunde, Vienna; PLAE, Inc., Berkeley, USA; and SS Cat San-Ta, Taishido, Setagaya-ku, Tokyo.

Playgrounds at the Crossroads

the concept has yet to achieve institutional recognition. There does not seem to be one full-time professional training course offered in play leadership and animation in the United States.

PREVENTIVE RISK MANAGEMENT

Children need to be challenged by their environment and to take risks in order to learn. It is an essential aspect of development (Jambor, 1986). At the same time, play environments must be safe, that is, injury free. To allow safe risk taking and to protect children socially, play leadership is a critical dimension of effective risk management. The interaction of physical setting, program, and leadership lies at the heart of any effective management model, which must be based on community involvement and public awareness (Moore et al., 1987; Moreland, McIntyre, Iacofano, & Goltsman, 1986). The prevailing idea of playgrounds as segregated places just for children must be challenged through broader programs that engage the whole community in playground-related community events.

NEW MEDIA

The results of action-research need to be packaged and disseminated in such a way that they will have a direct impact on decision makers and consumers (Zimring & Barnes, 1987).

Networking is nothing new to the multidisciplinary field of children's environments. Now, with the advent of electronic media, a more effective level of information exchange is possible that is not so dependent on face-to-face meetings, or, rather, it gives new, more precisely honed purposes to such meetings.

Documentation and transfer in the form of video has presented new possibilities for building a new kind of knowledge base. New visual media products will bring into the arena of discussion tacit knowledge that is the source of the deepest truth for many who work with children: human expression, emotional response, the subtleties of body language, and environmental interaction.

Such "data" cannot be adequately conveyed on paper. It dies in transmission. Audiences need to feel the joy of play, the sensuousness of settings, and the relationships of settings to dimensions of development: imagination, fine-muscle coordination, risk taking, social interaction, cognitive problem solving—all supported by differentiations of setting, leadership, animation, time, and materials.

Audiovisual media are paving the way to a future more accessible to the political power base of consumers. Internationally, this will help greatly to reduce the severe language barriers that exist in the field.[4] Visual/electronic

---

[4] For more information, contact the IPA VideoExchange, c/o Robin Moore, School of Design, Box 7701, North Carolina State University, Raleigh NC 27695-7701, USA.

media opens a powerful educational door in addition to the slower-moving pace of empirical research. The two approaches need to run together in counterpoint. The facts and figures of research can lend conviction to and broaden the base of demonstration projects. Demonstration projects can provide vehicles for broadcasting research results more widely, more powerfully, more vividly.

The principal need is not more research about what makes a good play environment but (1) a political, public education strategy to convince consumers and decision makers to pay attention to what we already know; (2) an institutional shift toward leadership, programming, and risk management; and (3) a nationwide upgrading of existing environments.

Designer Awareness

The design of an effective playground is an extremely challenging task. Design for winter use, for instance, is an issue requiring special attention (Thomsen & Borowieka, 1980; Wilkinson, Lockhart, & Luhtanen, 1980). How should designers approach this specialized field? The main requirement, as in any social design, is to involve representative users in a close working relationship over a long enough period so that a genuine understanding can evolve. There exists a well-developed methodology for design participation, which can not only result in higher quality, socially relevant settings, but also has important social and psychological benefits for children independent of the project at hand (Bakos, Bozic, & Chapin, 1987; Berkeley City, 1985; Childhood City Newsletter, 1980, 1981, 1982/3; de Monchaux, 1981; Hart, 1987; Gröning, 1986; Moore, 1978; Moore et al., 1987; Sanoff, 1986). Community involvement is the key to educational impact.

Having said this, it is also a fact that full participation is rarely possible because of the very real constraints of politics, time, and money, or simply because of contextual circumstances (a playground in a new development, for instance, where there is no existing population). In these situations, the designer must rely on professional expertise, but it must be informed by design research related to child development objectives.

Public/Private Partnership

In reviewing the new initiatives in public play environments of the last few years in the United States, it is clear that many of the most innovative programs are being generated by private nonprofit organizations willing to take substantial risks on behalf of children. But without municipal support, even the most innovative play programs can easily flounder. They cannot pay for themselves or accommodate children from families who cannot afford to pay— the children most in need. Government must be involved, and public funds must be applied if progress is to be made.

Playgrounds at the Crossroads 107

THE CHOICE

The choice is clear. In one direction is a negative path toward an increasingly conservative, highly proscriptive view of children's play, reinforced by tendencies that are already abroad in our society—the abandonment of recess in public schools for instance (Sutton-Smith, in press). This road leads toward the slow and painful degradation of the U.S. playground and its eventual demise. Some might say, "Good, it wasn't much use anyway."

The other road leads to public playgrounds that serve an important social, cultural, and educational role for children. For those living in high-density urban areas, it is literally the only place to go, good or bad. It is imperative that the bad be improved and the good be made better through creative problem solving. Research and development must be integral to this positive direction.

Playgrounds need to accommodate the full range of children's behaviors by offering a diversity of settings, including successful traditional settings. Research activity needs to focus on the content of settings rather than their form (Moore, 1966). Alternative models need to be adapted to the American context: playparks, adventure playgrounds, and urban farms are obvious candidates. Playgrounds must become places for people of all ages as zones of social vitality in the community. New public locations like shopping malls and airports should be promoted. At the same time, small individual play settings need to be scattered throughout the neighborhood (a swing on every street corner).

Childrens' play and its physical settings must be better understood and more highly valued by parents and the general public (Gaunt, 1987). Children are a critical group in society, their healthy thriving is everyone's business. Those involved directly in making decisions that affect the quality of children's environments (parents, educators, public officials, designers, manufacturers, park and recreation officials) carry the burden of responsibility.

APPENDIX: PLAY SETTING RESEARCH RECOMMENDATIONS

The seventeen setting types defined here derive from the action-research results of the Environmental Yard, later refined and added to in Moore *et al.* (1987), which, together with the findings of the Play for All Program, are the source of the following action-research recommendations to improve the physical quality of specific settings.

1. ENTRANCE/EXIT SETTINGS

Entrance/exit settings create and reinforce a sense of arrival and departure. They are places for hellos and goodbyes, with opportunities to meet, gossip, and hang out. They provide for pick-up/drop-off and delivery activities.

Action-Research Tasks:
- How do the drop-off/loading zone standards specified in Moore *et al.* (1987) work in practice, particularly with respect to wheelchair access?
- What arrangements of seating, bicycle racks, wheelchair access, bulletin boards, signs, litter receptacles, overhead shelter, and expressive features such as archways and flags and banners make the most effective settings?

2. PATHWAY SETTINGS

Primary pathways provide direct pedestrian routes connecting entrance/exit settings to centers of activity, important landmarks, indoor facilities, toilets, drinking fountains. telephones, etc.

Secondary pathways follow less direct routes, allowing children to wander and explore different settings at their own pace. They are a principal setting for hiding-and-chasing games.

Action-Research Tasks:

- What are appropriate dimensions, surfacing, and levels of accessibility[5] for secondary paths?
- What are the design and management criteria necessary for bicycles, to avoid conflict with other users?
- What are the most appropriate settings for different types of wheeled toys, by age group, including children with disabilities?
- What are reasonable standards and criteria for dimensions, surface treatments, edges and curbs, warning textures, and levels of accessibility for wheelchair and visually impaired users?

3. SIGNAGE AND DISPLAY SETTINGS

a. *Functional sign systems* contain four different types of signs associated with the design of primary pathways (Nordhaus, Kantrowitz, & Siembieda, 1984; Robinette, 1985). *Informational* signs present general information in words and graphics (for those who cannot read) about site layout, pathways, and the location of facilities (entry signs are an important subcategory). *Directional* signs, located at all entry and decision points, present information that indicates direction to a space or facility, change in route, or confirmation of correct direction. *Identification* signs present information in both words and pictographs indicating special features or facilities. *Regulatory* signs present notification of rules, requirements, warnings, and restrictions and are used for traffic delineation and control.

Action-Research Tasks

- What colors, configurations, icon systems, and locations work best for readability by different populations, including young children with limited reading comprehension, those whose mother tongue is not English, and visually impaired children and parents?

b. *Expressive/informative displays* use the walls, floors, ground surfaces, structures, ceilings, skywires, and roof lines of a playground site, to hang, suspend, and fly all manner of artwork, informational, cultural, and historical material.

Action-Research Tasks

- What arrangements work best, including new electronic media applications?

c. *Bulletin boards* display day-to-day information about playground programs and community events. An almost universal characteristic of bulletin boards is that they are usually scarce and too small.

Action-Research Tasks

- What configurations and formats provide maximum communication—especially for young children. Can electronic media applications help?

---

[5] The "levels of access" principle is used as a design concept to predict the degree of difficulty for wheelchair and other physically impaired users: level 1, "accessible"; level 2, "usable"; level 3, "difficult." The principle is fully described in Nordhaus, Kantrowitz, and Siembieda (1984).

Playgrounds at the Crossroads

4. FENCES, ENCLOSURES, AND BARRIERS

Fences, enclosures, and barriers protect vegetation and other fragile environments by directing pedestrian traffic flow. They define pathways, enclose activity areas, and define social settings. Enclosure is a primary means of differentiating and articulating the child's environment; for example, fences can double back on themselves to provide small social settings.

Action-Research Tasks
- Which enclosure alternatives work best and serve to (1) direct pedestrian flow, (2) protect vegetation, (3) create social enclosure, and (4) be visually attractive?

5. MANUFACTURED EQUIPMENT/PLAY STRUCTURE SETTINGS

Manufactured equipment/play structure settings primarily support motor development (Heusser, 1986). They are highly significant because even in the most diversified playground with many competing choices, they are well-liked (Moore & Wochiler, 1975) and attract both the highest density and greatest absolute level of use (Moore, 1986b). The most common items are (using industry terms) balance beams, climbers, enclosure structures, rocking equipment, slides, spinning equipment, swings, upper-body equipment, storage facilities, safety surfaces.

Because of burgeoning safety and liability issues, equipment settings have come under close scrutiny. Several countries have produced official guidelines and standards for play equipment: United States (United States Consumer Product Safety Commission [USCPSC], 1981), Australia (Standards Association of Australia, 1981, 1982a,b), Germany (German Standards Institute, 1985), New Zealand (Standards Association of New Zealand, 1986), and the United Kingdom (British Standards Institution, 1979). Canada is also preparing a set of standards.

Action-Research Tasks

Responsibility for many of the tasks specified below rests with the play equipment industry. Hopefully, the more progressive firms will link themselves to university-based research units so that programs of systematic research can be used to upgrade the industry's products.

- Is there an optimum level of complexity of configuration of manufactured equipment beyond which children become confused and distracted by too many choices?
- To what extent can the full range of large-muscle activity (balancing, bouncing, climbing, crawling, hopping, jumping, knee walking, lifting, pulling, pushing, rolling, skipping, sliding, sliding on the same level, spinning, swinging, and twirling) be integrated into a single piece of equipment?
- Can settings be developed where these behaviors can be supported by a continuously linked series of events?
- How can the primary dimensions of heat, light, resiliency, texture, color, and sound be integrated in equipment design?
- Can alternative settings be developed where challenge is either not based on height or where it is "graduated" in easy steps?
- What are some of the novel ways of incorporating movement into manufactured settings?
- How can the safety of manufactured equipment settings be improved by conducting studies of:
  -Entrapment configurations by size and shape of openings for various limbs?
  -Warning signs that code equipment by "degree of difficulty," possibly using color?
- How can reliable, detailed information on playground accidents be efficiently collected and analyzed?
- What setting characteristics best support the full range of impairments, including physical, learning, perceptual, mental, sensory, communicational, health-related, and social/emotional impairments?

- Do children respond best to primary colors, as is often assumed? If not, what are the most appropriate colors?
- What are the developmental disadvantages and benefits of thematic/figurative versus abstract equipment designs?
- What is the advisability of age separation and under what conditions might it be appropriate and useful?
- How can manufactured items be sized to fit the motoric and perceptual characteristics of very young children?
- Are "monumental" manufactured items that are much larger than the children using them inappropriate to their needs?
- What are the safety aspects of the areas around equipment locations, where circulation occurs and where equipment settings interface? The transition zone around swings is particularly important.
- How can playgrounds be made accessible by providing a hard surface for wheelchairs, cane users, and walkers, while at the same time providing a soft surface to protect against falls?
- How can detailed, routine site inspection programs be instituted as the cornerstone of effective risk management (Moore et al., 1987)? How are new construction materials, finishes, surfaces, and hardware, which are constantly appearing on the market (with unpredictable or unknown characteristics), to be researched?
- How can the experiences of progressive parks and recreation and public school agencies be collated as the next step in creating a set of national maintenance and inspection standards?
- How can the USCPSC guidelines be improved? Priority research topics include non-climbable enclosure height, slide gradients, chute rails, stair treads, exit and entry zones and chute materials; swing heights, seats, traffic flow barriers, setbacks, and accessibility; climber heights, rung size, free-fall zones; static versus dynamic balance events; balance height and linkage; upper-body events graduated challenge, linkage, mount–dismount arrangements and height; spinning events size and speed, surfacing, entrapment; rocking/spring mounted events; age groups and spring performance.

6. MULTIPURPOSE GAMES SETTINGS

Multipurpose games settings support formal ball games and informal kickabouts. Because they are large and flat, difficult design tradeoffs with other types of space-demanding settings are involved.

Informal ball play and games settings are less demanding on space and more flexible. Close observation of these settings (Moore & Wong, in press) indicates children's capacity for inventing adaptations of ball games to the characteristics of whatever setting is at hand (e.g., three-dimensional ball tag on play structures). Such constraints in fact force children to exercise ingenuity and are perhaps preferred.

Many games, whether traditional or "new," whether child or leader initiated, are adaptable to variable space constraints, especially with skilled playleaders (Orlick, 1978; Orlick & Botterill, 1975).

Action-Research Tasks
- How can traditional and "new" games be successfully adapted to small-scale settings?
- What alternatives are there to costly, well-drained, irrigated turf areas that will stand up to heavy use and not turn into hazardous, hard-baked dirt?

7. GROUNDCOVERS AND SAFETY SURFACES

Both soft and hard play surfaces are needed to support different types of play activity (Cooper Marcus, 1974). For children to have contact with nature, and in order to provide habitats for small animals, a choice of natural ground covers is needed. Options include turf;

Playgrounds at the Crossroads

unmown, rough areas of wild grasses and plants; carefully managed grassy areas suitable for crawling infants; and nonaccessible erosion control areas.

Because the majority of playground injuries are due to falls from equipment (USCPSC, 1981), much attention is being focused on the development of practical, reasonably priced alternative surfaces. The principal standard is the "under 200 g's" impact attenuation, conducted according to ASTM F-355/86 (Standard Test Method for Shock-Absorbing Properties of Play Surface Systems and Materials, American Society for Testing and Materials, 1986).[6]

Action-Research Tasks
- What are the surfacing requirements of outdoor play settings for infants and toddlers?
- How can managers of children's playgrounds get an immediate reading of impact attenuation of fall-absorbing surfaces so that necessary maintenance action can be taken?[6]
- How can standardized testing procedures for safety surfaces be implemented and consumers informed of the results?

8. LANDFORMS/TOPOGRAPHY

Landforms support varied interaction of the body in three-dimensional space, and varied circulation within and between spaces. Topographic variety stimulates fantasy play, orientation skills, hide-and-go-seek games, viewing, rolling, climbing, sliding, and jumping.

Action-Research Tasks
- How can the problem of erosion by foot traffic on slopes over a few degrees be solved?

9. TREES AND VEGETATION

Trees and vegetation constitute one of the most ignored topics in the design of public play environments. Vegetation is an intrinsically interesting play setting and a major source of play props, including leaves, flowers, fruit, nuts, seeds, and sticks (Moore, 1986c). It marks the passing of the seasons, introducing a sense of time into the child's environment. It stimulates exploration and discovery, fantasy, and imagination and provides an ideal setting for dramatic play (Kirkby, 1987) and hide-and-seek games (Talbot, 1985). "Specimen" plants are important orienting elements.

Trees and vegetation give greater spatial and textural variation to play settings (Moore, 1976). Indoor–outdoor transitions can be softened with vegetation—especially for people whose eyes adjust slowly to changing light levels and glare. Plantings used along paths create a complex sequence of texture, smell, light, shade, and color. Trees add a positive ambience to play settings through light modification, color, texture, fragrance, and softness of enclosure—esthetic impacts that both adults and children appreciate (Moore, 1989a). Broad-leaved deciduous trees can reduce the direct impact of heavy rain and extend the runoff period. Surface root systems bind the soil and help it resist erosion.

Children are especially attracted by a mix of natural and people-made elements (Mason, 1982; Moore & Wong, in press). Design should emphasize the integration of planting into play settings, rather than creating segregated "nature areas."

Action-Research Tasks
- What are the specific ways in which trees and vegetation can be integrated into play settings?
- What types of plants, methods of planting, and protection work best under different climatic conditions and site configurations?

---

[6] A safety surface resiliency tester has been developed. It is a head form that can be dropped from any height onto a surface to determine the G force of a fall. For more information, contact Paul Hogan, Playground Clearinghouse, Inc., 36 Sycamore Lane, Phoenixville, PA 91460-2921.

10. GARDENING SETTINGS

Gardens enable children to interact with nature, to learn about the ecological cycle, and to cooperate with peers. They stimulate social interaction, fine-motor skills, and sensory stimulation. Gardening is a powerful play-and-learning activity with specific but flexible design requirements. Because they are dependent on skilled leadership, gardening programs are rare in U.S. public parks and playgrounds, whereas in many European countries they are a common practice (Westland & Knight, 1982). Practical applications have been well documented (Ortho, 1978), including developments in the community gardening movement (Francis, Cashdan, & Paxson, 1984).

Action-Research Tasks
- What are the child development and educational impacts of gardening? How can the evidence be presented to child development experts and educators, to convince them of its value?

11. ANIMAL HABITATS

The two main categories of animals are domestic/farmyard, and wildlife. Animals stimulate a caring and responsible attitude toward other living things. They provide therapeutic effects and offer opportunities for learning about biology (Blue, 1986; *Childrens' Environments Quarterly*, 1984). Animals are a source of wonder and fascination; they are living things that children can interact with, talk to, and invest in emotionally. They provide companionship in nonthreatening ways and almost always come back for more contact. This can be critical for a child with limited self-esteem. Caring for animals can produce a strong sense of personal competence and pride in children, making animals a powerful socialization medium. Documented examples of childhood animal care are very strong (Moore, 1986a).

The most popular and easiest to care for domestic animals include rabbits, guinea pigs, hamsters, and chickens (Schools Council, 1974a). Larger farmyard animals include goats, sheep, pigs, ponies, and donkeys. They are often found on playgrounds in some countries (Westland & Knight, 1982).

Wildlife provides an important childhood experience (Leedy and Adams, 1982; Moore & Wong, 1984; Schicker, 1986). For purposes of programming and design, categories include:

a. *Nonharmful insects and insect-like organisms.* Caterpillars, butterflies, moths, ladybugs, beetles, pillbugs, spiders, millipedes, and snails are particularly attractive to children. The vast majority of insects are beneficial to the human race, do not bite, do not eat valuable materials or spread disease. They are an inevitable part of any vegetated setting.

b. *Birdlife.* It is difficult for children to make *close* contact with birds (unless caged); nonetheless, birds add movement, color, and song to play settings. Specific habitat requirements include high places for nesting, sources of nesting materials, and food-producing plants.

c. *Small animals, amphibians, and reptiles.* Salamanders, tortoises, squirrels, toads, mice, moles, snakes, and lizards are typical species. Each is adapted to specific habitat conditions that may be replicated through design (Moore & Wong, 1984). Gerbils are a popular caged animal.

d. *Pond life.* Fish and frogs and other pond organisms are very attractive to children (Moore, 1986b, and see Aquatic Settings below).

Vegetation and natural features such as ponds provide food and shelter essential to wildlife. Plants with fruits, cones, and seeds can be selected to attract birds, squirrels, and other wildlife (City of Seattle, 1986; Moore et al., 1987).

Action-Research Tasks
- What types of naturalistic habitats for small mammals can be most readily designed into play settings? The results of work that has been done in zoos need to be adapted to public playgrounds. It is a fertile area for experimentation.

12. AQUATIC SETTINGS

Water in all its forms is a popular, universal play material because it can be manipulated

Playgrounds at the Crossroads

in so many ways (splashed, poured, used to float objects) and mixed with sand, dirt, and vegetation. Water features and aquatic environments are highly valued by children because of their multisensory impact in sounds, textures, changes of state, and feelings of wetness (Moore, 1986a,b). Water both excites and relaxes; it adds a substantial esthetic dimension to any recreational setting. Children are strongly attracted to natural settings that range from a dew-covered leaf, to ponds, streams, and marshes. They support a variety of terrestrial and aquatic life that fascinate children, have a strong perceptual impact, and are vividly remembered for years (Moore, 1989a).

Other water settings include a hose in the sandpit, puddles, ponds, drinking fountains, bubblers, sprinklers, sprays, cascades, paddling, wading and swimming pools—places to cool off in hot weather—and post-rain settings (these deserve special design-research attention).

Action-Research Tasks
- What are the specific design criteria for water features relating to water movement, continuity of water flow, character of water channel, edge character (especially configurations that support maximum impact between users and setting while minimizing impact of users on the natural setting), and multiuse (skating/sliding in winter, for example)?
- Which configurations work best as waterplay/cool-off features?
- Which configurations work best for safety?

13. SAND/DIRT/SOIL SETTINGS

The younger the children, the more likely they are to play in dirt wherever they find it. Wood's (1976) highly detailed study provides overwhelming support for the developmental significance of classic dirt play. Using "props" such as a few twigs, a small plastic toy, or a couple of stones, children can create an imaginary world of their own in the dirt, around the roots of a tree for instance, or in part of a raised planter.

The sandbox is a refined and sanitized version of dirt play and works best if it retains the qualities of dirt play (intimate, small-group spaces, play surfaces, access to water and other small play props). Sand is an excellent medium for creative play and social interaction. It is easy to move and mold. It can be dug, sifted, sculpted, poured, thrown, and drawn upon. It is the ultimate loose part. Large sand areas enable children to engage in more expansive sand play and create imaginary landscapes using all manner of "found objects" (Hart, 1974; Moore, 1986a).

Action-Research Tasks
- What are the optimum means of managing sand settings? How can they be made accessible to children in wheelchairs?
- Can above-ground sand areas be developed for wheelchair users without transfer skills?
- What are the best means of enclosing sand play settings so that sand is kept in place and animals are kept out?
- How can children be kept from running through sand play settings (disturbing the sand play of others)?
- How can enclosures provide a psychologically calm atmosphere and provide shelf-like play surfaces and places on which to sit or "perch" with peers?

14. MANIPULATIVE SETTINGS, PLAY PROPS, AND ADVENTURE PLAY

Manipulative settings range from found objects in fixed settings to adventure playgrounds. Props include a wide variety of small natural and synthetic found objects, such as insects and small mammals, sticks and stones, bottle tops and popsicle sticks, logs, rocks, plant parts, sand, dirt, and scrap lumber, and larger manufactured items such as modular systems, wheeled toys, and dress-up clothes. They provide a low-cost method of enhancing existing play settings (Moore et al., 1987; Moore & Wong, in press). Their developmental significance has been demonstrated in several studies (G. T. Moore, 1985; Moore, 1966, 1974, 1986c; Moore & Wong, in press; Nicholson, 1971).

Using larger-scale props, children and trained leaders can transform a playground into a completely different, temporary setting (Playing and Learning in Adaptable Environments, in press).

Action-Research Tasks
- How can loose-parts systems and props be integrated into conventional playground and park settings?
- How can educators be convinced of the developmental value of manipulative settings?

15. GATHERING, MEETING, AND WORKING SETTINGS

To support social development and cooperative working relationships, children need small, comfortable gathering places where they can meet and work together in small (2–7), medium (7–15), and large (15+) groups. Such spaces are very often missing from public play areas (Cooper Marcus & Sarkissian, 1986). Parents, too, need comfortable places in which to sit where *they* can interact, but from which they can keep an eye on their children.

Architectural forms include benches, decks, patios, verandas, gazebos, and sitting circles. When used as "activity stations" in recreation or education programs, such settings need to have a strong identity and be located next to display settings so that products can be exhibited (Moore et al., 1987).

Action-Research Tasks
- What combinations of specific design characteristics (location, microclimatic comfort, social support, bodily support, multilevel configuration, enclosure, identity, materials, and physical dimensions) produce the best settings?

16. STAGE SETTINGS

Stages support performances, dramatic and fantasy play, and performance activities. They stimulate presentation of self, encourage teamwork, and foster a sense of community. They are places where local culture can be created. Architectural forms include campfire circles, mini-arenas, stages and arenas, groups of picnic tables, and amphitheaters.

Action-Research Tasks
- What forms of stage settings exist? How can their value be demonstrated?

17. FIELDHOUSE AND STORAGE SETTINGS

Fieldhouses function as program bases, storage facilities, communication centers, emergency/first aid posts, and toilet locations. Because of their cost they are sometimes hard to justify. They are a traditional setting in European playparks and adventure playgrounds. Proper storage space helps to reduce clutter that can limit activities. Accessible storage areas that are clearly defined, labeled, and properly placed will encourage children to clean up after their own activities (Adaptive Environments, 1980). Scandinavia offers a wide range of examples, most of which would have to be adapted to the harsh vandalism climate of most American cities. Storage is frequently overlooked in design programming and rarely researched, yet it makes a large difference to the viability of play programs that use loose parts and props. It should be designed as an integral part of the play environment.

Action-Research Tasks
- What are the minimum building requirements to support different kinds of users and programs?
- What are the essential characteristics of buildings and their management that protect them from vandalism damage in a harsh urban environment?

REFERENCES

Adaptive Environments. (1980). Environments for all children. In *Access information bulletin*. Washington, DC: National Center for Barrier-Free Environments.

Playgrounds at the Crossroads 115

American Society of Testing and Materials. (1986). Standard test method for shock-absorbing properties of play surface systems and materials. (F-355/86).
Andel, J. van. (1986). Physical changes in an elementary schoolyard. *Children's Environments Quarterly*, 3(3), 40–51.
Bakos, M., Bozic, R., & Chapin, D. (1987). Children's spaces: Designing configurations of possibilities. In C. S. Weinstein & T. David (Eds.), *Spaces for children: The built environment and child development* (pp. 269–288). New York: Plenum Press.
Balmforth, N., & Nelson, W. (1978). *Jubilee street*. London: British Broadcasting Corporation.
Becker, F. D. (1976). Children's play in multifamily housing. *Environment & Behavior*, 8, 545–574.
Bengtsson, A. (1972). *Adventure playgrounds*. London: Crosby Lockwood.
Benjamin, J. (1974). *Grounds for play*. London: National Council for Social Service.
Berkeley, City of. (1985). *Berkeley youth downtown planning project: Findings and recommendations*. (Report available from Moore Iacofano Goltsman, 1802 Fifth St., Berkeley, CA 94710.)
Björklid, P. (1982). *Children's outdoor environment: A study of children's outdoor activities on two housing estates from the perspective of environmental and developmental psychology*. Lund: Liber Förlag.
Björklid, P. (1984/1985). Environmental diversity on housing estates as a factor in child development. *Children's Environments Quarterly*, 1(4), 7–13.
Björklid, P. (1986). *A developmental-ecological approach to child-environment interaction*. Stockholm: Stockholm Institute of Education.
Blue, G. F. (1986). The value of pets in children's lives. *Childhood Education*, 63, 85–90.
Boehm, F. (1980). Youth farms. In P. F. Wilkinson (Ed.), *Innovation in play environments* (pp. 76–84). London: Croom Helm.
Boulding, K. (1956). *The image: Knowledge and society*. Ann Arbor: University of Michigan Press.
Boyce, W. T., Sobolewski, S., Springer, L. W., & Schaefer, C. (1984). Playground equipment injuries in a large, urban school district. *American Journal of Public Health*, 74, 984–986.
British Standard Institution. (1979). BS5696: Play equipment intended for permanent installation outdoors. London: Author.
Bruya, L., & Langendorfer, S. (in press). *Where our children play: Elemenetary school playground equipment*. Reston, VA: American Association for Leisure and Recreation.
Cambell, S. D., & Frost, J. L. (1985). The effects of playground type on the cognitive and social play behaviors of grade two children. In J. L. Frost & S. Sunderlin (Eds.), *When children play* (pp. 81–88). Wheaton, MD: Association for Childhood Education International.
Children and animals. (1984). *Children's Environments Quarterly*, 1(3).
Cobb, E. (1977). *The ecology of imagination in childhood*. New York: Columbia University Press.
Cooper, C. (1970). Adventure playgrounds. *Landscape Architecture*. October, 18–29, 88–91.
Cooper Marcus, C. (1974). Children's play behavior in low-rise, inner-city housing developments. In R. C. Moore (Ed.), *Man–environment interactions: Vol 12. Childhood city* (pp. 197–211). Washington, DC: Environmental Design Research Association.
Cooper Marcus, C., & Sarkissian, W. (1986). *Housing as if people mattered: Site guidelines for medium density family housing*. Berkeley, CA: University of California Press.
Derickx, C. (1985). Children's play in the city. In P. Heseltine (Ed.), *Play and playgrounds in Rotterdam: A research approach* (pp. 30–37). Birmingham, UK: Association for Children's Play and Recreation.
Duncan, J., Calasha, G., Mulholland, M. E., & Townsend, A. (1977). Environmental modifications for the visually impaired: A handbook. *Visual impairment and blindness*, 444–452.
Eriksen, A. (1985). *Playground design*. New York: Van Nostrand Reinhold.
Esbensen, S. B. (1979). *An international inventory and comparative study of legislation and guidelines for children's play spaces in the residential environment*. Ottawa: CMHC.
Francis, M. (1984/1985). Children's use of open space in Village Homes. *Children's Environments Quarterly*, 1(4), 36–38.

Francis, M., Cashdan, L., & Paxson, L. (1984). *Community open spaces*. Washington, DC: Island Press.
Fritid Stockholm (Stockholm Leisure Department). (1987). A political programme for Fritid Stockholm (English version, mimeo). Stockholm, Sweden: Stockholms Fritidsförvaltning.
Frost, J. L. (1985). History of playground safety in America. *Children's Environments Quarterly, 2*(4), 13–23.
Frost, J. L., & Klein, B. L. (1983). *Children's play and playgrounds*. Austin, TX: Playscapes International.
Frost, J. L., & Sunderlin, S. (1985). *When children play*. Wheaton, MD: Association for Childhood Education International.
Gaunt, L. (1987). Room to grow—in creative environments or on adult premises? *Scandinavian Housing and Planning Research, 4*, 39–53.
German Standards Institute (Deutsche Institut für Normung—DIN). (1985). Play equipment for children: Concepts, safety regulations, testing (DIN 7926—Parts 1–5). English translation, Milton Keynes: British Standards Institution (copies available from Kompan, Inc., 80 King Spring Rd., Windsor Locks, CT 06096).
Gröning, G. (1986). An attempt to improve a school yard. *Children's Environments Quarterly, 3*(3), 12–19.
Handicapped Adventure Playground Association. (1978). *Adventure playgrounds for handicapped children*. London: Author.
Hart, R. (1974). The genesis of landscaping: Two years of discovery in a Vermont town. *Landscape Architecture*, October, 356–362.
Hart, R. (1987). Children's participation in planning and design. In C. S. Weinstein & T. David (Eds.), *Spaces for children: The built environment and child development* (pp. 217–239). New York: Plenum Press.
Hayward, D. G., Rothenburg, M., & Beasley, R. R. (1974). Children's play and urban environments: A comparison of traditional, contemporary and adventure playground types. *Environment & Behavior, 6*, 131–168.
Heusser, C. P. (1986). How children use their elementary school playgrounds. *Children's Environments Quarterly, 3*(3), 3–11.
Holme, A., & Massie, P. (1970). *Children's play: A study in needs and opportunities*. London: Michael Joseph.
Iacofano, D., Goltsman, S., McIntyre, S., & Moreland, G. (1985). Project PLAE: Using the arts and environment to promote integration of all children. *California Parks and Recreation, 41*, 14–17.
International Association for the Child's Right to Play. (1977). *Declaration of the child's right to play*. Birmingham, UK: Author.
Jambor, T. (1986). Risk-taking needs in children. *Children's Environments Quarterly, 3*(4), 22–25.
Kirkby, M. A. (1987). *Young children's attraction to refuge in the landscape: An opportunity for dramatic play*. Landscape architecture thesis, University of Washington, Center for Planning and Research, Seattle, WA.
Lambert, J., & Pearson, J. (1974). *Adventure playgrounds*. Harmondsworth, Middlesex, England: Penguin.
Langley, J. D., Silva, P. A., & Williams, S. M. (1981). Primary school accidents. *New Zealand Medical Journal*, 336–339.
Leedy, D. L., & Adams, L. W. (1982). *A guide to urban wildlife management*. Columbus, MD: National Institute for Urban Wildlife Management.
Mason, G., Forrester, A., & Hermann, R. (1975). *Berkeley park use study*. Berkeley, CA: Department of Parks and Recreation.
Mason, J. (1982). *The environment of play*. West Point, NY: Leisure Press.
Miller, J. (1987). The work of the play leader. *Australian Parks and Recreation, 23*(2), 27–32.

Monchaux, S. de. (1981). *Planning with children in mind: A notebook for local planners and policy makers*. Sydney: New South Wales Department of Environment and Planning.
Moore, G. T. (1985). State of the art in play environment. In J. L. Frost & S. Sunderlin (Eds.), *When children play* (pp. 171–192). Wheaton, MD: Association for Childhood Education International.
Moore, G. T., Cohen, U., Oertel, J., & van Ryzin, L. (1979). *Designing environments for handicapped children*. New York: Educational Facilities Laboratories.
Moore, R. C. (1966). An experiment in playground design. Unpublished master's thesis, Massachusetts Institute of Technology, Department of City and Regional Planning, Cambridge, MA.
Moore, R. C. (1974). Patterns of activity in time and space. In D. Canter & T. Lee (Eds.), *Psychology and the built environment* (pp. 118–131). London: Architectural Press.
Moore, R. C. (1975). The place of adventure play in planning for children's leisure. In *Adventure playgrounds and children's creativity: Proceedings of the Sixth World Congress of the International Playground Association* (pp. 16–25). Birmingham, UK: International Playground Association.
Moore, R. C. (1976). The environmental design of children–environment relations. In *Children, nature and the urban environment. Proceedings of a Symposium-Fair* (Publication No. 19028, pp. 207–213). Darby, PA: U.S. Forest Experiment Station.
Moore, R. C. (1978a). Meanings and measures of child/environment quality: Some findings from the Environmental Yard. In W. E. Rogers & W. H. Ittelson (Eds.), *New directions in environmental design research* (pp. 287–306). Washington, DC: Environmental Design Research Association.
Moore, R. C. (1978b). A WEY to design. *Journal of Architectural Education, 31*(4), 27–30.
Moore, R. C. (1980a). Collaborating with young people to assess their landscape values. *Ekistics, 281*, 128–135.
Moore, R. C. (1980b). Learning from the Yard: Generating relevant urban childhood places. In P. F. Wilkinson (Ed.), *Play in human settlements* (pp. 45–75). London: Croom Helm.
Moore, R. C. (1986a). *Childhood's domain: Play and place in child development*. London: Croom Helm.
Moore, R. C. (1986b). Plant parts as play props. *Playworld Journal, 1*, 3–6.
Moore, R. C. (1986c). The power of nature: Orientations of girls and boys toward biotic and abiotic settings on a reconstructed schoolyard. *Children's Environments Quarterly, 3*(3), 52–69.
Moore, R. C. (1987). Streets as playgrounds. In A. Vernez-Moudon (Ed.), *Streets are public* (pp. 45–62). New York: Van Nostrand Reinhold.
Moore, R. C. (1989a). Before and after asphalt: Diversity as a measure of ecological quality in children's play environments. In M. Bloch & T. Pellegrini (Eds.), *The ecological context of children's play*. Ablex Publishing.
Moore, R. C. (1989b). Dance of life: Child development and the ecology of outdoor play. In M. Kurosaka (Ed.), *Resonance in nature*. Tokyo: Shisakusha.
Moore, R. C., Goltsman, S., & Iacofano, D. (1987). *The play for all guidelines: Planning, design and management of outdoor settings for all children*. Berkeley, CA: MIG Communications.
Moore, R. C., & Wochiler, A. (1975). An assessment of a redeveloped school yard based on drawings made by child users. In R. C. Moore (Ed.), *Man–environment interactions: Vol 12. Childhood city* (pp. 107–119). Washington, DC: Environmental Design Research Association.
Moore, R. C., & Wong, H. (1984). Animals on the Environmental Yard. *Children's Environment's Quarterly, 1*(3), 43–51.
Moore, R. C., & Wong, H. H. (in press). *Another way of learning: Child development in natural settings*. Berkeley, CA: MIG Communications.
Moore, R. C., & Young, D. (1978). Childhood outdoors: Toward a social ecology of the land-

scape. In I. Altman & J. Wohlwill (Eds.), *Children and the environment* (pp. 83–130). New York: Plenum Press.

Moreland, G., McIntyre, S., Iacofano, I., & Goltsman, S. (1986). The risky business of children's play: Balancing safety and challenge in programs and environments for all children. *Children's Environment's Quarterly*, 2(4), 24–28.

National Safety Council. (1985). *Accident facts: 1985 edition*. Chicago: Author.

National Safety Council. (1986). *Accident facts: 1986 edition*. Chicago: Author.

Neighborhoods as childhood habitats. (1984/5). *Children's Environments Quarterly*, 1(4),

Nicholson, S. (1971). How not to cheat children: The theory of loose parts. *Landscape Architecture*, 62, 30–34.

Nordhaus, R. S., Kantrowitz, M., & Siembieda, W. J. (1984). *Accessible fishing: A planning handbook*. Santa Fe, NM: New Mexico Natural Resources Department.

Olweg, K. R. (1986). The childhood "deconstruction" of nature and the construction of "natural" housing environments for children. *Scandinavian Housing and Planning Research*, 3, 129–143.

Orlick, T. (1978). *The cooperative sports and games book: Challenge without competition*. New York: Pantheon.

Orlick, T., & Botterill, C. (1975). *Every kid can win*. Chicago: Nelson-Hall.

Ortho Chemical (1978). *A child's garden*. San Francisco: Chevron Chemical Company. (Public Affairs Department, Box 3744, San Francisco, CA 94119).

Ostroff, E. 91978). *Humanizing environments*. Cambridge, MA: The Word Guild.

Ostroff, E., & Iacofano, D. (1982). *Teaching design for all people: The state of the art*. Boston: Adaptive Environments Center.

Participation 1. (1980). *Childhood City Newsletter* No. 22.

Participation 2: Survey of projects, programs and organizations. (1981). *Childhood City Newsletter*. No. 23.

Participation 3: Techniques. (1982/3). *Childhood City Newsletter*. 9(4)/10(1).

Petersen, J. (1985). The adventure playground in Denmark. In J. L. Frost & S. Sunderlin (Eds.), *When children play* (pp. 201–207). Wheaton, MD: Association for Childhood Education International.

Playing and Learning in Adaptable Environments. (in press). *Play scores*. Berkeley, CA: MIG Communications.

Rainwater, C. (1922). *The play movement in the United States*. Chicago: University of Chicago Press.

Rijnen, J. (1985). Sex differences in play. In P. Heseltine (Ed.), *Play and playgrounds in Rotterdam: A research approach* (pp. 30–37). Birmingham, UK: Association for Children's Play and Recreation.

Robinette, G. (1985). *Barrier-free site design: Anyone can go anywhere*. New York: Van Nostrand Reinhold.

Root, J. (1983). *Play without pain*. Melbourne: Child Accident Prevention Foundation of Australia.

Rutherford, G. (1979). *Injuries associated with public playground equipment*. Washington, DC: U.S. Consumer Product Safety Commission.

Safety in outdoor play. (1985). *Children's Environments Quarterly*, 2(4).

Sanoff, H. (1986). Planning outdoor play in the context of community politics. *Children's Environments Quarterly*, 3(3), 20–25.

Schicker, L. (1986). *Children, wildlife and residential developments*. Unpublished master's thesis, North Carolina State University, Raleigh, NC.

Schneekloth, L., & Day, D. (1980). *A comparison of environmental interactions and motor activity of visually handicapped and sighted children*. Blacksburg, VI: Virginia Polytechnic Institute and State Univesity. (mimeo).

Schools Council. (1974a). *Animal accommodation for schools*. London: English University Press.

Schools Council. (1974b). *The school outdoor resource area*. London: Longman.
Schoolyards. (1986). *Children's Environments Quarterly*, 3(3),
Seattle Department of Parks and Recreation (1986). *Guidelines for play areas: Recommendations for planning, design and maintenance*. Seattle, WA: Author.
Sebba, R., & Churchman, A. (1986). Schoolyard design as an expreession of educational principles. *Children's Environments Quarterly*, 3(3), 70–76.
Shaw, L. G. (1987). Designing playgrounds for able and disabled children. In C. S. Weinstein & T. David (Eds.), *Spaces for children: The built environment and child development* (pp. 187– 213). New York: Plenum Press.
Shier, H. (1984). *Adventure playgrounds*. London: National Playing Fields Association.
Standards Association of Australia. (1981). *Australian Standard 1924: Playground equipment for parks, schools and domestic use* (Parts 1 and 2). Sydney: Author.
Standards Association of Australia (1982a). *Australian Standard 2155-1982: Playgrounds—guide to siting and to installation and maintenance of equipment*. Sydney: Author.
Standards Association of Australia (1982b). *Australian Standard 2555-1982. Supervised adventure playgrounds: Guide to establishment and administration*. Sydney: Author.
Standards Association of New Zealand (1986). *NZS 5828: Part 1. General guidelines for new and existing playgrounds—equipment and surfacing*. Wellington, New Zealand: Author.
Sutherland, A. T., & Soames, P. (1984). *Adventure play with handicapped children*. London: Souvenir Press.
Sutton-Smith, B. (in press). What right do children have to play? Play as creativity v play as passion. In P. Heseltine (Ed.), *Play and creativity. Proceedings of the 10th World Conference of the International Association for the Child's Right to Play*. Stockholm, Sweden. London: International Association for the Child's Right to Play.
Sweeney, T. (1979). Playground accidents: A new perspective. *Trial*, 15, 40–44.
Sweeney, T. (1987). Playgrounds and head injuries: A problem for the school business manager. *School Business Affairs*, 53, 28–31.
Thomsen, C. H., & Borowieka, A. (1980). *Winter and play*. Ottawa: Central Housing and Mortgage Corporation.
Talbot. (1985). Plants in children's outdoor environments. In J. L. Frost & S. Sunderlin (Eds.), *When children play* (pp. 243–251). Wheaton, MD: Association for Childhood Education International.
U.K. Department of the Environment. (1973). *Children at play*. London: HMSO.
U.S. Consumer Product Safety Council. (1981). *A Handbook for public playground safety (vols 1 & 2)*. Washington, DC: Author.
van Vleit, W. (1983). Exploring the fourth environment: An examination of the home range of city and suburban teenagers. *Environment & Behavior*, 15, 567–588.
van Vleit, W. (1985). The methodological and conceptual basis of environmental policies for children. *Prevention in Human Services*, 4(1 & 2), 59–78.
Verkerk, J., & Rijmpa, S. (1985). Criteria for judging playgrounds. In P. Heseltine (Ed.), *Play and playgrounds in Rotterdam: A research approach* (pp. 38–43). Birmingham, UK: Association for Children's Play and Recreation.
Westland, C., & Knight, J. (1982). *Playing living learning: A worldwide perspective on children's Play*. State College, PA: Venture.
Whitehead, A. N. (1968). In T. Talbot (Ed.), *The world of the child*. New York: Doubleday/Anchor. (Original work published 1922)
Wilkinson, P. F., & Lockhart, R. S. (1980). Safety in children's formal play environments. In P. F. Wilkinson (Ed.), *Innovation in play environments* (pp. 85–96). London: Croom Helm.
Wilkinson, P. F., Lockhart, R. S., & Luhtanen, P. (1980). The winter use of playgrounds. In P. F. Wilkinson (Ed.), *Innovation in play environments* (pp. 103–122). London: Croom Helm.
Wood, D. (1976). *Early mound building: Some notes on kids' dirt play*. Raleigh, NC: North Carolina State University, School of Design (mimeo).

Wood, D. (1977). Free the children! Down with playgrounds! *McGill Journal of Education, 12,* 227–243.

Zimring, C., & Barnes, R. D. (1987). Children's environments: Implications for design and design research. In C. S. Weinstein & T. David (Eds.), *Spaces for children: The built environment and child development* (pp. 309–318). New York: Plenum Press.

5

Women and Urban Public Space

RESEARCH, DESIGN, AND POLICY ISSUES

KAREN A. FRANCK AND LYNN PAXSON

> And our bodies, learning the habit of careful deportment
> in public places, speak to us steadily and clearly, saying,
> *you are not free.*
> —Susan Griffin, *Rape: The Politics of Consciousness,* p. 77

The new and growing field of women and environments has focused almost exclusively on women's activities and needs in the home and the adjacent neighborhood with little research on women's use of urban public spaces.[1] The exceptions are studies of specific problems including crime and fear of crime (Gordon, Riger, LeBailly, & Heath, 1981), transportation (Cichoki, 1981; Fox, 1985), and some historical research (Cranz, 1981; Peiss, 1986; Stansell, 1986). Research on urban public spaces has also been growing (Carr, Francis, Rivlin, & Stone, in press; Francis, 1987; Francis, Cashdan, & Paxson, 1984; Whyte, 1980) but pays almost no attention to gender differences in the use of these spaces. Both areas of research are important, but they have not yet generated a theoretical perspective to guide future research on women and public space. The goal of this chapter is to develop just such a perspective.[2]

---

[1] For recent overviews of the literature on women and environments, particularly housing and neighborhoods, see Peterson (1987) and Franck (1988).
[2] The analysis of characteristics of public spaces and their use presented in this chapter and summarized in Figure 1 was initially developed by Lynn Paxson as part of her dissertation work. We are grateful to Setha Low and Dorothea Seelye Franck for their comments on an earlier draft of this chapter.

KAREN A. FRANCK • School of Architecture, New Jersey Institute of Technology, Newark, NJ 07102.   LYNN PAXSON • Environmental Psychology Program, City University of New York, Graduate Center, New York, NY 10036.

Although our primary focus is on contemporary women in western, industrialized countries, we believe the topic should be informed by a historical and cross-cultural view, which is presented in the first section of the chapter. Similarly, contemporary women's use of public space should be viewed in the context of their daily lives and experiences; salient aspects of these are reviewed in the second section of the chapter. A conceptual framework for studying the use of public space is outlined in the third section, where the essential characteristics of public spaces and a series of hypotheses are discussed along with findings from previous research. Possible future directions for education, policy, and design are outlined in the final section.

Our interest is in urban public spaces, indoors and outdoors, that are used by individuals on a temporary basis. Hence places intended primarily for wage work, education, or healthcare are excluded and stores, restaurants, museums, libraries, streets, plazas, parks, airports, stations, and public transit are included. We are concerned only with those activities that are place based in which people come face to face with strangers and with people who may be significantly different from themselves.

From early times until today and in societies throughout the world, women have been associated with and even restricted to the private space of the dwelling whereas men have had freer rein to frequent public spaces. This association of women with private spaces and men with public ones continues today in western industrialized society. Some writers have emphasized the physical and psychological vulnerability of women when they enter public spaces unaccompanied by men (Boys, 1984; Enjeu & Save, 1974; Hayden, 1984; Wekerle, 1981). Lofland (1984) questions the validity and the usefulness of this emphasis, suggesting that it is inconsistent with women's frequent use of urban public spaces and their enjoyment of urban public life. She concludes that although women do not enjoy the same "freedom of the streets" that men do, researchers need to avoid "overstating" both the "dangers and the delights" of city life for women or for men (p. 12).

However, it is also important to understand the context within which women do (or do not) use public spaces. Much of that context *does* constrain their activities and does limit the potentially positive aspects of their experiences. Women do use and enjoy public spaces unaccompanied by men, but only, in part, by overcoming various obstacles and following certain restrictions. Men may also feel constraints, but these seem to arise primarily from a concern about crime and are more closely related to particular places and times. That women still do not have the same "freedom of the street" as do men *is* significant. Finding ways to increase that freedom requires that we understand the ways in which women are constrained and the reasons why.

THEORETICAL AND HISTORICAL OVERVIEW

The following overview consists of four topics: a definition of "public" and "private"; the separation of spaces and sexes in other cultures; the "separation of spheres" ideal that developed in the 19th century; and women's participation in public life in the 19th century.

DEFINITION OF "PUBLIC" AND "PRIVATE"

Feminists writing about the designed environment have generally used the term "private" to refer to the space of the individual household, indoors and outdoors. All other spaces, indoors and outdoors, privately or publicly owned, are referred to as "public." A similar use of terms appears in anthropology but "private" is replaced by "domestic." Other analysts have introduced a third category, including the realm of the "social" (Arendt, 1958) or distinguishing among primary, secondary, and public territories (Altman, 1975). This chapter follows the former line of thinking, presuming the importance of the basic distinction between the space of the individual household and all other spaces in the urban environment, which are accessible to a greater number and a greater variety of people than the private household.

Three characteristics are often used to analyze the meanings of "public" and "private": access, agency of control, and interest (Benn & Gauss, 1983; Pitkin, 1981). The notion of legal ownership crosses all three characteristics (Benn & Gauss, 1983) so that what is publicly owned may still have restricted access and what is privately owned may have unrestricted access. Ownership, access, and control are all of key importance in analyzing public spaces. City streets, squares, and parks are usually both publicly owned and open to the entire population. Other spaces and buildings, privately owned and controlled, are open to the public but the owners may refuse or discourage entry by certain segments of the population (Brill, 1989; Forrest & Paxson, 1979). Examples are stores, shopping malls, and plazas owned by private corporations and built to receive zoning variances. Other buildings are both publicly owned and open to the public but the segment of the population actually using them may be restricted through self-selection or social control. Yet all these spaces—streets, squares, parks, stores, malls, plazas, libraries, and museums—are loosely called "public" and, in some sense and in varying degrees, they are.

SEPARATION OF SEXES AND SPACES

The assumption that women properly "belong" in or near the dwelling whereas men may have easy and frequent access to places distant from the dwelling where a greater number of people gather is characteristic of most societies throughout the world. Rosaldo (1980) cautions that this division of space and related activities by gender is a product of social processes, not biological ones, and that viewing gender only in contrasting terms limits our knowledge and enforces a concept of women as different and apart from men instead of in relationship with men and with other women. Also, although a sexual asymmetry in the domestic and public realms seems to be universal, the ways in which this is organized, the actual activities and relationships women and men pursue, and the meanings they ascribe to them differ among societies. A thoughtful distinction between domestic and public spaces continues to be a useful analytic device in anthropological research (Sharistanian, 1987a, b).

A sharp division between the private realm of the household and the public realm of political discourse was characteristic of life in ancient Athens and was extolled by Aristotle (Elshtain, 1974; Pitkin, 1981). The public spaces of the *polis* (city) were the highly valued realm of the free citizenry and therefore were only open to male citizens. Women and slaves were consigned to the less valued, but necessary, realm of the household, which was also the space of production. In 5th-century Athens, women were not permitted to enter many areas of the city, including the agora or central gathering space,[3] and a special police force restricted the movements of women (Keuls, 1986). The only daily occasion when well-bred women could leave their homes unchaperoned was to fetch water. This restriction of women continues in many Greek villages today (Hirschon, 1981) and in other Mediterranean villages where sharp gender divisions in use of space persist (Reiter, 1975).

SEPARATION OF SPHERES IN THE 19TH CENTURY

The division of the sexes in contemporary U.S. society dates most directly to the concept of "separate spheres," which first began to have a strong impact on middle-class families in the 19th century with the rise of industrialization, the movement of production to places distant from the household, and the employment of men in the paid labor force. Men were expected to pursue the activities of production and wage labor in the public sphere at some distance from the home while women were to remain in the domestic sphere taking all responsibility for homemaking and child care (Cowan, 1983). Although working-class women, particularly young, single women, also joined the labor force (Stansell, 1986; Scott & Tilly, 1975), society's *ideal* was that only men would do so and that women, certainly wives, would stay home. Prior to the 1840s, women's labor for production both in and outside the home had been socially acceptable, even desirable, and during colonial times, women were employed as butchers, silversmiths, and upholsterers, but by mid-century, occupations and professions that had been open to women were no longer open (Lerner, 1969).

Central to the "separate spheres" ideal were particular expectations about the desirable characteristics of women and a sharp distinction between the perceived characteristics of the public and private arenas. Women were to cultivate the virtues of piety, purity, submissiveness, and domesticity; they were to act as comforter, nurse, and keeper of moral values for their husbands and children (Welter, 1966). Whereas the public life of wage work, politics, and

---

[3] It is ironic that in architecture and urban design the agora is often idealized as a public open space when, in fact, its use was so severely restricted to the most powerful and prestigious segment of the population.

public gathering was considered harsh, competitive, and even immoral, the home was viewed as a refuge of peace, affection, and morality. The single-family house maintained by the housewife was idealized as a retreat from the competitive public realm (Davidoff et al., 1976). This ideal denied the social isolation of the wife, the existence of household work in the home, the tyranny of the husband, and the frequency of households without husbands or with wives doing wage work.

Industrialization allowed the "separate spheres" ideal to be realized at first by middle-class families in the 19th century but later, in the 20th century, by working-class families as well (Jackson, 1985). Until very recently, the assignment of women to the private domain of the home and men to public spaces of wage work and social gathering was assumed to be ideal.[4]

Industrialization in the 19th century also gave rise to a greater diversity of public spaces in urban settings that attracted a greater number and variety of people (Barth, 1980). Thus, places outside the individual dwelling became more public and the home became more private, as it lost its function of production and as its occupants became restricted to family members when the custom of housing servants, apprentices, and boarders declined (Laslett, 1973). The spatial privacy of the dwelling reached its peak with the twentieth-century proliferation of suburban single-family houses.

The related dichotomies of home/work, female/male, suburb/city (Saegert, 1981) continue to influence design, planning, and policy decisions as well as the activities and attitudes of household members. More specifically, they generate a spatial distance between the activities associated with "work" (including shopping and other services) from those associated with the home (homemaking and childcare). The ideology of separation of spheres not only misrepresents actual activities (that no "work" occurs at home and that home activities are independent of other services and facilities) but also makes those activities more difficult for both genders.

NINETEENTH-CENTURY WOMEN IN THE PUBLIC SPHERE

In the 19th century, women unaccompanied by men did participate in some activities located in the public realm. Most significantly, working-class women were unable to live according to the "separation of spheres" ideal realized by bourgeois women (Stansell, 1986). In the working class, single women were employed outside the home and many wives and mothers did wage work in the home—doing laundry or piecework or taking in boarders (Stansell, 1986). In tenement neighborhoods, the division between private household space and the public space of street and local store was not as clear as it was for the middle class: family life extended into the halls and streets.

[4] This arrangement and the spatial characteristics of city and suburb have been attributed to requirements inherent in capitalist production (MacKenzie & Rose, 1983; Markusen, 1981; McDowell, 1983) and to the reliance of capitalism on the purchase of consumer goods by individual households (Miller, 1983).

Neither working-class nor bourgeois women were free to venture alone to other parts of the city without difficulty. When they did so, men were likely to perceive their intentions as sexual regardless of their true intentions. Working women, more likely to be on the streets alone, were frequent targets of harassment (Stansell, 1986). In the 1830s, women unaccompanied by men did not enter even the most genteel restaurants and women did not frequent central business districts. Starting in the 1840s, the growth of department stores in downtown areas gave women from different classes an acceptable reason, and the necessary comfort, to be downtown (Barth, 1980). Department stores catered to women shoppers by providing reading rooms and dining rooms exclusively for women (Rothman, 1978).

In the 1840s and 1850s, women created and joined voluntary organizations in great numbers (Smith-Rosenberg, 1985). The goal of many of these organizations was to improve the working and living conditions of working-class women. The increase in the variety of public activities and public spaces in the 19th century appeared to provide women with a way to relate to society free of their subordinate position in the family (Dubois, 1975). This possibility, however, was purely illusory because women were expected to remain in the home. Women's suffrage offered another way women could be admitted to public life—through citizenship. However, the arguments given in favor of women's suffrage were still based on the Victorian role distinctions between women and men: women by virtue of their special characteristics could transform the public domain of politics into a more moral, more virtuous activity, thus repeating their domestic role (Elshtain, 1974).

Even though women participated somewhat in public life and used some public spaces, their activities were still sex segregated, their movements were still restricted when not accompanied by men, and their activities in public life were still an extension of their domestic responsibilities. When working-class women were employed outside the home, it was overwhelmingly in sex-segregated occupations (Stansell, 1986). And when bourgeois women formed their own clubs and volunteer organizations, they were for women only and many of their activities were still in the mode of caretaking for others. Also, clubs and organizations, although outside the domestic private setting, were only quasi-public and, at most, allowed their members to visit their beneficiaries (working-class women) in their homes. When women did use downtown public space unaccompanied by men, often by going to department stores, it was yet another extension of their domestic role and the spaces were frequented almost exclusively by women. Thus, although the location of women's activities began to extend beyond the home into more public spaces, women's reasons for being there and interpretations of the meaning of their presence were based on their private roles, either in terms of their sexuality or their domesticity.

CONTEMPORARY CONTEXT FOR WOMEN'S USE OF PUBLIC SPACE

Women's use of public space today should be viewed in the broader context of their early socialization, their daily activities and responsibilities, and their experiences and feelings in public spaces.

Socialization

From an early age, girls are encouraged to be less exploratory, more fearful, and less physically active than boys. Various studies reviewed by Saegert and Hart (1978) indicate that the spatial range of girls' activities beyond the home is smaller than that of boys and that girls' play is less likely to involve active manipulation of the environment. Parents and teachers discourage girls from exploratory activities and manipulation of the environment because these pursuits are considered masculine. Girls are also taught to take up less space, to cross their legs, and to smile more often (Henley, 1977). These same "rules" apply to the behavior of adult women in their use of public space.

Household Work and Childcare

Even though contemporary women are employed in the labor force in ever greater numbers, and are thereby using some public spaces in greater numbers, they continue to assume primary responsibility for housekeeping and childcare tasks. Research consistently shows that wives take primary responsibility for housekeeping. This is true whether or not they are employed outside the home (Hartmann, 1981; Miller and Garrison, 1982; Michelson, 1985). Berk's (1980) research suggests that the only task in which husbands made a substantial contribution was "outside errands." Women also have primary responsibility for childcare (General Mills, 1981; Hartmann, 1981).

Research by Schooler *et al.* (1984) indicates that because the wife is the central figure in maintaining the household, the psychological consequences of housework are greater for women than for men; these consequences are similar to those of paid employment. One consequence may be that women are concerned with household responsibilities when they are away from home ostensibly engaged in other activities, including using public spaces. Because of their household responsibilities, women are likely to have less leisure time to use public space. Michelson (1985) found that employed wives reported 40 fewer minutes a day spent in leisure activities than did their husbands.

Travel

Another daily activity that differs for women and men is travel. In a study of transit use in several cities, Guiliano (1970) reports that women use public transit more than men by a ratio of 2 to 1. Fox's (1985) research in suburbs shows that 57% of the women used cars for work trips compared with 73% of the men. Women's reliance on public transportation results from several factors: men are more likely to own cars (Fox, 1985), and in a household with one car where both spouses are employed, that car is usually used by the husband for travel to work (Cichoki, 1981; Pickup, 1984). Michelson's study reveals that regardless of mode of transportation, women's travel involves more other people and more purposes than does men's travel. Shopping and trips associated with childcare and the activities of children are more frequent for women than for men (Vanek, 1974).

Michelson (1985) found that women are also heavily responsible for grocery shopping. Similarly, Bowlby (1984) reviews research from the United States, Great Britain, and Sweden that indicates that women have the major role in grocery shopping whether or not they are employed. Indeed, shopping is one activity that takes women into public spaces but is still part of their domestic responsibility as homemakers.

Crime and Fear of Crime

In the United States and Canada, women report significantly more fear of crime than men (Riger and Gordon, 1981; Office of Solicitor General of Canada, 1985). This is despite the fact that women are less frequently victimized, with the exception of sexual assault, than are men.

Riger and Gordon (1981) found that women's fear was correlated with their perception of their own physical competence. When asked how strong they thought they were and how fast they thought they could run, 63% felt they were physically less competent than both the average man *and* the average woman. Women adopted two kinds of precautions to protect themselves from crime: isolation, or avoiding situations perceived as dangerous, and street savvy, such as judging carefully where to sit on a bus. In personal interviews, 41% of the women said they used isolation tactics all or most of the time or fairly often, compared with 71% of the men who rarely did so. Fear of crime was the best predictor of the use of isolation tactics.

Women's reports of how frequently they pursue various after-dark activities alone indicated that those activities that were pursued least often were *discretionary* ones, including going out for entertainment (Gordon *et al.*, 1981). For instance, 75% reported that they never go to the movies alone after dark. Activities that are less a matter of choice were less frequently avoided; only 25% reported that they never walk in their neighborhood alone after dark; 46% never use public transit alone after dark (the latter, however, is still a fairly high proportion).

The authors conclude that fear and its resultant precautionary behaviors considerably restrict women's freedom of movement, most particularly with regard to discretionary activities. Another precautionary measure women take is to behave in more vigilant ways; 50% of the women in the Gordon *et al.* sample (1981) reported that they "always" go out with a friend or two as a precaution, compared with 4% of the men; 58% avoided dressing in a provocative manner when out alone (compared with 25% of the men); and 81% reported making a point of being watchful and alert on the street (compared with 66% of the men). Men, however, were more likely to have taken a course in self-defense: 31% versus 17% of the women.

Following precautionary measures in using public spaces does not ensure safety. Schepple and Bart (1983) have examined the consequences the experience of sexual assault has for perceptions of safety. They found that if the attack took place in a situation the victim already believed to be dangerous, the victim was less likely to change her perceptions or her activities after the attack. Women who believed the attack circumstances to be safe were more likely to have severe reactions; 91% of those raped in a situation previously perceived to be safe reported subsequent feelings of danger that generalized well beyond the particular circumstances of the attack and some withdrew altogether from most social interaction. One explanation for this difference in subsequent feelings is that a person is able to regain a sense of control by blaming his or her own behavior. Without this opportunity to blame oneself, little if any sense of control is regained and, hence, everything may become more frightening. This research has wider implications: women's precautionary measures against all crime may be one way of exerting some control over an environment perceived as threatening.

Harassment

Less severe than physical attack but nonetheless significant in women's use of public space is the frequency with which women are approached by strange men. Such approaches range from friendly overtures to harmless exhortations to sexually explicit comments and actual touching. No thorough or systematic research exists on the frequency, location, or reasons for this behavior despite the fact that it is a daily occurrence in urban settings for many women. One small study based on interviews with and diaries of 20 single young residents of New York City suggests that women were approached twice as frequently by strangers as were men and that the most frequent type of interaction for women were sexual remarks and pick-up attempts. Over a five-day period one woman was approached 19 times; 16 of these incidents involved single males and 8 of these were clearly sexual (Nager & Nelson-Schulman, no date).

In interviews with 60 men who themselves had made remarks to the researchers in public, two German authors found that men were unable to explain the reasons for their behavior (Barnard & Schlaffer, 1981). Twenty percent of the men said that they do so only in the company of male friends. The authors also report that harassment declined in the late evening and during the night, indicating the symbolic nature of harassment. If approached at night, women could interpret such behavior as a serious threat, leading them to report it to the police.

Goffman (1977) has proposed that "hassling" women in public serves two purposes: at the least, it confirms gender identity; at most, it is the first step in a longer relationship. The rituals by which men confirm gender identity require that they do things that "can be seen as what a woman by her nature could not do" (p. 326). Goffman believes that this complementarity of gender relations is structurally deep-seated in the social construction of gender in this society. This is very likely true, but the manifestation of this complementarity through hassling of women in public severely limits women's right to use public space undisturbed.

The frequency of sexual attacks and sexual approaches of a purely verbal nature indicates how much women's sexuality makes them fair game to men in public spaces. Once they are in public, unaccompanied by men, women cannot claim as much right to privacy as men can. Moreover, men in looking at, commenting about, or molesting women are associating a *private* concern and an intimate activity, sex, with women's presence in *public* spaces. And women themselves make a similar association. As in the nineteenth century, when women are in public spaces they are still defined and perceived in terms of their sexuality, which is a private role. They are never free of this role as men are.

Restricted Mobility and Necessary Activities

This view of women's activities and experiences in public spaces suggests a variety of ways in which women's mobility is more restricted than is men's.[5] Women are more frequently engaged in housekeeping and childcare activities, which reduces the time they have available for the discretionary use of public spaces and for travel to public spaces distant from the domestic realm. They are more likely to be accompanied by small children, which may make the use of some public spaces difficult. Women's greater dependency on public transportation, and hence its availability and quality, also reduces the range and timing of their movement. In order to avoid sexual attack or other crimes, women restrict the times and the places they go to alone. When women are alone, their presence is more likely to be understood as sexual availability; women may consequently avoid certain locations or may reduce the amount of time they are in public spaces alone.

Another form of restriction concerns the type of activities women pursue when they do use public space. They are more likely to be engaged in necessary activities, that is, in activities related to their domestic role and are less likely to be engaged in discretionary activities. In addition, we believe women are more likely to feel they need an observable reason or "excuse" for being in a public space (Brown *et al.*, 1986; Forrest & Paxson, 1979). This could be eating, shopping, talking with a friend, even sunbathing or reading. Not only may this make their presence more justifiable, it may also signal that they are not open to overtures.

CONCEPTUAL FRAMEWORK FOR STUDYING WOMEN'S USE OF PUBLIC SPACE

The conceptual framework we propose to guide future research on women's use of public space consists of: (1) an understanding of public spaces as part of a network; (2) the concept of publicness; and (3) an analysis of the essential characteristics of public spaces and their use.

---

[5] The importance of restricted mobility in the lives of single parents is described by Leavitt (in press) and Leavitt and Saegert (1989).

No single public space can or should meet the needs of all users at all times; their variety is both necessary and valuable. In studying a particular public space or in theorizing about public spaces in general, it is important to consider the network or system of public spaces in which each space is embedded.

The concept of publicness refers both to the physical attributes of a space and, more important, to its social and behavioral features (Forrest & Paxson, 1979). Public spaces vary in the degree of publicness they possess and exhibit: the greater the diversity of people and activities allowed and manifested in a space, the greater its publicness. Diversity of people includes variation in age, race, ethnicity, class, gender, and "otherness," that is, other variations in appearance or behavior. A high degree of publicness also depends on the availability of different kinds of places within a space and on varying times of use. Diversity of activities and people does not mean that the more difference the better but rather that a range of diversity is tolerated and encouraged, even with respect to some "fringe" users and activities. The concept of publicness is based on the assumption that face-to-face interaction between diverse types of people is valuable and that many different public spaces should provide for such interaction or, at least, for the copresence of such diversity.

Our analysis of the characteristics of public spaces and their use consists of three classes of characteristics and one of use and users (see Figure 1). We believe that public spaces form a continuum and that no single characteristic used alone, such as the name of the type of space, can define this continuum. Figure 1 can be used to classify particular public spaces according to their individual characteristics and, thereby, to gauge their degree of publicness. (This possible use is indicated by listing Sites A through F across the columns.) Figure 1 can also be used to organize, in a systematic way, findings from past research or hypotheses for future research about different aspects of public space, including but not limited to women's use of it. That is how the figure is used in this chapter. Because very little research on women's actual use of public space exists, our hypotheses are tentative at best. Most of the findings that do exist concern outdoor spaces so we have concentrated on them, but the analysis is applicable to interior public spaces as well.

PROVISION AND MANAGEMENT OF PUBLIC SPACES

Characteristics of public spaces pertaining to provision and management include the name of the type of space and the reasons, stated and unstated, for its development. Some classifications of public open spaces are based primarily on the conventional names of the spaces (Francis, 1987). However, public spaces called by the same name exhibit important variations and classifying them by name tends to obscure that variety. Because one of our goals is to delineate a systematic way of handling and understanding that variety, we have made the name of a public space one of many characteristics. What a space is called reflects what the providers of the space envisioned and strongly influences how it is designed and, subsequently, how it is used. The name, in

SITES				SITE A	SITE B	SITE C	SITE D	SITE E	SITE F
PROVISION/MANAGEMENT	NAME/LABEL		Mall/Atrium Plaza Park Garden Lobby Port/Pier/Dock Block Walk-thru Other						
	HISTORY	Result of a Zoning Bonus or Incentive	Yes No Partially						
			Reason for Development						
	OWNERSHIP		Publically Private - Foundation Private - Corporation Private - Church/Institution Private - other						
	CONTROL		Police Security Guards (uniformed) Security (not uniformed) Signage Mechanical Other						
			Rules of Entry						
	MAINT.	Maintenance Provided By	Public Private Volunteer Other						
LOCATION	CONTEXT		Description of Physical Context						
			Description of Historical Context						
	AGE		Under 1 year 1-9 Years 1-15 Years 15-50 Years 50+ Years						
	SIMILAR SCALE		National Regional Community/Neighborhood Local/Block						
		Nearest Location of Similar Space/Activities	2 Blocks 5 Blocks 10 Blocks or more						
DESIGN	SIZE		Small Medium Large						
	QUALITIES		% Indoor % Outdoor						
			% Fixed Features % Manipulable Features						
			% Natural/Green % Built-up						
	OTHER ACCESS		Degree of Visual Access						
			Degree of Physical Access						
			Other Physical Characteristics						
USE/USERS	USE	Use/Activities (frequency by user type, time of day, groupings)	Use Categories						
	USERS	Users (frequency by use type, time of day, groupings)	User Categories						

Figure 1. Characteristics of public spaces and their use.

part, defines what the space is for and what behaviors are expected and accepted in it.

Reasons for creating a public space may be related to transportation, recreation, entertainment, education, commerce, health, setting a building apart, "cleaning up" a deteriorated area, or providing a visual amenity. Some public spaces, though intended and used primarily for one purpose, may be temporarily transformed for other uses: block parties, large street festivals such as Mardi Gras, and open markets in playgrounds or squares. Temporary uses can also transform a private space into a public one for the duration of that activity, as in yard sales. These temporary uses may attract more women users than do the fixed uses (Rivlin & Windsor, 1986).

Provision and management also include ownership and the history of the space's creation: when it was created; who funded, designed, and built the space; and what the space replaced. One important way ownership varies is whether the space is publicly or privately owned; a space or building that is public may be privately owned, as in places of entertainment and recreation like movie theaters, restaurants, stores, malls, plazas, and atriums. It is possible that women may feel more comfortable, when unaccompanied, in spaces that are privately owned, although this may also be a function of the design characteristics of privately owned spaces or of the amount of control users feel is directly exerted over the space by the owners. Maintenance is the ongoing aspect of provision and management. In some cases, maintenance is also the primary use, as in community gardens, where the primary activity is gardening.

Who controls a public space, how they do so (by vote, money, placement), and how they attempt to make the space safe and secure are all aspects of control. The latter varies from signage, to a public police force that is not always present, to guards in uniform who are always present, to security men who are not in uniform. Control may be directly exerted over entry to the space: by requiring payment or a ticket, as in museums and theaters; by removal of those deemed undesirable by those in control; by requiring users to have a key, as in some community gardens; or by having the space open only at certain hours.

Control exerted by the owner can be taken to an extreme in some public open spaces, such as Disneyland, where no aspects are left to chance or to the user's choice. Some urban spaces, including malls or atrium plazas, approach this level by requiring permits for entertainment such as bands or juggling, by refusing entrance to those people deemed undesirable, or by making those people feel uncomfortable or unwelcome when they do enter. Women who are not part of the undesirable group may feel more comfortable in such spaces but a proliferation of such spaces would mean a loss in the rights of others and the undermining of one reason for going to public spaces, which is the discovery of differentness. Payment for entry (theater) or for use (restaurant) or the expectation that one may purchase goods (stores) does limit the variety of users and thereby generates a kind of homogeneity. Plazas and atriums do not require such payment and yet through overt or subtle devices make clear that only potential consumers are welcome, thereby promoting a high degree of homogeneity.

Rules of entry adopted by the owner or the larger institution sometimes exclude women completely, as in mens' clubs, or may require them to remain separated from men, as in mosques and Orthodox synagogues. Such rules or institutional practices thus create public settings that are sexually segregated. Public environments vary in degree and type of segreation by sex (Wekerle *et al.*, 1981). Recent legal decisions in the United States have disallowed traditional men's clubs from retaining some of the privileges of being public spaces if they do not allow women to be full members. In the United States, spaces that are viewed as "public" by the courts are increasingly being required to allow women full and equal status with men.

Location of Public Spaces

Characteristics pertaining to location include the physical and historical context of the space, its age, its scale, and its location in a system of public spaces that ranges from the local/block level to neighborhood to regional and to national. Spaces created for these different scales do, and should, serve different needs and different users.

Women's greater involvement in the domestic sphere by virtue of their childrearing and homemaking responsibilities suggests that they are more likely to frequent public spaces near the home. Research does indicate that women are more likely, when not accompanied by men, to frequent local neighborhood open spaces than centrally located public open spaces (Rivlin, 1987). Similarly, research indicates that the neighborhood residents involved in the development and maintenance of neighborhood open spaces are more often women than men (Francis *et al.*, 1984). Open spaces in downtown business districts may be frequented less often by women partly because of their lower representation in the labor force. This is the reason Whyte (1980) gives for the 60% male, 40% female composition he found on average in mid-Manhattan plazas.

Physical Design of Public Spaces

Physical design characteristics include size; how much of the space is indoors or outdoors; type, location, and amount of natural amenities such as trees, shrubbery, water; type, location, and amount of built features including seating, tables, play equipment, services, and amenities that support and encourage particular types of activities such as eating, sitting, reading, writing, playing games; type and amount of physical and visual access into, out of, and within the space.

Many of these features may encourage women's use of a public space: if the space is indoors, if it has a high degree of visual access; and if it has amenities that support necessary activities or activities that can be "excuses" for being in the space. In a shopping center in Montreal where shopping is the major activity, women constituted a majority of the population observed, whereas in a multipurpose center that combined commercial and government offices and where fewer people reported that they were there to shop, the proportion of women was only 15% to 30% (Brown et al., 1986). (This difference in gender ratios may also have been due to the suburban location of the shopping center and the downtown location of the multipurpose center.) In observations of open spaces in Manhattan, Forrest and Paxson (1979) found that in the Citicorp Atrium where shopping is a primary "excuse," 51% of those present were women, whereas in Grand Central Station, only 31% were women. This situation, however, was largely determined by the high proportion of men adjacent to an Off Track Betting outlet, where only 5% of those present were women.

This last phenomenon is one of many examples of sex segregation in public spaces that arises from the accepted sex typing of activities (Wekerle et al., 1981), including betting, chess playing, and sports such as basketball, football, and baseball. Public spaces with amenities intended for activities that are predominantly pursued by men in this society will be less frequently used by women, except as spectators. Similarly, observations of 42nd Street between 7th and 8th Avenues in Manhattan where many sex-oriented bookstores, movie theaters, peepshows, and massage parlors are located, indicate that lone men outnumber lone women 7 to 1 during evening hours (Kornblum, 1978).

Ease of physical access by virtue of the design of the space or the route to it makes spaces more available to women especially when accompanied by children. A common attribute of many public spaces is the difficulties they present for people who are transporting small children in strollers or baby carriages and who may also be carrying other items (Boys, 1984; Women Plan Toronto, n.d.). Difficulties arising from various types of inaccessibility caused by poor design or problems with public transportation were *the* most frequent topics of discussion at the workhops held by the organization Women Plan Toronto. Stairways or other changes in level and the absence of ramps or escalators create significant obstacles. When escalators are present, signs may forbid strollers without indicating other means of access. Women are less likely to use public spaces with poor visual access, particularly parking garages or transit stations, and when they do so, are likely to be apprehensive.

The absence of facilities for infant care also causes difficulties, although this is changing at least in some airports. Public settings that young children frequent, such as waiting areas in airports and stations, have few facilities for children to enjoy, creating an additional burden for those adults with them, often women, to entertain them. (Some supermarkets and fast-food restaurants, however, are providing play equipment for children.)

A final design characteristic is the sexual stereotyping of women in public art, in historical landmarks, and in commercial advertising and pornography. In the commemoration of historic persons or events, women are almost completely absent. A survey of historic landmarks in Los Angeles showed that 99.7% of 299 landmarks reflected the contributions of Anglo-Americans and only 4% of them reflected the history of women, including Anglo-American women (Hayden, 1987). When women are portrayed in public monuments, it is primarily to symbolize justice, liberty, or some other grand, but impersonal, concept (Warner, 1985). The other way that women are depicted in public imagery is also impersonal, and degrading: that is as sex objects in posters, billboards, marquees, and other forms of advertising, which are sometimes pornographic. The latter public degradation of women may be one reason women avoid spaces where such advertising is pervasive (Kornblum, 1978). The lack of public recognition given to women's contributions to history and their impersonal presence in public imagery are other ways in which women are there but not seen (Lofland, 1975).

Use and Users of Public Spaces

Use of a public space is strongly influenced by its particular characteristics. The amenities of some public spaces support necessary or instrumental activities whereas those of other spaces support discretionary activities. We hypothesize that the former, such as streets, public transportation, and stores, are more frequently used by women unaccompanied by men than those spaces that support discretionary activities like parks, plazas, restaurants, and theaters. However, when those streets are adjacent to sexually oriented entertainment that is both targeted at men and degrading to women, few women are likely to be present on the street, particularly lone women. This indicates how carefully the combination of characteristics of a public space must be analyzed in studying differences in use by gender.

Even within spaces intended for discretionary activities, some are more supportive of task-oriented activities, albeit discretionary, and others support more diffuse activities. Examples of the former would be restaurants, theaters, museums, and libraries. It is our hypothesis that women, when alone or in the company of other women only, are more likely to use those spaces related to task activities.

Users, by virtue of their identity and their interaction or their lack of interaction with one another, define the use of the space. It may be that women, when alone or accompanied by other women or children only, are more likely to use public spaces that they know are used by people like themselves. When alone, women may be less likely to frequent spaces used mostly by couples or by people the potential woman user feels are very different from herself in economic, racial, or cultural background. (These hypotheses most likely apply primarily to spaces for discretionary activities.) This does not mean that *all* the other users must resemble her but, rather, that some of them must.

Some research conducted in New York City does indicate that public open spaces with a diversity of users also show a higher proportion of women present. A study of Bryant Park by the Project for Public Spaces (PPS; 1981) found that the upper terrace attracted the most diverse group of users in terms of age, race, and gender. This area also supported the greatest variety of seating options and the greatest variety of activities. Interviews also showed that women felt it was one of the most secure places in the park. Similarly, a PPS study of Exxon Minipark (1978) indicated that the area with the most women present was the focal point of the park and exhibited the most diversity in sexual and racial characteristics. Whyte (1980) surmises that among urban plazas "The most used places also tend to have a higher than average proportion of women" (p. 18). Diversity of users may encourage use by women when at least some of the users resemble the potential woman user.

Time of day is also likely to affect women's use of space. Because of both domestic responsibilities and fear of crime, women are less likely than men to frequent public spaces at dusk or after dark. Lunch time and departure from work may be more popular times for women to use public space because such times suggest necessary uses of space rather than discretionary ones. Research by the Project for Public Spaces (1981) indicates that on the 42nd Street Library steps, the percentage of women comes closest to that of men at 1 p.m. (44%). Similarly, in the Exxon Minipark's fountain area, women were approximately 50% of the users at 12 noon and also at 4 and 5 o'clock, whereas the percentages were much lower at other times of the day (Project for Public Spaces, 1978). Rivlin (1987) also notes that women make greater use of public spaces at peak hours.

Our discussion of the context for women's use of public space suggests several hypotheses about use in general. Women are less likely than men to be alone in public spaces, except in those spaces that are directly related to their domestic responsibilities or employment or that cater primarily to women. Compared with men, women are more likely to be with other people. Regardless of the type of space, women are less likely than men to be alone in the evening or at night. In most public spaces, women unaccompanied by men are more likely to be engaged in an activity, including eating, talking, shopping, walking, reading, and caring for children. Women are apt to be more sensitive to characteristics they perceive as making a space safe. They are also more likely to choose spaces that are already populated, particularly by other women. Altogether, they are likely to be more particular about the characteristics of the space and of the people using it (Whyte, 1980).

FUTURE DIRECTIONS FOR EDUCATION, POLICY, AND DESIGN

The lack of systematic research on women's use of public urban space necessitated that we propose hypotheses for future empirical investigation instead of just reviewing previous findings. This we have done in the preceding section; some additional research possibilities are indicated below. The research that does exist and the accumulated daily experiences of women do indicate, however, that women's use of public space is more restricted than is men's. In this sense women "are not free" (Griffin, 1986, p. 77). Because the sources of constraint on women's use of public urban space are so varied, the ways this constraint can be reduced are also varied.

DIRECTIONS FOR EDUCATION

Some of the restrictions placed on women stem from long-standing social expectations of sex role differences. Changing physical design or public policy without attempting to alter these expectations will do little to achieve greater freedom and enjoyment for women in using public space. Education, formal and informal, among adults and children, of oneself and others is also necessary.

Women and men, in their own behavior and in their socialization of children, can begin to question and to change patterns of behavior that restrict the actions and the freedom of girls and women. The extreme degree of self-containment and restraint of physical movement expected of girls may be lessening somewhat as girls participate more in athletics, but many advances can still be made by parents and teachers to encourage girls to be more active, outgoing, and exploratory. Adult women might begin to smile only when happy, to be more relaxed in demeanor, and to occupy public space more comfortably, even by reclining when appropriate (Henley, 1977).

Men can begin to respect women's right to use public spaces freely and without subtle or overt intrusions; men can refrain from undue staring and commentary and they can stop invading women's personal space when not invited (Henley, 1977). A more ambitious goal is for men to lessen their tendency to associate a woman's presence in a public place with her private, sexual life. Boys can be encouraged by parents and teachers to adopt similar attitudes—to accord women and girls the same right to space, public and personal, that they accord to one another.

The constraints on women's time imposed by childcare and housework tasks can be lessened and their freedom of movement and action increased with a greater assumption of these responsibilities by men; this also requires a change in the socialization of children and a change in the attitudes and behaviors of adult women and men.

Actions women can take individually include training courses in physical fitness and self-protection to improve not only their ability to protect themselves but, more important, their own feelings of physical strength. Encouraging one another to frequent safe places like particular parks, restaurants, and theaters would also be helpful. Much of women's reticence about frequenting public spaces when alone may not result from fear but rather from a social discomfort about being a lone woman among couples or groups of people. This reticence can be overcome, in part, by mutual support and encouragement. One of the advantages of some of the events and activities of the 1970s such as the Portland Women's Night Watch ritual (Griffin, 1986) was that it probably generated feelings of self-reliance and mutual support.

Women themselves can develop stronger feelings of self-reliance and self-confidence, but the threat of rape or other crimes nonetheless remains and needs to be addressed. It is essential that the solutions *not* be for women to limit their use of public spaces or to steel themselves to the difficulties of using them, both of which are based on women relinquishing their right to the freedom and pleasures of city life.

DIRECTIONS FOR POLICY

Two ideas have guided our thinking on policy and design: the principle of equal liberty (Kirp, Yudof, & Franks, 1986) and the concept of publicness described earlier.

The principle of equal liberty presumes the value of procedures that enable people to make decisions for themselves rather than specifying particular outcomes that must be reached (Kirp et al., 1986). The basic tenets of the principle are the availability of choices and the ability of people to choose among them. Ensuring greater availability of childcare is one way to increase women's opportunity to enjoy public space by decreasing some of their responsibilities. The solution, given the principle of equal liberty, is not federal financial support of childcare centers but rather cash allowances to parents to enable them to devise their own preferred solutions. However, much more fundamental changes are also needed, notably a significant lessening of the sexual division of labor. Men will have to share equally in childrearing and other domestic tasks; this may require radical changes in the organization of production (Pateman, 1983). What is also required is a closer connection between domestic spaces and other, more public settings that provide recreation, services, sources of employment, and opportunities for social interaction. This, in return, requires that zoning ordinances be changed when they enforce the isolation of residential land uses from commercial ones.

Increasing the range of choices available also means creating alternative scheduling of wage work through flextime and job sharing, frequent and safe public transportation at nonpeak hours, and ensuring that stores and other services are open during weekend and evening hours. The design and management of many public spaces are based on the assumption that all wage work occurs during daylight hours. A greater attempt to support the use of public spaces at other times would create greater choice and safer spaces.

The principle of equal liberty can also be applied to pornography and the sex stereotyping of women in advertising. Equal liberty does not mean censorship, which decreases choice, but rather the provision of funds, regulations, and procedures to increase choice and variety, particularly to counterbalance the existing bias of sexism. This might mean increasing the range of erotic imagery to include images that celebrate women's sexuality in ways that empower women (Diamond, 1985). It would involve women creating their own media, popularizing the work of women, and building up a women's culture (Steele, 1985).

The concept of publicness refers both to the observable variety of users and activities in a public space and to the desirability of such diversity. In regard to policy, a rich variety of public spaces that encourage diversity of users and uses should be maintained and, when possible, increased. The value premise of publicness is that people deemed by some to be socially undesirable are not universally so, especially when their presence does not infringe upon the presence of others. Although we would like to believe that spaces that support a high degree of publicness are the kind of places where different kinds of people come together entirely by choice, we do not think this is a realistic assumption. Therefore, we recommend some public spaces that will bring different types of people together by necessity is in public transit or shopping.

Two measures that are sometimes assumed to indicate the success of a public space are the number of people using the space (Whyte, 1980) and if the space is used by people conventionally considered socially acceptable. It is important *not* to adopt these same assumptions in the improvement of public spaces for use by women. Women's right to use and enjoy public spaces where they may seek and find solitude should not be strengthened by homogenizing the population of users of public urban spaces. The concept of publicness, like the principle of equal liberty, relies on a commitment to diversity and to the enhancement of individual choice.

DIRECTIONS FOR DESIGN

Until very recently, most urban public spaces were designed exclusively for able-bodied, young, or middle-aged men with an overemphasis on business, industry, and commerce (Mumford, 1956). Today, more attention is given to people with special needs such as the handicapped and to spaces that provide opportunities for recreation or relaxation. How these and other public spaces are best conceived and designed is the subject of recent writings (Carr *et al.*, in press; Francis, 1987). Although these are valuable, they do not address the need to make public spaces more pleasant for women.

Women's greater access to and enjoyment of public spaces requires, most fundamentally, a reduction in the sexual division of labor. Community design can aid in this by reducing the physical distance between private and public domains. For a very long time, the separation of public from private has disadvantaged women far more than it has men (Franck, 1985; Hayden, 1984). Greater use and enjoyment of public spaces by women (and others) requires the adoption of an alternative to the public/private dichotomy, that we conceptualize and design spaces as part of a private/public continuum in which those spaces that are relatively more private are enriched through their juxtaposition with more public ones and vice versa.

The extreme dichotomy between public and private domains that currently exists in many American communities is discussed in several feminist critiques of the urban environment (Franck, 1985, 1986; Hayden, 1984; Leavitt, 1985; Saegert, 1981; Wekerle, 1985; Wekerle & MacKenzie, 1985), and ways to connect public and private spaces and activities more closely are proposed.[6] These include the integration of social and other services into residential settings, the placement of sources of employment in or near residential areas, the provision of safe and available public transportation, and the careful design of a range

---

[6] Elshtain (1974), a political scientist, has analyzed the bifurcation between private households and public political discourse that consigns many moral issues to the private domain. She proposes a platform for noncoercive human discourse where concerns arising in the private household realm would be introduced into the realm of political discussion.

of outdoor spaces from shared to private. Other proposals include design and program suggestions to make downtown public space "more domestic" (Hayden, 1984) and the adoption of a Danish model of collective housing that provides complete private units as well as shared spaces for joint meal preparation and dining, for childcare, and for various types of recreation and social gathering (McCamant & Durrett, in press). All these attemps to bring public, or shared, spaces and facilities closer to the private household would allow easier and more frequent access to those spaces by women or men who are at home and by others whose mobility is restricted because they are children, elderly, handicapped, or do not have private cars.

Spaces associated with the performance of shopping and childcare tasks could be planned and designed as spaces that are to be enjoyed as well as used for instrumental tasks. This would include bus, train, and subway stations and spaces adjacent to or in shops and other facilities. Making these spaces enjoyable might include more and better seating facilities, visual amenities, and provision of information on community events or other topics. The point would be to allow women and men to take some discretionary time in public spaces while they pursue life maintenance responsibilities. To do that requires lessening the distinction between recreational and other types of public spaces and between recreational and other types of activities. The developers of shopping malls have taken such an approach by providing seating, cafes, and adjacent visual amenities, and recently owners of some laundromats have provided interior landscaping, tanning booths, and even first-run films. In Toronto, women envisioned ways they could meet and spend time with other women in small cafes or women's community centers and in local parks and plazas with drop-in daycare, places one could go to "without having to get a baby sitter and without being mistaken for a prostitute" (Women Plan Toronto).

Stores, parks, public transit, and public facilities can be made more physically accessible and more enjoyable for people accompanying children. Physical access as well as items and amenities that children enjoy should be considered. Airports or other waiting places could have play equipment; safe and pleasant private spaces for nursing or changing babies could also be provided. The provision of safe and well-maintained public toilets is a must for everyone. Visual access to public spaces is important for increasing women's sense of safety when occupying the space and for allowing them, and others, to view the activities and occupants of the space before entering.

The problem of crime in the United States is severe and research on it abounds, but attention to the location of particular types of crime and the particular characteristics of those locations is surprisingly sparse. One exception is research being conducted by Gerda Wekerle in Toronto on the design characteristics of locations where sexual assaults have occurred (Wekerle, 1987). Similar future research could well lead to building codes or other design requirements that would enhance the safety of public places for everyone.

Interior design to make public spaces safer and more pleasant for women and others who are alone is another consideration. Many restaurants still treat single diners as second-class citizens; alternatives should be explored. Some restaurants provided areas that allow single diners views of one another and the opportunity to engage in conversation if desired. Some hotels have assigned floors for women only; these are kept locked and have special amenities such as laundry, ironing facilities, and small lounges. Although we do not advocate increasing the number of sex-segregated spaces, in some cases they may be warranted, particularly when they allow a valuable degree of choice for both groups.

Finally, public spaces both indoors and outdoors can make particular women and women in general more visible and more respected through public art, monuments, and preservation of buildings and spaces that reflect women's cultural and social contributions. The efforts of Dolores Hayden and others in Los Angeles through the organization they have established, The Power of Place, is one example of work on this issue (Hayden, 1987). A public environment that demonstrates respect for women through its symbolic messages will help to increase women's right to use public space and their comfort in doing so.

EPILOGUE

The empirical basis for this chapter is small and our speculations have by necessity been plentiful. We have argued that in various ways women in public spaces are not free, we have indicated how and why that is the case, and we have suggested how it can be changed.

Things could be worse. In Margaret Atwood's novel *A Handmaid's Tale* (1986), the only use of public space permitted the main female character and others like her is grocery shopping, which she can only do accompanied by a female companion, always dressed in the same conspicuous costume that hides her figure and her features, following a prescribed route at prescribed times, and averting her eyes from all strangers. An alternative vision is created by Marge Piercy in *Woman on the Edge of Time* (1976), where a woman from the future is so free and easy in her movements and so confident in her use of space that a woman from today's world mistakes her for a man. In pursuing the topic of women and public space in research, education, design, or policy, what may be most important is developing an image of how things could be different and working to make that image true.[7]

REFERENCES

Altman, I. (1975). *The environment and social behavior*. Monterey, CA: Brooks Cole.
Arendt, H. (1958). *The human condition*. Chicago: University of Chicago Press.

---

[7] One way to develop such an image is to describe it in words in the form of a short story or vignette. See MacKenzie (1985) for an example. Franck (1988) has used this technique in architecture and social change courses.

Atwood, M. (1986). *The handmaid's tale.* Boston: Houghton Mifflin.
Barth, G. (1980). *City people: The rise of modern city culture in nineteenth-century America.* New York: Oxford University Press.
Benn, S. I., & Gauss, G. F. (1983). The public and the private. In S. I. Benn & G. F. Gauss (Eds.), *Public and private in social life* (pp 3–30). New York: St. Martin's Press.
Berk, S. F. (1981). The household as workplace. In G. R. Wekerle, R. Peterson, & D. Morley (Eds.), *New space for women* (pp. 65–81). Boulder, CO: Westview Press.
Bernard, C. & Schlaffer, E. (1981, May). The man in the street: Why he harasses. *Ms.*, pp. 18–19.
Bowlby, S. R. (1984). Planning for women to shop in postwar Britain. *Environment and Planning D, 2,* 179–199.
Boys, J. (1984). Women and public space. In Matrix Book Group, *Making space* (pp. 37–54). London: Pluto Press.
Brill, M. (1989). Transformation, nostalgia, and illusion in public life and public place. In I. Altman and E. H. Zube (Eds.), *Public Places and Spaces* (pp. 7–29). New York: Plenum Press.
Brown, D., Sijpkes, P., & Maclean, M. (1986). The community role of public indoor space. *Journal of Architecture and Planning Research, 3,* 161–172.
Bryant Park. (1980). *Intimidation or recreation, program development for increased park use.* New York: Bryant Park Restoration Corporation & Project for Public Spaces, Inc.
Carr, S., Francis, M., Rivlin, L. G., & Stone, A. (in press). *Public open spaces: Human qualities of the public environment of cities.* New York: Cambridge University Press.
Cichoki, M. K. (1981). Women's travel patterns in suburban development. In G. R. Wekerle, R. Peterson, & D. Morley (Eds.), *New space for women* (pp. 151–163). Boulder, CO: Westview Press.
Cowan, R. (1983). *More work for mother.* New York: Bani.
Cranz, G. (1981). Women in urban parks. In C. R. Stimpson, E. Dixler, M. J. Nelson, & K. B. Yatrakis (Eds.), *Women and the American city* (pp. 151–163). Chicago: University of Chicago Press.
Davidoff, L., L'Esperance, J., & Newby, H. (1976). Landscape with figures. In J. Mitchell & A. Oakley (Eds.), *The rights and wrongs of women* (pp. 139–175). New York: Penguin.
Diamond, S. (1985). Pornography: Image and reality. In V. Burstyn (Ed.), *Women against censorship* (pp. 40–57). Vancouver: Douglas & McIntyre.
DuBois, E. (1975). The radicalism of the woman suffrage movement. *Feminist Studies, 3,* 63–71.
Elshtain, J. B. (1974). Moral woman and immoral man: A consideration of the public-private split and its political ramifications. *Politics and Society, 9,* 453–473.
Enjeu, C., & Save, E. (1974). The city: Off limits to women. *Liberation,* July/August, 9–13.
Forrest, A., Grecni, J., Mesnikoff, W., & Paxson, L. (1979). *For people's sake: A study in grand Central Terminal* (Monograph). New York: City University of New York, Environmental Psychology Program.
Forrest, A., & Paxson, L. (1979). *Provision for people: Grand Central Terminal/Citicorp: Study II* (Unpublished monograph). New York: City University of New York, Environmental Psychology Program.
Fox, M. B. (1985). Access to workplaces for women. *Ekistics, 52,* 69–76.
Francis, M. (1987). Urban open spaces. In E. H. Zube & G. T. Moore (Eds.), *Advances in environment, behavior, and design* (pp. 72–106). New York: Plenum Press.
Francis, M., Cashdan, L., & Paxson, L. (1984). *Community open spaces.* Washington, DC: Island Press.
Franck, K. A. (1985). Social construction of the physical environment: The case of gender. *Sociological Focus, 18,* 143–170.
Franck, K. A. (1986). At home in the future: Feminist visions and some built examples. In

The spirit of home (pp. 260–269). Washington, DC: Association for Collegiate Schools of Architecture.

Franck, K. A. (1988). *Alternative futures, alternative buildings.* Unpublished research report, New Jersey Institute of Technology, School of Architecture, Newark, NJ.

Franck, K. A. (1988). Women's housing and neighborhood needs. In W. Van Vliet & E. Huttman (Eds.), *Handbook of housing and the built environment in the United States* (pp. 285–300). Westport, CT: Greenwood Press.

General Mills (1981). *Families at work.* Minneapolis: General Mills.

Giuliano, G. (1979). Public transportation and the travel needs of women. *Traffic Quarterly, 33,* 607–616.

Goffman, E. (1977). The arrangement between the sexes. *Theory and Society, 4,* 301–311.

Gordon, M. Y., Riger, S., LeBailly, R. K., & Heath, L. (1981). Crime, women and the quality of urban life. In C. R. Stimpson, E. Dixler, M. J. Nelson, & K. B. Yatrakis (Eds.), *Women and the American city* (pp. 141–157). Chicago: University of Chicago Press.

Griffin, S. (1986). *Rape: The politics of consciousness.* New York: Harper & Row.

Hartmann, H. (1981). The family as the locus of gender, family, and political structure. *Signs, 6,* 366–394.

Hayden, D. (1984). *Redesigning the American dream.* New York: W. W. Norton.

Hayden, D. (1987). *The power of place: A multi-ethnic historical itinerary for Los Angeles.* Paper presented at Berkshire Conference on Women's History, June, Wellesley College, Wellesley, MA.

Henley, N. (1977). *Body politics.* Englewood Cliffs, NJ: Prentice Hall.

Hirschon, R. (1981). Essential objects and the sacred. In S. Ardener (Ed.), *Women and space* (pp 72–88). New York: St. Martin's Press.

Jackson, K. T. (1985). *Crabgrass frontier: The suburbanization of the United States.* New York: Oxford University Press.

Keuls, E. C. (1986). *The reign of the phallus.* New York: Harper & Row.

Kirp, D. L., Yudof, M. G., & Franks, M. S. (1986). *Gender justice.* Chicago: University of Chicago Press.

Kornblum, W. (1978). *West 42nd Street study.* New York: City University of New York, Graduate Center.

Laslett, B. (1973). The family as a public and private institution. *Journal of Marriage and the Family, 35,* 180–191.

Leavitt, J. (1985). The shelter service crisis and single parents. In E. L. Birch (Ed.), *The unsheltered woman* (pp. 153–176). New Brunswick, NJ: Center for Urban Policy Research.

Leavitt, J. (in press). Two prototypical designs for single parents. In K. A. Franck & S. Ahrentzen (Eds.), *New households, new housing.* New York: Van Nostrand Reinhold.

Leavitt, J., & Saegert, S. (1989). *Housing abandonment in Harlem: The making of community households.* New York: Columbia University Press.

Lerner, G. (1969). The lady and the mill girl. *Midcontinent Studies Journal, 10,* 5–15.

Lofland, L. (1975). The "thereness" of women. In M. Millman & R. M. Kanter (Eds.), *Another voice: Feminist perspectives on social life and social science* (pp. 144–170). Garden City, NJ: Anchor.

Lofland, L. (1984). Women and urban public space. *Women and Environments, 6,* 12–14.

MacKenzie, S. (1985). No one seems to go to work anymore. *Canadian Women's Studies, 5,* 5–8.

MacKenzie, S., and Rose, D. (1983). Industrial change, the domestic economy and home life. In J. Anderson, S. Duncan, & R. Hudson (Eds.), *Redundant spaces in cities and regions* (pp. 157–199). London: Academic Press.

Markusen, A. (1981). City spatial structure, women's household work and national urban policy. In C. R. Stimpson, E. Dixler, M. J. Nelson, & K. B. Yatrakis (Eds.), *Women and the American city* (pp. 20–41). Chicago: University of Chicago Press.

McCamant, K., & Durrett, C. (in press). Cohousing Denmark. In K. A. Franck & S. Ahrentzen (Eds.), *New households, new housing*. New York: Van Nostrand Reinhold.
McDowell, L. (1983). Towards an understanding of the gender division of urban space. *Environment and Planning D, 1*, 59–72.
Michelson, W. (1985). *From sun to sun*. Totowa, NJ: Rowman & Allanheld.
Miller, J., & Garrison, H. H. (1982). Sex roles. *Annual Review of Sociology, 8*, 237–262.
Miller, R. (1983). The hoover in the garden. *Environment and Planning D, 1*, 73–87.
Mumford, L. (1956). Planning for the phases of life. In L. Mumford (Ed.), *The urban prospect* (pp. 24–43). New York: Harcourt Brace.
Nager, A. R., & Nelson-Shulman, Y. (no date). Women in public places. Unpublished manuscript, City University of New York, Environmental Psychology Program, New York.
Office of Solicitor General, Research and Statistics Group. (1985). *Female victims of crime, Canadian Urban Victimization Survey*. Ottawa: Author.
Pateman, C. (1983). Feminist critiques of the public/private dichotomy. In S. I. Benn & G. F. Gauss (Eds.), *Public and private in social life* (pp. 281–303). New York: St. Martin's Press.
Peiss, K. (1986). *Cheap amusements: Working women & Leisure in turn-of-the-century New York*. Philadelphia: Temple University Press.
Peterson, R. (1987). Gender issues in the home and urban environment. In E. H. Zube & G. T. Moore (Eds.), *Advances in environment, behavior and design* (pp. 187–218). New York: Plenum Press.
Pickup, L. (1984). Women's gender role and its influence on travel behavior. *Built Environment, 10*, 61–68.
Piercy, M. (1976). *Woman on the edge of time*. New York: Fawcett.
Pitkin, H. F. (1981). Justice: On relating private and public. *Political Theory, 9*, 327–352.
Project for Public Spaces. (1978). *Exxon Plaza Study*. New York: Author.
Project for Public Spaces. (1981). *Bryant Park: Intimidation or relaxation?* New York: Author.
Reiter, R. (1975). Men and women in the South of France. In S. Ardiner (Ed.), *Toward an anthropology of women* (pp. 252–282). New York: Monthly Review Press.
Riger, S., & Gordon, M. T. (1981). The fear of rape. *Journal of Social Issues, 37*, 71–93.
Rivlin, L. (1987). *Women and public space*. Comments made at workshop at the Annual meeting of the Environmental Design Research Association, June, Ottawa, Canada.
Rivlin, L., & Windsor, J. (1986). Found spaces and users' needs. Paper presented at International Association for People and Settings, July, Haifa, Israel.
Rosaldo, M. Z. (1980). The use and abuse of anthropology. *Signs, 5*, 389–417.
Rothman, S. M. (1978). *Woman's proper place*. New York: Basic.
Saegert, S. (1981). Masculine cities and feminine suburbs. In C. R. Stimpson, E. Dixler, M. J. Nelson, & K. B. Yatrakis (Eds.), *Women and the American city* (pp. 93–108). Chicago: University of Chicago Press.
Saegert, S., & Hart, R. (1978). The development of environmental competence in girls and boys. In M. Salter (Ed.), *Play: Anthropological Perspectives* (pp. 157–175). Cornwall, NY: Leisure Press.
Scheppele, K. L., & Bart, P. B. (1983). Through women's eyes: Defining danger in the wake of sexual assault. *Journal of Social Issues, 39*, 63–81.
Schooler, C., Miller, J., Miller, K., & Richard, C. (1984). Work for the household. *American Journal of Sociology, 90*, 97–124.
Scott, J. W., & Tilly, L. A. (1975). Women's work and the family in nineteenth century Europe. In C. E. Rosenberg (Ed.), *The family in history* (pp. 145–177). Philadelphia: University of Pennsylvania Press.
Sharistanian, J. (Ed.). (1987a). *Beyond the public domestic dichotomy*. Westport, CT: Greenwood Press.
Sharistanian, J. (Ed.). (1987b). *Gender, ideology, and action*. Westport, CT: Greenwood Press.
Smith-Rosenberg, C. (1985). Bourgeois discourse and the age of Jackson. In C. Smith-Rosenberg (Ed.), *Disorderly conduct* (pp. 79–89). New York: Oxford University Press.

Stansell, C. (1986). *City of women: Sex and class in New York, 1789–1860*. New York: Knopf.
Steele, L. (1985). A capital idea: Gendering in the mass media. In V. Burstyn (Ed.) *Women against censorship* (pp. 40–57). Vancouver: Douglas & McIntyre.
Vanek, J. (1974). Time spent in housework. *Scientific American, 231,* 116–120.
Warner, M. (1985). *Monuments and maidens: The allegory of female form.* New York: Atheneum.
Wekerle, G. (1981). Women and the urban environment. In C. R. Stimpson, E. Dixler, M. J. Nelson & K. B. Yatrakis (Eds.), *Women and the American city* (pp. 185–211). Chicago: University of Chicago Press.
Wekerle, G. (1985). Neighborhoods that support women. *Sociological Focus, 18,* 79–95.
Wekerle, G. (1987). *Women and public space.* Comments made at Workshop at the Annual meeting of the Environmental Design Research Association, June, Ottawa, Canada.
Wekerle, G., & Mackenzie, S. (1985). Reshaping the neighborhood as we age in place. *Canadian Women's Studies, 6,* 69–72.
Wekerle, G. R., Peterson, R., & Morley, D. (1981). Introduction. In G. R. Wekerle, R. Peterson, & D. Morley (Eds.), *New space for women* (pp. 1–34). Boulder, CO: Westview Press.
Welter, B. (1966). The cult of true womanhood: 1820–1860. *American Quarterly, 18,* 151–174.
Whyte, W. H. Jr. (1980). *The social life of small urban spaces.* Washington, DC: Conservation Foundation.
Women Plan Toronto. (no date). *Shared experiences and dreams.* Toronto: Women Plan Toronto.

6

Control as a Dimension of Public-Space Quality

MARK FRANCIS

INTRODUCTION

Public-space quality is attracting considerable attention. The number of new spaces has greatly expanded. At the same time, people are using existing and new public spaces in increasing numbers. As a result, the relationship of public spaces such as parks, plazas, and streets to the quality of urban life has attracted intense interest on the part of public officials, researchers, designers, and citizens (Hiss, 1987; Levine, 1984).

Several critical questions surround this public interest in the form and meaning of public space. How do public spaces support public culture and outdoor life? How does public space affect people's overall experience and satisfaction of living in towns and cities? What role do public spaces play in what Gehl (1987) has come to call the "life between buildings"? How can public spaces be best designed and managed to satisfy human needs and expectations? These concerns point to the need for expanded theory and improved practice in public space design and management.

A multiplicity of dimensions regarding public-space quality have been identified through past research and design and management practice (Francis, 1987b, 1988a; Goffman, 1963; Whyte, 1980). Several of these critical ingredients of successful public space are reviewed by other contributors to this volume. The purpose of the present chapter is to examine one important yet poorly understood dimension of public-space quality—people's right to control their use and enjoyment of public places. User control of public space is emerging

---

MARK FRANCIS • Department of Environmental Design, University of California-Davis, Davis, CA 95616. Research for this chapter was supported with grant #CA-D-EHT-4143-H from the University of California Agricultural Experiment Station.

from psychological and political theory and environmental design research as an essential ingredient for the success of urban places. It is part of an evolving public culture in the United States, where people are using outdoor space in greater numbers, with increased intensity, and for a wider range of activities than previously experienced in neighborhoods, on streets, and in urban centers.

Public spaces are participatory landscapes. Through human action, visual involvement, and the attachment of values, people are directly involved in public spaces. People claim places through feelings and actions. The public realm, as Lofland characterizes public space, is a publically perceived, valued, and controlled landscape. As pointed out by the Lennards (1984):

> a public space . . . is at once both stage and theater, for in public the spectators may at any moment choose to become actors themselves. Successful public places accentuate the dramatic qualities of personal and family life. They make visible certain tragic, comic and tender aspects of relationships among friends, neighbors, relatives or lovers.

It is this direct or symbolic human involvement that invites an examination of control as a critical element of the values attached to urban spaces.

This chapter considers several aspects of user control and participation in public space. The evolving nature of public life is first examined to point to the effect of changes in demography and leisure time on the use of public environments. The shift of designers away from a romanticized European image of public space to a more Americanized form of public environment is discussed. The differing and often competing interests of various publics such as space managers, users, city officials, and designers in controlling spaces is introduced to show how control affects American public space design and management.

Control as a psychological construct and participation concept is reviewed to point to the individual and social benefits of perceived and real control in public environments. The direct contribution of personal control is outlined utilizing a conceptual framework advanced by Lynch (1981) for making "good" urban environments. Lynch's five dimensions of control—presence, use and action, appropriation, modification, and disposition—are discussed in terms of their relevance to public-space quality. Gardening is employed as an example to illustrate how user control is an increasing part of residential and city life.

Several controversial issues are also reviewed, including the conflict between private interests and public needs, the growing role of public space as home for the homeless and other disadvantaged groups, and the effect of control on perceived safety. Design and management techniques that increase user control of streets, parks, and plazas are also reviewed. The chapter concludes with a discussion of some future policy and research implications of increasing user control over public space, including a research agenda for control with respect to public environments.

PUBLIC SPACE AND URBAN LIFE

Public spaces reflect ourselves, our larger culture, our private beliefs, and public values (Berman, 1986). Public space is the common ground where civility and our collective sense of what may be called "publicness" are developed and expressed. Our public environment serves as a reflection or mirror of individual behaviors, social processes, and our often conflicting public values.

An intense scholarly debate has raged for some time over the growth or decline of public life and culture. Strong positions have been drawn both for and against an increase in publicness in American life. Scholars such as Lofland (1973), Sennett (1977), and Brill (in Chapter 1, this volume) argue that American life has become more specialized, leading to a largely privatized society. Others, including Fisher (1981) and Glazer and Lilla (1987), observe that there is an expanding public culture and increased appetite for public space. This claim is supported by the commercial success of new festival marketplaces developed recently in many city centers and the increase in retail sales in downtowns and malls. Such evidence points to a renaissance taking place in both older as well as new types of public open spaces.

How does public life affect urban public space? Public life is evolving as part of a growing reaction to the privatization of American life. The isolation of suburban living, impersonal work environments, and the increased stress of modern life all contribute to an increased appetite on the part of many people for public space. The park or mall becomes a retreat, a form of refuge from the hectic daily schedule of appointments, faxing, car pools, and deadlines.

Many Americans still do not yet know how to use public space. People are often uncomfortable lingering for hours in a plaza watching the "place ballet," as Seamon and Nordin (1980) have characterized the changing life of dynamic public places in Europe. The behavioral rules are not clear for many types of public space. They are often limited at present to office workers sitting on benches during lunchtime periods and undesirables being discouraged from lingering for too long in a downtown plaza.

One of the most predominant forms of current public-space behavior can be characterized as recreational shopping, now a popular American family activity. The evening or weekend spent shopping in the mall or downtown marketplace is part of public life (Prus, 1987). Private developers have been quick to understand this consumer-oriented leisure activity by providing ample opportunities for food, performers, and benches. Public amenities and a highly articulated physical environment are used to support the browsing and buying behavior of recreational shopping. The rediscovery of the farmers' market, as reported by Robert Sommer in his chapter in this volume, is part of this trend, where people come together at the local park or downtown parking lot to buy fresh vegetables, meet friends, and exchange news with neighbors. Shopping is an important but still poorly understood aspect of public-space culture.

THE CHANGING FACE OF PUBLIC SPACE

Changes in public life are transforming the design and management of public spaces. Existing spaces have become more controlled by owners, managers, and designers. Who uses spaces has become a primary concern of private-space managers, with design and management being used in favor of affluent users and against less desirable users such as teenagers, the elderly, and the homeless.

The designer's romanticized view of European public space has also shifted with the realization that the Italian piazza does not fit American public-space culture (Brill, Chapter 1, this volume). As Chidister (1988, p. 40) points out, "Few, if any, of today's plazas achieve the concentration of vital political, commercial, religious, and social functions that characterized the medieval piazza. Today's public spaces are more amenity than necessity." Increased understanding of the limits of the "Euro-Urbanist" (Brill, Chapter 1, this volume) view of American public space has led some to a search for more appropriate design models for public space (Behl, 1987; Glazer & Lilla, 1987).

At the same time, new types of public spaces have been developed that respond to the changing public life of cities (Francis, 1987b). To address manager and owner concerns about undesirable uses and users, new types of spaces have been developed that often restrict public access and use. Examples include the lockable park that is fenced and closed at night and on weekends and the indoor atrium plaza designed to be visually separate from the street and patrolled by guards and closed-circuit cameras.

At the neighborhood scale, numerous community parks and gardens have been developed by neighborhood residents in response to the failure of some traditional public parks and playgrounds (Francis, Cashdan, & Paxson, 1984). These community-controlled sites also restrict access by fences and locks but several hundred keys are often checked out to neighborhood residents for a typical park. Community-controlled sites often experience equal or greater use and satisfaction than nearby public parks (Francis, 1987c), as was the case with a community garden and public park in downtown Sacramento, where the garden was found to be more highly valued by both users and nonusers on dimensions of beauty/visual quality, quality of facilities, and safety than the public park.

THE PUBLICS OF PUBLIC SPACE

A discussion of public space raises the question, Who is public space for? In reality, public space is the meeting ground of the interests of many diverse groups. Studying the needs and agendas of these different publics is important for understanding how public space is developed, used, and valued (Vernez-Moudon, 1987).

Zube (1986) distinguishes between three types of publics involved in the

Control as a Dimension of Public-Space Quality 151

Figure 1. Jefferson Market Garden—a community-controlled and -developed garden in New York City.

public landscape. The first are "professionals," who are involved in the development of plans and policies. The second he calls the "interested public"— those who perceive the plans as directly benefiting them. This group frequently has a direct role in shaping public space. The "general public" is the third category and it includes people who do not participate in making the plans or policies.

Using this framework as a starting point, a finer distinction of publics for public space can be proposed. At least five distinct groups or publics can be identified: *users, nonusers, space managers* and *owners, city officials,* and *designers* (see Table 1). Each has its own set of interests in controlling public space.

Users

Users are those who frequent public places and rely on them for passive and active engagement. Rarely are they asked their opinions or directly involved in designing or managing public spaces. The social failure of a number of public spaces points to the need to better articulate the needs of users and directly engage them in public-space design.

An example where lack of attention to user needs led to the eventual demolition of a redesigned plaza is Richard Serra's *Titled Arc* sculpture in the Federal Plaza in lower Manhattan (Storr, 1985). In this commissioned public art project designed without user input, the artist erected a large curved metal structure in the center of the plaza blocking direct access to the building entrance. The building occupants protested, eventually winning a court case to have the sculpture removed. Had the designer simply spent a lunchtime informally talking to and observing users of the plaza, he might have recognized the inappropriateness of his proposal.

Nonusers

Nonusers are another important and often neglected public space group. Many people pass by parks, plazas, and atriums on foot, in buses, and in cars without ever becoming users. How these sites are perceived is important for their overall value as public spaces. Studies of people's perception of places (Im, 1984; Zube, Sell, & Taylor, 1982) point to the importance of visual elements in landscape quality. A common problem with some new public places such as lockable parks and atriums is that they deny visual access to nonusers.

Space Managers and Owners

Space managers and owners represent a powerful and influential public space group. Either public (for example, a redevelopment authority) or private (for example, the owner of a building), these groups hire designers, strongly influence the assumptions that guide their work, and are responsible for the daily functioning of public spaces. In the past, some building owners have been interested in nonuse, discouraging public access to or ability to use a public place. Grace Plaza in New York City is a well-documented example (Carr, Francis, Rivlin, & Stone, in press). William Whyte (1980) has also documented several plazas that were purposely designed to discourage use by not providing comfortable seating.

Control as a Dimension of Public-Space Quality

TABLE 1. A FRAMEWORK OF THE PUBLIC INTERESTS IN PUBLIC SPACE

Major publics	Types	Public-space interests
Users	Age	Use
	Children	Recreation/leisure time
	Teenagers	Eating
	Adults	Shopping
	Elderly	Passive engagement
	Sex	Active engagement
	Male	Comfort
	Female	Visual quality
	Occupation/economic	
	Service	
	Professional	
	Unemployed/homeless	
Nonusers	Same as above	Visual quality
		Effect on
		Local economy
		Tax base
Managers/owners	Developers	Image
	Building owners	Cost
	Banks	Profit/return on investment
	Tenants	Maintenance
	Space managers	
	Guards	
	Investors	
	Stockholders	
Public officials	Planners	Economic development
	Zoning officials	Design quality
	Public-works engineers	Relationship of projects to
	Police department	standards, codes, and
	Fire department	guidelines
	Review bodies/commissions	
Designers	Landscape architects	Technical
	Architects	Aesthetic quality
	Planners	Client acceptance
	Urban designers	Liability
	Technical consultants	Recognition
		(awards, published projects)

PUBLIC OFFICIALS

Public officials are charged with the overall quality of the public landscape of towns and cities. City agencies typically responsible for public spaces include Departments of City Planning, Parks and Recreation, Real Estate, Public Works, etc. These agencies are faced with the difficult task of developing and maintaining new parks, streets, and squares as well as reviewing proposals for privately developed ones. An example of the complex and often competing role of public agencies in public space policy can be seen in New York City, where over a dozen agencies are involved in open-space policy. Many of these agencies were working against one another. Departments of Park and Recreation, Planning, General Services, and Housing Preservation and Development are all involved in development of parks, community gardens, and waterfront areas. Most are not familiar with each other's projects and efforts are often duplicated. At the same time, the New York City Department of Real Estate has sold city-owned property slated for open-space development at public auction to private developers for housing. These problems led the Mayor to appoint an interagency Open Space Task Force to better coordinate city policy. Other cities such as Boston and San Francisco have also established cross-departmental groups to better coordinate open-space and housing policy.

The trend to give private developers greater responsibility for providing open spaces has presented public officials with a difficult challenge. For example, indoor atrium spaces are being developed in many cities as part of the official requirement for providing public space. Yet many of these places are not accessible to the public. This led the City of New York to require that building owners post signs stating that spaces were open to the public. Another example of the complex relationship between public and private interests in public-space management can be seen in a recent controversy over Bryant Park in midtown Manhattan. The New York City Park Department developed an agreement with a private nonprofit corporation to take over the management of the park. The group then proposed allowing a private developer to build a large and exclusive restaurant in the park. After intense debate, the proposal was defeated by environmental groups; however, management of Bryant Park remains in private hands.

Designers

Designers, such as landscape architects, architects, and urban designers, play an influential role in shaping public space. Design often defines the behavioral rules of public space, communicating what is allowed and what is forbidden in open spaces. Fences, gates, edges, surfaces, and lack of amenities can communicate strong messages to users about the lack of hospitality of a space. On the other hand, a water feature that encourages touching, comfortable benches, and shade trees on a hot day can invite use.

CONTROL AS AN ENVIRONMENTAL CONCEPT

The goal of public control of the environment, as pointed out by J. B. Jackson (1984), is to "make favorable differences in the lives of the public." There is a long history in the United States of political and legal protection of the quality of the public environment. Examples of laws and regulations pro-

Control as a Dimension of Public-Space Quality   155

tecting the public landscape include the zoning of land use, general plans that control density, and design guidelines that control building heights.

Control of the public environment grows out of a tradition of community activism in the United States concerned with the enhancement of the civic environment (Zube, 1986). For example, in the late 19th century, numerous visual improvement societies existed for the protection and enhancement of public places. Local groups formed for the promotion of outdoor art and the development of town parks. These groups were also strong advocates for other types of civic improvements. Zube (1986) points out that by 1880 there were over 200 rural and community improvement associations in New England with more in other states. Cranz (1982) traces the influence of local concern for public health and improvement of the city in the early 20th century to the rise of the public playground, gymnasium, and schoolyard. The "city beautiful" movement was part of this social movement. Control as an environmental concept grows out of this tradition.

Environmental design research has also contributed useful information on the importance of the public environment. Research in the 1970s by William Whyte (1980) on use of urban plazas in New York City and subsequent studies (Gehl, 1987; Project for Public Spaces, 1981; Chidister, 1986) in diverse American and European cities identifies use as an important prerequisite to public-space quality. This perspective, simply stated, is that when a public space is heavily populated, it is successful.

However, a significant problem with use as a major indicator of success is the fact that activity alone is not a good gauge of the public values attached to a space. For example, the lunchtime use of an office tower plaza may be the result of a lack of meaningful alternatives. The space may be occupied but not loved. It is this deeper attachment to place that is ignored by a central focus on use as a measure of satisfaction.

More recently, concepts such as environmental meaning or one's connectedness to a place have been advanced as an important dimension of good public spaces (Carr *et al.*, in press; Francis, 1988a; Rapoport, 1982). The attachment of meaning to a public space can occur at several different levels. For example, human connectedness to a place can be at the individual level, as with a person experiencing a special event such as a wedding or memorable concert in a town park or public garden. Meaning can also be attached by a group to a public place, such as teenagers placing value on a certain street corner or an ethnic group's tradition of celebrating a festival on the same street at the same time every year. Meaning can also be at a national level as in the case of the millions of Americans and others who celebrate New Year's Eve in Times Square in New York City in their minds and through watching the events there on their television sets.

Another aspect of the attachment of meaning to a public space is through direct involvement in the designing or building of a place. Many examples of public spaces being designed with public participation now exist and those that have been documented through case study research point to the benefits of design participation (Iacofano, 1986). A current example is the design process for the North Park in Battery Park City in lower Manhattan. Gary Hack and Stephen Carr of Carr Lynch Associates are engaging residents in the design of the park through a variety of participatory techniques. The developers of the park, Battery Park City Authority, report that this participatory process has enhanced the sense of attachment of residents to this new, large-scale community. A similar participatory process used by Davis Design Research to develop a master plan for the expansion of Central Park in Davis, California, has resulted in the fostering of a sense of local ownership and advocacy for the master plan.

Direct involvement of users in the construction and maintenance of a place also may enhance meaning or attachment to a public place. Hart (1978) has documented the importance of children's building and modification of the landscape in child development. Hester (1985) involved Manteo, North Carolina, residents in the design and construction of a boardwalk along the town's waterfront. He found that their involvement in construction added to increased use of the waterfront and greater satisfaction with the project. Similar results have been documented in the case of community-built gardens in several New York City (Francis, Cashdan, & Paxson, 1984) and Boston (Warner, 1987) neighborhoods.

An ingredient of meaning is the concept of control or people's ability to directly influence their own use and experience of a place. In one of the most comprehensive discussions of the importance of freedom and control in open spaces, Carr and Lynch (1981) argue that user satisfaction is determined largely by one's ability to control one's experience of the place. They cite examples such as the territorial claims over open spaces by some groups, such as drug dealers, which in turn deny others their right of access and use.

CONTROL AS A PSYCHOLOGICAL CONSTRUCT

Control as a psychological concept has been a focus of considerable research and theoretical attention (Langer, 1975; Lefcourt, 1982; Wortman, 1975). The desirability of perceived control in a variety of situations has been found to be a prerequisite for a positive experience for some people (Burger & Cooper, 1979; Dougherty, 1988). Recently, Langer (1983) has conceptualized control to mean the "mindful process of mastering," which differs from previous views of control as achieving an outcome. Control has been defined in various ways in the social sciences, including the mindful process of mastery (Langer, 1983); efficacy (White, 1959); internal versus external control (Lefcourt, 1982); and process versus decision control (Tyler, Rasinki, & Spodick, 1985).

In person–environment studies, personal control has been found to be an important mediating variable in reducing stress (Ulrich & Simons, 1986) and the perception of crowding (Baldassare, 1979; Saegert, Mackintosh, & West, 1975). These studies support Lynch's (1981) suggestion that the environmental "fit" of a person and an environment is enhanced by the ability of a person to directly control or modify his or her environment. Retreating to a doorway at

Control as a Dimension of Public-Space Quality   157

a crowded bus stop or turning away from the person next to you on a crowded subway are examples of ways people adapt environments to fit their needs. When the ability to control the environment is reduced or eliminated, as in the case of an overcrowded apartment or noisy office environment, negative experiences such as stress or social withdrawal increase.

Territoriality is one key dimension of control. As defined by Altman (1975, p. 106), "Territoriality involves the mutually exclusive use of areas and objects by persons and objects." Brown (1987) reviews the structural characteristics of territoriality. Territories, she suggests, are a form of "markings" that promote display of personal identity and regulate social systems.

Altman (1975) distinguishes three types of territories that differ on dimensions of duration of occupancy and psychological centrality. Primary territories are settings such as homes and bedrooms, which are occupied for long periods of time and are central to their occupants. The last two types form the basis of a discussion of public space. Secondary territories such as a bar or neighborhood park are somewhat more accessible to a greater number of users but regular occupants exert some control over the space. These spaces take on a more collective ownership and shared public control. The third type is a public territory such as seats on a bus or a table in a restaurant, where occupancy is often determined on a "first come, first served basis" and for brief periods of time.

Applied to public space, the claiming of space by drug dealers or teenagers is an example of spatial territoriality in an urban park. For example, in a study and redesign of Exxon Mini Park in midtown Manhattan, Project for Public Space (PPS, 1981) found drug dealing to be a barrier to use of the plaza. The use of the plaza entry by drug dealers at lunchtime contributed to both underuse and misuse of the plaza. A redesign by PPS introduced food, comfortable seating, and a physical layout that provided for better visual surveillance by the plaza managers. As lunchtime use increased, the drug-dealing behavior shifted to other locations outside the plaza.

One reason people may be interested in more directly controlling places they use is that many parts of their everyday life are beyond their direct control. In a society where life has become anonymous and privacy is a legally guarded concept, some individuals and groups are working to create settings for greater public interaction and enjoyment. The concept of publicness or one's right to use the public environment has emerged as a central issue in urban design.

CONTROL AS A PARTICIPATION CONCEPT

Direct participation in designing, building, and managing environments has been found to increase user satisfaction in a variety of spaces including communities, the workplace, and open spaces such as parks and playgrounds (Wandersman, 1981). The effects of participation need to be more fully studied by environmental design researchers (Francis, 1985), but, clearly, participation in design has been found to increase a sense of attachment and ownership for many participants. For example, Iacofano (1986) reviewed several environmental design projects and found that participation was instrumental in fostering a sense of personal growth, self-actualization, and political efficacy.

Control has been advanced as an important goal of participation. Arnstein (1969), in an early and widely cited framework of citizen participation, suggests several levels of participation. In her "ladder of participation," citizen control is the ultimate goal of participation, followed by delegated power, partnership, placation, consultation, informing, therapy, and finally manipulation as decreasing degrees of participation and citizen power.

Hester (1987) cautions that participation does not always lead to equity and environmental justice. Like Arnstein, he points out that participation without real control over decision making can often lead to decreased environmental equity. Pateman (1970) argues that real environmental control implies a sharing of power. She attributes the limits of participation to basic structural problems of power and politics that often work against decentralized control over decision making. Politics and power have important influences on control.

This political view is useful for a discussion of public-space quality because it points out that control implies a sense of individual or group ownership or stewardship. When the degree of real or perceived control is limited, the amount of perceived responsibility over a place may be limited. For example, perceived control may reduce littering in a public plaza or reduce teenage graffiti in a neighborhood park by offering users a sense of caring for a place. Thus participation becomes a tool to achieve perceived control in public places.

CONTROL OF PUBLIC SPACE: A DEFINITION AND CONCEPTUAL FRAMEWORK

Kevin Lynch, in *Theory of Good City Form* (1981), offers a useful starting point for defining the importance of control in quality of place. He suggests that spatial control—or its absence—has strong psychological consequences such as contributing to anxiety, satisfaction, and pride. He proposes five forms of spatial control: presence, use and action, appropriation, modification, and disposition. A brief review of these rights is useful in understanding how control can be provided for in public space.

Presence is the right of access to a place. Without access, use and action are not possible. *Use and action* involve one's ability to use a space. *Appropriation* allows users to claim ownership, either symbolic or real, of a site. *Modification* is the right to change a space to facilitate use. *Disposition* is the ability to transfer one's use and ownership of a public place to someone else. Together, these spatial rights provide a conceptual definition of control in public space.

Following Lynch's framework, a preliminary definition of control of public places can be developed. *Control is the ability of an individual or group to gain access to, utilize, influence, gain ownership over, and attach meaning to a public place.*

TABLE 2. DIMENSIONS OF CONTROL IN PUBLIC ENVIRONMENTS

• Individual	• Group
• Symbolic	• Real
• Temporary	• Permanent
• Inclusionary	• Exclusionary
• One time	• Continuous

When conflicts arise between groups or individuals with competing interests, control becomes a process through which conflicts are identified, negotiated, and resolved.

Control can be either individual or group, as in the case of seniors or teenagers gathering in a park. Control can be real, as in the case of a group owning a site, or symbolic, as in a "Friends of the Park" group that takes on management responsibility for an open space. Control can also be temporary, existing for only certain times of the day, week, or year, or permanent, as in the complete control of a space. Control can be for one time only or continuous over a long period of time. Control can include or invite people into the process or place. It can also be exclusionary, restricting opportunities for involvement or use. Table 2 shows some dimensions of control in the public environment.

CONTROL IN THE PUBLIC LANDSCAPE: THE EXAMPLE OF GARDENING

The role of control in developing a satisfactory relationship to public space can be seen in one example—the growing interest in gardening as a recreational activity. A 1987 Gallup Poll found gardening to be the most popular of outdoor recreation activities surpassing jogging, swimming, fishing, and bicycling (National Gardening Association, 1987). Over 74 million American households reportedly garden, many on community sites. Americans spent $17.4 billion on their lawns and gardens in 1987. This represented a 23% increase from 1986 spending levels. The sharp increase in the number of garden supply and seed catalogues is further evidence of the increased public interest and involvement in gardening (Francis & Hester, 1987).

Several studies have begun to point out the psychological and restorative benefits of gardens and gardening (Altman & Wohlwill, 1983; Francis 1987c; Kaplan, 1973). Kaplan's study of community gardens in Ann Arbor, Michigan, found that gardening produced increased self-esteem and contributed to satisfaction with other aspects of people's lives. Kimber (1973), in a study of Puerto Rican gardens, reported that "gardens . . . represent social territories in which persons define their own places and express their self images" (p. 7).

This sense of symbolic ownership and control is a major motivation in the increasing number of community garden projects in U.S. communities. In a

TABLE 3. SOME CONCEPTUAL DIFFERENCES BETWEEN A COMMUNITY-CONTROLLED COMMUNITY GARDEN AND A CITY-CONTROLLED PUBLIC PARK[a]

Public park	Community garden
• Passive	• Active
• Quiet/relax	• Activity/work
• Be alone	• Get together
• Clean/neat	• Messy but cared for
• To look at	• To participate in
• Publicly controlled/managed	• User-controlled/managed
• Permanent	• Temporary
• Green attracts people	• People attract people
• Liked	• Loved

[a] Adapted from Francis (1987c).

study of ten community-developed garden and park sites in New York City (Francis et al., 1984), the desires to improve the appearance of the neighborhood and to grow fresh vegetables and flowers were the most frequently mentioned reasons people reported for getting involved in these projects. This intimate contact with and control over nature is one way urban residents create a sense of place for themselves. Other studies have identified as motivation both the visual preference for natural elements and vegetation (Schroeder, in press; Ulrich, 1979) and the active engagement gardening offers to people (Kaplan & Kaplan, 1987).

Community gardening as a human activity illustrates Lynch's framework. A garden must invite presence and be accessible. The process of gardening is both use and action—occupying a space and changing it. The gardener appropriates the space and directly modifies it through planting, pruning, and harvesting. The gardener is free to transfer the real or symbolic ownership of his or her plot to others.

In the previously cited study comparing perceptions regarding an adjacent community garden and public park in downtown Sacramento, control was found to be a key reason why both users and nonusers placed higher value on the gardens than the park (Francis, 1987b). Although fenced and locked, the gardens were valued by nonusers because they communicated a sense of caring for a place, something not communicated by the public park. Table 3 summarizes some conceptual and perceived differences between public parks and community gardens (Francis, 1987b).

The garden has also become part of the workplace with the advent of the employee garden popular in some corporate environments. For example, two insurance companies in Marin County north of San Francisco, Fireman's Fund and Amex Life Assurance Company, have set aside space for employee gardening. The garden site includes 15 plots but that does not satisfy the demand by employees who want space to raise vegetables and flowers. The companies put up the fence and supply the water; corporations such as Hewlett-Packard

Control as a Dimension of Public-Space Quality

in Palo Alto also have established employee gardening programs as part of their corporate landscape.

The expanded role of the urban garden as public space illustrates how gardens are becoming integrated into public life (Francis, 1988c). The garden is becoming part of the park, the plaza, the waterfront, the hospital, the homeless shelter, and housing for the elderly.

SOME CONTROL ISSUES WITH RESPECT TO PUBLIC SPACE

There are several control issues of concern to public-space users, designers, and managers. They include the growing privatization of public space by corporations and building owners, the increasing use of public spaces by the homeless and other disenfranchised groups, and the role of user ownership and accessibility in satisfactory relationships with public space. These issues help to illustrate the different ways control influences public space perception and use.

Private Interests versus Public Needs

Public spaces are becoming increasingly privatized by owners and managers (Kinkowski, 1981). The privatization of open space raises basic questions regarding what a public space is for and who it serves. Private interests, including merchants, bankers, developers, and property owners, are actively involved in the making and managing of public spaces. These groups frequently exert strong influence over public-space design and policy.

An example of how control relates to open space is a proposal to build a multistory building on the site of the New York City Coliseum, located on the southwest corner of Central Park. The building, as originally proposed, would cast a large shadow over the park and critics argued that this would change the park's use. Some cities such as San Francisco have adopted tough policies to guarantee solar access to existing public spaces, but New York City has not, pitting development interests against park advocates. Only after the Municipal Arts Society provided a simulated photograph showing the shadow cast over the park did the city force the developers to scale back the project. People's right to solar access and thus enjoyment of public space promises to continue to be a major urban policy issue in the future.

Public Space as Home

Public space has become home for many people. Although there have always been homeless people in public spaces in cities, the homeless are populating parks, open plazas, and streets in increasing numbers. A current example is Golden Gate Park in San Francisco, which is permanent home to some people who live in the park's wild areas and in vans and autos on its perimeter.

Figure 2. Public space as home. Fig Tree Park in Santa Barbara, California.

Cities such as Los Angeles and New York are struggling to find better solutions to housing for the homeless, yet the problem is still growing and there are no clear answers. Downtown Sacramento is redesigning many of its downtown open spaces to exclude homeless people without planning or concern for alternative settings or shelter. One large-scale attempt to solve the problem was the urban campground for the homeless constructed in Los Angeles. Only after being compared to a modern "concentration camp" was the idea abandoned. The ability of homeless people to have control over their lives and environment is a central part of the solution to this larger social problem.

PERSONALIZATION AND PUBLIC SPACES

The ability of people to change or modify a public space is also important. There are several ways users directly personalize public environments. Examples include the opportunity for people to garden in a public plaza or move furniture in a park to be able to sit in the sun. Other ways are through popular art such as murals (Sommer, 1983). The sides of buildings in ethnic neighborhoods such as Hispanic communities in Los Angeles are now dotted with murals expressing local culture and politics.

There also are subtle and indirect ways people personalize public spaces. As part of a fund-raising effort for a new plaza in downtown Portland, Oregon, residents contributed to the purchase of bricks. The plaza is now paved with the bricks that bear the names of the donors and, part of the use of the plaza includes people finding familiar names of friends or neighbors. A similar but more emotional activity can be observed at the Vietnam Veterans Memorial in Washington, D.C., where visitors discover the names of relatives killed in the

Control as a Dimension of Public-Space Quality

Figure 3. Discovering names in the Vietnam Veteran's Memorial Wall, Washington, D.C.

Vietnam War in the granite wall and often leave flowers, photos, and other mementos. Another recent example of personalization of public space that communicates meaning to people is the AIDS quilt touring public spaces in several U.S. cities. The patchwork quilt covering the length of two football fields includes 2,176 panels created by friends and family members of AIDS victims.

Personalization raises important questions about how public space is perceived by different publics. User maintenance of an open space, such as elderly residents planting a flower box in a housing project entrance, communicates a sense of caring for the environment. This has been supported by some studies of public open spaces. As we have seen, nonusers of a community garden project in downtown Sacramento were found to place high value on the garden because they "read" that the place was cared for (Francis, 1987c).

On the other hand, personalization can discourage participation or result in negative perceptions by some publics. For example, groups taking over a space such as the homeless camping on the Venice, California, beach is seen as a barrier for local residents to use and enjoy the public beach. Thus, personalization has qualitative dimensions that communicate messages of caring or neglect, access of restriction, and safety or fear.

ACCESSIBILITY

Access is an important prerequisite to realizing many other dimensions of public-space quality. For a space to be well used it must be accessible (Lynch, 1981). Access is also essential if people are going to be able to attach meaning to a public place. For example, teenagers' access to community places was found by van Vliet (1983) to be important for them to feel attached to a community. The access of the elderly to comfortable outdoor spaces provides opportunities for informal socializing and reduces a sense of isolation in housing projects.

Three types of access are important in public spaces. The first is the direct physical access to a plaza or park. Design devices such as doors, walls, and locked gates are being used by some public space designers and managers to physically block access to some spaces. Examples include lockable parks and atriums, now popular in corporate open-space design. Another form of access is social, where a space is open to different classes or types of users. For example, the City of Seattle surveyed public places, and found many to be inaccessible or poorly designed for children. A further example is public art, which is frequently not designed at a child's scale. A third type of access is visual, or the ability to see into a park or plaza. Visual access has been found by several researchers to be critical for people to feel safe and secure in a public place (Wiedermann, 1985). Nager and Wentworth (1976) found lack of visual access into Bryant Park to be a major barrier to people's use of the park. They also discovered that the visual barriers supported the role of the park as an active setting for drug dealing. Now over a decade after they made recommendations for removing some fences and lowering hedges on the borders of the park, park officials are implementing the recommendations after trying more expensive and less successful changes.

OWNERSHIP

Ownership is a direct form of spatial control. As sense of ownership increases, owner responsibility and concern for the quality of the environment often increases. Ownership can be either real or symbolic. Real ownership is when a space is legally owned by an individual, group, or corporation. The transfer of ownership from city government to private developers explains the increasing private control over public space. At the neighborhood scale, some parks and gardens have become owned as community land trusts by local residents who are legally responsible for preserving and maintaining the sites as permanent and publically accessible open spaces.

Symbolic ownership is a more common way users feel part of public places. The claiming of territory by teenagers populating benches in a park is one indicator of users' feeling a sense of ownership over a space. The results of perceived ownership have both positive and negative consequences. When ownership results in the exclusion of people who would like to use a space, access is denied. Ownership can also serve to invite people into a space by communicating a sense of caring or responsibility.

There are several direct benefits of ownership in community settings. Real or symbolic ownership of community gardens has been found to result in important psychological benefits such as increased self-esteem and satisfaction with significant aspects of people's lives (Kaplan, 1973; Kaplan & Kaplan, 1987). Home ownership increases positive attitudes of residents toward their neighborhood and fosters social contact.

SAFETY

To feel safe and secure in a space is also a prerequisite for space use (Stewart & McKenzie, 1978). Safety is a critical issue for the elderly and women in public spaces. Many women report not using parks and plazas because of fear of rape or other forms of physical violence (Wiedermann, 1985). An ability to feel a sense of control over a space, to be able to see in, to escape easily, or to gain assistance in times of crisis are examples of how a place can be made to feel more secure.

Urban vegetation contributes to one's sense of security and safety in public space. Schroeder (in press) reports on findings of a study in which people rated park photographs to determine perceived risk and safety. Long-view distances, open grassy areas, and water were associated with high degrees of perceived safety, whereas physical features such as dense vegetation, graffiti, and litter decreased the perception of safety. This concept supports physiological findings by Ulrich and Simons (1986) showing that scenes with vegetation promoted more relaxed and less stressful states than scenes lacking vegetation.

CONFLICT

The desire for diverse and often competing groups to control the design and management of a public place like a plaza or park will increase the amount of conflict in the development and management process (Berman, 1986). Yet conflict and negotiation are hallmarks of the democratic process and the concept of public space (Francis, 1987a). An example of the role conflict can play in urban design was the proposal to site the John Fitzgerald Kennedy Library in Harvard Square in Cambridge, Massachusetts, in the mid-1970s (Francis, 1975). The approval of the project was blocked because the developers did not let concerned community members participate in the design process, which could have led to a consensus plan and project approval. Instead, the developers chose to control the design process themselves and decided to relocate the project to an undeveloped part of Boston where the project could avoid public scrutiny.

SOME DESIGN AND MANAGEMENT OPPORTUNITIES FOR INCREASING CONTROL IN PUBLIC SPACE

Good design and management are central to making good public places (Project for Public Spaces, 1984). How can an understanding of the role of personal control in public-space quality be more fully integrated into the design and management process for public places?

The direct participation of users in the design and management process is one mechanism to increase control (Florin & Wandersman, 1984). As discussed earlier, participation can increase the perceived attachment of people to environments they have input in designing or managing. For example, Becker (1977) found that the ability to participate in both design and management was an important ingredient in resident satisfaction with housing projects. There are now well established and tested techniques for maximizing user participation in public environmental design (Iacofano, 1985). They include workshops, user consultancy, participatory mapping, and surveys. Participation is also a useful device in articulating and negotiating between the often conflicting values of different groups in public open-space design. Participation was employed successfully to clarify and resolve different design values between children and adults for a neighborhood playground in Davis, California (Francis, 1988b).

Another way to involve the public in public-space decisions is environmental simulation. Films or photographs are used to present the visual impacts of proposed development as part of the public debate over proposed new projects. This technique has been used recently to present visual simulations of development proposals in New York City and San Francisco on public television to invite public comment. Utilizing models, the UC Berkeley Environmental Simulation Laboratory, under the direction of Peter Bosselmann, has prepared public television programs showing the visual effects of new buildings proposed on the East Side and Times Square areas in Manhattan, downtown San Francisco, and the UC Berkeley campus. The films became part of the public review process for the projects, helping decision makers and the public evaluate the qualitative aspects of new development.

People's interest in having greater control of places they use has affected the form and management of both older and newer types of urban open spaces. Following a typology developed for this purpose (Francis, 1987c), some specific ways personal control can be integrated into streets, parks, plazas, and downtown public spaces can be identified.

STREETS

Streets are an important part of the public landscape of cities (see Nasar, Chapter 2, this volume). For neighborhood streets, resident efforts to control traffic speed and volume have been found by Appleyard (1981) and others to increase people's use of and attachment to streets they live on. A study of residential traffic control and street redesign in a West Germany city (Eubanks-Ahrens, 1985) found reduction or elimination of auto traffic greatly increased children's access to and use of streets.

Another way to increase people's sense of control over streets is the design of town trails, a mechanism used in many parts of Britain. Here streets serve as teachers of local history with an interpretive trail marked through areas of historic interest. School children, tourists, and local residents utilize the urban trail system to discover local architectural and cultural history (Goodey, 1975).

Neighborhood Parks

There are several ways people can be given a greater sense of control over neighborhood parks and playgrounds. Personal control can be applied to neighborhood parks and community open spaces through both symbolic and real ownership. Symbolic ownership can be achieved by initiating a "Friends of the Park" group or real ownership established when users own the park as a land trust. "Loose parts" such as natural elements can also be provided in playgrounds and neighborhood parks to support children's direct modification of the environment (Nicholson, 1971). These simple and low-cost elements serve to increase environmental competence and learning for children and teenagers (Hart, 1978; Hayward, Rothenberg, & Beasley, 1974).

Plazas and Downtown Public Spaces

Design devices can be employed by designers to invite direct physical control and modification of plazas and downtown spaces. One is the ability to touch or become actively engaged with water. Another is the movable chair, which Whyte (1980) has shown to help people adapt plazas to their own needs such as sitting in the sun, being alone, or sitting in a group. Also, office workers could be given the opportunity to garden in plazas, thus communicating to others a sense of caring for the space while reducing the maintenance costs for the owner. As we have seen, this has already been successfully tested in some corporate office parks in California.

Farmer's markets are being introduced into public open spaces, such as downtown streets and central parks, and give people an opportunity to have greater control over the quality of food they purchase. As Sommer states (Chapter 3, this volume), a farmers' market renaissance is taking place in many communities. Public spaces such as parks and plazas in small towns and large cities are being redesigned to include markets. For example, a major program element in the reconstructed Copley Square in Boston is the provision of space for a farmers' market in the plaza. Based on the great success of the Davis, California, farmers' market, a permanent plaza is being planned for the market in the town's central park.

Figure 4. Movable chairs in Western Plaza, Washington, D.C.—an example of opportunities for personal control in public spaces.

FUTURE DIRECTIONS FOR RESEARCH AND DESIGN

The effect of control on public environments raises several issues in need of further empirical study and design exploration. One example of research needed is a study of the role of control in the design, management, and use of different public-space types. Traditional spaces such as parks and playgrounds need to be examined, as do newer and more innovative environments, such as waterfront areas, transit malls, and everyday public spaces including steps to public buildings and streetcorners. For example, how can users be made to feel more a part of privately provided public spaces such as atriums and indoor plazas? How does the management of urban streets affect residents' perceived or actual control of streets? How can greater user control contribute to decreased vandalism or improved maintenance of public spaces?

Ownership and territoriality as outcomes of control need to be more deeply examined to determine how they impact on the quality of public environments. Both the interests of different publics in controlling public places and how control relates to the decision-making process require further study. New methods for expanding public involvement must be developed and tested. The social and psychological impact of involvement or exclusion from the decision-making process also requires careful examination.

Innovative design ideas must be developed to provide opportunities for people to directly shape and arrange spaces they use. Flexibility and change can be better provided for in the physical design of public spaces. Designers must recognize the changing and often evolutionary nature of public spaces, and owners and managers need to support such efforts by funding evaluation and redesign on a continuing basis (Francis, 1987b). Control needs to occupy a larger part of the overall agenda for environmental design research.

CONCLUSIONS

Public control has a long history of importance in civic improvement and will continue to shape the urban environment of the future. Public control also affects how the environment is used, perceived, and valued. Control is a mechanism by which people come to attach meaning—both positive and negative—to public places.

As seen in the research cited in this chapter, control of the public environment has both advantages and disadvantages. Control can contribute to a place being cared for or neglected. It can also nurture user responsibility for a place. Lack of control can foster a sense of neglect or disregard. Control by one individual or group can deny the right of access or use to other groups.

The process of making, managing, and changing public places needs to be an open democratic process engaging the ideas and interests of diverse individuals and groups. It is imperative that the design and management of public space remain part of the public arena. Only then can urban spaces become more fully integrated into our evolving public culture.

REFERENCES

Altman, I. (1975). *Environment and social behavior: Privacy, personal space, territory and crowding.* Monterey, CA: Brooks/Cole.

Altman, I., & Wohlwill, J. F. (Eds.). (1983). *Behavior & the natural environment.* New York: Plenum Press.

Appleyard, D. (1981). *Livable streets.* Berkeley, CA: University of California Press.

Arnstein, S. (1969). A ladder of citizen participation. *Journal of the American Institute of Planners.* 35, 216–224.

Baldassare, M. (1979). *Residential crowding in urban America.* Berkeley, CA: University of California Press.

Becker, F. C. (1977). *User participation, personalization, and environmental meaning: Three field studies.* Ithaca, NY: Cornell University, Program in Urban & Regional Studies.

Berman, M. (1986). Take it to the streets: Conflict and community in public space. *Dissent,* Fall, 33, 478–485.

Brown, B. (1987). Territoriality. In D. Stokols & I. Altman, (Eds.), *Handbook of environmental psychology* (Volume 1, pp. 503–532). New York: Wiley.

Burger, J. M., & Cooper, H. M. (1979). The desirability of control. *Motivation and Emotion, 3,* 381–393.

Carr, S., Francis, M., Rivlin, L., & Stone, A. (in press). *Public space for public life.* New York: Cambridge University Press.

Carr, S., & Lynch, K. (1981). Open space: Freedom and control. In L. Taylor (Ed.), *Urban open spaces* (pp. 17–18). New York: Rizzoli.

Chidister, M. (1986). The effect of context on the use of urban plazas. *Landscape Journal, 5,* 115–127.

Chidister, M. (1988). Reconsidering the piazza. *Landscape Architecture, 78,* 40–43.

Cranz, G. (1982). *The politics of park design.* Cambridge, MA: M.I.T. Press.

Dougherty, D. (1988). *Participation in community organizations: Effects of political efficacy, personal efficacy, and self-esteem.* Unpublished doctoral dissertation, Boston University, Boston, MA, Vol. 48, No. 10, Section A, p. 2578.

Eubanks-Ahrens, B. (1985). The impact of woonerven on children's behavior. *Children's Environments Quarterly, 1*, 39–45.

Fischer, C. (1981). The public and private worlds of city life. *American Sociological Review, 46*, 306–316.

Florin, P., & Wandersman, A. (1984). Cognitive social learning and participation in community development. *American Journal of Community Psychology, 12*, 689–708.

Francis, M. (1975). Urban impact assessment and community involvement: The case of the John Fitzgerald Kennedy Library. *Environment & Behavior, 7*, 373–404.

Francis, M. (1985). Research and design participation. In M. R. Beheshti (Ed.), *Design coalition team: Proceedings of the International Design Participation Conference* (pp. 211–221). Eindhoven, Netherlands: Department of Architecture and Planning.

Francis, M. (1987a). The making of democratic streets. In A. V. Moudon (Ed.), *Public streets for public use* (pp. 22–39). New York: Van Nostrand Reinhold.

Francis, M. (1987b). Some different meanings attached to a public park and community gardens. *Landscape Journal, 6*, 101–112.

Francis, M. (1987c). Urban open spaces. In E. Zube & G. Moore (Eds.), *Advances in environment, behavior & design*, (Vol. 1, pp. 71–106). New York: Plenum Press.

Francis, M. (1988a). Changing values for public spaces. *Landscape Architecture, 78*, 54–59.

Francis, M. (1988b). Negotiating between children and adult design values in open space projects. *Design Studies, 9*, 67–75.

Francis, M. (1988c). The urban garden as public space. Unpublished paper presented at the Future of Urban Open Space Symposium, University of California, Berkeley, October 29.

Francis, M., Cashdan, L., & Paxson, L. (1984). *Community open spaces*. Washington, DC: Island Press.

Francis, M., & Hester, R. (Eds.). (1987). *Proceedings of the Meanings of the Garden Conference*. Davis, CA: University of California, Center for Design Research.

Gehl, J. (1987). *The life between buildings*. New York: Van Nostrand Reinhold.

Glazer, N., & Lilla, M. (1987). *The public face of architecture: Civic culture and public spaces*. New York: Free Press.

Goffman, E. (1963). *Behavior in public places: Notes on the organization of gatherings*. New York: Macmillan.

Goodey, B. (1975). Urban trails: Origins and opportunities. *Journal of the Royal Town Planning Institute, 61*, 29–30.

Hart, R. (1978). *Children's experience of place*. New York: Irvington.

Hayward, D., Rothenberg, M., & Beasley, R. (1974). Children's play and urban playground types: A comparison of traditional, contemporary, and adventure playground types. *Environment & Behavior, 6*, 131–168.

Hester, R. (1985). Subconscious landscapes in the heart. *Places, 2*, 10–22.

Hester, R. (1987). Participatory design and environmental justice. *Journal of Architectural and Planning Research, 4*, 301–309.

Hiss, T. (1987, June 22, 29). Experiencing places. *The New Yorker*, pp. 45–68, 37–86.

Iacofano, D. (1986). *Public involvement as an organizational development process: A proactive theory for environmental planning program management*. Unpublished doctoral dissertation, University of California, Department of Landscape Architecture, Berkeley, CA, Vol. 48, No. 5, Section A, p. 1333.

Im, S. B. (1984). Visual preferences in enclosed urban spaces. *Environment & Behavior, 16*, 235–262.

Jackson, J. B. (1984). *Discovering the vernacular landscape*. New Haven, CT: Yale University Press.

Kaplan, R. (1973). Some psychological benefits of gardening. *Environment & Behavior, 5*, 145–161.

Kaplan, R., & Kaplan, S. (1987). The garden as restorative experience: A research odyssey.

In M. Francis & R. Hester (Eds.), *Proceedings of the Meanings of the Garden Conference* (pp. 334–341). Davis, CA: University of California, Center for Design Research.
Kimber, C. T. (1973). Spatial patterning in the dooryard gardens of Puerto Rico. *Geographical Review, 63*, 6–26.
Kinkowski, W. S. (1981). *The malling of America*. New York: Morrow.
Langer, E. (1983). *The psychology of control*. Los Angeles: Sage.
Langer, E. J. (1975). The illusion of control. *Journal of Personality and Social Psychology, 32*, 311–328.
Lefcourt, H. (1982). *Locus of control: Current trends in theory and research* (2nd ed.). Hillsdale, NJ: Erlbaum.
Lennard, S. H., & Lennard, J. L. (1984). *Public life in urban places*. Southamptom: Gondolier Press.
Levine, C. (1984, June). Making city spaces lovable places. *Psychology Today*, pp. 56–63.
Lofland, L. (1973). *A world of strangers: Order and action in urban public space*. New York: Basic Books.
Lofland, L. (in press). Social life in the public realm: A review essay. *Journal of Contemporary Ethnography*.
Lynch, K. (1981). *Good city form*. Cambridge, MA: M.I.T. Press.
Nagar, A. R., & Wentworth, W. R. (1976). *Bryant Park: A comprehensive evaluation of its image and use with implications for urban open space design*. New York: City University of New York, Center for Human Environments.
National Gardening Association. (1987). *Gallup Poll National Gardening Survey*. Burlington, VT: Author.
Nicholson, S. (1971). Theory of loose parts: How not to cheat children. *Landscape Architecture, 61*, 30–34.
Pateman, C. (1970). *Participation and democratic theory*. Cambridge: Cambridge University Press.
Project for Public Spaces. (1981). *What people do downtown: How to look at mainstreet activity*. Washington, DC: National Trust for Historic Preservation.
Project for Public Spaces. (1984). *Managing downtown public spaces*. Chicago: Planners Press, American Planning Association.
Prus, R. (1987). Developing loyalty: Fostering purchasing relationships in the marketplace. *Urban Life, 15*, 331–366.
Rapoport, A. (1982). *The meaning of the built environment*. Los Angeles: Sage.
Saegert, S., Mackintosh, E., & West, S. (1975). Two studies of crowding in urban public spaces. *Environment & Behavior, 7*, 159–184.
Schroeder, H. (in press). Research on urban forests. In E. Zube & G. Moore (Eds.), *Advances in environment, behavior & design* (Vol. 2). New York: Plenum Press.
Seamon, D., & Nordin, C. (1980). Marketplace as place ballet. *Landscape, 24*, 35–41.
Sennett, R. (1977). *The fall of public man*. New York: Basic Books.
Sommer, R. (1983). *Social design*. Englewood Cliffs, NJ: Prentice Hall.
Stewart, J., & McKenzie, R. L. (1978). Composing urban spaces for security, privacy & outlook. *Landscape Architecture, 68*, 392–398.
Stokols, D. (1987). Conceptual strategies of environmental psychology. In D. Stokols & I. Altman (Eds.), *Handbook of environmental psychology* (Volume 1, pp. 41–70). New York: Wiley.
Storr, R. (1985). Tilted arc. *Art in America*, September, *73*, 91–97.
Tyler, T. R., Rasinki, K. A., & Spodick, N. (1985). Influence of voice satisfaction with leaders: Exploring the meaning of process control. *Journal of Personality and Social Psychology, 48*, 72–81.
Ulrich, R. S. (1979). Visual landscapes & psychological well being. *Landscape Research, 4*, 17–19.
Ulrich, R. S., & Simons, R. F. (1986). Recovery from stress during exposure to everyday

outdoor environments. In J. Archea *et al.* (Eds.), *Proceedings of the 17th Environmental Design Research Association Conference* (pp. 115–122). Washington, DC: Environmental Design Research Association.
van Vliet, W. (1983). An examination of the home range of city and suburban teenagers. *Environment & Behavior, 15,* 567–588.
Vernez-Moudon, A. (Ed.). (1987). *Public streets for public use.* New York: Van Nostrand Reinhold.
Wandersman, A. (1981). A framework of participation in community organizations. *Journal of Applied Behavioral Science, 17,* 27–58.
Warner, S. B. (1987). *To dwell is to garden.* Boston: Boston University Press.
White, R. W. (1959). Motivation reconsidered: The concept of competence. *Psychological Review, 66,* 297–333.
Whyte, W. H. (1980). *The social life of small urban spaces.* Washington, DC: Conservation Foundation.
Wiedermann, D. (1985). How secure are public open spaces? *Garten + Landschaft, 85,* 26–27.
Wortman, C. (1975). Some determinants of perceived control. *Journal of Personality & Social Psychology, 31,* 282–294.
Zube, E. H. (1986, April). *Public landscapes and public values.* Lecture given at the Department of Geography, University of Victoria, Victoria, British Columbia, Canada.
Zube, E. H., Sell, J. L., & Taylor, J. G. (1982). Landscape perception: Research, application, and theory. *Landscape Planning, 9,* 1–33.

7

The Emergence of Environment–Behavior Research in Zoological Parks

JANAEA MARTIN AND
JOSEPH O'REILLY

INTRODUCTION

Animal–environment research in the zoological park dates back to the turn of the 20th century. In 1896, Robert Garner proposed that enclosure design be based upon the scientific examination of biological and social behavior of animals. There also is a tradition of informal investigations of the physical environment in designing for keeper safety and for solving problems involving human interaction with physical elements of zoological parks. However, systematic environment–behavior research within zoological parks has emerged only quite recently.

HISTORICAL CONTEXT OF ZOOLOGICAL PARK DEVELOPMENT

A fascinating history of the relationship between "animals and architecture" is provided by David Hancocks (1971). His work indicates that modern-day zoological gardens trace their historical origins to China, Egypt, India,

---

JANAEA MARTIN • Program in Social Ecology, University of California-Irvine, Irvine, CA 92717. JOSEPH O'REILLY • Mesa Public Schools, 545 North Stapley Drive, Mesa, AZ 85203. Background research by the first author was supported, in part, by a Faculty Development Grant from Wabash College, Crawfordsville, Indiana, and by National Institute of Mental Health Grant T 32 MH 16868.

Mexico, and Europe, where elaborate animal collections were maintained amidst majestic architectural creations. Early European menageries were built by royalty to create a mood sympathetic to an animal's mythical/legendary history and its country of origin. Later, public European menageries included side shows, concerts, and various displays. The Menagerie du Jardin des Plantes, however, included a zoological museum, a museum of comparative anatomy, botanical and geological museums, and a library by the year 1841.

The Zoological Society of London was formed in 1826 and the New York Zoological Society in 1895. Goals of the New York society included instruction, recreation, wildlife protection, and zoological research and publication. In the following year, Garner developed his enclosure recommendations based upon considerations of appropriate space, temperature, and physical materials (see Hancocks, 1971). The first example of the "barless zoo," was opened by Carl Hagenbeck at the Hamburg Zoo in 1907 and included landscaping devices such as hidden moats, concrete mountains, and panoramic vegetation.

The American Association of Zoological Parks and Aquariums (AAZPA) was formed in 1924 and grew from a membership of 30 to approximately 5,240 in 1988 (Boyd, 1988). The association oversees a professional registration program for members, an accreditation program for zoos and aquariums, and a species survival plan for endangered species. More recently, a Consortium of Aquariums, Universities and Zoos (CAUZ) was formed to further collaborative research efforts.

Thus, modern zoological parks emerged from various historical lines including an exhibition tradition related to country ot origin as well as to heightening the entertainment value of animals. However, they also have evolved within traditions of scientific study and publication and of research-based enclosure design.

THE CONTEMPORARY CONTEXT OF ZOOLOGICAL PARKS

Zoo staff often consider their facilities to be a last refuge for endangered species and attempt to provide the kinds of habitats that will allow those species, especially if endangered, to sustain themselves and to reproduce. They know captive breeding programs will only aid total conservation efforts in a small way. Thus, many believe it is through their role as educators that they can best affect those who will eventually be responsible for the ultimate fate of animal species through land-use policy decisions (Block, 1986; Liebhardt & Faust, 1975; Rabb, 1985).

A vast expansion in the availability of zoological parks has occurred since the 1930s. For example, there were 55 public zoos identified in the United States in 1931, but by 1988 the number had increased to 135 accredited zoos. The growing popularity of American zoos and aquariums is reflected in annual attendance rates that by 1988 totaled well over 110 million visitors (Boyd, 1988). The pattern is much the same at the international level.

The ability to meet the recreational needs of a community is one key to the enormous popularity enjoyed by zoological parks. The opportunity to view exotic species of animals in outdoor settings is considered central to that popularity. Closely aligned with the recreational aspect of the zoo visit are the entertainment elements associated with it. Yet the issue of zoo "entertainment" provokes both intense controversy and considerable ambiguity on the part of zoo professionals (Segal, 1984). On the one hand, many feel it is important to maintain the entertainment component for the zoo experience to be considered "fun." On the other hand, some worry that the entertainment aspect detracts from the seriousness of the message that zoos want to impart about the plight of the many species they exhibit.

Since the late 1800s, zoos have been at the center of a variety of scientific research projects related to animal behavior. More recently, zoological parks also have become settings for research on humans as well as animals. Like museum research, visitor research in zoos has evolved from simple demographic surveys for marketing purposes to more sophisticated investigations of visitor perceptions and visitor behavior in relationship to exhibit design and park-management strategies.

DESIGN AND ENVIRONMENT–BEHAVIOR RELATIONSHIPS

Effective zoological park design must respond to the needs of three primary groups affected by design outcomes—animals, visitors, and staff. Each of these primary groups in turn consist of smaller subgroups that have differential responses and effects on the zoological park setting. For example, different species of animals have varying biosocial and physical requirements; different subgroups of visitors have diverse goals, objectives, expectations, and abilities to interact with the environment; and staff perform a variety of functions that require different facilities and supports in order to accomplish their jobs effectively. Zoo research generally focuses on only one of these three groups at a time. Approaches that focus on two or more of these groups are unusual, and integrative approaches that focus on all three groups are extremely rare. What follows is a discussion of research that examines each of these interrelationships within the context of the zoological park environment.

Animal–Environment Research

Although Robert Garner recommended attention to space, temperature, and physical materials as early as 1896, there was an obviously limited interpretation of design solutions responsive to those considerations. According to Boice (1981), there have been extremely few studies dealing with the relationship of enclosure design and animal behavior.

Currently, there are two approaches that attempt to respond to the relationship between the needs of animals and their captive zoo environments. One approach emphasizes the creation of naturalistic environments (Hancocks,

1980; Heidiger, 1964) and the other emphasizes the creation of behavioral opportunities paralleling those available in an animal's natural habitat (Markowitz, 1982).

Much of the early naturalistic design has been based upon intuition, informal anecdotes, and personal preferences (Hancocks, 1980). However, comparative research within natural habitats such as that of Jane Goodall and a few empirical studies within zoo exhibits (Maple, 1981; Maple & Stine, 1982; Shettel-Neuber, 1986; Timson, 1978) have often supported these intuitive assumptions. There have, however, been instances in which assumptions about the creation of more "natural" design have failed to evoke the appropriate behavioral response in animals. Calip (1978) unexpectedly found that gibbons who had been provided a net simulating vines for brachiated movement preferred to use bars instead. It appears that naturalistic exhibits result in higher satisfaction for visitors and staff, but the difference for the animal may be dependent upon the amount of designed behavioral opportunity between "old" and "new" exhibits (Shettel-Neuber, 1988).

A second focus of animal–environment study goes beyond the naturalistic look of exhibits to include the promotion of "species appropriate" behavior. This is accomplished by "reintroducing" ways for animals to experience excitement and stimulation through simulated predator-prey type relationships (Markowitz, 1982). Food delivery systems are designed whose operation is contingent upon behavioral performance. For example, interactive "games" are developed whereby an animal may gain food through successful competition with humans. This approach is compatible with environment–behavior research, also to be discussed later, that suggests visitors spend more time at, and enjoy exhibits more, when the animals are active. In addition, visitors are most satisifed with exhibits that provide either direct (e.g., children's zoos) or indirect (e.g., interactive exhibits) contact with animals.

Examination of effects that visitors have upon animals is a relatively new area of research. However, some philosophical ideas exist about the appropriate designed relationships. Hancocks (1971) notes:

> Animals, for example should never be looked down upon. Not only are there unwholesome psychological connotations in such a viewpoint, but it can be disturbing for an animal to have potentially dangerous enemies at such an unnatural vantage point . . . it can also make animals look ridiculous: giraffes . . . lose the majesty of their height, and look like quaintly patterned mice. (p. 145)

Michelmore (1975a) also maintains that the metaphor "we look down on what we despise and look up to what we admire" is true in zoo exhibition. Architects such as Coe (1986, 1987) and others involved in "landscape immersion" approaches to zoo design have used these conceptualizations to guide the layout and structure of exhibits (Green, 1987). Unfortunately, the assumptions underlying this philosophy have not been directly tested and the ability of design based upon these assumptions to engender greater visitor "respect" for animals may only be inferred (e.g., Birney, 1988; Derwin & Piper, 1988).

There are recent attempts to examine the effect that social and physical features existing outside the exhibit have upon animal behavior (Mitchell, Soteriou, Towers, Kenney, & Schumer, 1987). Observations of golden-bellied mangabeys suggest that threat behavior from one animal toward other animals of the same and different species; toward visitors, keepers, and researchers; and toward environmental sounds may be evoked by the act of visitors illicitly feeding other animals. In addition, threat behavior is evoked in some animals by the proximity of construction sounds. However, these findings must be considered tentative. Two of the observed pairs of mangabeys had been relocated to the cages where observations were made only one week before the study was begun. Effects of relocation stress, in this instance, cannot be separated from other environmental variables.

VISITOR–ENVIRONMENT RESEARCH

Zoo professionals have historically focused upon the behavior and environmental needs of the animals in their care. Consequently, they tend to know much less about the behavior of one of the most frequently found species in the zoo—humans. What is known about human behavior in these settings is primarily descriptive and site specific. Very little data are available that allow for the understanding and general prediction of human behavior in zoo settings. However, an emerging interest in this research area, the availability of researchers trained and concerned about issues related to visitor behavior, and a strong link to museum and recreation research, have resulted in a growing body of research about human behavior in zoological parks. What follows is an overview of that research.

Demographics

Zoo visitors have generally been found to have a higher education level and socioeconomic status than the average person. They also are likely to be involved in community activities and to live near the zoo (Hood, 1984; Reed & Mindlin, 1963; Wheeler, 1980). However, group composition and attendance frequency are perhaps more significant than education and socioeconomic status in their impact upon behavior. Most visitors come to the zoo in small family groups consisting of 2 to 5 people (Joslin *et al.*, 1986; Reinhardt, 1986; Wheeler, 1980). Although local residents may attend a zoo repeatedly, the majority of visitors may be attending a specific zoo for the first time (Wheeler, 1980).

Unfortunately, too much emphasis on these simple profiles may lead to the neglect of important subpopulations of visitors such as children, the physically limited, the elderly, the poor, and ethnic populations. Failure to recognize the needs of these populations could preclude their full pariticpation in the zoo visit and/or lead to lower visit satisfaction and quality. For example, one zoo assumed it was meeting the needs of children until empirical evidence indicated that children encountered several obstacles to full participation including visual barriers, competing sources of stimulation, and educational material geared to adults (Martin & O'Reilly, 1982).

The underrepresentation of a demographic group such as the elderly or an ethnic population in zoo attendance may be the result of inappropriate physical and/or programmatic design (e.g., graphics presented only in English), or it could also mean that such groups simply do not want to visit zoological parks. For example, of 85 people interviewed in a New Orleans retirement home, only 16 had been to a zoo in the past two years (Verderber, Gardner, Islam, & Nakanishi, 1988). Reasons for this result are not entirely clear; however, results do indicate a need to closely examine a group's use or nonuse of facilities in order to ensure that barriers to visiting are minimized.

Motivation

People often mention recreational and/or educational purposes for their zoo visit (Martin & O'Reilly, 1982; Myers, 1987; Wheeler, 1980). Although these purposes are not contradictory in an informal learning environment such as a zoo, the emphasis accorded each may vary depending on the visitor type. Hood (1985) found that frequent visitors are primarily interested in opportunities to learn, to be challenged by new experiences, and to do something worthwhile with their leisure time. Occasional visitors, who make up the largest group of visitors, value social interaction with family and friends, active participation, and feeling comfortable in the leisure surroundings.

Rosenfeld (1982) created an experimental "mini-zoo" adjacent to a science museum and found that most visits were fun-oriented and child-centered. They also provided "private social experiences" for the family groups participating. Similarly, in a national survey of zoo visitors, Cheek (1973) found that 40 percent of respondents indicated that a primary zoo activity was "getting to know [their] children better."

In summary, there appear to be two major motivational aspects guiding zoo visits. Members of some visitor groups want a learning experience and to focus primarily on zoo animals. Others want a recreational focus with educational experiences that are facilitated within a family-interaction context. Thus, group composition is an important variable for understanding the motivation of individual members, and it has implications for both zoo design and research applications. Therefore, zoos should be aware that visits are often child centered (Martin & O'Reilly, 1982) and that, in addition to interests in recreation and education, family groups are often concerned about interactions among group members (Hill, 1971; Joslin et al., 1986; Rabb, 1969; Wolf & Tymitz, 1979).

Orientation

The ways in which visitors orient themselves in a zoological setting appear to be based upon the purpose of the zoo visit and the kinds of orientation aids provided. Those who come to the zoo for a designated purpose such as to see a specific animal, to participate in a specific activity, or to see a particular exhibit generally do not rely on orientation aids such as signs or maps. Visitors who come with a more general purpose in mind (e.g., for a pleasant outing) are much more in need of orientation and circulation cues.

For example, 60% of a sample questioned about the kind of information that would have been most helpful to them prior to the beginning of their visit indicated the need for information about what was available to see. An additional 20% indicated the need for information about how to travel around the facility (Shettel-Neuber & O'Reilly, 1981, p. 5). The emphasis on what is available to be seen, rather than on how to get around, may result from a "wandering" exploratory strategy reportedly used by visitors (Rosenfeld, 1982; Shettel-Neuber & O'Reilly, 1981). Along these lines, providing a previsit orientation has been found to increase visitor learning in museums (Screven, 1986).

In addition to a preorientation, visitors may benefit from redundant orientation cues of various types. Signs, maps, docents, and directional information may best serve visitor needs when they are provided throughout the zoo because such information is repeatedly needed and no single device is universally favored (Bitgood & Patterson, 1986). These results, in both zoos and museums, are consistent with cognitive research suggesting that a framework for organizing and integrating material makes that material more memorable and easy to learn.

Circulation

There have been relatively few published studies of visitor circulation conducted specifically in zoos. The available literature is often anecdotal in nature or consists of unpublished and/or proprietary studies examining circulation as part of a larger project. For example, when studying children's use of a zoo, Martin and O'Reilly (1982) reported that a majority of sampled family groups followed one major path around the zoo's perimeter. Thus, many missed exhibits in the central area of the zoo. Similarly, Martin, O'Reilly, and Albanese (1983) identified heavily traveled routes and frequently encountered nodes in order to determine the most favorable placement of exhibit viewing opportunities.

Another study examining both orientation and circulation (Shettel-Neuber & O'Reilly, 1981) found that the majority of visitors maintained the "right-turn bias" repeatedly observed in museums and other exhibition settings, (e.g., Melton, 1933). The result was assumed to be influenced by the spatial layout of the setting. Spatial features, such as the closest visible exhibit or directional sign, have been observed to impact turning behavior in other zoo settings (Bitgood, Benefield, Patterson, Lewis, & Landers, 1985).

Graphics

Zoo graphics include signs that are used to orient and cue spatial behavior and those that provide educational information. Zoos often are designed with an intended viewing order for the sequential presentation of information or for the placement of species within themed geographic zones. It is considered vital, therefore, that signs reinforce the conceptual and spatial framework presented. Orientation signs also are used by visitors who want to be sure they do not miss anything and for locating essential visitor services like bathrooms and water fountains.

From an educational perspective, signs have traditionally been the basic way in which information about animals is presented to the public (Rabb, 1975). Because having educational experiences are important goals for many visitors, and providing those experiences are also primary goals for zoos, if signs are ineffective, the quality of the visit may suffer.

Orientation and educational signs also are important for economic reasons. People who see more of the zoo and who read signs tend to have longer visits (Serrell, 1980) and people who stay longer tend to spend more money on concessions. Zoos often rely on such sales to provide operational revenue; therefore, effective signage can mean a more stable economic base for a zoo.

Unfortunately there has been little published research on the relationship between graphic presentations and effects upon orientation and circulation within zoo settings. Most available research is entirely site specific. For example, although Martin, O'Reilly, and Albanese (1983) conducted studies of circulation graphics as part of the master planning process, their specific findings (e.g., location for sign placements) cannot be generalized to other zoos. However, the methodology used for locating exhibit viewing opportunities could be adapted to other settings.

Educational or "informational" graphics have typically been considered the core of graphic systems, even though many people do not read traditional zoo signs. The number who read signs has been found to vary across zoos and to range from 10% to 33% (Bitgood, Patterson, & Benefield, 1988; Roper, Bitgood, Patterson, & Benefield, 1986; Serrell, 1980; Wolf & Tymitz, 1979) and to range within the same zoo from 16% to 34% depending upon the exhibit (O'Reilly & Martin, unpublished).

A number of studies have examined factors that influence readership. The number of words in the text has been found to have an inverse relationship to readership (Borum & Miller, 1980; Hodges, 1978; Robinson, 1930). For example, one researcher broke a 150-word label into three 50-word labels and increased readership by as much as 35%.

The sign format also affects readership, but the evidence for type of format is contradictory. For example, it has been found that the outline form increases readership and that a few short paragraphs rather than outlines or longer text are more successful (Pliskin, 1980). This discrepancy might be due to a lack of consistency in topics presented, to the length of the initial text, or to other contextual effects. Nonuniform signs stimulate interest (Rabb, 1975) and the test signs were probably different from the other existing signs. Additional format factors include the size and font of letters, proximity to the exhibit (Bitgood, Nichols, Pierce, Conroy, & Patterson, 1986), size of the background (Hodges, 1978), and catchy titles (Rabb, 1969).

Graphic content also influences whether or not a sign is read. Serrell's (1980, 1981, 1982) work in this area is exemplary. Her studies indicate that concrete, visually verifiable information, properly placed, and written at an appropriate language level is more often read and leads to more pointing and reading aloud than other types of information. Based on these findings, Serrell developed short labels with high visual content and compared them with traditional labels. The new signs elicited significant increases in sign reading, responses to interviews, and performances on short quizzes.

Short graphic texts may be generally read more frequently but they have one distinct disadvantage—they are short. There are a variety of visitors with differing information needs, and curators who desire to present more detailed, scientific data. Therefore, contemporary graphic systems may use "layered" information that combines signs of short, catchy content with signs of somewhat longer text. Exhibit signs are varied both in content and in style to maximize novelty and visitor interest. More detailed information is found at information stations and in compact visitor guides where the most in-depth information on species and habitats is presented (Martin, O'Reilly, & Albanese, 1983).

Extended Educational Environments

Graphic presentations represent only one aspect of the educational efforts of zoo professionals. Additional approaches include both on-site and off-site educational programs. These programs are designed with attention to the influence that environmental context has on the impact of conservation education.

Because family groups do constitute such a large proportion of zoo visitors, programs like HERPlab, a family educational laboratory, have been created and tested (White & Marcellini, 1986). Mean stay lengths were considerably longer than those reported as averages for zoo and museum exhibits (cf. Brennen, 1978; Rosenfeld, 1982; Wolf & Tymitz, 1979). A majority of visitors were able to give specific examples of what they had learned and many reported that activities had increased their respect and appreciation for wild animals. Fifteen percent reported that the experience reinforced family relationships; however, no objective measures of family interaction were recorded.

A popular perspective maintained by zoo professionals is that the exhibition of unfamiliar domestic and exotic animals provides an understanding about the relationship between human beings and animals. Others, like Sommer (1972) suggest that zoos may be teaching inappropriate animal stereotypes. A previously mentioned controversy surrounds the use of live animals in "shows" or "demonstrations." Some feel that the use of animals in this way creates an image of wild animals as potential "pets" and undermines conservation education. Others maintain that live animal demonstrations are powerful educational adjuncts that utilize the important aspects of concrete, sensory learning (Hood, 1986).

An attempt to examine these issues was made by assessing an educational outreach program. Measurements were taken both before and after the program presentation (Hilker, 1986; Wakeman, 1986). The study sampled fourth through sixth graders at both urban and rural schools. Results indicated significant changes in tested knowledge regarding the understanding of issues related to extinction. Although mean responses were reported to indicate that live animals were more beneficial in dispelling the pet image than other techniques used, results were not statistically significant. In addition, differential results were not reported for those presentations made with and those made without animal contact. The interpretation of these results is thus unclear.

Exhibit Behavior

A number of variables have been found to influence attraction to an exhibit—animal activity, an animal infant, interactive devices, variety in exhibit design, open areas, natural settings, and water features (Bitgood et al., 1985). Children are often the first to lead a group to an exhibit and, although parents may make other important decisions, children also appear to control the pattern and pace of exhibit visits (Brennan, 1978; Rosenfeld, 1982). For children, animal color, movement, size, and pattern, as well as the presence of other children and water elements, may play a major role in attraction to an exhibit (Martin & O'Reilly, 1982).

The influence of these variables is consistent with research results on esthetic preference and interest in natural settings. Ulrich (1983) indicated that natural settings are associated with such elements as complexity, focal points, ground surface texture, threat/tension, deflected vistas, and water. There have only been a few studies directly related to these elements and their relationship to exhibit preference and interest. One area of apparent conflict between esthetic preference and zoo research findings is that even though caged exhibits provide very strong focal points, they are not often preferred, except perhaps by children (Martin & O'Reilly, 1982). This would suggest an age–culture relationship in which children have such preferences because the age preference for complexity and/or the cultural preference for "natural environments" has not yet overridden the perceptual preference for a focal point. These relationships, obviously, require further study.

In addition, the dislike of threatening or dangerous stimuli found in response to natural settings may be moderated by the "built aspects" of the zoo setting such that tension or threat may be stimulating. For example, people have been attracted to a glassed viewing area where a lioness stalked and pounced at visitors. Children standing by the glass screamed and jumped back but spent a long period of time at this exhibit. Thus, excitement and preference for an exhibit may be enhanced by situations in which an animal acts in a threatening manner but where any real threat or danger is removed.

Deflected vistas (Ulrich, 1983), "mystery" (Kaplan & Kaplan, 1978), or "anticipation" (Cullen, 1961) refers to blocking the line of sight so that it appears that new landscape information is just beyond the bounds of the observer's visual field. In zoo design, multiple viewing areas that cannot be seen from each location are purported to increase viewing satisfaction and viewing time (Bitgood, Patterson, & Benefield, 1988). Water elements have been found to be dominant features in preferred landscapes (Zube, Pitt, & Anderson, 1975). In addition, the attraction of children to water has also been noted in the zoo literature (e.g., Martin & O'Reilly, 1982). These results suggest that exhibit designs incorporating strong water elements are likely to be preferred over those that do not.

In general, utilizing principles of esthetic preference associated with natural settings may provide more generalizable explanations for research results related to exhibit preferences. These principles may also provide a valuable theoretical framework for shaping future research.

Once attracted to an exhibit, visitors typically spend very little time before moving on to the next area. Visitors at the Brookfield Zoo were found to average about 90 seconds per exhibit (Brennan, 1978). Similar results have been obtained at other zoos (O'Reilly & Martin, unpublished; Rosenfeld, 1982), and even less time has been recorded in some museum settings (e.g., Beer, 1987). Visitors also tend to interact with other group members, often by asking or answering questions, and not to interact with other groups or traditional signs (Brennan, 1978; Wolf & Tymitz, 1979).

Exhibit behavior research has primarily been descriptive of conditions at specific zoos and little has been done to empirically measure how people respond to the different exhibits housing the same species. Recently, however, three comparative studies have been undertaken that are notably different from previous research.

Shettel-Neuber (1988) compared two new naturalistic exhibits with two older exhibits that housed the same species. Interestingly, comparisons revealed no consistent, clear-cut differences in animal and visitor behavior between the "old" and the "new" naturalistic exhibits. However, the new exhibit design did result in more positive attitudes toward the exhibit on the part of visitors and staff alike.

A second study compared visitor reaction to common exhibits across 13 zoos (Bitgood, Patterson, & Benefield, 1988). Visitor behavior was found to be very uniform from zoo to zoo. The exhibit characteristics most highly related to visitor viewing included animal activity, animal size, presence of an infant animal, proximity to the animal, visibility of the animal, lack of a competing exhibit within sight, and, possibly, richness of exhibit content. These results suggest a tie to environmental esthetics principles of complexity and mystery, outlined by Ulrich (1983).

A third study (Finaly, James, & Maple, 1988) took a more rigorous, experimental approach to examining exhibit affects on perceptions by analyzing responses to slides of 8 different species. Each species was shown in caged environments, in naturalistic exhibits, and in the wild. In ratings on 11 semantic differential scales, exhibit type generally had a significant effect on animal attributes. Overall, the more confined the animal, the less positively it was rated.

These three studies provide important advancements in environment–behavior research related to zoological parks. The first study provided multiple methodologies for examining broader contextual relationships. All three studies examined the same species across different settings, and the third study manipulated perceptual variables under controlled conditions.

Zoological Visit Outcomes

Zoo professionals anticipate that zoo experiences will result in improved attitudes toward animals and conservation and in the acquisition of new knowledge about the lives and habitats of the animals exhibited.

Studies examining exhibit viewing effects on attitudes are contradictory. Current evidence suggests that context both does influence attitudes toward the animal (Rhoades & Goldsworthy, 1979) and that it does not (Swensen, 1984, as cited in Finlay, Woehr, & Maple, 1984). Though contradictions may result from differences in methodology, because a main goal of zoos is to promote a conservation ethic and positive attitudes toward animals, it is important that attempts be made to eliminate these apparent contradictions.

As previously mentioned, zoo professionals often assume positive correlations between opportunities to view live animals in exhibits or in animal demonstrations and resulting educational impacts. Some data suggest that the issue is much more complex, at least in the case of children, than ordinarily assumed. Birney (1986) conducted a study comparing the knowledge acquired about wildlife by sixth graders who were randomly assigned to either a trip to the zoo or a trip to a natural history museum. Results indicated no significant differences between the two groups in terms of their overall knowledge of wildlife, their knowledge of feeding behavior, or their knowledge of defensive behavior. There were, however, differences in the kinds of characteristics that were recalled about animals. Significantly more children who visited the zoo cited the behavior of an animal as memorable, whereas significantly more children who visited the museum recalled structural adaptations and environmental elements. Results suggest that contextual elements such as static displays of the museum versus dynamic displays of the zoo are important determinants of the kind of learning that occurs.

Additional results from this study partially supported Sommer's (1972) contention that zoos may actually create misperceptions and inappropriate animal stereotypes. Children in Birney's study believed that captive animals were "safe" and would not harm humans, that captive animals were "calm" and "tame," and that wild animals "do crazy and uncontrolled things."

Exhibit design and educational programming are merging most closely in newer projects like the Primate Discovery Center at the San Francisco Zoo and Jungle World at the Bronx Zoo. (Burks, 1985; Conway, 1986). These exhibits provide multilevel viewing of naturalistic exhibits combined with engaging graphics, interactive educational components, and informal research space within the facility. They have been built with the concept of formal evaluation as an integral part of the design process and with the idea that a certain proportion of exhibits may be modified, deleted, and recreated on an ongoing basis. The built-in evaluation process and flexibility for modification is similar to the approach called for by researchers in other building programs. It recognizes the dynamic nature of the environment–behavior transaction and the necessity for responding both to changing animal and changing human needs.

Taken together, these studies and trends in exhibit research and design provide support for contentions that exhibits themselves and special educational programs promote learning about wild animals. They are beginning to demonstrate the methods necessary to examine the more complex questions about what is learned and point to specific environmental factors that help to determine what is learned. They also suggest that additional research will be necessary to help focus on the relationships intended to convey conservation information.

STAFF–ENVIRONMENT RESEARCH

Other than the informal research with keepers and other key staff that is conducted by architects in the process of exhibit design, almost no environment–behavior research with zoo staff has been performed. The one exception will be reported in the next section. Semistructured input by staff through the use of architectural survey forms and unstructured input obtained through informal discussions have been used to incorporate a problem-solving approach to exhibit-design concerns. Although the importance of staff input to the design process is generally recognized (Faust & Rice, 1978; Turnage & Hewitt, 1984), a systematic research approach has not yet been forthcoming.

INTEGRATING RESEARCH ON ANIMALS, VISITORS, AND STAFF

Only one study could be found that incorporates the behavior of all three zoo user groups in the research design. Shettel-Neuber (1986) conducted an intensive postoccupancy evaluation and comparison of animal enclosures at the San Diego Zoo that included behavior mapping, exhibit timing, visitor tracking, visitor and staff questionnaires, and visitor and staff interviews. One of the major implications from this study is that by using a model of user-group interaction that includes the physical environment as a focus, a framework for systematic inquiry and for examining relevant issues of zoo functioning can be provided.

FUTURE DIRECTIONS OF RESEARCH

The emergence of systematic environment–behavior research in zoological parks is relatively recent in origin but is built upon historical precedents of scientific inquiry and publication. The major problems facing environment–behavior research in zoological parks are those frequently associated with other types of environment–behavior research. Specifically, much of the research is descriptive in nature, is site specific, lacks methodological consistency, and is atheoretical in nature. These problems make it difficult to develop a body of generalizable results that demonstrate sound reliability and validity.

METHODOLOGICAL ISSUES

Although much of the research reported in this review is problematic in the ways described above, several recent studies have begun to address these problems (e.g., Birney, 1986; Bitgood et al., 1988; Finaly et al., 1988; Shettel-Neuber, 1988). Some of these studies involve examinations of responses to the same species across a number of settings. This approach allows for identification of environment–behavior relations that typify successful exhibits. Similarly, some employ more rigorous laboratory and field methodologies, such as random assignment of groups to conditions and manipulation of specific variables under controlled conditions. These methods help to refine our knowledge about factors responsible for conveying specific information to visitors. Finally, some have performed exhibit evaluations using pre/post techniques that are replicated in a variety of settings to allow for the identification of common features that appear to predict successful exhibits. Perhaps most significantly, these studies suggest important connections between zoo research and theoretical work in areas such as environmental perception and environmental esthetics.

THEORETICAL ISSUES

For the most part, zoo research has been driven by the need to solve short-term, practical problems rather than by the need to develop or test theory. However, Finlay et al. (1988) have demonstrated the important link between zoo research and environmental perception. If this work were extended, and guided by research in landscape perception, a model might be developed to predict perceptions of exhibit quality and affective reactions to exhibits that are based upon measures of the physical setting. Such a model would be an important contribution to exhibit development and design. There are numerous models and techniques of landscape assessment (Daniel & Vining, 1983; Zube, Sell, & Taylor, 1982) that could serve as the basis for developing more general principles of exhibit assessment.

Similarly, R. Kaplan (1975) and S. Kaplan (1975) propose an environmental preference model that posits four components of a preferred setting—coherence, legibility, complexity, and mystery. Intuitively, these may be characteristics that describe a successful circulation system. Because successfully navigating the zoo is associated with visit satisfaction it may be possible to examine and predict zoo preference based on these factors. In addition, R. Kaplan's (1983) work suggesting that certain behaviors of urban dwellers are motivated by a need for contact with nature may provide a partial explanation for zoo attendance. Examination of these theoretical links could potentially provide a foundation for explaining and predicting much of visitor behavior in zoological parks.

Research related to exhibit attractiveness also suffers from a lack of theoretical perspective. Work in environmental esthetics (e.g., Ulrich, 1983) might provide a conceptual framework for more predictive studies of what attracts people to exhibits. All esthetic principles derived from research in natural settings may not be applicable to "naturalistic" environments created in zoos; however, there is a great deal of overlap in characteristics found to be attractive in zoo settings and the principles of esthetic preference. Exploration of the conceptual and perceptual boundaries between "natural" and "naturalistic" settings might prove provocative.

RESEARCH OPPORTUNITIES

Several research opportunities exist within the context of zoological parks. For example, the large numbers of family groups visiting zoological parks provide unique opportunities for environment–behavior research related to family interaction patterns. In addition, because first-time visits to a zoological park often constitute involvement with a seminovel environment, research on orientation, way finding, and exploratory behavior is most appropriate. Likewise, the impact that other people may have in terms of modeling traffic direction and the effect of density on orientation and circulation has seldom been reported. Examination of these relationships to circulation and their resulting implications for design would be valuable contributions to the research literature.

The study of environmental cognition also could benefit from research on circulation within zoological parks. Zoos could provide a novel setting for examining cognitive mapping processes, the development of spatial frames of reference across the life span, and spatial problem solving. In addition to the potential theoretical significance, such investigations could lead to the design of circulation and graphic systems that would make zoos more legible for their various visitor populations. Such research also could influence spatial arrangements and other design decisions because underutilized or missed areas may negatively affect the quality of the zoo visit and result in reduced revenue.

Zoos are often perceived as adding to the social or cultural value of a community. Kaplan (1983, p. 154) maintains that "nature fulfills human needs in diverse ways." The large number of visitors in attendance at zoological parks, and the strong civic support provided to such facilities, suggests positive links between visits and the quality of urban life. However, there is very little empirical evidence to support this claim. Similarly, it is maintained that wilderness experiences have psychological benefits (Kaplan & Talbot, 1983). An important question is "Do zoo visits have similar positive outcomes?" These may be exciting and challenging arenas for future research.

Current research on work environments would provide new information on environment–behavior relations when set in the context of a zoological park. It would be valuable to understand how this unique work environment impacts the behavior and attitudes of employees who are one part of the total system that makes up the zoo setting.

Overall, zoological parks are rich settings in which to conduct investigations of various relationships central to environmental design problems. Thus, zoos can provide many opportunities for important contributions to the larger body of environment–behavior theory and research.

Acknowledgments

The authors would like to offer special thanks to Jerry Hurst of the San Diego Zoo Library for her assistance with this project.

REFERENCES

Altman, I., & Wohlwill, J. F. (Eds.). (1983). *Behavior and the natural environment*. New York: Plenum Press.
Beer, V. (1987). Great expectations: Do museums know what visitors are doing? *Curator, 30*, 206–215.
Birney, B. (1986). Comparing exhibit influences on children's knowledge of wildlife as a result of field trips to a zoo versus a natural history museum. *Annual Proceedings of the American Association of Zoological Parks and Aquariums*, 377–387. Wheeling, WV: American Association of Zoological Parks and Aquariums.
Birney, B. (1988). Brookfield zoo's "flying walk" exhibit: Formative evaluation aids in the development of an interactive exhibit in an informal learning setting. In J. Martin & J. O'Reilly (Eds.), *Environment and behavior* (Vol. 20, pp. 416–434). Newbury Park, CA: Sage Publications.
Bitgood, S., & Patterson, D. (1986). *The prompting of label reading in zoos and museums*. Report to the Alabama Zoological Society, April.
Bitgood, S., Benefield, A., Patterson, D., Lewis, D., & Landers, A. (1985). Zoo visitors: Can we make them behave? *Annual Proceedings of the American Association of Zoological Parks and Aquariums*, pp. 419–432. Wheeling, WV: American Association of Zoological Parks and Aquariums.
Bitgood, S., Nichols, G., Pierce, M., Conroy, P., & Patterson, D. (1986). *Effects of label characteristics on visitor behavior* (Tech. Rep.). Jacksonville, AL: Jacksonville State University, Psychological Institute.
Bitgood, S., Patterson, D., & Benefield, A. (1988). Exhibit design and visitor behavior: Empirical relationships. In J. Martin & J. O'Reilly (Eds.), *Environment and behavior* (Vol. 20, pp. 474–491). Newbury Park, CA: Sage Publications.
Block, R. (1986). Endangered species—beyond teaching warm feelings. *Annual Proceedings of the American Association of Zoological Parks and Aquariums*, 179–183. Wheeling, WV: American Association of Zoological Parks and Aquariums.
Boice, R. (1981). Captivity and fertilization. *Psychological Bulletin, 89*, 407–421.
Borum, M., & Miller, M. (1980). To label or not to label? *Museum News, 58*, 64–67.
Boyd, L. (Ed.) (1988). *Zoological parks and aquariums in the Americas* (1988–1989 ed.). Wheeling, WV: American Association of Zoological Parks and Aquariums.
Brennan, T. (1976). Visitor watching: What people do at the zoo. *Brookfield Bison*, August–September, 1–8.
Burks, M. (1985). Primate discovery center: Integration of education and animal exhibitry. *Annual Proceedings of the American Association of Zoological Parks and Aquariums*, 69–71. Wheeling, WV: American Association of Zoological Parks and Aquariums.
Calip, T. (1978). Cage utilization by the white-handed gibbon. In C. Crocket & M. Hutchins

(Eds.), *Applied Behavioral Research at the Woodland Park Zoological Gardens* (pp. 181–198). Seattle, WA: Pika Press.
Cheek, N. H. (1973). People at the zoo. *Animal Kingdom, 76,* 9–14.
Coe, J. (1986). Environment–behavior research in zoological parks workshop. In J. Wineman, R. Barner, & C. Zimring (Eds.), *The Cost of Not Knowing: Environmental Design Research Association Conference* (p. 375). Washington, DC: Environmental Design Research Association.
Coe, J. (1987). *Return to Eden.* Paper presented to the American Association of Zoological Parks and Aquariums, Portland, OR, September.
Conway, W. G. (1986). Jungleword, concept and execution. *Annual Proceedings of the American Association of Zoological Parks and Aquariums,* 325–333. Wheeling, WV: American Association of Zoological Parks and Aquariums.
Cullen, G. (1961). *Townscape.* New York: Reinhold.
Curtis, L. (1968). *Zoological park fundamentals.* Washington, DC: National Recreation and Park Association.
Daniel, T., & Vining, J. (1983). Methodological issues in the assessment of landscape quality. In I. Altman & J. Wohlwill (Eds.), *Behavior and the natural environment* (pp. 39–84). New York: Plenum Press.
Derwin, C., & Piper, J. (1988). The African Rock Kopje Exhibit: Evaluation of interactive and interpretive elements. In J. Martin & J. O'Reilly (Eds.), *Environment and behavior* (Vol. 20, pp. 435–451). Newbury Park, CA: Sage Publications.
Faust, C., & Rice, D. (1978). *Design handbook.* Unpublished manuscript, Zoological Society of San Diego, San Diego, CA.
Finlay, T., James, L., & Maple, T. (1988). People's perceptions of animals: The influence of zoo environment. In J. Martin & J. O'Reilly (Eds.), *Environment and behavior* (Vol. 20, pp. 508–528). Newbury Park, CA: Sage Publications.
Finlay, T., Woehr, D., & Maple, T. (1984). *Evaluation techniques in zoo environments: Visitor attitudes and animal behavior.* Paper presented at the Southeastern Psychological Association Conference, New Orleans, LA, March.
Green, M. (1987, December). No rms, jungle vu. *The Atlantic Monthly,* pp. 62–78.
Hancocks, D. (1971). *Animals and architecture.* London: Hugh Evelyn.
Hancocks, D. (1980). Bringing nature into the zoo: Inexpensive solutions for zoo environments. *International Journal for the Study of Animal Problems, 1,* 170–177.
Heidiger, H. (1964). *Wild animals in captivity: An outline of the biology of zoological gardens.* New York: Dover.
Hilker, K. (1986). Exotic cats as teachers: Stress and pet image—how do we cope? *Annual Proceedings of the American Association of Zoological Parks and Aquariums,* 392–397. Wheeling, WV: American Association of Zoological Parks and Aquariums.
Hill, C. (1971). An analysis of the zoo visitor. *International Zoo Yearbook, 11,* 158–164.
Hodges, S. (1978). *An ecological approach to the study of zoo visitor behavior: Implications for environmental management and design.* Paper presented at the Southern Psychological Association Conference, Atlanta, GA, April.
Hood, M. (1984). The role of audience development in strategic planning. *Annual Proceedings of the American Association of Zoological Parks and Aquariums,* 97–103. Wheeling, WV: American Association of Zoological Parks and Aquariums.
Hood, M. (1985). Marketing to new audiences—or, prospecting for trends to the year 2000. *Annual Proceedings of the American Association of Zoological Parks and Aquariums,* 507–513. Wheeling, WV: American Association of Zoological Parks and Aquariums.
Hood, M. G. (1986). Animals as marketing tools: Not pros and cons, but hows and whys. *Annual Proceedings of the American Association of Zoological Parks and Aquariums,* 399–401. Wheeling, WV: American Association of Zoological Parks and Aquariums.
Joslin, P., Grunauer, S., Napilatano, G., Nichols, M., Sarris, A., Steadman, A., & Urbanick,

R. (1986). A demographic profile of zoo visitors. *Annual Proceedings of the American Association of Zoological Parks and Aquariums,* 276–283. Wheeling, WV: American Association of Zoological Parks and Aquariums.

Kaplan, R. (1975). Some methods and strategies in the prediction of preference. In E. Zube, J. Fabos, & R. Brush (Eds.), *Landscape assessment: Values, perceptions and resources* (pp. 118–129). Stroudsburg, PA: Dowden, Hutchinson & Ross.

Kaplan, R. (1983). The role of nature in the urban context. In I. Altman & J. Wohlwill (Eds.), *Behavior in the natural environment* (pp. 127–161). New York: Plenum Press.

Kaplan, S. (1975). The role of nature in the urban context. In E. Zube, J. Fabos, & R. Brush (Eds.), *Landscape assessment: Values, perceptions and resources* (pp. 92–101). Stroudsberg, PA: Dowden, Hutchinson & Ross.

Kaplan, S., & Kaplan, R. (1978). *Humanscape: Environments for people.* Belmont, CA: Duxbury Press.

Kaplan, S., & Talbot, J. (1983). Psychological benefits of a wilderness experience. In I. Altman & J. Wohlwill (Eds.), *Behavior in the natural environment* (pp. 163–201). New York: Plenum Press.

Liebhardt, F., & Faust, C. (1975). A comprehensive tool for zoo survival. In A. P. G. Michelmore (Ed.), *Zoo design: First international symposium on zoo design and construction* (pp. 18–22). Paighton, England: Paighton Zoological and Botanical Gardens.

Maple, T. (1981). *Evaluating captive environments.* Paper presented before the American Association of Zoo Veterinarians, Seattle, WA, June.

Maple, T., & Stine, W. (1982). *American Journal of Primatology Supplement, 1,* 67–76.

Markowitz, H. (1982). *Behavioral enrichment in the zoo.* New York: Van Nostrand Reinhold.

Martin, J., & O'Reilly, J. (1982). Designing zoos for children: An alternative approach. *Knowledge for design: Proceedings of Environmental Design Research Association, 13,* 339–346.

Martin, J., & O'Reilly, J. (Eds.). (1988). Special issue: Zoological parks and environment-behavior research. *Environment and behavior.* Newbury Park, CA: Sage Publications.

Martin, J., O'Reilly, J., & Albanese, C. (1983). *Master plan and exhibit development plan.* Tucson: Brooks & Associates.

Melton, A. (1933). Some behavior characteristics of museum visitors. *Psychological Bulletin, 30,* 720–721.

Michelmore, A. P. G. (1975a). Proverbs from Paighton. In A. P. G. Michelmore (Ed.), *Zoo design: Proceedings of the First International Symposium on Zoo Design and Construction* (pp. 6–8). Paighton, England: Paighton Zoological and Botanical Gardens.

Michelmore, A. P. G. (Ed.). (1975b). *Zoo design: Proceedings of the First International Symposium on Zoo Design and Construction.* Paighton, England: Paighton Zoological and Botanical Gardens.

Mitchell, G., Soteriou, S., Towers, S., Kenney, L., & Schumer, C. (1987). Descriptive accounts of the behavior of breeding and non-breeding pairs of Golden-bellied Mangabeys. *Zoo Biology, 6,* 391–399.

Myers, D. G. (1987). Market research on the bright side. *Western Regional Proceedings of the American Association of Zoological Parks and Aquariums,* 392–394. Wheeling, WV: American Association of Zoological Parks and Aquariums.

Pliskin, J. (1980). The effects of copy format on reading behavior and learning. *Oklahoma City Zoo Journal.*

Rabb, G. (1969). The unicorn experienced. *Curator, 12,* 258–262.

Rabb, G. (1975). Signs—essential links to the public. *Annual Proceedings of the American Association of Zoological Parks and Aquariums,* 140–144. Wheeling, WV: American Association of Zoological Parks and Aquariums.

Rabb, G. B. (1985). Facing up to conservation education. *Annual Proceedings of the American Association of Zoological Parks and Aquariums,* 17–20. Wheeling, WV: American Association of Zoological Parks and Aquariums.

Reed, T., & Mindlin, A. (1963). Where do visitors come from? *International Zoo Yearbook, 3,* 43–46.
Reinhardt, H. (1986). Demographics of current and future American populations. *Annual Proceedings of the American Association of Zoological Parks and Aquariums,* 799–801. Wheeling, WV: American Association of Zoological Parks and Aquariums.
Rhoads, D., & Goldsworthy, R. (1979). The effects of zoo environments on public attitudes toward endangered wildlife. *International Journal of Environmental Studies, 13,* 283–287.
Robinson, E. (1930). Psychological problems of the science museum. *Museum News, 8,* 9–11.
Roper, J., Bitgood, S., Patterson, D., & Benefield, A. (1986). Post-occupancy evaluation of the predator house at the Birmingham Zoo. *Visitor Behavior, 1,* 4–5.
Rosenfeld, S. (1982). A naturalistic study of zoo visitors at an interactive mini-zoo. *Curator, 25,* 187–212.
Sausman, S. (Ed.). (1982). *Zoological park and aquarium fundamentals.* Wheeling, WV: American Association of Zoological Parks and Aquariums.
Screven, C. (1986). Exhibitions and information centers: Some principles and approaches. *Curator, 29,* 109–137.
Segal, J. L. (1984). Animal show survey results. *Annual Proceedings of the American Association of Zoological Parks and Aquariums,* 374–379. Wheeling, WV: American Association of Zoological Parks and Aquariums.
Serrell, B. (1980). Looking at zoo and aquarium visitors. *Museum News, 59,* 37–41.
Serrell, B. (1981). Zoo label study at the Brookfield Zoo. *International Zoo Yearbook, 21,* 54–61.
Serrell, B. (1982). Education in zoos and aquariums. In S. Sausman (Ed.), *Zoological park and aquarium fundamentals* (pp. 13–18). Wheeling, WV: American Association of Zoological Parks and Aquariums.
Shettel-Neuber, J. (1986). *Zoo exhibit design: A post-occupancy evaluation and comparison of animal enclosures.* Unpublished doctoral dissertation, University of Arizona, 47 (4), section B, p. 1473.
Shettel-Neuber, J. (1988). Second- and third-generation zoo exhibits: A comparison of visitor, staff, and animal responses. In J. Martin & J. O'Reilly (Eds.), *Environment and behavior* (Vol. 20, pp. 452–473). Newbury Park, CA: Sage Publications.
Shettel-Neuber, J., & O'Reilly, J. (1981). *Now where? A study of visitor orientation and circulation at the Arizona Sonora Desert Museum.* Tucson: University of Arizona, Department of Psychology.
Sommer, R. (1972). What do we learn at the zoo? *Natural History, 81,* 26–29, 84–85.
Timson, R. (1978). *Activity patterns and play sequences of captive caracals.* Paper presentation before the Animal Behavioral Society, Seattle, WA, June.
Turnage, J., & Hewitt, D. M. (1984). The role of the hospital keeper. *Zoonooz, 57,* 17.
Ulrich, R. S. (1983). Aesthetic and affective response to natural environment. In I. Altman & J. Wohlwill (Eds.), *Behavior and the natural environment* (pp. 85–125). New York: Plenum Press.
Verderber, S., Gardner, L., Islam, D., & Nakanishi, L. (1988). Elderly persons' appraisal of a zoological environment. In J. Martin & J. O'Reilly (Eds.), *Environment and behavior* (Vol. 20, pp. 492–507). Newbury Park, CA: Sage Publications.
Wagner, R. O. (1986). State of the association address. *Annual Proceedings of the American Association of Zoological Parks and Aquariums,* 1–5. Wheeling, WV: American Association of Zoological Parks and Aquariums.
Wakeman, B. N. (1986). An evaluation of zoo educational techniques (including the use of live animals). *Annual Proceedings of the American Association of Zoological Parks and Aquariums,* 390–393. Wheeling, WV: American Association of Zoological Parks and Aquariums.
Wheeler, L. (1980). *Arizona-Sonora Desert Museum demographic study.* Tucson: University of Arizona, Department of Psychology.
White, J., & Marcellini, D. (1986). HERPlab: A family learning center at the national zoological park. *International Zoo Yearbook, 24/25,* 340–343.

Wolf, R., & Tymitz, B. (1979). *Do giraffes ever sit? A study of visitor perceptions at the National Zoological Park*. Washington, DC: Smithsonian Institution, National Zoological Park.

Zube, E., Fabos, J., & Brush, R. (Eds.). (1975). *Landscape assessment: Values, perceptions and resources*. Stroudsburg, PA: Dowden, Hutchinson & Ross.

Zube, E., Pitt, D., & Anderson, T. (1975). Perception and prediction of scenic resource values in the northeast. In E. Zube, J. Fabos, & R. Brush (Eds.), *Landscape assessment: Values, perceptions and resources*. Stroudsburg, PA: Dowden, Hutchinson & Ross.

Zube, E., Sell, J., & Taylor, J. (1982). Landscape perception: Research, application & theory. *Landscape Planning, 9*, 1–33.

8

Urban Parks
RESEARCH, PLANNING, AND SOCIAL CHANGE

JEFF HAYWARD

INTRODUCTION

Urban parks are community assets. They provide a convenient setting for a broad variety of leisure and recreational activities, as well as enhancing the image and perceived value of the community. Urban parks can serve the needs and interests of all kinds of people and many subgroups of the population: young and old, groups and individuals, affluent and poor, male and female, athletic or not, and all ethnic and cultural groups. This wide appeal makes city parks a tremendous asset—in a social and behavioral sense as well as a physical sense—to the quality of urban life.

Some observers will be quick to point out that urban parks fall short of this positive aura. Instead of reducing problems, parks have *caused* problems; instead of being a "melting pot" for a neighborhood's diverse populations, parks seem to *create* social tensions. Thus, people often decide whether to use a park on the basis of who else goes there (friends, people they fear, families, drug sellers, police patrols), rather than landscape features or recreational opportunities. And, unfortunately, the physical quality of a park may depend on the political clout of the neighborhood more than on the needs and interests of the park's users.

Ambivalence and controversy about urban parks may have been common throughout their history. One school of thought holds that parks reflect trends in society (e.g., today's trends include drug problems, privatization of land, alienated youth, physical fitness), but problems and controversies are more likely to surface here because these settings are in full view to the public and accountable to public opinion. For example, if crime is a problem in a particular

---

JEFF HAYWARD • People, Places & Design Research, 4 Allen Place, Northampton, MA 01060.

neighborhood, crime will also occur in the local parks; however, these incidents will often be more salient and have a long-term effect on people's perceptions of the parks, even if the crime rate is lower in the park than it is in the adjacent neighborhoods.

This blending of social perceptions and physical environment makes urban parks a fascinating focus for the field of environmental design research. Parks are *valued by the public;* they have *explicit design goals*—such as providing a natural landscape as an esthetic, perceptual, and behavioral contrast to the urban environment; and they are frequently *undergoing small-scale changes* (renovating, repairing, adding, or eliminating facilities) that are influenced by public perceptions and behavior patterns. Therefore, in addition to offering a rich opportunity for studying the relationships between social issues and physical environments, urban parks also offer a productive and welcome opportunity to apply the results of research for public benefit.

Research can offer insights to important planning questions: What do people want? What activities should be encouraged through design, and which should be discouraged? How has the community changed since the time when its neighborhood park was designed? Are the needs the same now as then? What is the public's image of a park and what attitudes do people have that affect park use?

This chapter addresses these questions in the context of an issue that is central to the field of environmental design research—the relationship between research and planning for a public environment. It will also present a conceptual overview of urban park planning, examining the relationship between planning for organized recreation as well as for passive recreation and interpretation. Over the last several decades, much of park planning has been rooted in a facilities-oriented approach (tending to support active and organized recreation); this review will illustrate the need for a complementary approach that speaks to a wider segment of the public, emphasizing interpretive and cultural experience in addition to facilities.

THE CONTEXT FOR CHANGE

The history of urban parks reveals that not only have parks differed in size and type, but the design intentions and social purposes of parks have varied. In the 19th century, parks were planned as "pleasure gardens"—some formal gardens and a strong emphasis on bringing natural landscape features (e.g., meadows, rolling hills, woods, ponds) into an urban setting. Over time, emphasis on active recreational facilities has changed the face, if not the spirit, of many urban parks by imposing features such as playground equipment, ballfields, golf courses, tennis courts, and hockey rinks (Cranz, 1978).

In recent decades, parks have apparently not been meeting the needs of the public at large—at least that is the message from the design research field, which has been studying social change in parks in terms of vandalism, nonuse, crime, negative image, and barriers to park use (Godbey, 1985; Gold, 1972; Hayward & Weitzer, 1984). But not all parks have been deteriorating, and it seems clear that the relationship with the immediate neighborhood and the perceived quality of the physical environment are critical to successful urban parks (Hester, 1984; Palmer, 1984). The vitality of urban spaces—plazas, "open space," streets, and parks—is created through use, and use is encouraged by behavior-based design (Francis, 1987; Kaplan, 1980; Whyte, 1980), allowing for sitting, viewing, informal socializing, and eating.

Demographic changes in society are also affecting park use: there are more older people and they are healthier and more active; the "baby boom" generation is reaching middle age, creating a substantial demand for family activities and programming for children (the "baby boomlet"); two-career households and the increase in single-parent households are creating pressures on leisure time and make it more important that local urban parks provide accessible recreation opportunities.

Lifestyle changes are equally important to consider. For example, concern for physical fitness and health is reflected in the large numbers of people who use parks for jogging and walking. Patterns of urban recreation are also being affected by changes in values and attitudes toward work, the trend toward more social acquaintances and fewer close personal relationships, and a greater emphasis on self-fulfillment and expressive values rather than instrumental values (Johnson & Field, 1984). Research topics and planning initiatives are responding to these changes in society by considering the needs of population subgroups and urban lifestyles (Kaplan, 1983; Kornblum, 1987; Talbot & Kaplan, 1984).

To reflect on the relationships between leisure behavior and park design issues, it will be useful to examine recent planning trends, and then to consider some actual examples or case studies of urban parks research.

BEHAVIOR-BASED TRENDS IN PARK PLANNING

Urban parks are usually designed (or renovated) with an explicit rationale of serving the public's needs and interests. One obvious rationale emphasizes *active recreation*—landscape architects and planners are directed to accommodate recreational needs through ballfields, tennis courts, swimming pools, playgrounds, bicycle paths, jogging paths, fitness courses, ice skating rinks, and so on. Another common rationale is the idea of *"nature in the city"*—planning naturalistic park features to enhance people's appreciation and enjoyment of nature. This model emphasizes passive experience and the park as a visual/ esthetic resource; activities that might be encouraged include picnicking, sitting and relaxing, nature walks, watching birds and other animals, reading, or sunbathing.

Historically, these two themes of park planning have experienced periods of greater or lesser popularity, and at times have seemed to be in conflict with each other. However, it is clear that these are enduring and important themes over the last century at least. In the 19th century, Frederick Law Olmsted consciously designed park areas for active play, separated from naturalistic-passive areas. Over time, active recreation facilities have increased in response to the rise of organized sports such as baseball, football, basketball, soccer, golf, and hockey. It was not unusual for new facilities or ballfields to take over meadows and woods. Undeveloped parkland was also considered fair game for other municipal priorities, such as a new school or fire station.

In recent decades, with the emergence of the environmental movement and concerns about the lack of "open space" to serve as a buffer against increasing urban development, there has been considerable sentiment for preserving natural areas of parks; nature trails, picnic areas, flower gardens, and quiet ponds are frequently more popular than ballfields (although vocal public support for such activities is usually less visible and organized than it is for sports). This trend is reflected in a variety of ways, including school curriculum units and field trips concerning ecology in parks, as well as the popularity of community gardening programs in parks and other undeveloped spaces.

Building on the coexistence of these potentially conflicting themes, it is useful to consider the ways in which park planning and recreational programming have responded to changes in the patterns of public interest. Several planning trends and initiatives suggest interesting new patterns of park development and use such as waterfront parks and plazas, interpretive parks, and cultural programming.

Diversification

New urban parks are being created, and existing ones are being redesigned, to take on new roles. For example, urban plazas have been designed or redesigned for public use (in contrast to the sterile and clean corporate image they used to have). Lawrence Halprin's cascading fountain plaza in Portland, Oregon, and the Citicorp atrium in New York City are examples of spaces that were explicitly designed for the public to use rather than to look at. They contrast with, for example, the noted Seagram Building on Park Avenue in New York, which created a landscaped plaza several stories above the street (accessible to the building's occupants), but with virtually no usable public space at ground level. In part, the trend to create small parks and usable public plazas has been a response to an increasing demand for leisure opportunities—especially for opportunities that can be experienced as part of everyday activities, not requiring a separate trip to a park (Talbot, Bardwelt, & Kaplan, 1987).

Of course, there has been diversity among urban parks for a long time: parks have included recreational facilities as well as formal gardens, reflecting pools, and historic structures. But diversification has been occurring at a larger scale—in the types of parks created, not only the types of features planned in a conventional park. Chicago, Denver, and other cities have created botanical gardens as park-like settings for educational/interpretive purposes as well as for social outings. San Antonio, Baltimore, Toronto, and many other cities have created waterfront park developments, integrating leisure activities such as walking, shopping, visiting museums, and sightseeing in the same place where the city used to turn its back to the water. Miami, Indianapolis, and Washington, D.C., have created major zoos ("zoological parks")—a popular place for families and an alternative to highly active forms of recreation.

Other new developments in park planning include "art parks"—where outdoor sculpture or earthworks are a principal theme—and "sports parks" where organized recreational facilities are concentrated, with appropriate amenities such as bleachers or a stadium, refreshments and other concession stands, restrooms, and parking lots. Many museums, especially art museums and children's museums, are capitalizing on outdoor space to create park-like settings for their visitors.

This diverse array of parks can be tied together by a common theme: a response to the public's increased appetite for leisure activities and the interest in alternative forms of leisure beyond those that are offered in conventional urban parks. Also, in many cases, it probably seemed easier to create an entirely new type of park than to invest money in an existing one that was characterized by a negative image and perceived social problems.

INTERPRETATION

Among the new developments in parks, many are considered "interpretive environments"—places that combine a leisure setting with an educational or cultural experience. Zoos, botanical gardens, art parks, historic sites, museum parks, aquariums, and arboreta have grown significantly as a result of public interest and support. In part, these developments can be correlated with a more affluent society, one with a shorter work week and more leisure time; they can also be linked with the maturation of a college-educated "baby boom" generation and their interest in family-oriented outings.

A broad definition of interpretation is that it promotes public understanding and appreciation, assists visitors to pursue their interests in the park, and helps to accomplish management goals for use of the resource (Sharpe, 1982). The "tools" of interpretation include exhibits, signage, pamphlets and brochures, maps, media presentations, and personal interpretation such as demonstrations and guided walks. Although there has been a field of work focused on these topics,[1] especially interpretation of nature, it has had little relationship with the field of environmental design research, nor have interpretive projects been very evident in urban parks (except at nature centers). However, within the last decade, the field of interpretation has consciously expanded beyond environmental education, ecology, and talks at national monuments. It has

---

[1] The primary professional organization in the United States representing the field of interpretation, is the National Association for Interpretation (NAI) (formerly the Association of Interpretive Naturalists [AIN] and the Western Interpreters Association [WIA]). This organization sponsors conferences, publications such as a journal and newsletter, and communication among practitioners as well as universities that offer graduate training.

expanded to become associated with cultural and historical interpretation—e.g., explanations of early American life at outdoor history museums, such as Old Sturbridge Village and Colonial Williamsburg. The field is also expanding to include exhibits, tours, and media presentations at any site where the public is attracted to a leisure-educational experience (e.g., Cyclorama exhibits about the Civil War battles in Atlanta and Gettysburg or corporate interpretation such as a simulated tour of the Hershey chocolate factory in Hershey, Pennsylvania).

In urban parks, the use of interpretation is growing but is still in its infancy. Designers and planners are discovering that people are interested in informal educational opportunities such as learning the names of trees and shrubbery, understanding the role of parks for urban wildlife, and finding out about the history of a park, for example, how it has changed and what people used to do there. This trend is likely to produce more outdoor exhibits, including signage and graphics, more historical restorations, as well as interpretive programming such as guided nature walks, horticulture programs, and collaborations with schools.

Cultural Programs

A third behavior-based trend in park planning has a considerable history, but is experiencing a resurgence. Urban parks have long been the setting for music concerts (e.g., a band playing in the gazebo at holiday events), but they are now used for rock concerts, Philharmonic-in-the-park concerts, children's theater shows, mimes and jugglers, kite-flying contests, ethnic festivals, and community fairs.

Urban parks offer many advantages for cultural events: they can host free events and activities designed to serve a diverse audience, easy access, low-cost maintenance, flexibility in the size of crowd that can be accommodated, an attractive setting, and opportunities for compatible activities such as picnicking and people watching.

Design considerations for cultural programming have often been the responsibility of park maintenance staff because they focus on needs pertaining to portable stages, electrical supply, truck access, temporary banners, booths, and so on. However, these considerations are also becoming more explicit as park managers have more experience with such programming, and landscape architects can respond with creative solutions to persistent problems.

To examine these behavior-based trends in actual practice and to elaborate on the partnership between environmental design research and urban park planning, the next sections of this chapter present two case studies: research for a new master plan for a large multiuse park and research for planning and evaluation purposes concerning an innovative urban historical park.

CASE STUDY: A LARGE, MULTIUSE URBAN PARK

Franklin Park, located in the Roxbury section of Boston, was designed by Frederick Law Olmsted in 1885. Its 520 acres include major recreation facilities (golf course, ballfields, and a stadium, although some of these features were not in the original design), as well as a modest zoo and extensive natural areas (woods, ponds, and rolling hills). A map of this park, Figure 1, illustrates the multiuse character of its design; some areas, such as the Playstead, are intended for active sports and recreation and other areas, such as the Wilderness, offer undeveloped spaces intended for escape, solitude, and passive enjoyment of park land.

This park suffers from problems that are typical of many urban parks, most notably crime and physical deterioration. The original design is basically intact, but many physical features have deteriorated to the point where they are no longer usable. Lack of care has created a negative public image.

Franklin Park and other large urban parks were created with donations and purchases of land when cities were much less developed, and they tend to reflect different attitudes and conceptions of outdoor recreation. As park planners attempt to upgrade or renovate these parks, serious consideration has to be given to the needs and recreational lifestyles of today's public. Is it appropriate to "restore" a park to its original design as if it were an architectural landmark, preserving a particular era or designer? Should the suggestions of today's recreationists be implemented, requiring major changes to bring the park in line with current needs?

In the case of Franklin Park and others designed by the Olmsted firms, the original design intent was thoughtful and well planned. But even though Olmsted's designs are considered "classics," are they so timeless that they serve the community well 100 years later? For example, one section of this park is called The Wilderness. Considering the problems with crime and people's fear of going into unused areas with no surveillance, this section gets little use. Should it be redesigned to be more accessible, or should it remain an unmanaged forest offering a different kind of experience with nature, but being perceived by most people as an area to be avoided?

Another section of the park, the children's zoo, is undergoing substantial renovation and new construction. Are these new buildings and developments incongruous with the "country in the city" theme that influenced park designs in the late 19th century? Or are they a logical extension of the intent to provide an interesting leisure experience for families and children—in fact, an alternative to conventional recreational activities?

RATIONALE FOR A NEW MASTER PLAN

There is a strong consensus that Franklin Park has deteriorated over the last several decades. Some say that this is related to the social change in the area; that is, the Roxbury neighborhood used to be a middle-class area but has changed to a lower-income and primarily black community. Although parks in upper-income areas continued to be maintained and cared for, this one deteriorated and was the scene of vandalism and crime. It has had a reputation for muggings and rapes; a dead body suggested murders in the park; cars were stolen and brought there to be salvaged for parts; old cars were abandoned

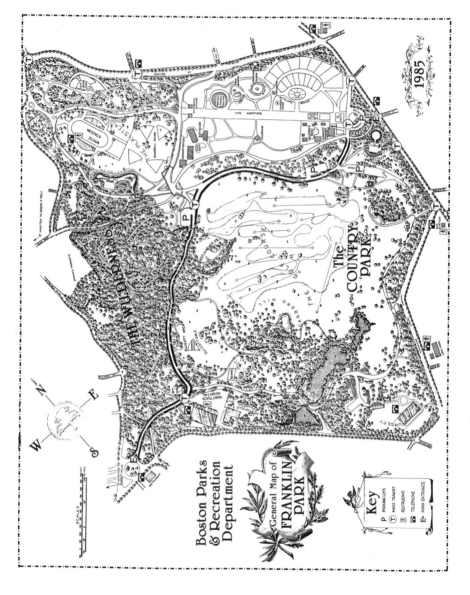

Figure 1. Map of Franklin Park, Boston, Massachusetts.

Urban Parks

there; a building containing a refreshment stand and rest rooms was dismantled and not replaced.

A community-based group, the Franklin Park Coalition, has worked very hard over the last ten years to improve the condition of the park. In cooperation with the city of Boston's Parks and Recreation Department, its members helped to improve park management, security, and maintenance and secured thousands of dollars from foundations to renovate structures in the park.

Recently, as part of a statewide initiative to renovate or restore significant Olmsted park projects, Franklin Park was selected for attention. A master planning team[2] was chosen to work with the state agency and with the community, analyzing and synthesizing a wide range of issues including historic value, community use and perception, maintenance, and recreational needs. As part of this process, a user analysis and community survey was commissioned to represent the needs, interests, and attitudes of the community as a whole (Hayward, 1987).

Planning Issues

It was generally agreed that a successful master plan should retain the character and overall design integrity of Olmsted's plan while also recognizing the interests of the current community and the need to reverse a declining image. The planning team was especially concerned that public hearings were attracting only a narrow segment of the community who were voicing special interests and that a systematic survey was needed to broaden their understanding of who is using the park, what activities need to be accommodated, and what local reaction might be to some possible design initiatives.

There was a particular need to explore the issue of "active" and "passive" recreation. The Olmsted design had created a separate area for active sports and games (The Playstead), which contrasted with less-developed areas for appreciating nature or passive, relaxing activity (ponds, The Wilderness, The Circuit Walk). The Meadow, originally intended as a multi-use open space on "natural" rolling terrain, had been converted to a golf course some time ago. Should this original design intent be preserved? Is it compatible with today's lifestyles and recreational pursuits? How extensive are passive recreational activities in the park? Although active use of the park tends to be organized and visually obvious (baseball games, soccer, golf), it was not known whether these activities are more prevalent or less common than use of the park by small groups for casual or unstructured recreation.

Another important planning issue focused on conflict and potential conflicts in the park. Public hearings and casual observation suggested that there were some tensions between different user groups, and it was important to

---

[2] The Franklin Park Master Plan was commissioned by the Olmsted Historic Landscape Preservation Program, Department of Environmental Management, Commonwealth of Massachusetts; The Halvorson Company of Boston, Massachusetts, was hired to design the Master Plan and to coordinate research, public meetings, and other related services.

identify the nature and extent of these problems so that design solutions might aim toward resolving rather than perpetuating such conflicts. For example, is it possible to accommodate the needs of teenagers and young adults who want places to "hang out" without compromising the community's perception that such groups create an unsafe atmosphere in the park? Or how serious is the conflict involving increased picnicking and cookouts, as family groups encroach on the golf course? Do residents from different sides of the park (two sides are predominantly black, lower-to-middle income; one side is changing to white middle-class) limit their use to their own side of the park, or do they feel free to use park features and opportunities throughout the park?

RESEARCH STRATEGY

To address these and other planning issues, a research strategy was developed to obtain information about current patterns of park use as well as about community opinion, recreational interests, and perceptions about the park and park users. Two complementary research methods were selected to collect appropriate data: observations in the park, using a behavioral mapping procedure, and telephone interviews with a random sample of neighborhood households.

Observations

Observations were designed to provide information about actual park use: how many people were using each of a dozen "areas" of the park, what activities were occurring, and whether the behavioral pattern of park use might suggest problems or priorities for planning. Observers completed a total of 30 rounds through the park, varied by time of day and day of week, resulting in a count of 7,337 persons observed.

Interviews

Interviews with neighborhood residents were conducted by telephone during evenings and weekends. This method allowed contact with park users as well as "nonusers" (those who had not visited the park in the previous 12 months) and sought information about activities engaged in and/or observed in the park, the image of the park including strengths and weaknesses, conflicts, changes perceived in recent years, interest in the history of the park, and reactions to possible improvements. The sample of 125 persons represented a fair distribution of ages, sexes, socioeconomic characteristics, and household types.

RESEARCH RESULTS

This research produced a substantial base of information for the master planning process and strengthened the role of community participation and dialogue with the planners. Three aspects of the results are highlighted here: image, passive recreational activities, and the potential role of interpretive information.

Image

Neighborhood residents enjoy Franklin Park. They like the easy access to open space as well as the chance to be in a natural setting. The park is valued because it is a good place to take children to, have picnics and cookouts, and relax and see other people enjoying themselves, and because it is a good setting for community festivals and seasonal events.

People frequently acknowledge that Franklin Park has had a troubled image. But this research confirmed the sense that the park is "coming back"— 72% of the sample said they had noticed changes in the park over the last several years, and four-fifths of these people described the changes as positive; a few people said they had only recently started using the park again, indicating an improved image and sense of safety. Unfortunately, the "image" of a place changes slowly, and the old image of Franklin Park still hangs on—the image of a place that is unsafe and poorly maintained. Rumors of drug dealing and major crimes in the park a few years ago continue to inhibit park use.

Passive Recreation

The distinction between "active" and "passive" recreation can be artificial and misleading (Kaplan, 1984). However, it serves a useful purpose in planning studies such as this one because public hearings are often dominated by sports enthusiasts who suggest major repairs or improvements to facilities, whereas people who use the park for passive enjoyment tend to be underrepresented in the public discussions about planning decisions.

In Franklin Park, "passive" activities are by far the most common uses of the park. Systematic observations revealed that the five most common activities are picnicking, walking, sitting/relaxing, children playing, and sitting in a car; together these activities accounted for 70% of all people observed in the park. A similar result was obtained from interviews, where people reported the most common activities as walking, picnicking, going to the zoo (the zoo area was not included in observations), playing golf, and jogging (these results combined answers about what people do there and what else they see there). The top three activities were the only ones reported by more than 50% of the sample.

The broad interest and occurrence of passive recreational activities—such as sitting, picnicking, walking, listening to music, watching children play, looking at animals in the zoo, sunning, flying kites, taking pictures, etc.—means that this type of use should be a strong influence in park planning. This emphasis suggests some strong parallels with Olmsted's original design and may help to make a stronger case for historic preservation.

On the other hand, active recreation is also an important part of the public's

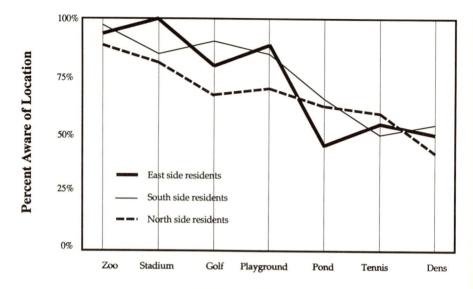

Park Features and Locations

Figure 2. Users' awareness of features of Franklin Park.

use of this park. The research results indicate that improvements and repairs to ballfields, the golf course, and tennis and basketball courts may be warranted, but should be done in a way that does not undermine the use of the park by a public seeking relaxation and passive experience.

Interpretive Information

Park users from the local neighborhood are reasonably well informed about Franklin Park. As illustrated in the accompanying graph, Figure 2, people are more aware of "developed" facilities such as the zoo, stadium, and golf course clubhouse. They are less familiar with the "undeveloped" or wooded areas of the park, including a large pond, tennis courts located next to a wooded picnic area, and old stone bear dens. Analysis of the pattern of knowledge revealed that residents have incomplete knowledge about features that are farther away from their "side" of the park. These differences suggest that there is a need for better information about the park, which could be provided through maps, interpretive signs, and/or information booths.

Interpreting a park—explaining its features, history, and opportunities for use—offers an alternative way of communicating with park users; the usual approach is a series of signs proclaiming "Don't. . ." or "No Swimming Allowed." In an effort to enforce rules and regulations, park officials may assume that bluntly stated messages are the best form of communicating with the public. However, this approach does nothing to reinforce the positive image and attitude that they would like the park to have, and it is unrealistic to assume that restrictive messages will be completely successful in an environment that is sought out for its freedom from supervision and routine. By contrast, interpretive signs and graphics are designed to enhance people's understanding and appreciation of a park through spatial orientation, information about the landscapes and plant materials, and even the history of how the park was used. We mistakenly assume that people want such information in a botanical garden or arboretum but not in public parks.

In Franklin Park, a park-wide system of information about the park could significantly enhance the appeal of the park, the extent of its use, and the perceptions of its users. Research shows that people want more information about the park and that the lack of information inhibits the extent of their use. Recent efforts to provide interpretation through a Park Ranger program (offering informative and supervised activities such as horseback riding lessons and walking tours of the park) have clearly enhanced the image and perceived security of the park; results from this research suggest that there is a greater demand for interpretive information and orientation and that a noticeable response to this demand is likely to produce positive long-term benefits.

APPLYING RESEARCH RESULTS TO THE DESIGN PROCESS

The user analysis of Franklin Park is helping to inform the process of developing a new master plan. Historic preservation and original design intent are important considerations in this Olmsted park, but planners recognized the need to understand the current community and its perceptions and patterns of park use. Thus, systematic information from local residents is helping to supplement other community discussions and public hearings.

The results from this study are not intended to prescribe specific actions or design decisions, but they do serve to represent the broad range of park users and neighborhood residents who are and will be affected by changes in the park. Paralleling the fact that landscape architects conducted a thorough analysis of the *physical* condition of the park, this analysis of social and behavioral conditions becomes a resource and stimulus to the planning process. For example, how can the image of the park be improved? Why do people still feel unsafe in this park even though it has the lowest crime rate of any major park in Boston? Is the public only interested in more facilities or do they care about the undeveloped "natural" landscape too? Such questions will continue to be important as planning decisions are faced, but they are now informed by a systematic source of public opinion and behavioral data.

Although this research had primarily focused on describing present uses and attitudes at one point in time, park planners requested that the analysis include recommendations about significant problems, possible approaches to those problems, and comparative information from other similar park studies.

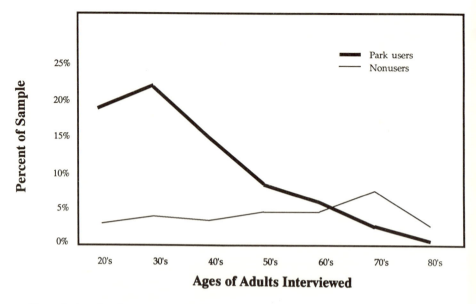

Figure 3. Age distribution of adults interviewed about Franklin Park: Users and nonusers.

These recommendations included the need for substantial visible improvements, facilitating the use of the park for passive and unstructured recreational activities, accommodating active recreation such as jogging and bicycling, continuing the trend of restricting through-traffic on park roads, reinforcing the perception and use of a "main entrance," accommodating the use of this park for major community festivals, providing more information about special features in the park, and, ultimately, maintaining Olmsted's original distinction between an active, developed area of the park as contrasted with undeveloped, wooded areas. The form of these recommendations was such that they suggested broad issues and directions without prescribing specific design solutions. In this way, designers and planners can consider a variety of ways of addressing the issues, based on comprehensive information about physical characteristics of the site, management needs, future maintenance concerns, design integrity, and relative costs of improvements.

The issues raised by this case study offer several parallels with other studies of urban parks. For example, the great majority of park users are interested in passive and unstructured activity—a result that contrasts with the conclusion one might draw from most public hearings where special interests often focus on facilities for sports and other forms of exercise. Another common finding is that the majority of park users are young adults and families; middle-aged and older adults are likely to be less frequent users or nonusers (see Figure 3).

The Franklin Park study also offers unique and community-specific results, such as the feedback about how the image appears to be improving. However, it will be useful to consider a different type of urban park, to provide a broader context of the types of environments that are being created for public use.

CASE STUDY: LOWELL, MASSACHUSETTS, URBAN HISTORICAL PARK

Lowell, Massachusetts, was one of the most remarkable examples of urbanization. A new city founded in 1822, it transformed farmland into a thriving industrial city of 30,000 people in less than 20 years. At the threshold of the Industrial Revolution, Lowell was the first comprehensive effort in North America to design and build a humane, livable community to serve the needs of a large manufacturing industry (in this case, based on textiles). Corporations built mill complexes with nearby housing, churches, and urban amenities. However, its heyday was relatively short-lived, as competition from southern mills caused a continuing decline in New England's textile industry in the latter half of the 19th century.

By the 1920s, the textile industry collapsed entirely in Lowell, resulting in high unemployment and economic stagnation. The city had been left with a legacy of obsolete mill buildings, canals that became health hazards, and substandard housing. After more than 100 years of decline, a renaissance here seemed unlikely. Still, in the mid-1970s local leaders proposed a "cultural park" concept, seeking to recognize the historical significance of the buildings as well as the entire urban design. "The cultural park concept was based on the notion that the city, itself, should be seen as a park—not in the traditional sense of a green, open space—but as a place where people could enjoy themselves through the sounds and smells and sights that can be found in an ethnic neighborhood or a culturally diverse street" (Peskin, 1985).

The concept of the city as a cultural/historical park implied an emphasis on recreation and leisure as well as on historical appreciation. As the concept gained support, Lowell was designated a National Historical Park and a State Heritage Park (see Figures 4 and 5). Local, state, and federal planning focused on creating an enjoyable leisure experience for residents and visitors, including activities such as self-guided walks, rides on trolleys and canal boats, picnicking, interpretive programs, and ethnic festivals.

The Need for Research

Because Lowell's economic revitalization depended, in part, on creating new recreation and tourism, planners were especially intent on understanding the interests, behavior patterns, numbers, and types of people who would be attracted. An early economic impact analysis compiled information from other historical and interpretive sites in the region, focusing on how many visitors attended, their demographics, and the behavioral characteristics of their visits. For example, the analysis predicted that children would constitute less than 20% of the park's visitors, a statistic that was based on other sites that specialize

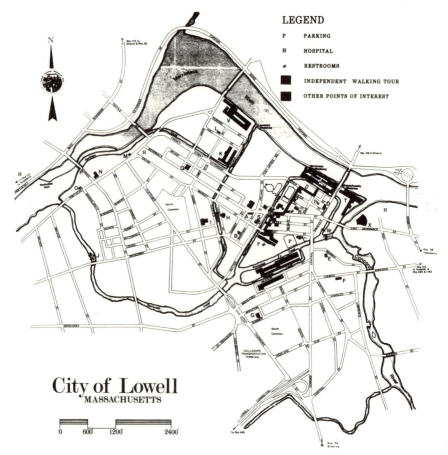

Figure 4. Map of Lowell, Massachusetts, urban historical park.

in historical interpretation. This type of information helped to guide physical planning as well as planning for activities and events.

After the park began to take shape, other research was commissioned. A study of local residents' perception of the park revealed that their negative image of the city was gradually being replaced by a more positive and supportive attitude. By 1983, a substantial amount of restoration had occurred and there were several developments that were open for use, including a visitor center, guided tours, and interpretive sites such as canal gates, a riverside park, mill buildings, and worker housing. Information about the visiting public was needed to evaluate the implementation of facilities, themes, and orientation materials; to investigate the need for new recreational or interpretive facilities; and to inform several aspects of future planning.

Urban Parks

Figure 5. Typical guided tour of Lowell's historical park.

RESEARCH STRATEGY

One of the major challenges for research was to represent the visitor's experience of Lowell, ranging from image and expectations to patterns of use and satisfaction. Consequently, the research strategy called for contacts with visitors before, or at the beginning of, their visit as well as follow-up contact after a visit. It was expected that this approach—focusing on visitors' experiences and demographic and behavioral profiles—would serve as an evaluation of the overall park concept, a baseline against which future development could be measured, and a way of informing planning and management decisions.

Two related studies were designed to obtain information about park users: a "visitor experience" study and a "visitor center evaluation." In the visitor experience study, randomly selected park visitors were interviewed at their point of arrival, at a large free parking lot or a paid parking garage (rate of cooperation was approximately 95%). At the completion of this interview, visitors were asked for a home address or phone number (alternating groups) for the purpose of a follow-up contact. This study was conducted in the fall season of one year and the summer season of the following year, resulting in a sample of 442 visitors for an initial interview and a follow-up rate (postvisit contact) of 63%.

The second study, a visitor center evaluation, was designed to investigate the use and effectiveness of visitor orientation and also to explore the reliability of demographic profiles with the visitor experience study. Randomly selected visitor groups were interviewed as they exited from the visitor center (rate of cooperation was approximately 90%), resulting in a sample of 321 park visitors. Comparison of this sample with the other study showed high reliability on demographic variables (when controlling for seasonal variation) in terms of geographic origin and distance to home, percentage of repeat visitors, group size, and percentage of groups with children. The only exception to this pattern was that Lowell residents were less likely to use the major parking lots and were therefore slightly underrepresented in the visitor experience study; however, they were slightly overrepresented in the visitor center evaluation because local residents also used the visitor center for advance information (in anticipation of visiting the park) and to use facilities such as the water fountains and restrooms.

In general terms, this research focused on independent visitors to the park, including distant visitors as well as local residents, but it did not include large groups of school children or adult bus tour groups in the fall.

RESEARCH RESULTS

Increasing numbers of park users, several hundred thousand per year, had already demonstrated the popularity of this park concept. This research confirmed such broad public appeal in terms of visitor experiences and enjoyment. Beyond this popularity, however, there were important questions about what types of visitors are using the park, their interests, reactions to the park concept, and whether some types of visitors are being served better than others. Therefore, these highlights of the research results focus on the visitor profile and interests in historical interpretation.

Profile of Park Users

The Lowell historical park (a combined experience of the National Historical Park and the Heritage State Park) is a regional attraction. Half of the visitors come from within a 30-mile radius, and others come from New England or live elsewhere in the United States but are traveling or visiting friends in New England. Analysis of demographic and behavioral patterns identified two major "user groups." One user group, *intentional visitors*, are those who come

Urban Parks

to Lowell because they are interested in the blending of the subject matter with a leisure experience. As a reason for coming, they are more likely to cite "historical importance of the sites," "personal interest in Lowell," and "personal interest in the textile industry." Thus, they arrived with better-than-average knowledge about the interpretive themes and are more interested in paying attention to exhibit material and guided tours. As a broad generalization, they think of their visit as educational as well as entertaining.

A second type of park user, *casual visitors*, come to the Lowell park because it sounds like an interesting experience—citing reasons such as "it's something to do," "vacationing," or "friends recommended it." These park users often decide to visit on impulse, rather than planning it in advance, and they arrive with less specific knowledge about interpretive themes and park opportunities (although there is general awareness of the historical nature of the park). They are likely to be interested in recreational opportunities and events more than exhibits, although they also like active interpretive programs (including guided tours, trolley and canal boat rides, costumed role playing at some sites, etc.) because of the entertainment value of these experiences.

Casual visitors were more common in the summer, whereas intentional visitors dominated in the fall. Families with children were also more common in the summer (37% of groups contained at least one child under 18, compared with 22% in the fall), but they were not always casual recreational visitors. Because casual visitors (families as well as adult groups) viewed this park experience as an outing, they looked for things to do in addition to the tours, such as picnics in a natural setting beside a canal, concerts, and performances. Interestingly, they expected to spend more time at the park than did intentional visitors.

Interest in Interpretation

The results of this research also demonstrated the broad interest in interpretation among both major user groups. Visitors enjoyed themselves and found that they also learned a great deal about the Lowell story and its historical significance to the nation.

Both the federal and the state park programs declare their commitment to visitor interpretation, and their success is quite evident. Follow-up contacts with visitors revealed that at least 94% recalled three of the five major themes in Lowell (water power, industrial revolution, and immigrants as workers), and at least 58% recalled the other two themes (city planning and capital investment methods). Awareness of these themes was demonstrated by visitors' ability to discriminate them from a list of general historical themes—five from Lowell and five from Boston (e.g., historic architecture, the development of democratic principles in America). With this base of understanding the park and its concept, visitors said that they were likely to return again, doing more and enjoying the experience again.

Part of the success of the park's interpretive efforts can also be attributed to successful orientation, both spatial and conceptual. The decision to have a central visitor center provided an excellent way to attract people. It serves as a beginning point for tours and creates a setting for exhibits, a bookstore, and audiovisual programs. The visitor center was often cited as the feature that was most helpful in understanding what the whole park was about, and it contained several effective aids to orientation such as a multi-image slide show (interestingly, a large map on one wall was recalled and mentioned by an impressive 39% of the visitors after they returned home!). Brochures and pamphlets about the park were also helpful, but they were mentioned primarily as aids to *spatial* orientation and had relatively little impact on *conceptual* orientation compared with the tour guides and the visitor center.

APPLICATION TO PLANNING AND MANAGEMENT

Based on questions and priorities from both the National Park Service and the Heritage State Park program, this research was designed to inform decision-making on a variety of topics such as interpretive services, seasonal operations, program planning, facilities planning, fees for services, promotion and publicity, and information management. Although these applications are quite different, they depend on similar information about visitors. Therefore, to be accepted by planners and incorporated into their decisions, scientifically acceptable procedures and good reliability in the data were essential. To "demystify" the research methods and provide a foundation for later acceptance of the results, staff members from the park agencies were required to participate in the data collection, after training and supervision. It seems likely that this decision was a useful strategy to enhance the application and understanding of results.

In general, the response to a systematic visitor analysis and evaluation study has been rewarding. Federal and state planners are using the information to reinforce or revise priorities for physical development, publicity, orientation, staff management, and budgeting. Geographic, demographic, and behavioral data about park users is being shared with merchants and business organizations in Lowell, leading to collaboration for improved visitor services as well as benefits to the city.

Defining the principal user groups—intentional and casual visitors—has been a useful contribution, providing a context for evaluating existing efforts as well as the feasibility of new initiatives. For example, the significant numbers of "casual visitors" and families suggested the viability of starting a children's museum in Lowell. If park users were only interested in historical interpretation, and if the park's primary audience was older adults (common at other historical sites and museums), then the results would have run counter to planning a new family attraction.

Recommendations from the research were widely circulated within the park agencies and distributed to the designers of new exhibits as well as to the local business community. As the quantitative and qualitative results are assimilated into ongoing planning and management, it is clear that the focus on "visitor experience"—a topic that seemed esoteric to some and ambiguous to others—provided the best framework for a comprehensive analysis of the park's concept and implementation.

FUTURE DIRECTIONS FOR DESIGN RESEARCH

Studying the public's perception and use of urban parks is fascinating as well as problematic. In this section, some of the strengths, weaknesses, and unique circumstances of this research are considered.

First, there are a variety of advantages to studying urban parks. As a general type of environment, urban parks are most often perceived as community assets, and this public support makes it easier to obtain information about people's use and opinions of a park. Thus it is common to achieve a participation rate of 90% or higher for face-to-face interview studies and a rate of 70% or more for telephone interviews. Parks also benefit from a high degree of awareness and at least moderate knowledge: people know where the parks are and have a basic awareness of the park's features (e.g., recreation facilities, gardens, or special natural features). For the validity of research, it is important to have this broad base of cooperation so that all segments of the community can be represented.

Another advantage—more theoretical than practical—is that parks are conceptually ambiguous in the public's mind. People often say that it's hard to have a mental map of a park, and they're not able to name or describe its natural features. In one sense this presents a problem for research that is trying to probe the public's knowledge and image of a park. In a broader sense, however, it is quite helpful because it allows people to think freely about space use, other types of users, potential conflicts in activities, and so on. People can imagine *change* in a park in a way that they couldn't if they were thinking about a building.

Research on urban parks benefits from the opportunity to explore a broad range of theoretical issues. In addition to studying recreational behavior, parks offer opportunities to explore landscape perception, economic issues such as the benefits of parks on real estate prices and the resulting municipal tax income (More, Stevens, & Allen, 1982), and innovative applications of behavioral mapping methods to investigate 24-hour park use (More, 1985).

A continuing strength is the cooperation and overlap between researchers and landscape architects—not only are designers requesting and applying the results of research, but they are also a growing constituency in the Environmental Design Research Association, which is an ongoing forum for professional communication on this topic.

Of course, there are weaknesses and unmet challenges in urban parks research too. Foremost among these is the lack of a consistent taxonomy of recreational uses and interests. Studies with similar objectives (e.g., to describe the pattern of urban recreation activities) have yielded different results, apparently depending on the questions asked and the interests of the researchers

(Heywood & Mullins, 1985; Hayward & Weitzer, 1983). More work in this direction is warranted because a useful taxonomy would aid in comparing across parks as well as in communicating with designers.

Future research in this area will continue to face a theoretical and political problem: the persistent conception among recreation managers and planners that sports facilities are the primary need and purpose of urban parks. It seems fair to speculate that the present field of recreation, and many of today's recreation professionals, were heavily influenced by the postwar growth in organized sports and active recreation facilities. Society as a whole, however, is exhibiting the need for a much more diversified approach to recreation planning. Thus, for example, we cannot afford to treat passive recreation and interpretation as afterthoughts or optional amenities in park design. We have seen that they are the primary interest of a sizable majority of park users. Recognizing society's needs and lifestyles and accommodating significant behavior-based planning trends are the ultimate challenges for research and planning in urban parks.

How can environmental design research on urban parks assist and stimulate the planning process? What roles can researchers play in improving the quality and extent of recreational opportunities and, ultimately, the quality of urban life? Can research help implement social change? This final section suggests some strategies that appear to be useful in advancing the relationship between research and planning.

User Analysis

One of the most significant roles that researchers can play is to work within the planning process for a specific park, for example, on a master plan or feasibility study. At the same time that landscape architects or planners work on a physical analysis of the park, the researcher can be conducting a social–behavioral analysis of park users and nonusers. During this phase, the researcher's role is to identify the public's needs and interests, analyze and interpret public opinion, and facilitate the process of clarifying issues that will affect people's perception and use of the park. Specific activities or tasks may include attendance at public meetings, community surveys, observation of park use, and identification of user groups.

Design Review

Researchers can also assist the planning process and help to advocate user needs by participating in a design review. This role may be as minimal as an informal session to review and comment on design proposals, extrapolating some results from a user analysis to predict the degree of success of those proposals. However, this role can also be more systematic and welcomed by designers as an opportunity to gauge public reaction before publicizing their plans. For example, a community survey could be used to assess possible design proposals, or a display of alternative designs could be held in public places such as banks, libraries, and post offices; reactions can be assessed by "ballots" on specific design issues.

EVALUATION

Management-oriented research can also be useful in assessing needs, setting priorities for long-range planning, identifying weaknesses and programs with little public benefit. This research strategy can be appropriate at any time and does not have to be conducted within the boundaries and constraints of a specific design process. Evaluation research may investigate patterns of attendance at programs or events, awareness and participation among various subgroups of the population, and the balance between user benefits and potential negative impacts on the site.

EXPERIMENTATION

Research opportunities are often presented as "one-shot case studies"— do a survey and present a report. However, there could be significant benefits to the field if researchers could capitalize on longer-term relationships with urban park agencies. One obvious benefit would be the ability to apply and test research results over time. Experimentation would require a process of partially implementing new plans, using mock-ups, single-session test programs, or a gradual schedule of renovation. Such a process may or may not require new research at each stage, but it would at least suggest a framework for seeking information about public use and opinion and would put a researcher in a position to assist with ongoing decision making.

EDUCATION AND COMMUNICATION

Environmental design research as a field and park user surveys in particular are not so widely recognized that they are automatically considered a normal part of planning processes. Therefore, this additional role emphasizes the need to communicate with planners, design professionals, and recreation professionals concerning the uses and value of research. Urban parks research has helped to inform planning and design decisions, it has represented the needs and interests of the public in a way that is much more credible than public hearings, and it has been sensitive to issues of social change that must be accommodated if we expect to reduce conflict and enhance the role of parks in society. Clearly, this area of research has been fruitful and it should be the subject of dialogue with related fields so that it will endure and improve.

REFERENCES

Cranz, G. (1978). Changing roles of urban parks: From pleasure garden to open space. *Landscape, 22,* 9–18.

Francis, M. (1987). Urban open spaces. In E. Zube & G. Moore (Eds.), *Advances in environment, behavior & design* (pp. 71–206). New York: Plenum Press.

Godbey, G. (1985). A model of non-use of urban leisure services. In *1985 national outdoor recreation trends symposium II* (pp. 90–108) Clemson, SC: Department of Parks, Recreation and Tourism Management.

Gold, S. (1972). Non-use of neighborhood parks. *Journal of the American Institute of Planners, 3*, 369–378.

Hayward, D. G., & Weitzer, W. (1983). Understanding urban park users: A key to effective planning and management. *Parks & Recreation Resources, 2*(2), 24–27.

Hayward, J. (1987). *Franklin Park user analysis.* Northampton, MA: People, Places and Design Research.

Hayward, J., & Weitzer, W. (1984). The public's image of urban parks: Past amenity, present ambivalence, uncertain future. *Urban Ecology, 8,* 243:268.

Hester, R. (1984). *Planning neighborhood space with people.* New York: Van Nostrand Reinhold.

Heywood, J. L., & Mullins, G. W. (1985). *Urban forest recreation participation in Columbus and Franklin County, Ohio.* Columbus, OH: Ohio State University, Ohio Agricultural Research and Development Center.

Johnson, D. R., & Field, D. R. (1984). Social and demographic change: Implications for interpretation. In G. E. Machlis & D. R. Field (Eds.), *On interpretation: Sociology for interpreters of natural and cultural history* (pp. 111–125). Carvallis OR: Oregon State University Press.

Kaplan, R. (1980). Citizen participation in the design and evaluation of a park. *Environment & Behavior, 12,* 494–507.

Kaplan, R. (1983). The role of nature in the urban context. In I. Altman & J. F. Wohlwill (Eds.), *Behavior and the natural environment* (pp. 127–161). New York and London: Plenum Press.

Kaplan, R. (1984). The impact of urban nature: A theoretical analysis. *Urban Ecology, 8,* 189–197.

Kornblum, W. (1987). *Conceptual planning for recreation at Battery Park City.* Report to the Battery Park City Authority, City University of New York, Graduate Center, New York.

More, T. A. (1985). *Central city parks: A behavioral perspective.* Burlington, VT: University of Vermont, School of Natural Resources.

More, T. A., Stevens, T., & Allen, P. (1982). The economics of urban parks: A benefit/cost analysis. *Parks and Recreation, 17*(8), 31–33.

Palmer, J. F. (1984). Neighborhoods as stands in the urban forest. *Urban Ecology, 8,* 229–241.

Peskin, S. M. (1985). *Lowell, Massachusetts—Preservation key to revitalization* (Project Monograph). New York: Institute for Urban Design.

Sharpe, G. (1982). *Interpreting the environment* (2nd ed.). New York: Wiley.

Talbot, J. F., Bardwelt, L. V., & Kaplan, R. (1987). The functions of urban nature: Uses and values of different types of urban nature settings. *Journal of Architectural and Planning Research, 4*(1), 47–63.

Talbot, J. F., & Kaplan, R. (1984). Needs and fears: The response to trees and nature in the inner city. *Journal of Arboriculture, 10,* 222–228.

Whyte, W. H. (1980). *The social life of small urban spaces.* Washington, DC: Conservation Foundation.

9

The Attractiveness and Use of Aquatic Environments as Outdoor Recreation Places

DAVID G. PITT

INTRODUCTION

SIGNIFICANCE OF WATER-BASED OUTDOOR RECREATION

Water is a dominant feature in many environments. The United States, a nation of some 2.3 billion acres, has approximately 110 million acres of water surface, 3.6 million linear miles of rivers and streams, approximately 100,000 miles of coastal and Great Lakes shoreline, over 100,000 natural lakes, 2.5 million farm ponds, and a land area submerged under man-made reservoirs that exceeds the size of New Hampshire and Vermont combined. Roughly one-third of the U.S. population lives within five miles of a public lake, river, stream, or coastal shoreline (Lime, 1983).

Outdoor recreation engagements (those intrinsically rewarding behaviors committed by an individual or group of their own personal and free choice during nonobligated time [Driver & Tocher, 1970]) constitute a growing sector of water and water-related land resource use. One-fourth of all outdoor recreation is water-dependent; two-thirds of all public recreation areas contain a body of water or are adjacent to accessible water. Among Americans over 11 years of age, one-third swim, fish, and boat at least once each year and between 10% and 20% canoe, kayak, or raft on a river, ice skate, hunt waterfowl, or sail at least once each year (Lime, 1983).

DAVID G. PITT • Landscape Architecture Program, University of Minnesota, St. Paul, MN 55108.

RECREATIONAL USE OF AQUATIC ENVIRONMENTS: A TRANSACTION OF
PEOPLE AND ENVIRONMENT

Water-related recreational behaviors inherently involve a transaction of people and environment (Ittelson, 1973). The nature and quality of the recreational experience resulting from this transaction depend on salient attributes of the environment, characteristics of the recreationists involved, and the psychological, social, physical, and managerial context within which the experience occurs (Litton, Tetlow, Sorensen, & Beatty, 1974).

The Environment

Environment can be construed as both a source of attraction and a setting in which human behavior occurs. For example, many passive recreationists are attracted to a riverine environment simply to view and enjoy scenery. Other people engage in recreational behaviors on or near the river (e.g., fishing, canoeing, swimming) that may or may not be related to attractiveness values. Active recreationists may construe the river as a behavior setting that affords the opportunity to realize the particular package of psychological outcomes (e.g., companionship, nature study, skill testing, solitude) they associate with a given activity (Driver & Brown, 1978). Finally, an aquatic environment can be cast from the perspective of environment as both source of attraction and behavior setting. For example, a visitor to northern Minnesota's Boundary Waters Canoe Area (BWCA) may find the BWCA provides the attractions necessary to realize the meaning of a sought-after communion with nature but be upset by the mosquito infestation encountered while camping in a densely vegetated site protected from wind. A transactional perspective on water-based recreation also views environment as containing social as well as physical dimensions. Environmental attractiveness and the suitability of environment as a behavior setting may be determined by who is present as much as they are by what is present.

The Participant

The characteristics of people involved in the transaction profoundly affect its nature. Knowledge of the permanent characteristics a participant brings to a transaction is critical to understanding its meaning.

The Context

A specific individual may transact with a given environment in entirely different contexts resulting in very different recreational experiences. Contextual changes have psychological and social as well as physical dimensions. Variation in the psychological context of transaction occurs when an individual's knowledge of, attitude toward, or intention with respect to a specific environment change. Social context is determined by who else is involved in the transaction as well as the range of events that precede, accompany, or succeed the transaction. Physical contextual changes involve variation in such dimensions as people's physical position relative to an environment and their rate and mode of travel through the environment.

The psychological, social, and physical contexts of environmental transactions may be products of pure happenstance or they may be created by the actions of individuals deliberately attempting to influence the nature of the transaction and the quality of the experience (e.g., a landscape architect redesigning a road to reduce the speed at which a riverine landscape is experienced or a naturalist providing interpretative information about an adjacent grove of trees). Thus, context must also include a managerial dimension that describes the extent to which the environment, the individual, or the other contextual elements have been deliberately altered by people, planners, and managers trying to influence the nature of the transaction (Driver & Brown, 1978).

OUTLINE OF CHAPTER

This chapter uses a transactional model of people interacting with environments from different psychological, social, physical, and managerial contexts as a framework to examine the recreational experience of aquatic environments. Lakes, rivers, and coastal waters and their associated land resources are examined as sources of attraction as well as settings for water-dependent outdoor recreation behavior. The chapter examines pertinent characteristics of environment, recreationists, and context as these three sets of characteristics frame recreational transactions with aquatic environments in predominately rural or natural settings. The chapter concludes by identifying directions for future research.

SPECIAL CHARACTERISTICS OF AQUATIC ENVIRONMENTS THAT FRAME THE TRANSACTION

As places where the transaction of people and environments occurs, aquatic areas have physical characteristics that clearly differentiate them from terrestrially based places. Several social, economic, legal, and political institutions guide the conduct of transactions. As land-based animals, humans use a wide spectrum of technological innovation to adapt what is essentially a terrestrial existence to an aquatic regime. Finally, the unique attraction of people to water establishes several dimensions that frame recreational transactions with aquatic environments.

PHYSICAL CHARACTERISTICS

Perceptual Clues on the Presence of Water

The presence of water in the environment is more complex than simply the existence of lakes, streams, rivers, bays, and so forth. Rather, water leaves its signature in the landscape as it affects and is affected by landform and vegetation. The edge between water and land is a visual element that receives equal attention with water features, *per se*, in the comprehension of aquatic environments (Gratzer & McDowell, 1971; Shafer, Hamilton, & Schmidt, 1969). Perception of aquatic environments depends not just on salient features of water, but also on the relationship water and the space immediately above the water surface have with their enclosing landforms, vegetation, or structures. The flow of water through the hydrologic cycle inextricably links the physical, chemical, and biological properties of aquatic environments with characteristics of adjacent terrestrial ecosystems.

Geographic Scale as a Determinant of Aquatic Environment Character

The landform and vegetative patterns that influence the physical character of an aquatic environment extend over large geographic areas. Regional distribution of geologic formations, climate, soils, and vegetative communities establishes a regional character for riparian and other aquatic environments. Because the character of any single aquatic environment is affected by regional patterns of geology, climate, soil, and vegetation, and because the experience of any specific aquatic place is temporally and spatially bounded by the experience of adjacent landscape, any given aquatic environment can be comprehended only as it exists within a hierarchically nested regional setting (Litton et al., 1974).

The Flow of Negative Externalities across the Water Surface

To the extent that the effects of events in one part of an aquatic environment spill over into other parts, recreation behavior in aquatic environments involves two sets of direct and indirect costs: internal costs directly associated with the recreationist's choice of when, where, and how to use the environment (e.g., costs of renting a boat to fish); and external costs imposed by the actions of others spilling over into the desired recreational setting (e.g., cost of gasoline to drive to another lake because a preferred lake contains too many boats for the type of desired fishing experience and the anxiety of not being able to fish in a preferred setting). The physical dimensions of external costs for recreationists in aquatic environments are often more intensive and ubiquitous than in terrestrial systems because water dissolves and transports nearly everything, nearly everywhere. The flat, open character of most lacustrine environments provides little protection from the social dimensions of negative externality (Field & Martinson, 1986). Escaping undesirable behavior of others on a lake often means physically leaving the area. The winding channels, thick bank vegetation, and narrow, steep corridors of many riverine systems provide screening that mitigates negative spillover effects among river user groups. However, the flow of the river accentuates the potential for stationery users (e.g., shore anglers) to experience negative social externalities generated by river floaters because the river continually brings people into and out of view. Depending on channel width and flow direction, stationery users would expect to encounter repeated, uninvited violations of their behavior setting. The existence of externalities establishes behavioral incentives wherein recreationists attempt to avoid the assumption of costs generated by other users' behavior, resist internalizing their own spillover costs, and prefer to have costs associated with negative externalities assumed by others or by society.

Fragility and Irreversibility

Aquatic environments contain at least two sets of natural resource values: management values, in which the environment is viewed as a developable resource, and preservation values, in which the environment is viewed as a protected healthy ecosystem (Sagoff, 1985). Realization of management values generally implies some form of resource development, as when a boating resource value is developed on a lake by building a boat launch ramp and public dock. Preservation values, on the other hand, involve intrinsic values of the environment. Preservation values associated with aquatic environments are fragile because they are often easily destroyed, especially in the process of developing management values.

To the extent that the development of management values results in the elimination of fragile preservation values, aquatic environmental managers are continually faced with decisions concerning nontrivial irreversibilities (Krutilla & Fisher, 1975). Individuals seeking management values push for their development until the internal marginal cost of development equals internal marginal return. As more management values are developed, more preservation values are destroyed. The remaining preservation values become more scarce and, therefore, more valuable, assuming at least constant demand. Each additional unit of management value development produces a decreasing marginal return on management value investment at an increasing marginal cost in foregone preservation values. The social welfare incentive is to stop management value investment when the total (i.e., individual plus social) marginal gain of management value development equals the total marginal costs of management value development plus the total marginal costs of preservation value loss. Unfortunately, the calculus of preservation value estimation has yet to be developed. As extramarket values, preservation values are under-represented in explicit policy decision making, producing a bias in favor of behaviors associated with management values. Over time, the nontrivial irreversibilities associated with this management value bias leads to a decline of aquatic environmental resources.

INSTITUTIONAL CHARACTERISTICS

Institutions are the social structure through which society organizes and executes its activities. The laws, regulations, customs, and habits spawned by the economic, political, legal, religious, and family systems that bind a society together establish limits and create incentives for prescribed patterns of aquatic resource use.

Common Property and Public Trust

Throughout most of the United States, navigable surface waters and the land thereunder are held in public trust by state governments. In exercise of this trust, the public can use navigable waters as common property for navigation, commerce, fishing, swimming, boating, general water-related recreational uses, and the preservation of esthetic and ecological values. Because nearly all aquatic environments contain waters that meet the judicial definition of navigable waters (able to float a 6-inch log), aquatic environments can be described as common property resources wherein property rights cannot or have not been distributed among users. The fact that property rights have not been distributed means that virtually nobody can be restricted from using the resource without some form of collective action. When each individual's use subtracts from the quantity available to others or lowers resource quality below a critical threshold for viable use by others, the incentive among individuals is to obtain first use and resist policies designed to restrain individual use. Even when the deleterious long-term consequences of an action are known, the incentive of more immediate short-term gain leads the individual to pursue a long-term suboptimal behavior pattern (Johnston, 1988). Because all users of the resource pursue their short-term instincts, individuals who buck the pattern in favor of the more optimal long-term pattern find themselves at a competitive disadvantage with respect to resource availability. Such mentality produces a social trap that leads eventually to resource depletion. Resolution of the trap dilemma involves collective action by all users (Hardin, 1968).

The inability to exclude users from a commonly held aquatic environment produces little incentive for users to be individually concerned or active in policies to enhance or restore resource quality, since nobody can be precluded from enjoying the benefits of such policies. Rather, the incentive is for individual users to "ride free" on the efforts of others, especially where the number of users is large (Johnston, 1988).

The high costs of exclusion are often associated with the evolution of a heritage of multiple use. Seeing no way to limit access of any sector of the public to publicly owned resources, managers often naturally assume the operating philosophy of providing the greatest good for the greatest number over the longest time. The heritage of multiple use often prevails long after the discovery of documented negative externalities flowing among user groups.

The juxtaposition of commonly held aquatic environments and privately owned property can introduce property rights conflicts. Public access programs enable exercise of public trust use rights, but they can also introduce nuisance and trespass problems for riparian landowners. Transient recreationists often hold motivations for resource use and perceptions of management strategy

Aquatic Environments as Outdoor Recreation Places

appropriateness that are considerably different from those of riparian landowners (McAvoy, 1982).

Multiple Jurisdictions and the Boundary Issue

The boundaries of an aquatic environment and its contributing land area rarely follow the boundaries of political geography. Boundary issues arise when the costs and benefits of an activity or decision affecting resource use are not contained within the jurisdiction making the decision (Johnston, 1988). For example, while the Chesapeake Bay drainage basin includes portions of Maryland, Virginia, West Virginia, the District of Columbia, Delaware, Pennsylvania, and New York, over half of the Bay proper is contained in Maryland. Of the rivers flowing into the Chesapeake Bay, the Susquehanna contributes the largest single amount of total freshwater inflow and over 50% of the total nitrogen and phosphorous nutrient inflow (U.S. Environmental Protection Agency, 1983). Yet, the Susquehanna flows through only 15 miles of Maryland before meeting the tidal flats of the Chesapeake. Clearly, a majority of the generators of the external costs associated with nutrient enrichment in the Susquehanna River inflow are residents of Pennsylvania and New York. A majority of the recipients of these externalities are residents of Maryland and Virginia. Recreational management of aquatic environments is further complicated by multiple functional as well as political jurisdictions. In Maryland, for example, direct responsibilities for planning, implementing, and enforcing management strategies for the Chesapeake Bay are shared among the various counties contiguous to the Bay, four departments of state government, the U.S. Army Corps of Engineers, and the U.S. Coast Guard.

TECHNOLOGICAL ADAPTATIONS TO EXTEND TERRESTRIAL EXISTENCE INTO AQUATIC ENVIRONMENTS

Human use of aquatic environments generally requires development and use of technology to extend a terrestrially based existence into an aqueous regime. To a large extent, technology is used not to alter environmental elements or systems to fit human needs but rather to fit patterns of human life into the parameters of the aquatic environment. Boats, for example, extend bipedal locomotion and other forms of terrestrial activity onto the water surface. Variation in the level and type of technology employed by recreationists in their transactions with aquatic environments affects the characteristics of the transaction's social context, producing an asymmetrical antipathy and source of conflict among recreationists employing different levels of technology (Heberlein, 1977). The effects of technological asymmetries among recreationists will be further identified in a subsequent section of this chapter.

Technological developments or adaptations can also be instrumental in generating demand for transactions between people and aquatic environments, as well as altering human perception of environment. For example, the incidence of river floating through the Grand Canyon increased dramatically in the years immediately following development of the inflatable rubber raft for use in World War II (Nash, 1977). Development of the wind surfboard and the growing popularity of windsurfing as a sport is transforming Hood River, Oregon, formerly a lumber town of 4,600, into a *mecca* of windsurfing. The growing popularity of the sport has altered local residents' perception of the regularly occurring 60 miles per hour wind gusts that previously were viewed as a menace (Baker & Huck, 1987).

THE ATTRACTION OF WATER

Water has a magnetic attraction in the environment that is unrivaled by other materials or elements. Human response to aquatic environments emanates from the sound, smell, taste, and feel of water, as well as from the sight of it (Litton *et al.*, 1974). The presence of water nearly always enhances human perception of scenic beauty or preference in rural and urban settings (Ulrich, 1983).

Cognitive Differentiation of Aquatic Environments

A growing body of literature suggests that people differentiate in their minds between landscapes that contain water and those that do not. Furthermore, there appear to be cognitively different types of aquatic environments. For example, cluster analysis of data generated from the Q-sorting of 56 photographs of rural and exurban western New England landscapes on the basis of perceived similarity yields seven discrete categories of landscape, including farms, meadow and woods, open water, wetlands and stream, forested hills, towns, and industrial areas (Palmer & Zube, 1976). Cluster analysis of two sets of rural Kentucky stream-related landscapes rated on a semantic differential of beautiful–ugly produces a cluster of scenes containing heavily dissected and thickly vegetated landscapes through which swiftly flowing water is a dominant feature and a cluster of scenes depicting placid pools of water, often in a panoramic setting (Dearinger, 1979). Nonmetric factor analysis of 70 color slides of water-related landscapes from six different states yields a waterscape typology containing four orthogonal dimensions: (1) mountain waterscapes containing waterfalls and rushing mountain streams; (2) swampy areas containing stagnant creeks covered with algae and slime, streams with brown water, and lakes with prominent swamp features near the shoreline; (3) rivers, lakes, and ponds with no particularly outstanding features; and (4) large bodies of water wherein water extends to the horizon. Among 259 subjects, 73% of the variance in preference for these scenes can be explained simply by correctly classifying the scenes according to this cognitive waterscape typology (Herzog, 1985). Finally, factor analysis of scenic value Q-sortings of the same photographs used in the Palmer and Zube (1976) study by different subjects yields a landscape typology containing 10 orthogonal dimensions. Of these 10 dimensions, four describe the presence of water in the landscape, including: (1) rushing water wherein water is depicted as flowing swiftly over strong and irregular contours, through thick forested vegetation and in relatively steep, narrow valleys; (2) wetlands having poorly defined shorelines and containing wide expanses of vegetation that irregularly covers broad expanses of water; (3) placid river valleys containing gentle or calmly moving rivers, flanked by high vegetation and strongly contoured landform; and (4) undifferentiated open water wherein large, open water is the dominant and most extensive feature and land is a minor bordering element in the distant background (Amedeo, Pitt, & Zube, in press).

Two points emerge from these studies. Among the two studies comparing riparian and nonriparian landscapes (Amedeo *et al.*, in press; Palmer & Zube, 1976), landscapes containing water consistently constitute unique components of the subjects' landscape typology. Secondly, strong concordance exists among the content of the waterscape categories emerging from the four studies conducted with four different sets of subjects in three different settings. The stability of these content categories suggests that aquatic environments in rural and natural settings can be cognitively differentiated into rushing or flowing streams; wetlands; lakes, ponds, pools, or placid stretches of rivers having strong land borders but lacking the eutrophic conditions of a wetland; and large open expanses of water.

Dimensions of the Attraction

Several hypotheses offer explanations for the near-universal attraction of people to aquatic environments. As viewed from a "naturalness of human existence" perspective, humans have an innate desire to return to the natural environment of the phylogenetic past (Sitte, 1965). Repeated contact with nature aids in coping with the intransience and complexities of contemporary life (Stainbrook, 1969). Some authors attach Freudian significance to human relationships with Earth-mother, suggesting vaginal symbolism in the landscape painter's fascination with deep gorges created by river valleys as they pass through ridges (Shepherd, 1961). The naturalness of human existence hypothesis finds empirical support in several landsacpe perception studies that repeatedly find preference for natural versus man-made landscapes (Ulrich, 1983), a preference within man-made settings for the presence of natural elements (Brush & Palmer, 1979), an increase in preference for the same scene when its label is changed from a man-made to a natural connotation (Hodgson & Thayer, 1980); feelings of anxiety and sadness associated with the presentation of urban scenes but more positive affective responses to natural scenes (Ulrich, 1979); and low galvanic skin response and high alpha brain-wave production associated with the viewing of natural scenes and the opposite physiological responses associated with urban scenes (Ulrich, 1981). From this perspective, the presence of water, the quintessential element of nature, symbolizes the former existence of humans in a more natural setting.

Habitat theory of landscape aesthetics poses a link between aesthetic appeal and the ability of a place to satisfy human biological needs (Appleton, 1975). In this sense, human fascination with aquatic environments is explained by the fact that while we can survive for weeks without food, shelter, or succoring, our existence without water is measured in days.

A variation of habitat theory suggests that the habitat of prime importance to human perception of landscape is that which cradled human evolution—the savanna of east Africa (Dubos, 1980). Savanna landscapes are characterized by extensive grasslands, irregularly interspersed with groves of trees whose canopies barely overlap and in which there is minimal undergrowth. Periods of precipitation extremes produce water bodies that regularly vary in size (Odum, 1971). The irregularly shaped water bodies follow the landform contours and serve as the focal point of life in the savanna. Tree groves frame expansive views to the horizon across both grassland and water. Empirical tests of the savanna preference hypothesis find young children preferring savanna landscapes over landscapes from other biomes. With increasing age and experience, preference for the savanna is replaced by preference for the familiar (Balling & Falk, 1982). Numerous studies show strong preferences for landscapes possessing savanna-like attributes: parks containing biomorphically shaped water bodies, open grassy areas, visually penetrable groves of trees, and expansive views to the horizon (Daniel & Boster, 1976; R. Kaplan, 1977; Shafer et al., 1969; Zube, Pitt, & Anderson, 1975). In this context, water symbolizes the focal point of human existence in the specific natural setting that nurtured human evolution—the savanna of east Africa.

Prospect-refuge theory proposes a relationship between aesthetic preference and landscapes that would have afforded the opportunity to fulfill Lorenz's (1952) notion of "seeing without being seen" during human evolution (Appleton, 1975). The theory posits the existence of three types of symbols in the landscape: hazard, prospect, and refuge. Hazards are symbolized as animate or inanimate threats (e.g., a predator, another human, meteorological phenomena, fire) to human existence during the species' evolution occasioned by some external incident; natural or artificial impediments (e.g., expansive water bodies, walls) that do not of themselves initiate an incident threat; and chronic deficiencies that threatened the satisfaction of human biological needs during evolution. Prospects are symbolized by conditions that would have afforded direct or indirect opportunities to view the landscape and the hazards it beheld during evolution. Refuge provides opportunities wherein a creature could have escaped the impending peril that accompanied any of the hazards and removed itself from the view of animate objects likely to generate a potential hazard. The prospect and the hazard aroused attention and generated tension as the evolving species surveyed its environment. The refuge provided opportunity to resolve the conflicts and anxieties aroused by the prospect and the hazard. The capacity to read prospect, hazard, and refuge into the landscape—to "see without being seen"—allowed the evolving human to fulfill basic biological needs. Although no longer critical to human survival, the predisposition toward processing of environmental information against the criteria of hazard, prospect, and refuge provide for contemporary humans a source of aesthetic satisfaction (Appleton, 1975).

Aquatic Environments as Outdoor Recreation Places

Water is specifically represented in all three environmental components of prospect-refuge theory. As a flat, unvegetated surface, water affords ample direct prospect in the landscape. One's gaze directly across the water surface, especially from an elevated perspective, is unimpeded and provides opportunity to detect presence of incident hazards. Indeed, the line where water and land meet often directs the view. Indirect prospect finds classic expression in aquatic environments in the form of elevated shorelines and rivers or lake bodies that disappear around protruding points of land (i.e., the "deflected vista").

For early humans lacking the technology needed to extend their existence onto the water surface, water also symbolized an impediment hazard—it prevented bipedal locomotion. Water retarded human flight from animate hazards and prevented hunting and gathering of food clearly evident on the opposing shore. Strongly contoured landforms located immediately adjacent to the water's edge (e.g., a sheer rock wall) symbolized inanimate threats to survival as well as affording direct or indirect prospect. The interplay of water and its enveloping land mass, the undulation of the shoreline, and the presence of riparian vegetation provided evolving humans with ample refuge. Humans could flee along the often open shoreline, following a path that eventually took them around a river bend or into an adjacent embayment and consequently out of the prospect of an animate hazard. Alternatively, one could duck into riparian vegetation and find a hiding place that would afford prospect back across the water surface. Contemporary waterscape perception studies find attention often focused on the shoreline (Gratzer & McDowell, 1971) and preference associated with the amount and crispness of shoreline present in a view (Shafer *et al.*, 1969; R. Kaplan, 1977).

Many of the psychological correlates of landscape preference uncovered by recent empirical studies are strongly manifest in aquatic environments. Mystery represents the prospect of gaining further information about a scene should the observer change location (Kaplan & Kaplan, 1982). In aquatic environments, mystery is classically expressed by the deflected vista of a river or other water body flowing around a bend or point of land (Herzog, 1985).

In natural settings, riparian environments often contain a configuration of water, landform, and vegetation possessing the visual and spatial organization needed to provide the observer with a coherent and legible image of an identifiable place (Kaplan & Kaplan, 1982). Visual complexity is often high but ordered by geomorphic or biologic process (e.g., water rushing over boulders in a stream producing intermittent patterns of whitewater). The presence of water functions as an interconnected matrix enabling the observer to integrate multiple focal points visually and mentally (Ulrich, 1983) that are created by patterns of water, landform, and vegetation. The protrusion of geologic and vegetative material through the water surface at varying distances from an observer and the undulation of shoreline vegetation and landform establish strong notions of near and far. These depth cues heighten esthetic appreciation of aquatic environments (Ulrich, 1983). The flow of the water, together with the flow of space strongly defined above the water surface by surrounding landform and riparian vegetation, lures the observer into further visual and mental, if not physical, exploration of the scene. Given the technology necessary to extend human existence onto a water surface, the generally fine surface texture of water, coupled with shoreline pathways, provide ample locomotion affordances to further explore the spatial and visual qualities of the aquatic environment.

CHARACTERISTICS OF PARTICIPANTS ENGAGED IN THE TRANSACTION

As settings for recreational behavior, aquatic environments possess physical and institutional characteristics that incite and facilitate social conflict. The near-universal magnetism of water makes aquatic environments places where people want to be. The common-property nature of ambient water resources is a source of potential conflict because the multiple use heritage of common pool resources precludes exclusion of users without collective action. Conflicts exist between public trust and private property. The flat, open nature of aquatic environments makes it difficult to separate incompatible uses by means other than distance or time. Uses reflecting management values almost inherently conflict with uses reflecting preservation values. The special relationship that streams, rivers, lakes, and ponds enjoy with their watersheds introduces potential conflict between on-site and off-site users. The dissonance of political and physical geography associated with aquatic environments means that the parties involved in the conflict may reside in jurisdictions having different legal perspectives on the conflict. Finally, since some form of technology is needed to accommodate nearly every human use of aquatic environments, conflict may arise with respect to type and level of technology involved.

Whether these potential conflicts materialize depends in large part on the characteristics of the uses and users present in a given aquatic environment and the psychological, social, physical, and managerial context in which the recreationist-environment transaction occurs. This section explores recreationist characteristics that are useful in understanding the transaction of people and aquatic environments in rural and natural settings, which are relatively stable across transactions. It will be followed by a discussion of contextual issues.

Socioeconomic Characteristics

Much of the early literature dealing with the transaction of people and natural environments in the context of recreational experience focused on the role of socioeconomic characteristics in shaping the transaction. Although these studies linked outdoor recreation patterns to age, income, occupation, residence, and life cycle, the combined effect of these relationships generally explains less than 30% of the variance in general outdoor recreation activity (see

Manning, 1986, for a review of this literature). Perceptions of landscape scenic value among diverse socioeconomic and demographic groups are also generally characterized by strong intergroup concordance (Zube et al., 1974; Zube, Pitt, & Evans, 1983).

Subsequent studies have refined the objectives and methods of inquiry to produce more specific relationships for water-based recreation events. Income has been identified as a necessary but insufficient predictor of activity choice pattern in that it limits participation in activities with high costs (Lucas, 1964). Surveys of water-based recreationists in rural and natural settings generally characterize participants as having above-average incomes and at least four years of post-high school education (Lime, 1986). The type of education completed by recreationists affects their perception of landscape quality and the choice of attributes to which they attend in their environmental transactions (Buhyoff & Leuschner, 1978; R. Kaplan, 1973).

Age has been strongly and inversely associated with activities requiring physical strength and endurance (Kelly, 1980). For example, water skiing is most prevalent among young adults between 18 and 29 years of age (McDonough & Field, 1979), whereas fishing draws participants from all ages but especially older adults (Field & Martinson, 1986). While approximately half of those recreationists who travel on rivers and streams in kayaks, canoes, rafts, innertubes, or small motorboats are under 30 years of age, they begin their participation in these activities at a later age than do hunters, anglers and wilderness users (Lime, 1986). While teenagers exhibit stronger preferences for social contact in beach settings than other age cohorts (Hecock, 1970), older recreationists at a developed reservoir setting are less likely than younger visitors to experience serious crowding problems (Gramann & Burdge, 1984). Age also affects perception of landscape attractiveness. Unlike the scenic value perceptions of teenagers and adults, the perceptions of young children (6 to 10 years old) are indifferent to the presence of nature and unrelated or only weakly related to the presence of rugged topography and adjacent incompatible land uses (Zube et al., 1983).

People engaged in occupations requiring high energy expenditure tend to seek recreation activities requiring low energy expenditure (Bishop & Ikeda, 1970), and among river recreationists, professional or white-collar occupations predominate (Lime, 1986). Some studies report a white-collar predisposition toward natural beaches and beaches without human influences (Hecock, 1970). Discrepancies exist between the perceptions of people using an aquatic environment as a recreation behavior setting and those whose occupations involve managing the setting (Wellman, Dawson, & Roggenbuck, 1982).

The experience preferences and behavior patterns of water-based recreationists are related to their demographic characteristics. For example, housing unit density of the home environment relates directly to preferences for solitude in the recreation experience (Knopp, 1972) and the extent to which people view recreation as a means of escaping their neighborhoods (Knopf, 1976). Recreationists living in heavily burglarized neighborhoods view recreation as an "opportunity to experience a secure, trustful social environment" (Knopf, 1983,

p. 214). Fishermen seeking escape from distractions of the home environment spend a longer period of time each day fishing than fishermen not seeking escape (Wellman, 1979). Among river recreationists, the length of the trip from the home environment to the riverine setting in which the recreation experience is bimodal; many trips occur within 75 miles of home and many trips require one-way travel distances of several hundreds of miles (Lime, 1986). Whitewater enthusiasts travel further from home to pursue their activity than do more casual river users (e.g., anglers and swimmers) (Field & Martinson, 1986; Peterson, Lime, & Anderson, 1981).

CULTURE AND ETHNICITY

Studies examining perception of landscape scenic value among diverse groups are characterized by strong intergroup concordance (Daniel & Boster, 1976; Zube et al., 1974, 1983), even when the groups cross nationalities (Zube & Pitt, 1981). On the other hand, preferences for extreme Arctic landscapes vary dramatically between Eskimo and non-native residents (Sonnenfeld, 1967). Cultures structured around extended families (e.g., Mexican-American) encounter difficulties fitting their camping styles and structures into the nuclear-family-based facility design of American campgrounds (Hoots, 1976). The disparity among these findings is partially explained by examining the extent of difference between the cultures being compared (Zube & Pitt, 1981). Thus, people from strongly divergent cultures are likely to reap different experiences from their transactions with aquatic environments.

Atlhough some authors relegate differences in outdoor recreation activity participation patterns among blacks and whites to socioeconomic status or social class, studies controlling for social class status report persistent black–white differences. Blacks are reported to be less likely to engage in or prefer boating, fishing, swimming, canoeing, hunting, and sightseeing and are more likely to seek engagements in urban rather than rural or natural settings. Blacks are also reported as desiring further public expenditure for recreation to be devoted to urban rather than rural parks, more facilities rather than more land, more indoor as opposed to outdoor facilities, and inland rather than waterfront sites (see Wendling, 1980, for a review of this literature). What emerges from these findings is a general absence of blacks from recreational transactions involving aquatic environments in rural or natural settings.

Studies of landscape perception find similar effects attributable to ethnic variation. A group of center-city blacks in Hartford, Connecticut, for example, do not share the prevailing normative bias toward natural environments and natural elements within built environments (see earlier discussion on the attraction of water). Rather, the tendency of these blacks and native Virgin Island residents responding to scenes of the Virgin Island coastline was to prefer landscapes in which structures are pronounced (Pitt, Zube, & Palmer, 1980; Zube & Pitt, 1981).

Childhood Experiences

Several studies implicate childhood experiences as strong determinants of both recreational activity patterns of adults and perception of landscape quality (Yoesting & Christensen, 1978). Car campers, for examples, can be differentiated from backpackers on the basis of whether they camped as children and if so, the predominant style of camping they experienced (Burch & Wenger, 1967). The range of landscape types to which people are exposed as children is a significant determinant of their perceptions of landscape quality as adults (Zube et al., 1974). Landscape exposure occurs through socialization in the home environment (Aiello, Gordon, & Farrel, 1974), as well as through children's literature (Marcus, 1977).

Psychological Characteristics

Recreationists bring their personalities to their transactions with aquatic environments. The individuality of personality produces personal styles of transaction both in the sense of what a recreationist chooses to do in a given environment and in the way an individual identifies and attends to salient attributes of the environment (Knopf, 1987). Personality traits relate to motivation for recreation behavior (Driver & Knopf, 1977), variation in landscape preferences (Macia, 1979; Sonnenfeld, 1967), and recreation behavior choice among children (Bunting & Cousins, 1985) and adults (McKechnie, 1974). Responses on a wilderness-urbanism environmental attitude scale (Hendee, Catton, Marlow, & Brockman, 1968) are related to management preferences among river recreationists in Dinosaur National Monument (Schreyer, Roggenbuck, McCod, Royer, & Miller, 1976) and perceptions of crowding among floaters on the Green and Yampa Rivers in Utah (Schreyer & Roggenbuck, 1978). Users characterized by a purist wilderness perspective are more sensitive to crowding than are individuals desiring more urban amenities in their outdoor activities. Recent work tends to examine personal style of environmental transaction as manifestations of more general dispositions such as locus of control, cognitive flexibility, cognitive complexity, primary orientation, and arousal or sensation-seeking tendencies (Knopf, 1987).

CONTEXTUAL INFLUENCES ON TRANSACTIONS

Several characteristics of both the environment and the participant fluctuate from one transaction to another. These situational constraints may be products of the psychological context a participant bring to a particular transaction, variations in the social and physical contexts of the transaction, or differences in the level and type of management that has been applied to either the environment or the participant.

PSYCHOLOGICAL CONTEXT OF THE TRANSACTION

Recreationists bring at least four sets of situation-specific psychological dimensions to their transactions with aquatic environments. From one transaction to another with the same environment, participants can change their motivation or intention with respect to the transaction, their level of experience or specialization associated with realizing a given motivation in a specific setting, their familiarity with a given setting, and the level and type of information they have about the physical and social characteristics of the setting.

Motivation

As noted earlier, participation in recreation activities is valued more for the psychological outcomes or consequences that accrue as a result of an experience in a specific environmental setting (Driver & Tocher, 1970). More than one outcome can and usually does contribute to the definition of an experience; and any given outcome may contribute to the definition of more than one experience (Driver & Brown, 1978).

Among recreationists transacting with aquatic environments in rural and natural settings, research has focused on the motivations of people engaged in fishing (Knopf, Driver, & Basset, 1973), river floating (Schreyer & Roggenbuck, 1978; Ditton, Fedler, & Graefe, 1983; and Schreyer, Lime, & Williams, 1984), and waterfowl hunting (Vaske, Fedler, & Graefe, 1986). Motivation profiles of river floaters are consistent across different settings (Knopf, Peterson, & Leatherberry, 1983). More important for purposes of this chapter, differences in motivation profiles among recreationists using a single, aquatic environment are related to perceptions of crowding (Ditton et al., 1983; Schreyer & Roggenbuck, 1978) and conflict among user types (Driver & Basset, 1975).

Experience Level

The level of experience a recreationist has either with a specific aquatic environment or a specific type of activity affects the nature of transactions between people and aquatic environments. For example, people who have visited the Boundary Waters Canoe Area more than four times report extensive changes in their use patterns (change in time of use, choice of campsite, and selection of entry access point; Anderson, 1980). Floaters on 13 rivers throughout the United States were stratified into groups based on their experience in river floating, *per se*, and their experience in floating on a particular river. Significant differences exist among these groups in terms of how they transacted with a given river (e.g., length of trip, type of craft), motivations for floating on the river, subjective evaluations of the experience, perceptions of conflict with other river users, and perception of different management levels and types (Schreyer et al., 1984). Among fishermen, level of specialization is directly associated with tolerance for encounters with people engaged in other activities (Bryan, 1988). Length of experience in a particular aquatic environment has been linked to differences in motivation for river floating (Knopf & Lime, 1984) and to perceptions of crowding among river floaters (Ditton et al., 1983), canoeists (Anderson, 1980), and open-water boaters (Colton, Pitt, Morgan, & Chaney, 1979; Vaske, Donnelly, & Heberlein, 1980). Floaters and boaters with a longer history of use across various settings are also more sensitive than novices to crowding (Ditton et al., 1983) and changes in environmental quality (Anderson, 1980; Vaske et al., 1980). Compared with novice river runners, more experienced runners tend to rely less on socially provided information sources in development of river trip norms and expectations, and more on their own personal experiences (Cockrell & McLaughlin, 1982).

Familiarity

As exposure to a given aquatic environment increases, an affective person–environment bond emerges. This bond differentiates that environment from others (Knopf, 1987) and results in the environment being cognitively represented and processed more on the basis of past experience than on its physical attributes (Tuan, 1974). As exposure increases, the recreationist "begins to make more subtle environmental differentiation, to develop a more complex, well-defined set of expectations from the environment, to adopt a narrower definition of what forms of behavior are appropriate, and to formulate less flexible opinions about how the area should be managed" (Knopf, 1987, p. 806).

With few exceptions (Wellman & Buhyoff, 1980), landscape perception research reports links between familiarity and preference. Adults consistently report favoring familiar biomes (Balling & Falk, 1982), environments similar to the home (Deardon, 1984; Sonnenfeld, 1967), and natural environments wherein they have lived or recreated for considerable periods (Deardon, 1984). These general findings extend into aquatic environments. Among residents of New York State's coastal zone, variability in subject reports of familiarity among diverse coastal scenes accounts for a significant amount of variance in preference (Nieman, 1980). Repeated exposure to a bog environment increases visitor perceptions of its visual quality. The effect of exposure is stronger for repeat bog visitors than for first-time visitors (Hammitt, 1981).

Information

Recreationists having different levels of formal education, different life experiences, or varying levels of experience of familiarity with either a specific activity or a specific environmental setting would be expected to bring different sets of information to a transaction. One would expect these information set differences to affect human transaction with rural and natural aquatic environments. In addition, variations in the level and type of information provided recreationists immediately prior to, during, or immediately succeeding a transaction will significantly affect their experiences with an aquatic environment.

Information programs are effective in modifying wilderness area camping norms of Boy Scouts (Dowell & McCool, 1986), visitor propensity to engage in environmentally depreciative behavior (Oliver, Roggenbuck, & Watson, 1985), and the distribution of use patterns among different settings (Krumpe & Brown, 1982). Something as simple as changing the name of an area can dramatically affect recreationist behavior intentions (Fedler & Kuss, 1986) and use patterns (More & Buhyoff, 1979). Information programs are most successful in altering recreation behavior in natural environments: (1) with visitors having little experience with a specific environment; (2) when they discuss a wide variety of topics, including site characteristics, use levels, backcountry norms, and related backcountry activities; and (3) when they are delivered to the visitor early enough to affect setting choice decisions (Roggenbuck & Berrier, 1982). Not all recreationists, however, will favorably receive such efforts as increased signing or information pamphlets. Some recreationists may view the effects of these programs as creating rather than resolving problems of overuse and user conflict (Roggenbuck & Berrier, 1982).

Human perception of aquatic environments can also be affected by information provided during the transaction. The appearance of a *New York Times* feature story on the erosion process as a naturally occurring phenomenon is associated with a dramatic shift in public opinion with regard to strategies for altering the erosion of Niagara Falls (Zube, 1980). Changing the label on a riparian landscape from lake or pond to reservoir or irrigation significantly lowers judgments of scenic value (Hodgson & Thayer, 1980). Similarly, informing subjects that the interesting orangish pattern present in a forested scene is a beetle infestation significantly lowers their perceptions of scenic value (Buhyoff & Leuschner, 1978).

SOCIAL CONTEXT OF THE TRANSACTION

People are rarely alone in their transactions with aquatic environments. The presence of others introduces two sources of social context that influence the nature of the transaction: the social group with whom the recreationist is affiliated during the transaction and the individuals and groups the recreationist encounters during the transaction.

Social Group Affiliation

Even in a wilderness setting wherein people's motivations may be oriented toward solitude and a solitary experience, visitation to parks, beaches, lakes, and rivers is characterized by group behavior, with individuals having to attend to the desires and norms of the group (Knopf, 1987). Among river recreationists, group size is larger than among other recreationists (Lime, 1986). Commitment or attention to group norms may be stronger than commitment to personal desires with respect to an environmental transaction (Knopf, 1983). For example, among waterfowl hunters on the Chesapeake Bay and river floaters on the Buffalo River in Arkansas, intragroup and intergroup contact enhances the hunting experience (Vaske et al., 1986; Ditton et al., 1983). Among river floaters, members of the float trip groups to which floaters belong serve as a primary referent for normative belief development concerning the float trip (Cockrell & McLaughlin, 1982). Group affiliation similarly affects landscape preferences (Deardon, 1984).

Groups move freely from activity to activity without disintegration of structure or peer norms, and within a group, many activities are substitutable (see Manning, 1986, and Knopf, 1983, 1987, for reviews of literature on the effects of social group affiliation). However, changing the nature of the group produces variation in the perception of appropriateness and rate of participation among activities, as well as variation in the satisfactions to be derived from the transaction. Thus, individuals behave differently in the same setting, depending not only on what is happening at that point in time but also on the nature of the group to which they belong at that time.

Group size and composition depend not only on primary group affiliation (e.g., family, friendship, and mixed family/friendship constituents) but also on psychological outcome expected from the transaction. For example, among participants in the 1979 National River Recreation Study conducted by the USDA Forest Service, river recreationists seeking quiet and/or escape experiences are more likely to belong to small, primary (i.e., family and friendship-related) groups. Those seeking group adventure participate in large groups consisting of individuals who may or may not be familiar with one another but have a desire to share what they have learned, be a part of a group, and talk with varied people (Heywood, 1987).

Behavior norms within an aquatic environment may be influenced by social groups other than those to which an individual currently belongs (Knopf, 1983). Individuals attempting to change group affiliation will pursue normative recreation behavior patterns of the sought-after group. Over time, the patterns of higher-status groups diffuse among groups of lower status. That working-class people living in a white-collar community would emulate the recreation activities of white-collar workers more than working-class people living in working-class neighborhoods demonstrates the significance of activities, values, and norms of the prevailing social system on individual behavior patterns (Knopf, 1983).

The emulation of significant others may lead an individual or group to unknowingly engage in depreciative behavior. Many forms of depreciative behavior differ from other but acceptable types of behavior only in the context in which they occur (Pitt & Zube, 1987). At the same that society carefully preserves the cliff inscriptions of American Indians, it also publicly supports the reshaping and preservation of Mt. Rushmore's cliffs, marvels at the man-made tunnel cut through a giant Sequoia tree, and become outraged when rock out-crops are defaced by a spray paint artist or trees are initialized by knife-wielding whittlers (Williams, 1976). In one context, a behavior pattern is permitted and even encouraged while in another context, the pattern may result in incarceration. Often, the only contextual differences are imperceptible administrative rules and regulations with which the visitor may be unfamiliar. Having witnessed and possibly participated in a normatively acceptable behavior pattern in a similar molar physical environment, the visitor fails to perceive that such behavior has been administratively deemed inappropriate.

Encounters with Others

Early attempts to examine the effects of recreationists' encounters with others during transactions with a natural environment posited a linear inverse relationship between quality of the transaction (as measured by participant-reported estimates of satisfaction derived from the transaction) and the number of encounters experienced (Fisher & Krutilla, 1972). Subsequent empirical investigations find measures of user density and self-reports of encounter volume related to perceived crowding but, at best, unreliable direct correlates of the satisfaction recreationists derive from their transactions with aquatic and terrestrial environments throughout the United States. Because the voluntary, nonobligatory nature of recreation suggests that water-based recreationists are unlikely to report low levels of satisfaction from their transactions with natural environments (Heberlein & Shelby, 1977), more recent work focuses on crowding perceptions among water-based users.

Relationships between density and crowding depend on the environmental disposition and encounter expectation and preferences of the participant, and three dimensions of the psychological context of the transaction (motivation, experience level, and information set). (See Graefe, Vaske, & Kuss, 1984; Manning, 1986; and Shelby & Heberlein, 1986, for reviews of this literature.) River floaters possessing a "purist" perspective toward wilderness values are more sensitive than their urbanist counterparts to crowding as a function of encounter density. The crowding sensitivities of river recreationists, as well as waterfowl hunters, vary with the participant's expectations and preferences for contact with others. Water-based recreationists are more tolerant when encounter densities exceed their preferences than when densities exceed their expectations (Shelby & Heberlein, 1986). River floaters, anglers, and canoeists having experience motivations related to solitary experiences report crowding occurring at lower densities of encounters. Water-based recreationists with more extensive experience either in a particular activity or with a particular setting report higher crowding sensitivities than their inexperienced or novice counterparts. Encounter norms become increasingly more tolerant of the presence of others as the name of the setting in which encounters occur changes from wilderness to semiwilderness and developed recreation, or as the name of the experience changes from wilderness whitewater trip to scenic whitewater trip and social recreation trip (Manning, 1986).

The level of technology employed by water-based recreationists persistently affects individual perceptions of encounters with others. Given an identical number of interpersonal or interparty contacts, water-based recreationists employing higher levels of technology in their activities (motorized canoes or motorboats as opposed to paddling canoes or paddle rafts) tend to disrupt the experiences of their lower technology counterparts more than lower technology recreationists disrupt high technology recreationists. Paddle canoeists report enjoying their encounters with other paddlers but disliking encounters with motorized canoeists who enjoy or do not mind encounters with others whether they operate paddle or motorized craft (Adelmann, Heberlein, & Bonnickson, 1982; Lucas, 1964).

Explanations for the existence of asymmetrical antipathy (Heberlein, 1977) among recreationists employing different levels of technology in their transactions focus on differences in motivations (Jackson & Wong, 1982) that are not revealed by normative patterns of encounter behavior. Paddlers may view the existence of motors in wilderness as antithetical to their personal construct of a wilderness experience. Motorized canoeists' motivations are obviously indifferent or positively associated with the presence of motors. To motor-craft operators, the seemingly pleasant behavior of encountered paddlers (e.g., smiling or waving) reveals little of the paddlers' anxiety (Adelmann *et al.*, 1982). Asymmetrical antipathy often results in displacement. Low-technology participants persistently encountering high-technology participants are the first to leave an environment in search of another setting wherein their expectations might be more fully realized (Catton, 1983).

Behavioral crowding, or the spillover of behavioral consequences among parties of recreationists (Gramann, 1982), adversely affects the nature of the environmental transaction. The crowding perceptions of reservoir visitors relate directly to their reports of encountering reckless boating (Gramann & Burdge, 1984). Anglers and streamside residents object to canoeists because of the latter's inconsiderate behavior (Driver & Basset, 1975). River floaters are sensitive to the number of encounters in which behavior of those encountered is considered disruptive (Titre & Mills, 1982). Experienced visitors to the Boundary Waters Canoe Area who have changed entry points, campsite locations, or entry days feel that failure to change their behavior patterns would have resulted in their encountering noisy people in large groups, seeing litter along the shore and at portages, and seeing and camping at heavily used and worn-out campsites at which birch trees have been vandalized. All of these behavioral consequences and behavior traces are perceived as detracting from their recreational experience (Anderson & Brown, 1984). Numerous additional studies directly link crowding perceptions and general deterioration of the spillover effects of other people's behavior such as the presence of litter (Lucas, 1980), environmental disturbance associated with previous use by others (Vaske, Graefe, & Dempster, 1982), the size of other groups encountered (Lime, 1972), and the noise generated by others (Womble & Studebaker, 1981).

Finally, the spatial–temporal location of encountering others influences the effect of an encounter on perceived crowding. Wilderness visitors are more sensitive to encounters in interior wilderness areas than they are in peripheral areas (Stankey, 1973). Group members spatially located on the edge of their group are more sensitive to encounters with other groups than those having more central locations (Womble & Studebaker, 1981). Whereas seeing an increasing number of boats within 300 feet of an observation boat is inversely related to boater satisfaction, an increasing number of boats in the distance is positively related to satisfaction (Pitt, Chaney, & Colton, 1981). Boaters report adverse reactions to increasing encounter densities only when the proximity of the encounters precludes their ability to pursue desired activities on a particular body of water in a prescribed direction of travel (Colton et al., 1979). Similarly, the crowding perceptions of river floaters are most sensitive to having to queue up for passage through rapids (Titre & Mills, 1982). Floaters whose experiences are diminished by encounter density feel more strongly that encounter levels exceed their preferences at campgrounds and take-out locations rather than at in-stream locations (Ditton et al., 1983). Encounter norms are lower at campsite locations relative to in-stream locations (Roggenbuck & Bange, 1983).

PHYSICAL CONTEXT

Several aspects of the discussion concerning encounters with others also implicate physical context as a potential determinant of enjoyment derived from recreational transactions with aquatic environments in rural or natural settings. For example, the studies on asymmetrical antipathy in encounter norms among recreationists employing different levels of technology (Adelman et al., 1982; Lucas, 1964) also implicate mode of travel as a factor influencing the recreational experience. As previously noted, motorized and nonmotorized recreationists differ in their experiential motivations and encounter norms. To the extent that users are more perceptive of environmental deterioration attributable to styles of use other than their own (e.g., hikers more perceptive of trail damage created by cyclists than by other hikers), mode of travel will also affect perceptions of resource quality (Graefe et al., 1984). User experiences are affected by physical traces of other people's behavior, such as litter (Lucas, 1980), environmental disturbance (Vaske et al., 1982), and noise (Womble & Studebaker, 1981). To the extent that recreationists draw inferences from these traces about functional density and the ability the environment affords to realize desired motivations and expectations, inferences about the social context of the transaction and the ability to achieve objectives emanating from the social or psychological contexts can be gleaned from the physical arrangement of elements in the environment (Hammitt, 1983; Womble & Studebaker, 1981). Finally, within a given recreational experience, encounter norms and the perception of an encounter with other recreationists depend on the physical setting in which the encounter occurs (Ditton et al., 1983; Pitt et al., 1981; Roggenbuck & Bange, 1983). Within a river-floating experience, encounters at campsites are evaluated differently than are those occurring on the river.

Contextual changes in water quality also influence the nature of a recreational transaction with an aquatic environment in a rural or natural setting. Although there is a tendency among some recreationists to "overrate" water quality at settings they have already selected for use (Moser, 1984), perceptions of pollution and other descriptors of water quality (e.g., transparent, clean, healthy) correlate with objective measures of water quality (Coughlin, 1976).

Water-quality perception among recreationists is multisensory, including visual evidence of the presence of algae, scum, suds, foam, debris, or dead fish on the water surface; odor; and perceived water clarity (Moser, 1984). Neither visitors to nor riparian owners along lakes experiencing different levels of nutrient enrichment have difficulty recognizing nutrient-rich water (Coughlin, 1976). However, anglers are often unaware of the presence of toxic chemical pollutants, which leave no physical trace in the water (Udd & Fridgen, 1986). Although recreationists can discern polluted waters from clean waters (at least as the pollution is physically manifest in the water), the existence of pollution bears little relationship to waterscape preference (Coughlin, 1976). The effects of objective or perceptual measures of pollution on use patterns are unclear. Several studies report no relationship between actual use of perceptions of use suitability and objective pollution estimates (Moser, 1984; Udd & Fridgeon, 1986) or perceptual estimates (Coughlin, 1976). Other studies (Cowdin, 1986; see Coughlin, 1976, for a review of other studies) find pollution perceptions related to use suitability ratings only when the use involves direct water contact.

Managerial Context

In aquatic environments, managerial context exists in three forms: (1) strategies designed to "harden" the setting in which a transaction occurs to increase its ecological resiliency and capacity to accommodate use; (2) direct regulation of recreationist behavior, such as spatial and/or temporal use zoning, prohibition of specific uses, or restrictions on use intensity in general; and (3) modification of user behavior by means of indirect controls or suggestions of control (e.g., programs designed to alter user behavior by influencing the type and level of information that is processed in the psychological context of a transaction or by creating peer pressure for behavioral change as a result of involving users in the management process (Lime, 1975).

The effectiveness of management strategies in influencing recreationist behavior and the response of different recreationists to the transactional intrusions inherent in different forms of managerial context are mixed. Hardening a setting, for example, may involve site modifications that decrease soil erosion potential on a trail. Recreationists are more likely to perceive these strategies as inappropriate environmental modifications as the strategies are introduced into more remote wilderness or backcountry settings. Wilderness users express preferences for low-standard rather than high-standard wilderness trails (Anderson & Manfredo, 1986; Manning, 1986). Recent literature on user reaction to direct regulation of backcountry recreationist behavior (see Anderson & Manfredo, 1986; Manning, 1986; and McAvoy, 1982) suggests that (1) most visitors favor use limitation in the context of a setting that has been degraded by overuse; (2) first-come, first-served and reservation systems are preferred over lotteries and environmental skills testing as methods for rationing use allocation; (3) requiring users to predetermine and adhere to a fixed travel route or itinerary is unpopular among backcountry recreationists; (4) users are split but tend to slightly favor surface zoning by mode of travel; (5) users are split but tend to oppose restricting access to heavily used settings; and (6) proposals to limit party size are generally accepted by wilderness users but are resisted by river floaters.

As discussed earlier in this chapter, the information set established for a recreational transaction by management activity can change both the recreationist's perception of and behavior patterns within an aquatic environment. Care must be exercised in implementing information programs to avoid introduction of informational intrusions into the transaction. Wilderness users and river floaters, for example, appreciate receipt of brochures and pamphlets outlining the environment they will use (Lime & Lucas, 1977). They do not all appreciate, however, constant reminders during a transaction of where they are, where they are supposed to go, and how they are supposed to behave (Anderson & Manfredo, 1986). Some recreationists may view information programs as activating latent demand for recreational experiences, increasing use intensity, and thereby creating rather than solving problems (Roggenbuck & Berrier, 1982).

FUTURE DIRECTIONS OF RESEARCH

The transactional model provides a useful structure for integrating existing research findings into a more coherent understanding of recreation behavior in aquatic environments. The model simplifies the integration process by categorizing findings based on their relevance to understanding the discrete contributions of environmental attributes, participant characteristics, and contextual issues in the transaction of recreationists with aquatic environments. The model also inherently complicates the integration process by insisting that the character of recreational transactions in aquatic environments can be fully understood only as the interaction of factors attributable to environment, participant, and context. Many of the research needs outlined below emerge from the failure of existing studies to examine recreational experience comprehensively and explicitly as a transaction of environment, participant, and context. As a prelude to assessing future research needs, five trends that have emerged from existing studies and are likely to characterize water-based recreation in rural and natural settings over the next two decades are examined.

Trends in Water-Based Recreation

Involvement by a Wider Segment of Society

The characteristics of recreationists transacting with aquatic environments will become more diverse. The broadening of the participatory base is a function of several factors, including increased discretionary time and income, greater desire to include leisure, recreation, and physical fitness into lifestyles, flexible work schedules, improved water quality and public access to water, the emergence of new primary social units within society (e.g., single-parent families;

Aquatic Environments as Outdoor Recreation Places   241

gays and lesbians), increased availability of facilities, services, and technologies needed to extend our terrestrial existence into aqueous regimes, and growing social norms concerning aquatic environments as desirable and fun places (Field & Martinson, 1986; Lime, 1986). This trend will complicate future research pertaining to the transactional experience of aquatic environments by diversifying the characteristics of participants involved in the transaction, diversifying the psychological and social contexts in which these transactions occur, and diversifying the managerial context of the experience as managers seek new tools to cope with the social, psychological, and environmental consequences of greater participant diversity.

Aging of Water-Based Recreationists

As the post-World War II baby boom generation matures, the median age of water-based recreationists will rise, resulting in a move away from strenuous activities toward experiences involving more passive endeavors. As the baby boomers continue to start and rear their families, experiences focusing on the family as a social group will grow in importance. More aged recreationists for the future are likely to be more physically fit than their contemporary age cohorts. However, the rising median age will produce a greater proportion of water-based recreationists having ambulatory and physical limitations (Lime, 1986). Population aging, then, will alter participant characteristics, change the mix of experience motivations sought by water-based recreationists, affect the composition of the social group with whom participants engage in environmental transactions, and require a managerial context capable of accommodating the characteristics of a pool of participants more physically limited.

Increasingly Experienced Recreationists

As a greater segment of society shifts toward water-based recreation, experience levels among participants will increase. A more specialized participant pool will become more discriminating in its definition of a quality recreational transaction with aquatic environments (Lime, 1986). These changes in the psychological context of the transaction will require future researchers to reformulate the criterion measures of transactional quality as experienced by recreationists and to explicitly incorporate experience level as a contextual element.

Increased Use of Advanced Technology

The development of advanced technology is increasing the range of activities in which water-based recreationists may engage. "As the microchip hits the water" (Field & Martinson, 1986), the emergence of technology oriented toward individualized encounters with aquatic environments will increase (e.g., motorized jet ski or surfboard, inexpensive sonar fish-finders, more sophisticated scuba and hunting equipment). These changes will have direct effects on the psychological context of water-based recreation behavior (i.e., motivation); they will affect the manner in which recreationists encounter (i.e., social context) one another, possibly resulting in greater displacement of low-technology participants; and they are likely to exacerbate the direct and indirect environmental quality effects of water-based recreation (Catton, 1983).

Increased Conflict among Water-Based Recreationists

An increasing pool of water-based recreationists possessing more physical limitations but an increasingly more diverse mix of motivations and experience levels and an expanded array of technology to use in pursuing their intentions will result in greater conflict among recreationists in aquatic environments (Field & Martinson, 1986). A more contentious aquatic environment has direct implications on the social context of recreational transactions. Social conflict among participants will also alter managerial context as management interventions (both direct and indirect) attempt to resolve user and use incompatibilities.

RESEARCH NEEDS

Existing water-based recreation research is incomplete in its failure to consider environmental attributes, participant characteristics, and contextual elements from a comprehensive transactional perspective. Preceding sections of this chapter describe what is known about the effects of discrete components of the transactional model on recreational experiences in aquatic environments. For the most part, however, the findings emerge from studies that examined recreational experience as a function of one or a limited number of the transactional model components.

More recent research has employed multidimensional perspectives that simultaneously examine, for example, the influence of motivation, experience level, familiarity, demographic characteristics, managerial context, and encounters with others on the quality of the river-floating experience in 13 environmental settings (Schreyer *et al.*, 1984). Even in this relatively comprehensive perspective, however, there is no mention of specific physical, institutional, or perceptual attributes of the 13 environments, no discussion of participant characteristics (other than demographic), no consideration of the information participants brought to or received during their experiences concerning behavioral norms and expectations and environmental perceptions, and no mention of the social groups with whom subjects participated in their river-floating experience.

Thus, there exists a general need to cast future water-based recreation research in a transactional perspective that better reflects the interaction of environmental attributes, participant characteristics, and psychological, social, physical, and managerial dimensions of the context of participation. The following comments discuss more specific needs with respect to studying the effects of environment, participant, and context on the nature of recreational transactions with aquatic environments.

Respecification of Criterion Measures of Quality

The recreation literature has relied extensively on participant-reported measures of satisfaction as criterion indices of the quality of recreational transactions with aquatic environments. The environmental perception literature generally uses an evaluative appraisal or a globally referent preferential judgment (as opposed to a statement of preference relative to a specific intention) as a measure of environmental attractiveness. Both criterion measures of quality need to be reconsidered.

The satisfaction derived from recreational experiences is a multidimensional phenomenon requiring multidimensional analysis. Recreationists may be pleased with their intraparty experiences and may be satisfied with the level and type of encounters they experienced with other recreationists, but they may be upset by a management decision to close a favorite but badly deteriorated picnic site. The magnitude of satisfaction with the intraparty and interparty experiences may be strong enough to mask negative reactions to management changes, producing a high global assessment of satisfaction and leaving managers to believe the public has accepted their decision.

Satisfaction can be conceptually distinguished from dissatisfaction (Stankey & McCool, 1984). Future research must differentiate between satisfaction and dissatisfaction as criterion measures of quality of transaction. The multiple dimensions of both satisfaction and dissatisfaction need further specification. The factors included in defining the multidimensionality of both criteria must move beyond the current focus on encounters with other recreationists in the social context of the transaction to include elements of the psychological, physical, and managerial context, individual characteristics of the participants, and conditions in the environment wherein the transaction occurs (Catton, 1983; Stankey & McCool, 1984). Routine procedures must be defined to operationalize the multidimensionality of both satisfaction and dissatisfaction in the context of recreation research.

In assessing environmental attractiveness as it relates to recreational transactions with aquatic environments, the psychological, social, and physical context of the transaction must be considered. This involves a shift from currently used evaluative appraisals to preferential judgments cast in the psychological, social, and physical contexts of participant intentions, social group affiliation, encounter norms, and participant mode of travel that prevail during the transaction.

More Specific Consideration of Environment Attributes

The environmental perception literature contains a strong tradition of explicitly considering environmental attributes as they contribute to the formation of environmental attractiveness (Zube, Sell, & Taylor, 1982). Through the Recreation Opportunity Spectrum (ROS), the recreation literature conceptually incorporates the influence of environmental setting attributes on recreation experience and divides these attributes into physical–biological, social, and managerial components (Clark & Stankey, 1979; Driver & Brown, 1978). As previously described in this chapter, considerable attention has focused on social and managerial aspects of the environmental settings of outdoor recreation. However, other than replicating studies across settings (e.g., Schreyer *et al.*, 1984; Williams & Knopf, 1985), the recreation literature pays little explicit attention to the influence of physical–biological setting attributes on recreation behavior and an insufficient amount of attention to the long-term consequences of recreation behavior on physical–biological setting attributes (Catton, 1983).

Current attempts to consider physical–biological attributes of recreation opportunity settings use the primitive–urban continuum of the ROS (Driver & Brown, 1978) as a means of conceptualizing the spectrum of opportunities in which different types of recreational experiences occur. Recent empirical work undermines the validity of a primitive–urban continuum as a basis for recreationists' psychological representations of environment. Among river floaters on 42 rivers through the United States, environments can be characterized on the basis of waterflow intensity and trip duration, but not on the basis of the primitive–urban continuum (Williams & Knopf, 1985). Furthermore, experience motivations (Knopf *et al.*, 1983) and encounter expectations (Shelby, 1981) are consistent across different points on the continuum.

The philosophy and procedures of research cited earlier in this chapter on cognitive differentiation of aquatic environments hold promise of being able to more validly and sensitively depict participants' psychological representations of water-based recreation places. An understanding of recreationists' perceptual typologies of waterscapes would enable researchers to relate to aquatic environments in the same terms as participants. Attributes more salient to a participant's environmental constructs could be investigated in conjunction with the participant's characteristics and psychological, social, physical, and managerial contexts of participation.

Focus on Individual Differences

There is a need to return to the early recreation research models, in which individual differences received considerable attention. However, rather than dredging for the effects of socioeconomic or demographic differences on activity preferences, this work needs to focus on personality, developmental, and cultural/ethnic effects on the formation of environmental perception and recreation experience norms. Personality measures emanating from such constructs as locus of control, cognitive flexibility, cognitive complexity, privacy seeking, and arousal or sensation-seeking need to be factored into judgments of environmental attractiveness, responses to various factors in the environment or social context of a transaction, and explanations of on-site behavior (Knopf, 1987). International currency markets have helped develop an international tourism market in the United States. As more foreign tourists visit the attractions of the United States aquatic environments, cross-cultural studies of environmental perception, and recreation behavioral norms will become increasingly important to understanding and facilitating the transactions of this market segment with aquatic environments. Coupled with a renewed focus on developmental aspects of environmental perception and norm formation, the cross-cultural studies will shed light on the relative importance of innate tendencies as opposed to learning in the formation of response to aquatic environments (Knopf, 1987).

Reformulation of Contextual Elements

Previous sections of this chapter have documented the contributions of differences in psychological, social, physical, and managerial context toward explaining variation in attractiveness perceptions, behavioral norms, and on-site behavior of water-based recreationists. Some of these contextual elements need reformulation.

In formulating the psychological context of transaction, two aspects of motivation need to be reconsidered. Some of the identified motivational factors used in previous research have subsequently been characterized as having multidimensional components. For example, the motivation of escaping civilization has been refined into several dimensions including intimacy with selected others, solitude with respect to the presence and observation of others, anonymity, reserve (avoiding self-disclosure), seclusion, and not neighboring (Hammit & Brown, 1984; Twight, Smith, & Wassinger, 1981). These findings suggest a need for further refinement of motivational measurement methodology because responses to the global statement of escaping civilization will depend on which dimension of escape a respondent uses. Motivational research also tends to cluster subjects based on responses to the scale that most potently captures motivation. Just as satisfaction is multidimensional, so also is motivation—participants do not pursue experiences for one reason alone. Thus, methodologically, motivational research needs to focus on defining the constellation of motivations that characterize a particular experience.

Two other aspects of psychological context, experience level and information set, need clarification. The plethora of research on experience level is encouraging, especially given its conceptual and empirical saliency to recreation transactions in aquatic environments. However, the call to focus on the perceptions and norms of more experienced participants (because novices have little basis for comparison and are likely to emulate their more seasoned peers) (Driver, Brown, Stankey, & Gregoire, 1987) leaves unanswered the equity issue of ignoring the specific needs and characteristics of the newcomer. The needs of novices pose unique issues for the managerial contexts of future transactions because the responsibility of acculturating novices to the social norms of a transaction falls largely on the novice's peers and the manager. The shift of older people with more physical limitations into water-based recreation suggests that managers will need more definitive characterizations of future recreationists if they are to assimilate segments of special populations into their management schema. Studies of latent demand for environmental transactions in aquatic environments are needed to characterize those most likely to enter the ranks of the water-based recreationist. The work documenting the effects on recreational transactions of information transmitted from manager to participant needs to be continued. However, the effects of additional sources and types of information (e.g., peers, media, events preceding the transaction) also need investigation.

Research investigating the effects of social and managerial context on recreational transactions needs refinement. The characteristics and dynamics of the social group with which participants are affiliated need to be examined relative to styles of interpersonal exchanges (both informational and behavioral) and their effects on norm development and enforcement. Little is known about how transactional norm development is affected by within-group social dominance hierarchies or propensity by individual group members to conform to group norms. Measurement of encounter norms needs to more sensitively reflect variation in the behavioral and physical consequences of an encounter (Gramann, 1982) and the timing and location of an encounter within a participant's planned itinerary (Shelby & Heberlein, 1986). Given the documented effects of information programs, site hardening, direct regulation of participant behavior, and other management activities on recreational transactions with an aquatic environment, it seems advisable in future research to explicitly state the managerial context of those transactions being investigated.

Technological Assessment

Given the fact that most human transactions with aquatic environments require some level of technology, an assessment of current and future technology seems particularly important to understanding water-based recreational behavior. Few would have anticipated the dramatic effects cited earlier in this chapter of advances in wind-surfing technology on the transactions of Hood River, Oregon, residents with their wind-swept environment. Better technological forecasting is needed to anticipate the character and extent of infusions of new technology into the transactions of recreationists with aquatic environments. Further focus is needed on the sources of asymmetrical antipathies among recreationists employing different levels of technology. Strategies to mitigate the negative externalities realized by low-technology participants need to be investigated. Technological advancements in water-related recreation must also be examined in terms of their direct and indirect consequences on the quality of aquatic environments and their comprehensive spillover effects into adjacent terrestrial biomes (e.g., the economic development boom associated with windsurfing in Hood River, Oregon).

Monitoring and Longitudinal Studies

Much of the existing outdoor recreation research relies on cross-sectional data gathered from a particular set of experiences of a group of people in a specific setting at one point in time. Cross-sectional analyses are unable to systematically examine inherent environmental or behavioral changes that occur on a daily, weekly, seasonal, annual, and cyclical basis. The effects of inherent environmental changes need to be incorporated into research seeking the identification of environmental setting attributes salient to recreational transactions. Although the environmental impacts of discrete recreational transactions are relatively low, the cumulative effects of many transactions over time can be substantial. Cumulative effects often manifest themselves only through monitoring of environmental conditions from a baseline characterization. As recreationists gain experience with a particular transaction or environment, their perceptions, attitudes, and behaviors with respect to environment change. The feedback of environmental change on setting attribute saliency, the cumulative environmental impacts of recreational transactions, and the effects of environmental or transactional experience are best examined through monitoring of aquatic environmental conditions and longitudinal studies of recreation behavior in aquatic environments.

From Discovery to Justification

Much of the research on water-based recreation in rural and natural settings has emerged from a discovery context—involving "tabular analyses of opinion polls . . . dedicated to the formation of information and conjecture." Very little of the existing work has been cast in the context of justification— "the process of validating new knowledge, new theories and new hypotheses. Studies involving working hypotheses that formalize conjecture and force it to the test are the exception rather than the rule" (Knopf, 1986, p. 305). Both discovery and justification are important dimensions of theory building with respect to recreational transactions in aquatic environments, and a balance is needed between discovery and justification. However, greater emphasis needs to be placed on testing conjecture if universalities of recreation behavior in aquatic environments are to emerge.

REFERENCES

Adelman, B. J. E., Heberlein, T. A., & Bonnickson, T. M. (1982). Social psychological explanations for the persistence of a conflict between paddling canoeists and motorcraft users in the Boundary Waters Canoe Area. *Leisure Sciences, 5*(1), 45–61.

Aiello, J. F., Gordon, B., & Farrel, T. S. (1974). Description of children's outdoor activities in a suburban residential area: Preliminary findings. In D. H. Carson (Ed.), *EDRA5: Man-environment interactions: Evaluations and applications—the state of the art in environmental design research* (Vol. 12, pp. 157–196). Stroudsburg, PA: Dowden, Hutchinson & Ross.

Amedeo, D., Pitt, D. G., & Zube, E. H. (1989). Landscape feature classification as a determinant of perceived scenic value. *Landscape Journal, 8*(1), in press.

Anderson, D. H. (1980). Long-time Boundary Waters' visitors change use patterns. *Naturalist, 3*(4), 2–5.

Anderson, D. H., & Brown, P. J. (1984). The displacement process in recreation. *Journal of Leisure Research, 16*(1), 61–73.
Anderson, D. H. & Manfredo, M. J. (1986). Visitor preferences for management actions. In R. C. Lucas (Ed.), *Proceedings—National Wilderness Research Conference: Current research*, (USDA-Forest Service General Tech. Rep. No. INT-212, pp. 314–319). Ogden, UT: Intermountain Research Station.
Appleton, J. (1975). *The experience of landscape*. New York: Wiley.
Baker, N. J., & Huck, J. (1987, August 24), A boardhead's paradise. *Newsweek*, p. 59.
Balling, J. D., & Falk, J. H. (1982). Development of visual preference for natural environments. *Environment and Behavior, 14*, 5–28.
Bishop, D. W., & Ikeda, M. (1970). Status and role factors in the leisure behavior of different occupations. *Sociology and Social Research, 44*, 190–208.
Brush, R. O., & Palmer, J. F. (1979). Measuring the impact of urbanization on scenic quality: Land use change in the northeast. In G. Elsner & R. S. Smardon (Eds.), *Our national landscape* (USDA-Forest Service General Tech. Rep. No. PSW-35, pp. 358–364). Berkeley, CA: Pacific Southwest Forest and Range Experiment Station.
Bryan, H. (1977). Leisure value systems and recreational specialization: The case of trout fishermen. *Journal of Leisure Research,9*(3), 174–187.
Buhyoff, G. J., & Leuschner, W. A. (1978). Estimating psychological disutility from damaged forest stands. *Forest Science, 26*, 227–230.
Bunting, T. E., & Cousins, L. R. (1985). Environmental dispositions among school-aged children: A preliminary investigation. *Environment and Behavior, 17*, 725–768.
Burch, W. R. Jr., & Wenger, W. D., Jr. (1967). The social characteristics of participants in three styles of family camping (USDA Forest Service Research Paper No. PNW-48). Portland, OR: Pacific Northwest Forest and Range Experiment Station.
Catton, W. R., Jr. (1983). Social and behavioral aspects of carrying capacity in natural environments. In I. Altman & J. F. Wohlwill (Eds.), *Human behavior and environment: Advances in theory and research: Vol. 6. Behavior and the natural environment* (pp. 269–306). New York: Plenum Press.
Clark, R. N., & Stankey, G. H. (1979). Determining the acceptability of recreational impacts: An application of the Outdoor Recreation Opportunity Spectrum. In R. Ittner, D. R. Potter, J. K. Ayee, & L. Anschell (Eds.), *Recreational impact on wildlands* (pp. 32–42; USDA-Forest Service Report No. R-6-001-1979). Portland, OR: Pacific Northwest Forest and Range Experiment Station.
Cockrell, D., & McLaughlin, W. J. (1982). Social influences on wild river recreationists. In D. W. Lime (Ed.), *Forest and river recreation: Research update* (Miscellaneous Publication 18-1982, pp. 140–145). St. Paul, MN: University of Minnesota, Agricultural Experiment Station.
Colton, C. W., Pitt, D. G., Morgan, J. M., III, & Chaney, T. H. (1979). Behaviors and perceptions of recreational boaters. In *First Annual Conference on Recreation Planning and Development: Proceedings* (pp. 171–179). New York: American Society of Civil Engineers.
Coughlin, R. E. (1976). The perception and valuation of water quality: A review of research method and findings. In K. H. Craik & E. H. Zube (Eds.), *Perceiving environmental quality: Research and applications* (pp. 205–227). New York: Plenum Press.
Cowdin, N. P. (1986). Conceptions and behaviors of recreationists regarding water quality in Rocky Mountain National Park. In R. C. Lucas (Ed.), *Proceedings—National Wilderness Research Conference: Current research* (USDA-Forest Service General Tech. Rep. No. INT-212, pp. 241–244). Ogden, UT: Intermountain Research Station.
Daniel, T. C., & Boster, R. S. (1976). *Measuring landscape aesthetics: the scenic beauty estimation method* (USDA-Forest Service Research Paper No. RM-167). Fort Collins, CO: Rocky Mountain Forest and Range Experiment Station.
Deardon, P. (1984). Factors influencing landscape preferences: An empirical investigation. *Landscape Planning, 11*, 293–306.

Dearinger, J. A. (1979). Measuring preferences for natural landscapes. *Journal of the Urban Planning and Development Division, ASCE, 105,* 63–80.
Ditton, R. B., Fedler, A. J., & Graefe, A. R. (1983). Factors contributing to perceptions of recreational crowding. *Leisure Sciences, 5,* 273–288.
Dowell, D. L., & McCool, S. F. (1986). Evaluation of a wilderness information dissemination program. In R. C. Lucas (Ed.), *Proceedings—National Wilderness Research Conference: Current research* (USDA-Forest Service General Tech. Rep. No. INT-212, pp. 494–500). Ogden, UT: Intermountain Research Station.
Driver, B. L., & Basset, J. R. (1975). Defining conflicts among river users: A case study of Michigan's AuSable River. *Naturalist, 26,* 19–23.
Driver, B. L., & Brown, P. J. (1978). The opportunity spectrum concept and behavioral information in outdoor recreation resource supply inventories: A rationale. In H. G. Lund, V. J. LaBan, P. F. Ffolliott, & D. W. Robinson (Eds.), *Integrated inventories of renewable natural resources* (USDA-Forest Service General Tech. Rep. No. RM-55, pp. 24–32). Fort Collins, CO: Rocky Mountain Forest and Range Experiment Station.
Driver, B. L., Brown, P. J., Stankey, G. H., & Gregoire, T. C. (1987). The ROS planning system: Evolution, basic concepts and research needed. *Leisure Science, 9,* 201–212.
Driver, B. L., & Knopf, R. C. (1977). Personality, outdoor recreation and expected consequences. *Environment and Behavior, 9,* 169–193.
Driver, B. L., & Tocher, R. C. (1970). Toward a behavioral interpretation of recreational engagements with implications for planning. In B. L. Driver (Ed.), *Elements of outdoor recreation planning* (pp. 9–31). Ann Arbor, MI: University Microfilms.
Dubos, R. (1980). *The wooing of the earth.* New York: Scribners.
Fedler, A. J., & Kuss, F. R. (1986). An examination of the effects of wilderness designation on hiker attitudes. In R. C. Lucas (Ed.), *Proceedings—National Wilderness Research Conference: Current research* (USDA-Forest Service General Tech. Rep. No. INT-212, pp. 308–313). Ogden, UT: Intermountain Research Station.
Field, D. R., & Martinson, K. (1986). Water-based recreation participation. In The President's Commission on Americans Outdoors (Ed.), *A literature review* (pp. 49–58). Washington, DC: U.S. Government Printing Office.
Fisher, A. C., & Krutilla, J. V. (1972). Determination of optimal capacity of resource-based recreation facilities. *Natural Resources Journal, 12,* 417–444.
Graefe, A. R., Vaske, J. J., & Kuss, F. R. (1984). Social carrying capacity: An integration and synthesis of twenty years of research. *Leisure Sciences, 6,* 395–431.
Gramann, J. H. (1982). Toward a behavioral theory of crowding in outdoor recreation: An evaluation and synthesis of research. *Leisure Sciences, 5*(2), 109–126.
Gramann, J. H., & Burdge, R. J. (1984). Crowding perceptions determinants at intensively developed outdoor recreation sites. *Leisure Science, 6*(4), 167–186.
Gratzer, M. A., & McDowell, R. D. (1971). *Adaptation of an eye movement recorder to esthetic environmental mensuration* (Research Rep. No. 36). Storrs, CN: University of Connecticut, Agricultural Experiment Station.
Hammitt, W. E. (1981). The familiarity-preference component of on-site recreational experiences. *Leisure Sciences, 4,* 177–193.
Hammitt, W. E. (1983). Toward an ecological approach to perceived crowding in outdoor recreation. *Leisure Sciences, 5,* 309–320.
Hammitt, W. E., & Brown, G. F. Jr. (1984). Functions of privacy in wilderness environments. *Leisure Sciences, 6,* 151–166.
Hardin, G. (1968). The tragedy of the commons. *Science, 162,* 1243–1248.
Heberlein, T. A. (1977). Density, crowding, and satisfaction: Sociological studies for determining carrying capacities. In *River recreation management and research.* (USDA-Forest Service General Tech. Rep. No. NC-28, pp. 67–76). St. Paul, MN: North Central Forest Experiment Station.

Heberlein, T. A., & Shelby, B. (1977). Carrying capacity, values, and the satisfaction model: A reply to Greist. *Journal of Leisure Research, 9* 142–148.
Hecock, R. D. (1970). Recreation behavior patterns as related to site characteristics of beaches. *Journal of Leisure Research, 2,* 237–250.
Hendee, J. C., Catton, W. R., Jr., Marlow, C. O., & Brockman, C. F. (1968). *Wilderness users in the Pacific Northwest—their characteristics, values and management preferences* (USDA-Forest Service Research Paper No. PNW-61). Portland, OR: Pacific Northwest Forest and Range Experiment Station.
Herzog, T. R. (1985). A cognitive analysis of preference of waterscapes. *Journal of Environmental Psychology, 5,* 225–241.
Heywood, J. L. (1987). Experience preferences of participants in different types of river recreation groups. *Journal of Leisure Research, 19*(1), 1–12.
Hodgson, R. W., & Thayer, R. L. (1980). Implied human influence reduces landscape beauty. *Landscape Planning, 7,* 171–179.
Hoots, T. A. (1976). Vandalism and law enforcement on National Forest lands. In *Vandalism and outdoor recreation.* (USDA-Forest Service General Tech. Rep. No. PSW-17, pp. 20–23). Berkeley, CA: Pacific Southwest Forest and Range Experiment Station.
Ittelson, W. H. (1973). *Environment and cognition.* New York: Seminar Press.
Jackson, E. L., & Wong, R. A. G. (1982). Perceived conflict between urban cross-country skiers and snowmobilers in Alberta. *Journal of Leisure Research, 14*(1), 47–62.
Johnston, G. A. (1988). The role of economics in natural resource and environmental policy analyses. In G. Johnston, D. W. Freshwater, & P. Favero (Eds.), *Natural resource and environmental policy analysis.* Boulder, CO: Westview Press.
Kaplan, R. (1973). Predictors of environmental preference: Designers and clients. In W. F. E. Preiser (Ed.), *Environmental design research* (pp. 265–274). Stroudsburg, PA: Dowden, Hutchinson & Ross.
Kaplan, R. (1977). Preference and everyday nature: Method and application. In D. Stokols (Ed.), *Perspectives on environment and behavior: Theory, research and application* (pp. 235–250). New York: Plenum Press.
Kaplan, S., & Kaplan, R. (1982). *Cognition and environment.* New York: Praeger.
Kelly, J. R. (1980). Outdoor recreation participation: A comparative analysis. *Leisure Sciences, 3,* 129–154.
Knopf, R. C. (1976). *Relationships between desired consequences of recreation engagements and conditions in home neighborhood environments.* Unpublished doctoral dissertation, University of Michigan, Ann Arbor. Dissertation Abstracts International, 37/06A: 3897.
Knopf, R. C. (1986). Wilderness attitudes and behavior research—from here to where? In R. Lucas, (Ed.), *Proceedings—National Wilderness Conference: Current research,* (USDA-Forest Service General Tech. Rep. No. INT-212, pp. 305–307). Ogden, UT: Intermountain Research Station.
Knopf, R. C. (1987). Human behavior, cognition and affect in the natural environment. In D. Stokols & I. Altman (Eds.), *Handbook of environmental psychology* (pp. 783–825). New York: Wiley.
Knopf, R. C., Driver, B. L., & Basset, J. R. (1973). Motivations for fishing. In *Human dimensions in wildlife programs* (pp. 28–41). Washington DC: Wildlife Management Institute.
Knopf, R. C., & Lime, D. W. (1984). *A recreation manager's guide to understanding river use and users* (USDA Forest Service General Tech. Rep. No. WO-38). Washington, DC: U.S. Department of Agriculture-Forest Service.
Knopf, R. C., Peterson, G. L., & Leatherberry, E. C. (1983). Motives of recreational river floating: Relative consistency across settings. *Leisure Sciences, 5,* 231–255.
Knopp, T. B. (1972). Environmental determinants of recreational behavior. *Journal of Leisure Research, 4,* 129–138.
Krumpe, E. E., & Brown, P. J. (1982). Redistributing backcountry use through information related to recreational experiences. *Journal of Forestry, 80,* 360–362.

Krutilla, J. V., & Fisher, A. C. (1975). *The economics of natural environments.* Baltimore: Johns Hopkins University Press.
Lime, D. W. (1972). *Large groups in the Boundary Waters Canoe Area—their numbers, characteristics, and impact.* (USDA Forest Service Research Note No. NC-142). St. Paul, MN: North Central Forest Experiment Station.
Lime, D. W. (1975). Sources of congestion and visitor dissatisfaction in the Boundary Waters Canoe Area. In *Proceedings, Quetico-Superior Foundation 1975 Institute on the Boundary Waters Canoe Area* (pp. 68–82). Ely, MN: Quetico-Superior Foundation.
Lime, D. W. (1983). Water, water, everywhere for Americans at play. In J. Hayes (Ed.), *Using our natural resources, 1983 yearbook of agriculture* (pp. 326–335). Washington, DC: U.S. Government Printing Office.
Lime, D. W. (1986). River recreation and natural resource management: A focus on river running and boating. In The President's Commission on Americans Outdoors (Ed.), *A Literature Review* (pp. 137–150). Washington, DC: U.S. Government Printing Office.
Lime, D. W., & Lucas, R. C. (1977). Good information improves the wilderness experience. *Naturalist, 28*(4), 18–20.
Litton, R. B., Jr., Tetlow, R. J., Sorensen, J., & Beatty, R. A. (1974). *Water and landscape: An aesthetic overview of the role of water in the landscape.* Port Washington, NY: Port Washington Press.
Lorenz, K. Z. (1952). *King Solomon's ring.* London: Methuen.
Lucas, R. C. (1964). *The recreational capacity of the Quetico-Superior area* (USDA-Forest Service Research Paper No. LS-15). St. Paul, MN: Lake States Forest Experiment Station.
Lucas, R. C. (1980). *Use patterns and visitor characteristics, attitudes and preferences in nine wilderness and other roadless areas* (USDA Forest Service Research Paper No. INT-253). Ogden, UT: Intermountain Forest and Range Experiment Station.
Macia, A. (1979). Visual perception of landscape: Sex and personality differences. In G. H. Elsner & R. C. Smarron (Eds.), *Proceedings of Our National Landscape Conference* (USDA-Forest Service General Tech. Rep. No. PSW-35, pp. 279–285). Berkeley, CA: Pacific Southwest Forest and Range Experiment Station.
Manning, R. E. (1986). *Studies in outdoor recreation.* Corvallis, OR: Oregon State University Press.
Marcus, L. S. (1977). Within city limits: Nature and children's books about nature in the city. In *Children, nature and the urban environment* (USDA-Forest Service General Tech. Rep. No. NE-30, pp. 83–88). Upper Darby, PA: Northeastern Forest Experiment Station.
McAvoy, L. (1982). Management techniques preferred by user and landowners along a state river. In D. W. Lime (Ed.), *Forest and river recreation: Research update.* (Miscellaneous Publication No. 18-1982, pp. 20–25). St. Paul, MN: University of Minnesota, Agricultural Experiment Station.
McDonough, M. H., & Field, D. R. (1979). *Coulee Dam National Recreation Area: Visitor use patterns and preferences.* Seattle, WA: University of Washington.
McKechnie, G. E. (1974). The psychological structure of leisure: Past behavior. *Journal of Leisure Research, 6,* 27–45.
More, T. A., & Buhyoff, G. (1979). *Managing recreation areas for quality experience: A theoretical framework* (USDA Forest Service Research Paper No. NE-432). Upper Darby, PA: Northeastern Forest Experiment Station.
Moser, G. (1984). Water quality perception, a dynamic evaluation. *Journal of Environmental Psychology, 4,* 201–210.
Nash, R. (1977). River recreation: history and future. In *River Recreation Management and Research Symposium Proceedings* (USDA-Forest Service General Tech. Rep. No. NC-28, pp. 2–7). St. Paul, MN: North Central Forest Experiment Station.
Nieman, T. J. (1980). The visual environment of the New York coastal zone: User preferences and perceptions. *Coastal Zone Management Journal, 8,* 45–62.

Odum, E. P. (1971). *Fundamental of ecology* (3rd ed.). Philadelphia: W. B. Saunders.
Oliver, S. S., Roggenbuck, J. W., & Watson, A. E. (1985). Education to reduce impacts in forest campgrounds. *Journal of Forestry, 83*, 234–236.
Palmer, J., & Zube, E. H. (1976). Numerical and perceptual landscape classification. In E. H. Zube (Ed.), *Studies in landscape perception* (pp. 43–57). Amherst: University of Massachusetts, Institute for Man and Environment.
Peterson, G. L., Lime, D. W., & Anderson, D. H. (1981). *Attraction of recreationists to rivers: A nationwide review* (USDA-Forest Service General Tech. Rep. No. NC-63, pp. 18–26). St. Paul, MN: North Central Forest Experiment Station.
Pitt, D. G., Chaney, T. H., & Colton, C. W. (1981). A perceptually based definition of valued boating environments on the tributaries of the Chesapeake Bay. *Landscape Research, 5*(3), 19–21.
Pitt, D. G., & Zube, E. H. (1987). Management of natural environments. In D. Stokols & I. Altman (Eds.), *Handbook of environmental psychology* (pp. 1009–1042). New York: Wiley.
Pitt, D. G., Zube, E. H., & Palmer, J. F. (1980). *Regional and demographic perspectives on landscape perception.* Paper presented at annual meeting of Council of Educators on Landscape Architecture, Madison, WI, August, 1980.
Roggenbuck, J. W., & Bange, S. P. (1983). *An assessment of the float trip carrying capacity of the New River Gorge National River.* Blacksburg, VA: Virginia Polytechnical Institute and State University, Department of Forestry.
Roggenbuck, J. W., & Berrier, D. L. (1982). A comparison of the effectiveness of two communication strategies in dispersing wilderness campers. *Journal of Leisure Research, 14*(1), 77–79.
Sagoff, M. (1985). Fact and value in ecological science. *Environmental Ethics, 7*, 99–116.
Schreyer, R., Lime, D. W., & Williams, D. R. (1984). Characterizing the influence of past experience on recreation behavior. *Journal of Leisure Research, 16*(1), 34–50.
Schreyer, R., & Roggenbuck, J. W. (1978). The influence of experience expectation on crowding perceptions and social-psychological carrying capacities. *Leisure Sciences, 4*, 373–394.
Schreyer, R., Roggenbuck, J. W., McCool, S. F., Royer, L. E., & Miller, S. (1976). *The Dinosaur National Monument whitewater river recreation study.* Logan, UT: Utah State University, Department of Forestry and Outdoor Recreation, Institute for the Study of Outdoor Recreation and Tourism.
Shafer, E. L., Jr., Hamilton, J. F., Jr., & Schmidt, E. A. (1969). Natural landscape preferences: A predictive model. *Journal of Leisure Research, 1*, 1–19.
Shelby, B. (1981). Encounter norms in backcountry settings: Studies of three rivers. *Journal of Leisure Research, 13*(2), 129–138.
Shelby, B., & Heberlein, T. A. (1986). *Carrying capacity in recreation settings.* Corvallis, OR: Oregon State University Press.
Shepherd, P., Jr. (1961). The cross valley syndrome. *Landscape, 10*(3), 4–8.
Sitte, C. (1965). Greenery within the city. In C. Sitte (Ed.), *City planning according to artistic principles* (pp. 167–185; C. R. Collins & C. C. Collins, Trans.). New York: Random House. (Original work published 1889.)
Sonnenfeld, J. (1967). Environmental perception and adaptation level in the Arctic. In D. Lowenthal (Ed.), *Environmental perception and behavior* (Department of Geography Research Paper No. 109, pp. 42–59). Chicago, IL: University of Chicago.
Stainbrook, E. (1969). Human needs and the natural environment. In *Man and nature in the city* (pp. 1–6). Washington, DC: U.S. Department of the Interior, Bureau of Sport Fisheries and Wildlife.
Stankey, G. H. (1973). *Visitor perception of wilderness recreation carrying capacity* (USDA-Forest Service Research Paper No. INT-142). Ogden, UT: Intermountain Forest and Range Experiment Station.
Stankey, G. H., & McCool, S. F. (1984). Carrying capacity in recreational settings: Evolution, appraisal and application. *Leisure Sciences, 6*, 453–473.

Titre, J., & Mills, A. S. (1982). Effect of encounters on perceived crowding and satisfaction. In D. W. Lime (Ed.), *Forest and river recreation: Research update* (Miscellaneous publication No. 18-1982, pp. 146–153). St. Paul, MN: University of Minnesota Agricultural Experiment Station.

Tuan, Y. F. (1974). *Topophilia: A study of environmental perception, attitudes and values.* Englewood Cliffs, NJ: Prentice-Hall.

Twight, B. W., Smith, K. L., & Wassinger, G. H. (1981). Privacy and camping: Closeness to the self vs. closeness to others. *Leisure Sciences, 4,* 427–441.

Udd, E., & Fridgen, J. D. (1986). Angler's perceptions of toxic chemicals in rivers and sport fish. In R. C. Lucas (Ed.), *Proceedings-National Wilderness Research Conference: Current research* (USDA-Forest Service General Tech. Rep. No. INT-212, pp. 245–250). Odgen UT: Intermountain Research Station.

Ulrich, R. S. (1979). Visual landscapes and psychological well-being. *Landscape Research, 4,* 17–23.

Ulrich, R. S. (1981). Natural versus urban scenes: Some psycho-physiological effects. *Environment and Behavior, 13,* 523–556.

Ulrich, R. S. (1983). Aesthetic and affective response to natural environments. In I. Altman & J. F. Wohlwill (Eds.), *Human behavior and environment: Vol. 6. Behavior and the natural environment* (pp. 85–125). New York: Plenum Press.

U.S. Environmental Protection Agency. (1983). *Chesapeake Bay: A framework for action.* Annapolis, MD: Author.Vaske, J. J., Donnelly, M. P., & Heberlein, T. A. (1980). Perceptions of crowding and resource quality by early and more recent visitors. *Leisure Sciences, 3,* 367–381.

Vaske, J. J., Donnelly, M. P., & Heberlein, T. A. (1980). Perceptions of crowding and resource quality by early and more recent visitors. *Leisure Sciences, 3,* 367–381.

Vaske, J. J., Fedler, A. J., & Graefe, A. R. (1986). Multiple determinants of satisfaction from a specific waterfowl hunting trip. *Leisure Sciences, 8,* 149–166.

Vaske, J. J., Graefe, A. R., & Dempster, A. (1982). Social and environmental influences on perceived crowding. In L. K. Canon (Ed.), *Proceedings of The Wilderness Psychology Group Conference* (pp. 211–227). Morgantown, WV: West Virginia University.

Wellman, J. D. (1979). Recreational response to privacy stress: A validation study. *Journal of Leisure Research, 11,* 61–73.

Wellman, J. D., & Buhyoff, G. J. (1980). Effects of regional familiarity on landscape preferences. *Journal of Environmental Management, 11,* 105–110.

Wellman, J. D., Dawson, M. S., & Roggenbuck, J. W. (1982). Park managers' prediction of the motivations of visitors to two National Park Service areas. *Journal of Leisure Research, 14,* 1–15.

Wendling, R. C. (1980). Black/white differences in outdoor recreation behavior: State-of-the-art and recommendations for management and research. *Proceedings—social research in national parks and wildland areas* (pp. 106–117). Atlanta, GA: U.S. Department of the Interior, National Park Service.

Williams, D. R., & Knopf, R. C. (1985). In search of the primitive-urban continuum: The dimensional structure of outdoor recreation settings. *Environment and Behavior, 17,* 351–370.

Williams, M. L. (1976). Vandals aren't all bad. In *Vandalism and outdoor recreation* (USDA-Forest Service General Tech. Rep. No. PSW-17, pp. 46–50). Berkeley, CA: Pacific Southwest Forest and Range Experiment Station.

Womble, P., & Studebaker, S. (1981). Crowding in a national park campground: Katwai National Monument in Alaska. *Environment and Behavior, 13,* 557–573.

Yoesting, D. R., & Christensen, J. E. (1978). Reexamining the significance of childhood recreation patterns on adult leisure behavior. *Leisure Sciences, 1,* 219–229.

Zube, E. H. (1980). *Environmental evaluation: Perception and public policy.* Monterey, CA: Brooks/Cole.

Zube, E. H., & Pitt, D. G. (1981). Cross-cultural perceptions of scenic and heritage landscapes. *Landscape Planning, 8,* 69–87.

Zube, E. H., Pitt, D. G., & Anderson, T. W. (1974). *Perception and measurement of scenic resources in the Southern Connecticut River Valley* (Publication No. R-74-1). Amherst, MA: University of Massachusetts, Institute for Man and Environment.

Zube, E. H., Pitt, D. G., & Evans, G. W. (1983). A lifespan developmental study of landscape assessment. *Journal of Environmental Psychology, 3,* 115–128.

Zube, E. H., Sell, J. L., & Taylor, J. G. (1982). Landscape perception: Research application and theory. *Landscape Planning, 9,* 1–33.

10

Managing Parks as Human Ecosystems

GARY E. MACHLIS

INTRODUCTION

It is late spring in a western national park. As the air and soil warm with longer days, the snow melts, and the alpine meadows are increasingly uncovered. Bear move in the lower valleys, and backpackers begin a yearly migration along their favorite routes to camping sites at the high elevations. As the spring turns to early summer, the number of employees and visitors climb, gift shops and restaurants open, the payrolls grow, electricity, water, and gasoline consumption rise. Underground, sewer systems flow at increased rates, leach fields swell, wildflowers break through along roadways and trails. The pace of life in the park quickens, for the deer, elk, fish, and people.

Parks have their particular rhythms, and members of *Homo sapiens*—visitors, local residents, rangers, concessioners, and bureaucrats—are part of them. To manage without a sense of these rhythms is unrealistic, myopic, poor husbandry in the agricultural sense, and perhaps dangerous. The purpose of this chapter is to argue a particular theory of park management, that is, the value in managing parks as human ecosystems. Park management involves an endless series of often difficult decisions, most with tradeoffs and unforeseen consequences. A sound theoretical framework can be invaluable for making environmental choices that are coherent, far-sighted, and effective. In this respect, sound theory is a very necessary and practical tool.

GARY E. MACHLIS • Department of Forest Resources, College of Forestry, Wildlife, and Range Sciences, University of Idaho, Moscow, ID 83843. Portions of this chapter are adapted from "The Human Ecology of Parks" by Gary E. Machlis, Donald R. Field, and Fred L. Campbell. *Leisure Sciences* 4(3):195–212, 1981, and *The state of the world's parks: An international assessment for resource management, policy, and research* by Gary E. Machlis and David L. Tichnell, 1985, Boulder, CO: Westview Press.

First, several key assumptions about people and parks are presented, derived from the disciplines of sociobiology, anthropology, ecology, and sociology. Following is a brief description of the ecological perspective—the roots of human ecology and the key variables and processes human ecology addresses. This perspective is then applied specifically to parks.

Next, the role of people in park management is examined in more detail, first focusing on visitors and then the local communities that are often interdependent with national parks. Efforts to model park ecosystems are discussed and the need to include people in these models is argued. Finally, the implications of the material—especially for research—are suggested.

KEY ASSUMPTIONS

The rationale for managing parks as human ecosystems is simple: *increased ecological understanding of people can lead to better management of both people and park resources.* Several assumptions underlie this argument, and these are discussed below.

Assumption 1. Homo sapiens is both natural and cultural. A significant portion of human social behavior is biologically determined. *Homo sapiens* is also a unique species, with special traits that make it wide-ranging, dominant, and capable of wide behavioral variation.

Support for this assumption comes from the emerging discipline of sociobiology, as well as anthropology and sociology. The sociobiologists argue that when social behavior is related to natural selection, an organism should behave so as to maximize the fitness of its genes—that is, its ability to reproduce. Studies of parent–child relations, sibling rivalry, and kin networks in higher primates and man have selectively supported this idea (Barash, 1982). Biological evolution has set broad constraints on *Homo sapiens'* behavior, and within these constraints, culture and environment steer our course. These constraints can be considered to be *biosocial demands*, and must be met. Examples include nutritional minimums, the long period of infant care in humans, the need to order sexual relations (Burch & DeLuca, 1984).

This suggests that there are a set of human behaviors in parks that are predictable and universal. Such common regularities, such as the need for sustenance, shelter, and protection of the young, may guide significant portions of human behavior in parks.

Yet, our species *is* different; our conspecifics are varied. Humans have the unique capability of complex language and can communicate (with the written word) across time as well as space, unlike other social animals (Chomsky, 1972). We use symbols that transmit emotional messages as well as information and have myth and religion to guide our behaviors into morally approved channels. Our technologies, even among the most nonindustrialized human populations, are powerful and complex, and among industrial societies they are characterized by immense inputs of energy, resources, and information. And our organizational skills are unparalleled in nature: humans have complex hierarchies, intricate rules or norms for behavior, the ability to assume several different social roles almost simultaneously, and so forth.

Hence, we find around us wide variety in certain behaviors. Consider food habits:

> Americans eat oysters but not snails. The French eat snails but not locusts. The Zulus eat locusts but not fish. The Jews eat fish but not pork. The Hindus eat pork but not beef. The Russians eat beef but not snakes. The Chinese eat snakes but not people. The Jale of New Guinea find people delicious. (Robertson, 1981, p. 62)

Other behaviors—the way we work, make love, fight, play, and so on—are also culturally specific.

Hence, there are a set of human behaviors in parks that are widely divergent, socially influenced, and relatively fluid and changing. For example, in a time-budget study of foreign visitors at Grand Canyon National Park, significant differences were found between Japanese and European tourists relative to the time spent in certain visitor activities (Machlis & Wenderoth, 1982). Likewise, activities such as cross-country skiing, kayaking, and high-impact camping may rise and fall in popularity and social approval.

Assumption 2. Homo sapiens is ecologically interdependent with the natural world and can best be understood from this perspective.

As the anthropologist Robert Redfield (1963) noted, all societies have world views, that is, visions outward from themselves that explain and describe their role and responsibilities. Western industrialized societies, with a history of technological, scientific, and economic expansion, largely share a view characterized by human exceptionalism and an exuberance for exploiting nature (Catton & Dunlap, 1980; White, 1967).

In contrast to this dominant western world view is the ecological perspective, which assumes a connectedness between human values, human behavior, and the environment. This is not a new or widely held paradigm, though it is gaining support as the complexity of man's role on earth becomes more apparent. Rene Dubos in his book *The Wooing of Earth* (1980) states:

> The ecological image of human life that is now emerging is in part a consequence of concern for environmental degradation. It has also been influenced by the development of new scientific disciplines such as cybernetics, information sciences, general systems theory, and hierarchy theory. Its more profound origin, however, is the increased awareness of the intimate interdependence between human beings and their total environment. (p. 146)

This assumption is powerful, for once adopted, it demands humility—from resource managers, from visitors, from our expectations of what park management can and cannot do. The eruption of Mt. St. Helens, beach erosion on Fire Island, the etching of monuments by acid rain, all remind us of the difficulty in managing nature to meet human objectives.

With these assumptions—(1) *Homo sapiens* is a biological species with certain biosocial behaviors, yet unique in its cultural variation, and (2) part of a much wider web of nature—we turn to the details of an ecological perspective applied first to human activity generally, and then to park management specifically.

THE ROOTS OF HUMAN ECOLOGY

The roots of human ecology lie primarily in general ecology, sociology, and anthropology, as documented by comprehensive literature reviews (e.g., Bruhn, 1974; Micklin, 1977). Frederick Clements' influential work *Plant Succession* (1916) began the formal development of ecological principles, and the ecologists' work was soon applied to human activity; sociologists spearheaded the effort.

The application of general ecological principles to human activity was sparked by sociologists at the University of Chicago, where, in the 1920s and 30s, the field of sociology experienced rapid growth. The appeal of the ecological viewpoint lay in the wide intellectual scope it offered. Sociologists Park and Burgess drew analogies between natural and human communities, describing society's symbiotic and competitive relationships as an organic web (Faris, 1967).

The aggregate, or community, was the common ecological unit of analysis, and it became the appropriate unit of analysis for human ecology as well (Hawley, 1950, 1968). Park and Burgess used Chicago as a "social laboratory." Their students gathered data throughout the city, resulting in an analytic emphasis on mapping. Maps were made of occurrences of crime, juvenile delinquency, tenant residences, and so forth. Figure 1 is an example; the city of Columbus is divided into economic areas to reveal the geographic distribution of wealth.

Space and time became key descriptors of community structure. McKenzie defined human ecology as "the study of the spatial and temporal relations of human beings as affected by . . . forces of the environment" (1968:41). The Chicago School also used maps to learn about community structure, using the distribution of services to define the boundaries of a rural community. Recently, Hawley has provided a unified and systematic rendering of this perspective in *Human Ecology: A Theoretical Essay* (Hawley, 1986).

THE HUMAN ECOLOGICAL PERSPECTIVE

The essence of this general approach is a recognition of *Homo sapiens* as a part of nature; the human ecosystem is its basic unit of analysis. The human ecosystem is defined by the interaction of *population, social organization,* and *technology* in response to *environment* (Catton, 1987; Duncan, 1964). These are in effect human ecology's "master variables"; their interaction is human ecology's major concern.

For the human ecologist, it is the behavior of aggregates that is of special

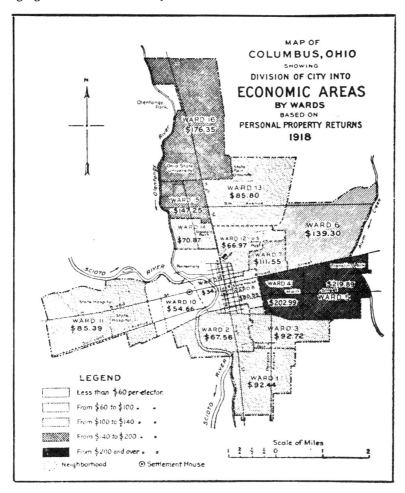

Figure 1. Economic areas of Columbus, Ohio. (From Hawley, A. H., *Roderick D. McKenzie on human ecology*. Chicago: University of Chicago Press, 1968, p. 58.)

interest—whether it be the study of Tsembaga tribesmen, the analysis of Chicago neighborhoods, or efforts to measure the impact of camping parties on alpine habitat. As Vayda and Rappaport (1976) state,

> The units important to ecologists are populations (groups of organisms living within a given area and belonging to the same species or variety) communities (all of the populations within a given area), and ecosystems (either individual organisms, populations, or communities, together with their non-living environments). (p. 22)

Human ecosystems are dynamic and adaptive; that is, the relations linking human populations to the environment can change over time. As Micklin (1977) and Hawley (1986) suggest, the analytic problem for ecological analysis is to explain these variations in adaptation. Human ecology asks, what conditions give rise to adaptive change? Why do some ecological units adapt more readily than others? What strategies of adaptation are available, and what are their consequences?

"Adaptation" is a crucial term here. The biologist's concept of adaptation has at least two meanings: evolutionary genetic change and mechanisms used by organisms during their lifespan to cope with the environment (Ricklefs, 1973). Although evolutionary genetic change has been influential (the sociobiological argument), short-term adaptation within the human ecosystem is largely based on the importance of coping. Unlike other species, humans engage in adaptation that includes a large measure of conscious choice. Bennett (1976) writes:

> The rational or purposive manipulation of the social and natural environments constitutes the human approach to Nature: the characteristics of this style of adaptation must, it seems to me, become the heart of any approach to human ecology that concerns itself with the question of what people want and how they go about getting it, and what effects this has had on themselves and Nature. (p. 3)

In summary, a human ecological approach treats *Homo sapiens* as part of nature, deals primarily with aggregate units of analysis, and attempts to describe and understand the biosocial and social processes of adaptation.

The human ecological perspective, like all others, has its limitations. Early efforts at human ecology overemphasized the importance of spatial relationships and were often blatantly deterministic in outlook (Young, 1983). Biological metaphors such as niche, succession, and species can be misused (Rosa & Machlis, 1983). The human ecosystem is an attractive unit of analysis, but the definition of system boundaries is often difficult to accomplish. Likewise, the simultaneous treatment of several variables makes analysis a complicated and rigorous activity.

Yet much of human behavior, from political conflict to energy conservation, from the aging of the baby boom generation to forest management, can be usefully examined from this ecological perspective. Next, we shall try to see if human ecology can be applied specifically to parks and provide useful information to park managers.

THE HUMAN ECOLOGY OF PARKS

What would we need to ecologically understand a national park in order to wisely manage it? The question is broad but not vague, for it asks us to list the key variables in a human ecology of parks. What kinds of ecological information are critical for park management?

First, we need detailed knowledge of the park's biophysical environment. We would need to document energy flows (from sunlight to electricity), eco-

Managing Parks as Human Ecosystems

system processes such as eutrophication and nitrogen fixing, the abundance and distribution of the various plant and animal species, and the inventory of physical structures (from geological to man-made).

Second, we would need to describe the social organization of the park. What biosocial demands are important? What social institutions (such as the courts and schools) impact the park, and what specific organizations (such as the NPS, concessions, Christian Ministry in the Parks) are operating? The social norms for behavior at campgrounds, visitor centers, staff offices, and roadways would all need to be recorded.

Third, we would need information about the various human populations that use the park, including visitors, staff, and others. Especially for visitors, we would document various sociodemographic characteristics such as age, sex, income, ethnic group, and occupation. Detailed information would be collected on where they go and what they do while visiting the park. We would describe the various social institutions that help bring visitors and staff to the park—colleges, airlines, highway systems, travel agencies, and so forth. For different visitor subpopulations, we would want to be aware of key cultural elements that guide behavior—norms brought with individuals or groups when they entered the park.

Fourth, even if we had all this information, we would need to understand the interactions *among* all these components (if the price of fuel rises, will backcountry visitation drop and wildflower regeneration increase?) In other words, we would have to document the adaptation process. Figure 2 outlines our data so far.

Fifth, having amassed all this information, we would still find our knowledge inadequate, for the park ecosystem is likely to change over time. Data collected in early spring may be a poor indicator of winter characteristics, and spring 1989 will be very different from spring 1969 and spring 2009. Hence, we would need careful documentation of all the aforementioned variables over time.

Sixth, even if we had all *this* information, we would find ourselves not fully ready to manage. Parks are not often biological or socioeconomic islands, and we would need to know the relationship of the park to its surrounding region. As Hart, in *A Systems Approach to Park Planning* (1966) states,

> Within a given land area all parks, no matter how large they may be, or for what purpose they were established, are related to each other, to the use of resources in the landscape which includes them, and to the society which supports them. (p. xi)

The earlier variables of population, organization, environment, and technology are relevant. So, seventh, we would need to describe the regional population—its settlement pattern, migration rates, age structure, and so on. We would need to understand the workings of regional organizations such as county and state governments, economic development commissions, large corporations, and local communities. We would need detailed information on how regional ecosystems are linked to park ecosystems—airsheds, watersheds, elec-

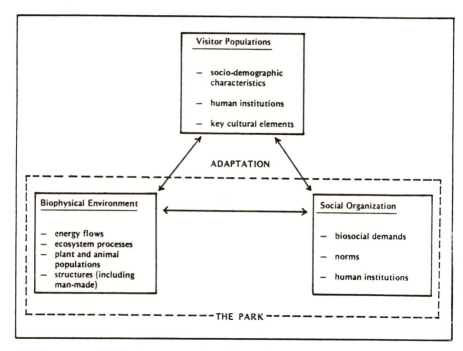

Figure 2. A view of the park ecosystem.

tric power grids, wildlife ranges, and so forth. We would require knowledge of regional technology—industrial, communication, and transportation activities in particular. And, like before, we would need to understand the interactions between these variables and how the entire system changes over time.

If we knew all this might it not improve our ability to be good stewards of park resources? Yes, but in all likelihood, such an enormous database is impossible to develop and maintain for a national park. The value of such a framework lies in highlighting what we know and don't know and suggesting new kinds of what Lindbloom and Cohen (1979) called "usable knowledge." It serves as a kind of checklist against which we can measure our understanding. And high on that checklist will be an understanding of the role people play in park ecosystems.

PEOPLE AS A DOMINANT IN PARKS

Beginning in the 1970s, this ecological perspective was applied to leisure and recreation. Cheek and Burch (1976) suggested that the physical environment is important in understanding leisure behavior and that behavior is characterized by peoples' recreational activities and the spaces and times in which these activities occur. Cheek, Field, and Burdge (1976) emphasized that people recreate in social groups. They suggested that, through shared meanings, social groups attach qualities to physical spaces that transform them into recreation settings. Thus, activities, space (physical place or social setting), and time are key variables in studying recreation behavior.

Drawing on these approaches and the earlier tradition of human ecology, Machlis and colleagues (Machlis, Field, & Campbell, 1981; Machlis & Field, 1984; Machlis & Tichnell, 1985) have tried to describe and analyze parks as a special type of "human ecosystem," organized and structured around recreation and resource preservation. In this system, park visitors are the primary resource users. Their behavior—their natural history—affects park resources. Thus, understanding human activities over space and time should be useful to park managers.

The argument treats *Homo sapiens* as the dominant species in most park ecosystems. Two varieties are particularly important: visitors, both from near and far, and locals that live near and are interdependent with park ecosystems. We first examine visitors.

The management of visitors would be relatively easy if they were homogeneous—same length of stay, activities, impact upon the resource, and so forth. In some parks—French regional ones, African wildlife reserves during the Colonial era, Yellowstone and Yosemite before 1900—this has largely been the case. Yet in a culturally heterogeneous society and an interdependent world like ours, such faith in the idea of an "average visitor" will be misplaced. To treat visitors as a single collective is an oversimplification of the park ecosystem, and it can result in less than best management.

For most national parks, there is some diversity in the kind of people who visit. Figures 3–6 provide illustration. They are from a series of visitor studies conducted at over 15 U.S. national parks and are based closely on the Chicago school's approach to the analysis and display of data (Machlis & Dolsen, 1988a, b). The figures illustrate how sociodemographic characteristics can vary within and between park ecosystems. The age structure of the visitor population shows a distinctive pattern at both locales (note the high proportion of older visitors in the fall at Shenandoah). The geographic distribution of visitors' origins shows the national and regional distributions typical of the U.S. park system; regardless of "crown jewel status," surprisingly few parks share similar maps.

This diversity is translated into differential behaviors and impacts upon the park ecosystem. Large groups may heighten per capita impact in the backcountry (such as soil compaction), yet improve efficiencies in the frontcountry (less per capita gasoline consumption, staff contact time, campsite space, and so on). Frontcountry densities (in this case, the main highway cutting through North Cascades National Park) tend to concentrate visitation. Activities may be age graded, with the young and old separated by pace, timing, and interests. Ethnic groups may stake claim to certain park territories, cultural resources, even times of day or season (Lee, 1972).

From an ecological perspective, the cumulative impact of these visitors is

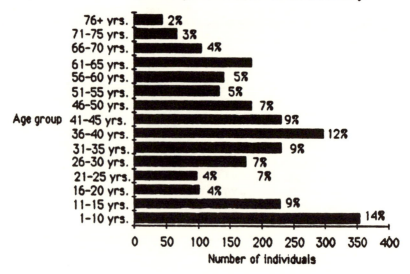

Figure 3. Visitor ages, Yellowstone National Park.

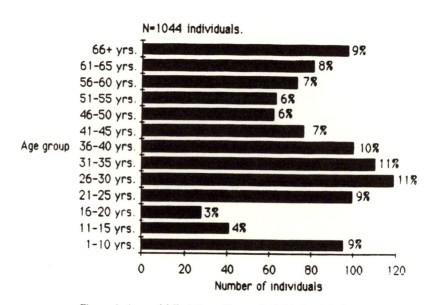

Figure 4. Ages of fall visitors, Shenandoah National Park.

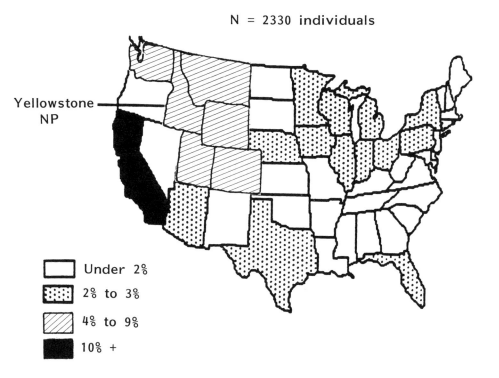

Figure 5. Proportion of visitors from each state, Yellowstone National Park.

to increase the volume, rate, and complexity of resource flows (energy, nutrients, materials, and information), as well as concentrating wastes and leading to other adverse impacts. Likewise, visitors result in important commodity exchange and political support, necessary to keep the fiscal budget, concessioner investment, park policies, staff and physical infrastructure in place. Indeed, without visitors, most national parks would quickly revert to simple land banks ripe for withdrawal or scientific preserves drastically limited in size and number (Nicholson, 1974).

A second important human population is represented by the local communities adjacent to or nearby national parks. Often these communities are interdependent with the park and rely on a flow of visitors (and their vacation dollars) for their livelihood. Such economic dependencies almost always develop into political linkages, as the community's economy becomes intertwined with park policy.

Where conflicts arise, the impacts of local communities may have signif-

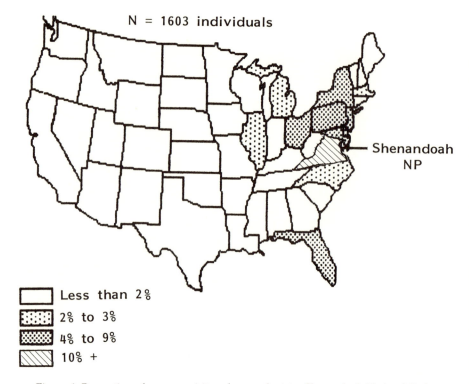

Figure 6. Proportion of summer visitors from each state, Shenandoah National Park.

icant consequences to the park ecosystem. There is significant evidence emerging from the fields of environmental sociology and conservation biology. In a recent study of threats to 98 national parks in 49 countries (Machlis & Tichnell, 1985), the role of local populations emerged as critical and often threatening. Table 1 shows that of the ten most reported threats, at least half are related to local communities. Three-quarters of the parks suffered from poaching, and over half were threatened by local attitudes, conflicting demands, and human harassment of wildlife.

A second piece of evidence comes from a human ecological analysis of Virunga National Park in Zaire. Mugangu-Trinto (1983) analyzed the evolution of local habitat over time, focusing on the energy flow within ecosystems. The park was set aside to protect the mountain gorilla. Management has attempted to remove local people from the park ecosystem. In a region of limited resources, such efforts have met with resistance: 36 wardens have been murdered by poachers. Local populations ("ecosphere people," in Raymond Dasmann's (1974) terms) have been forced from the system; foreign elites ("biosphere people") carefully shepherded through the park. The attempt to remove locals has led to a population explosion of large herbivores freed from their traditional

TABLE 1. TEN MOST REPORTED THREATS

Threat	Resource subsystem	Respondents (percent of total respondents; $n = 95$)
Illegal removal	Animal life	76
Lack personnel	Management	74
Removal of vegetation	Vegetation	61
Erosion	Soil	60
Local attitudes	Management	55
Conflicting demands	Management	55
Fire	Vegetation	52
Human harassment	Animal life	51
Loss of habitat	Animal life	49
Trampling	Vegetation	48

human predators—with overgrazing, trampling, erosion, and ecological imbalance the result. Outside the park, cashcropping and survival agriculture on a limited land base result in unstable systems as well. Clearly, parks like Virunga are linked to the socioeconomic and ecological regions around them.

A third example is the current struggle to protect China's giant panda. The giant panda is dependent entirely upon bamboo for food. Because bamboo grows abundantly throughout the animal's range, it usually provides a dependable food source. But every 40 to 120 years, depending on the species, most bamboo in an area flowers and dies. The seedlings these plants produce take 10 to 15 years to grow large enough to provide food. In evolutionary terms, this synchronous flowering may benefit the panda. It provides an ecological "crunch" that intensifies natural selection, forces the panda to migrate, and mixes the gene pool.

But today pandas have no place to go: villages, forestry operations, farms, and roads are encroaching from below, and alpine habitat—nothing more than rock and ice—extends above the panda's forested range. Now, when the bamboo dies, pandas are often trapped on small, forested "islands" of dwindling habitat (Machlis & Johnson, 1987). Human settlement patterns, local economic alternatives, and cultural norms regarding resource use will have a great impact on whether this situation is reversed.

MODELING PARK ECOSYSTEMS TO INCLUDE HUMANS

As we move from conceptualizing to applying the human ecological perspective, one of the key intellectual resources may be the recent advances in knowledge about systems and the increased ability to model them.

Systems thinking is not particularly new, dating from Aristotelian philosophy and science. Von Bertalanffy first proposed his general systems theory in 1937 (Von Bertalanffy, 1968), and several general treatments exist (e.g., Ashby, 1956; Miller, 1978; Weinberg, 1975). Miller in his *Living Systems* (1978), argues that for systems at various levels—from organism to society—there are certain key functions, and their interactions are predictable.

There is a paradox, however: systems understanding is crucial to wise management, yet Gödel's Theorem suggests that no system can fully understand itself, because more components are required to analyze and understand than simply function. We avoid the paradox by emphasizing models, simplified conceptions of real-world systems.

The process of modeling is intuitive and remains largely a high-tech art form. Such models can take many shapes, and unfortunately no universal language of systems modeling has emerged. Howard Odum (1983) suggests a three-step process involving definition of boundaries and sources, definition of key components, and description of key relationships. Once developed, such conceptual models can be quantified—in flows of energy, material, information, or money.

Several models have been developed that relate to specific elements of park ecosystems. This is often because the species assemblages of parks are unique and parks offer a database not found elsewhere. Predator–prey models developed for Isle Royale (Beyer, Harris, & Ryan, 1979; Blackwell, 1983), recreational use models (Romesburg, 1974), and fire management models at Glacier (Kessel, 1976) are examples. Wright (1979) attempted to use a computer simulation model to predict potential visitation to developing national parks in Alaska.

A more limited number of models have been developed expressly to analyze or better understand full park ecosystems. DeBellevue, Odum, Browder, & Gardner (1979) attempted to model the energy flows in and out of Everglades National Park in an effort to measure its contribution to the economy of the region. Parton and Wright (1975) developed a simulation model to analyze the effect of resource management strategies on the physiographic structure of Cape Hatteras National Seashore. Parton, Wright, & Risser (1980) utilized a computer simulation model to examine the impact of establishing a tall-grass prairie national park in central Kansas.

The construction of diagrammatic models is an integral step in the process used to develop mathematical and computer models. A diagrammatic model is essentially an outgrowth of a conceptual model. The conceptual model embodies the mental thoughts on how a system is structured; the diagrammatic model is a picture of that construction (Hall & Day, 1977). For that reason, diagrammatic models can be very useful in explaining system structure and communicating that to others. Nonetheless, the literature on purely diagrammatic models is meager. Hale and Wright (1979) used this approach to analyze the marine ecosystem at Glacier Bay National Park. Wright (1981) used a similar approach to look at wolf-moose habitat interactions at Denali National Park.

Such modeling has tentatively been applied to parks, though rarely include social variables. For example, the model of Everglades National Park (Figure 7) (DeBellevue, Odum, Browder, & Gardner, 1979) treats social and economic

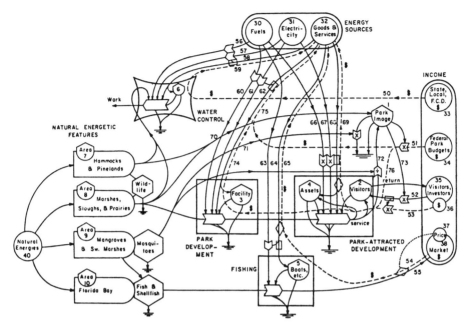

Figure 7. Systems model, Everglades National Park. (From DeBellevue et al., 1979.)

variables as having significant influence, including an intriguing component entitled "park image." The linkages between visitors and natural features are far from direct; park management serves a coordinating function. At first, the complexity is discouraging, but the model reflects only a small portion of the variables discussed earlier.

As a precursor to more quantitative efforts, Wright and Machlis (1985) have attempted to create a series of conceptual models of parks as human ecosystems. Figure 8 is the overall model for the park ecosystem. Although most subsystems within the park ecosystem are interdependent, several patterns emerge. Several subsystems act as storage components (air, water, soil, cultural resources), others as producers (vegetation) or consumers (animals), and others are combinations of these functions (support infrastructure and visitors).

The support infrastructure is a major interface between the natural and social systems, with linkages to all other subsystems. It also is a major linkage to outside the park. Many of the important flows are materials, and a number of these are one-way, suggesting major pathways rather than smaller cycles. The support infrastructure has the most diverse set of relevant flows; cultural resources is the most isolated.

A great deal needs to be accomplished before these and other models can be directly useful to resource management in national parks. The development of ecological modeling has generated much publicity, met with some successes, and engendered many criticisms. Common complaints have been that there

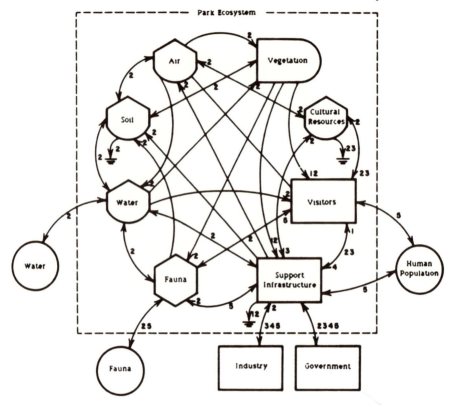

Figure 8. Overall model for park ecosystem. Specified diagram of park ecosystem. The notation is based on H. T. Odum's *Systems ecology: An introduction* (New York: Wiley, 1983). The shapes imply storage, production, and consumption functions, and the numbered arrows refer to flows of (1) energy, (2) materials, (3) information, (4) money, and (5) individuals. The ⚌ symbol represents a sink. (Adapted from R. G. Wright and G. E. Machlis, *Models for park management: A prospectus*, Cooperative Park Studies Unit Report CPSU/UI SB85-1. Moscow: University of Idaho, 1985, p. 20.)

has been too much emphasis put on the development of elaborate models of unreal systems, that overly simplistic models have been created to study complex systems that therefore have no relation to reality, that modelers often do not understand the systems they are modeling, and finally that the benefits and potentials of models have too often been oversold (Woodmansee & Lauenroth, 1983).

Agee and Johnson (1988) are pessimistic:

> Complex ecosystem models that incorporate either human culture or nonhuman biological components accurately are not likely to emerge in the near future, if ever.

Conceptual efforts must include feedback mechanisms as well as threshold effects, and quantitative models must be tested against real-world systems. Only a small percentage of the needed data are actually available for any park. Yet human ecological models of parks, developed for use by resource management specialists, seem technically feasible and worth the effort. Such models may be to the 1990s park manager what a species list was to the ecologist of the 1950s: a basic working tool for research and decision making. They are the logical outgrowth of theoretical human ecology applied to parks.

FUTURE DIRECTIONS IN RESEARCH

These remarks are not definitive—they provide only a single perspective for further thinking about visitors and parks. Yet a particularly ecological research agenda emerges. The basic outline might include the following:

1. Some visitor behavior is predictable, some is highly varied. The discovery of these patterns is important to resource management. All the social sciences—anthropology, sociology, psychology, geography, and economics—can contribute. The key is to treat behavior as biological *and* cultural and develop research strategies to sort out the influence of culturally specific variables and biosocial demands.
2. There is a basic minimum ecosystem knowledge that is required of wise resource managers. This minimum understanding includes biophysical and sociological knowledge. A large and coherent database is required, suggesting focused, long-term study. The research model is that of the Hubbard Brook studies of the last two decades (see Bormann and Likens, 1979); monitoring techniques need to be developed. Institutional cooperation and long-term funding are critical.
3. Visitor–resource interactions can be examined fruitfully if first considered as adaptive responses. The natural history approach described earlier remains viable, and it could be extended to include studies of local populations. The cultural meaning of park resources, as well as local demography and economic alternatives, seem crucial variables.
4. Visitors and local communities exert significant influence on park ecosystems, and they need to be integrally considered in resources management planning. The impact of park management upon visitors and local communities is also of importance. The metaphor that parks are "islands" will need to be replaced with a more realistic view of park boundaries.
5. The development of park models may provide a significant management tool for resource managers within the next decade. These models must include both social and biological parameters.

Underlying this agenda is the critical need to forge a real intellectual link between the natural and social sciences. This will not be easy. One example is the difficulty of integrating rural development and conservation efforts in the Third World. Elsewhere we have written:

Traditional and contemporary theories of development skirt such environmental issues, and conservation biology has refrained from including sociopolitical variables in its models. A synthesis is needed, whereby both biological and social variables are explicitly considered. We suggest that a human ecological perspective might be fruitful, and argue that flows of energy, materials, information, wealth, and populations, are critical variables. (Machlis & Tichnell, 1987, p. 255)

CONCLUSION

In his "Solving for Pattern" (1981), the American poet-farmer Wendell Berry tells us of the "irony of methods," whereby sanitation systems pollute, medical cures cause disease, and social reforms lead to corruption. Instead, he argues for a *pattern* of solutions, interdependent and effective. Berry's prescription is for farmers; it has wider usefulness as a practical guide for managing parks as human ecosystems. Indeed, the occupational metaphor for a park manager may not be the bureaucrat, scientist, public relations specialist, politician, or policeman, but the family farmer, who must manage resources and people with care and wisdom or suffer the consequences. Berry writes:

> A good solution accepts given limits, using so far as possible what is at hand. The farther-fetched the solution, the less it should be trusted . . . A good solution improves the balances, symmetries, or harmonies within a pattern—it is a qualitative solution—rather than enlarging or complicating some part of a pattern at the expense or in neglect of the rest.
>
> A good solution solves more than one problem, and it does not make new problems. I am talking about health as opposed to almost any cure, coherence of pattern as opposed to almost any solution produced piecemeal or in isolation . . . A good solution will satisfy a whole range of criteria; it will be good in all respects.
>
> Good solutions have wide margins, so that the failure of one solution does not imply the impossibility of another.
>
> A good solution always answers the question, How much is enough? A good solution should be cheap, and it should not enrich one person by the distress or impoverishment of another.
>
> Good solutions exist only in proof, and are not to be expected from absentee owners or absentee experts. Problems must be solved in work and in place, with particular knowledge, fidelity, and care, by people who will suffer the consequences of their mistakes. Practical advice or direction from people who have no practice may have some value, but its value is questionable and is limited.
>
> It is the nature of any organic pattern to be contained within a larger one. And so a good solution in one pattern preserves the integrity of the pattern that contains it.
>
> Our ability to make such [solutions] depends on virtues that are specifically human: accurate memory, observation, insight, imagination, inventiveness, reverence, devotion, fidelity, restraint. Restraint—for us, now—above all: the ability to accept and live within limits; to resist changes that are merely novel or fashionable; to resist greed and pride; to resist the temptation to "solve" problems by ignoring them, accepting them as "trade-offs," or bequeathing them to posterity. A good solution, then, must be in harmony with good character, cultural value, and moral law. (pp. 134–145)

To ignore Berry's wisdom—because of its clarity, its lack of scientific jingoism, for whatever reason—and to manage parks without a sense of rhythm and organic wholes is restrictive, unenthusiastic, and myopic. If park resources are precious resources, it may also be harmful. To learn about and care for parks as Berry would husband a good farm is to be humane and wise.

REFERENCES

Agee, J. K., & Johnson, D. R. (1988). *Ecosystem management for parks and wilderness: Workshop synthesis*. Seattle, Washington: Institute of Forest Resources.

Ashby, W. (1956). *Introduction to cybernetics*. New York: Wiley.

Barash, D. P. (1982). *Sociobiology and behavior* (2nd ed.). New York: Elsevier.

Bennett, J. W. (1976). *The ecological transition: Cultural anthropology and human adaptation*. New York: Pergamon Press.

Berry, W. (1981). *The gift of good land*. San Francisco: North Point Press.

Beyer, W., Harris, D., & Ryan, R. (1979). A stochastic model of the Isle Royale Biome. *Rocky Mountain Journal of Mathematics. 9*, 3–18.

Blackwell, C. (1983). Some new results in resource management oriented natural process dynamics modelling. In W. Lauenroth, G. Skogerboe, & M. Flug (Eds.), *Analysis of ecological systems: State of the art in ecological modelling. Developments in environmental modelling 5* (pp. 69–74). New York: Elsevier.

Bormann, F., & Likens, G. E. (1979). *Pattern and process in a forested ecosystem*. New York: Springer-Verlag.

Bruhn, J. G. (1974). Human ecology: A unifying science? *Human Ecology, 2*, 105–125.

Burch, W. R., Jr., & DeLuca, D. R. (Eds.). (1984). *Measuring the social impact of natural resource policies*. Albuquerque: University of New Mexico Press.

Catton, W. R., Jr. (1987). The world's most polymorphic species. *Bioscience 37*, 413–419.

Catton, W. R., Jr., & Dunlap, R. E. (1980). A new ecological paradigm for post-exuberant sociology. *American Behavioral Scientist 24*, 15–47.

Cheek, N. H., Jr., & Burch, W. R., Jr. (1976). *The social organization of leisure in human society*. New York: Harper & Row.

Cheek, N. H., Jr., Field, D. R., & Burdge, R. J. (1976). *Leisure and recreation places*. Ann Arbor, MI: Ann Arbor Science Publishers.

Chomsky, N. (1972). *Language and mind*. New York: Harcourt Brace Jovanovich.

Clements, F. E. (1916). *Plant succession*. Washington, DC: Carnegie Institute.

Dasmann, R. F. (1974). Biotic provinces of the world. (IUCN Occasional Paper No. 9). Morges, Switzerland: International Union for the Conservation of Nature.

DeBellevue, E., Odum, H. T., Browder, J., & Gardner, G. (1979). Energy analysis of the Everglades National Park. In Linn, R. M. (Ed.), *Proceedings of the First Conference on Scientific Research in the National Parks* (Vol. 1, pp. 31–43). Washington, DC: National Park Service.

Dubos, R. (1980). *The wooing of earth*. New York: Scribner's.

Duncan, O. D. (1964). Social organization and the ecosystem. In R. Faris (Ed.), *Handbook of modern sociology*. New York: Rand McNally.

Faris, E. L. (1967). *Chicago sociology: 1920–1932*. Chicago: University of Chicago Press.

Hale, L., & Wright, R. G. (1979). *The Glacier Bay Marine Ecosystem: A conceptual ecological model*. Anchorage: National Park Service, Alaska regional office.

Hall, C., & Day, J. (1977). Systems and models: Terms and basic principles. In C. Hall & J. Day (Eds.), *Ecosystems modelling in theory and practice* (pp. 5–36). New York: Wiley.

Hart, W. J. (1966). *A systems approach to park planning*. Morges, Switzerland: International Union for the Conservation of Nature.

Hawley, A. H. (1950). *Human ecology: A theory of community structure.* New York: Ronald Press.
Hawley, A. H. (1968). *Roderick D. McKenzie on human ecology.* Chicago: University of Chicago Press.
Hawley, A. H. (1986). *Human ecology: A theoretical essay.* Chicago: University of Chicago Press.
Kessel, S. (1976). Gradient modelling: A new approach to fire modelling and wilderness resource management. *Environment Management, 1,* 39–48.
Lee, R. G. (1972). The social definition of outdoor recreational places. In W. R. Burch, Jr., N. H. Cheek, Jr., & L. Taylor (Eds.), *Social behavior, natural resources and the environment.* New York: Harper & Row.
Likens, G. E. (Ed.). (1985). *An ecosystem approach to aquatic ecology.* New York: Springer-Verlag.
Lindbloom, C. E., & Cohen, D. K. (1979). *Usable knowledge: Social science and social problem solving.* New Haven, CT: Yale University Press.
Machlis, G. E., & Dolsen, D. E. (1988a). *Visitor Services Project Report 14: Shenandoah National Park.* Moscow, ID: University of Idaho, Cooperative Park Studies Unit.
Machlis, G. E., & Dolsen, D. E. (1988b). *Visitor Services Project Report 15: Yellowstone National Park.* Moscow, ID: University of Idaho, Cooperative Park Studies Unit.
Machlis, G. E., & Field, D. R. (Eds.). (1984). *On interpretation: Sociology for interpreters of natural and cultural history.* Corvallis, OR: Oregon State University Press.
Machlis, G. E., Field, D. R., & Campbell, F. L. (1981). The human ecology of parks. *Leisure Sciences, 4,* 195–212.
Machlis, G. E., & Johnson, K. (1987). Panda outposts. *Parks* (Sept./Oct.), *61* (9–10), 15–16.
Machlis, G. E., & Tichnell, D. L. (1985). *The state of the world's parks: An international assessment for resource management, policy, and research.* Boulder, CO: Westview Press.
Machlis, G. E., & Tichnell, D. L. (1987). Economic development and threats to national parks: A preliminary analysis. *Environmental Conservation 14,* 151–156.
Machlis, G. E., & Wenderoth, E. L. (1982). *Foreign visitors at Grand Canyon National Park: A preliminary study.* Moscow, ID: University of Idaho, Cooperative Park Studies Unit.
McKenzie, R. D. (1968). The neighborhood: A study of local life in the city of Columbus, Ohio. In A. H. Hawley (Ed.), *Roderick D. McKenzie on Human Ecology* (pp. 51–93). Chicago: University of Chicago Press.
Micklin, M. (1977). *The ecological perspective in the social sciences: A comparative overview.* Paper presented at the Conference on Human Ecology, December, Seattle, WA.
Miller, J. G. (1978). *Living systems.* New York: McGraw-Hill.
Mugangu-Trinto, E. (1983). *A new approach for the management of Zairean national parks.* Moscow, ID: University of Idaho, Cooperative Park Studies Unit.
Nicholson, M. (1974). What is wrong with the national park movement? In H. Elliott (Ed.), *Second World Conference on National Parks* (pp. 32–37). Morges, Switzerland: International Union for the Conservation of Nature.
Odum, H. T. (1983). *Systems ecology.* New York: Wiley.
Parton, W., & Wright, R. G. (1975). The use of models in environmental impact analysis. In G. S. Innis (Ed.), *New directions in the analysis of ecological systems.* (Simulation Councils, Proc. Ser. 5, pp. 83–92). New York: Elsevier.
Parton, W., Wright, R. G., & Risser, P. (1980). Simulated grazing responses on the proposed Prairies National Park. *Journal of Environmental Management, 4,* 165–170.
Redfield, R. (1963). *Peasant society and culture.* Chicago: University of Chicago Press.
Ricklefs, R. E. (1973). *Ecology.* Portland, OR: Chiron Press.
Robertson, I. (1981). *Sociology* (2nd ed.). New York: Worth Publishers.
Romesburg, H. (1974). Scheduling models for wilderness recreation. *Journal of Environmental Management, 2,* 159–177.
Rosa, E. A., & Machlis, G. E. (1983). Energetic theories of society: An evaluative review. *Sociological Inquiry, 53,* 152–178.
Vayda, A. P., & Rappaport, R. A. (1976). Ecology, cultural and noncultural. In P. G. Richerson

& J. McEvoy III (Eds.), *Human ecology: An environmental approach*. North Scituate, MA: Duxbury Press.

Von Bertalanffy, L. (1968). *General systems theory*. New York: Braziller.

Weinberg, G. M. (1975). *An introduction to general systems theory*. New York: Wiley-InterScience.

White, L., Jr. (1967). The historical roots of our ecologic crisis. *Science, 155*, 1203–1207.

Woodmansee, R., & Lauenroth, W. (1983). Modelling reality: Fact, fancy, and fiction. In W. Lauenroth, G. Skogerbo, & M. Flug (Eds.), *Analysis of ecological systems: State of the art in ecological modelling 5* (pp. 39–42). New York: Elsevier.

Wright, R. G. (1979). The use of simulation models in projecting potential visitation to new national parks in Alaska. In R. Linn (Ed.), *Proceedings of the First Conference on Scientific Research in the National Parks* (pp. 1067–1076). Washington, DC: National Park Service.

Wright, R. G. (1981). *A conceptual simulation model of moose-wolf habitat interactions at Mt. McKinley National Park*. Moscow, ID: University of Idaho, Cooperative Park Studies Unit.

Wright, R. G., & Machlis, G. E. (1985). *Models for park management: A prospectus*. Moscow, ID: University of Idaho, Cooperative Park Studies Unit.

Young, G. L. (Ed.). (1983). *Origins of human ecology*. Stroudsburg, PA: Dowden, Hutchinson & Ross.

11

Solitude for the Multitudes
MANAGING RECREATIONAL USE IN THE WILDERNESS

GEORGE H. STANKEY

INTRODUCTION

Wilderness evokes many impressions—pristine nature, spectacular scenery, wildlife in its natural habitat. And solitude. A solitary backpacker silhouetted along a mountain ridgeline exemplifies the image of wilderness as a setting of solitude, where one is alone in the midst of primitive natural conditions. The imagery is backed by law: the 1964 Wilderness Act, the legal foundation for the protection and management of wilderness, states that such areas will have "outstanding opportunities for solitude or a primitive and unconfined type of recreation." Indeed, Lucas (1985) reports that 85% of the wilderness visitors he surveyed rated "to experience solitude" as an important wilderness appeal.

But image and attitude often differ from reality and behavior. Both the idiosyncratic actions of wilderness visitors as well as their collective behavior raises questions about the importance of solitude. The stereotypic solitary backpacker is, in fact, rare; few wilderness users travel alone. Recreational use in most wildernesses is highly concentrated; as much as 90% of the use in some areas enters on only 10% of the entry points, with most users concentrated along only 10% of the total trail milage (Hendee, Stankey, & Lucas, 1978).

Rising use levels have led to concerns that wilderness is being "loved to death." Anecdotal evidence of a growing crisis in overuse of wilderness abounds. Rod Nash cites the case of a father who returns to climb Mt. Whitney with his son in 1972, a repeat of a visit the man had made in 1949 with his father. Then, however, his father and he were only the sixth and seventh people

---

GEORGE H. STANKEY • Department of Leisure Studies, Kuring-gai College of Advanced Education, Lindfield, New South Wales 2070, Australia.

to sign the summit register that year; in 1972, his son and he were the 259th and 260th registrants that day! (Hendee *et al.*, 1978).

To provide an understanding of the cultural basis from which the meaning of wilderness has evolved, I will briefly review the history and development of the concept and its eventual codification into law. We then turn to a review of the conceptual framework within which solitude and crowding in wilderness can be studied. Various studies reporting on wilderness solitude and crowding are reviewed. Finally, a discussion of the management options available to maintain or restore desired levels of privacy among visitors is outlined, followed by a discussion of future directions for needed research.

HISTORICAL EVOLUTION OF THE WILDERNESS CONCEPT

"In Wildness is the preservation of the World" intoned Transcendentalist Henry David Thoreau at the Concord Lyceum in 1851. Rooted in his statement was the conviction that wild nature—wilderness—nurtured the growth of society's finer qualities: creativity, sensitivity, and spirituality. The vast wilderness landscape of North America was to be valued because it offered abundant opportunities where these higher states of human endeavor might be fostered.

Such views marked the beginning of a period in American history in which undeveloped nature became viewed as a national treasure rather than as a liability to be overcome. Such a conception was long in the making and continues yet today. The nation's Judeo-Christian origins provided an intellectual foundation that encouraged and justified conquering the wilderness. The wilderness was conceived of as the polar notion to civilization, the antonym of paradise. "The story of the Garden (of Eden) and its loss," Nash (1982) writes, "imbedded into Western thought the idea that wilderness and paradise were both physical and spiritual opposites."

But imbedded in these generations of antipathy toward the wilderness was a sense of ambivalence as well. Although early Christian thought fostered a conception of wilderness as a threat to society's spirituality, it simultaneously recognized wilderness as the place where one could cleanse one's self preparatory to meeting God in the absence of the distracting influences of civilization. This countervailing conception of wilderness persisted; even the Puritans valued the wilderness as a sanctuary to which they could retreat in order to pursue their beliefs, although it is unlikely they appreciated the paradox involved (Nash, 1982).

By the time Thoreau made his pronouncement, a variety of factors had helped begin the move toward a more beneficent view of wilderness. The growth in scientific understanding of nature, begun between the 11th and 13th century in Europe, provided an alternative perspective to the teleological model of nature's form and function. The wild sweep of the Alps was the product of eons of erosion and uplift, not an expression of a wrathful God. Art and literature changed; the ordered, sculptured landscapes of Versailles were replaced by a preference for the wild and natural; literary figures able to live with nature came to be heroes.

The appreciation of wilderness also grew from a concern that the apparently boundless reaches of wild country were in fact limited. Impressed by the great loss of wildlife in the West as well as the adverse effects of white civilization on Indian culture, George Catlin, an artist and lawyer, called for creation of "a nation's Park, containing man and beast, in all the wild and freshness of their nature's beauty!" This was in 1832; only 60 years later, the once seemingly endless wilderness frontier of America was officially declared closed as the 1890 Census revealed a nation where urban residents outnumbered rural. In a startlingly short time, the American wilderness had become a scarce landscape.

In response to growing concerns to preserve examples of the landscape that had helped shape the American character, steps were taken to preserve some areas in their natural state. Yellowstone National Park in 1872 was the first notable action, although the preservation of wilderness had little to do with it. Later, in 1890, President Benjamin Harrison signed into law an act establishing Yosemite National Park in California, the first national preserve set aside consciously to protect wilderness values (Nash, 1982).

The early years of the new century saw wilderness attract broad public attention as a public issue. John Muir, a Scottish machinist turned wilderness evangelist, had already gained national notoriety in the efforts to protect Yosemite. A 1908 proposal by San Francisco to dam the Tuolumne River, thereby flooding the spectacular Hetch Hetchy Valley within the Park in order to provide the city with fresh water, sparked a five-year battle to preserve the integrity of the Park's natural features. Muir was a leading figure in the battle, publishing a stream of articles to mobilize public opposition. In the end, the dam was built and Hetch Hetchy was flooded. But the threats of development to America's remaining wilderness lands were crystallized by the Hetch Hetchy controversy and public awareness was heightened.

The auspicious combination of individuals and events continued. In 1920, Arthur Carhart, a landscape architect with the U.S. Forest Service, convinced his superiors to forego the development of Trappers Lake in Colorado, retaining instead the area's primeval characteristics. Four years later, forester Aldo Leopold's recommendation that a portion of the Gila National Forest in New Mexico be preserved from development was accepted, and the nation's first area explicitly labeled as wilderness, the 574,000-acre Gila Wilderness, was established. In 1926, the Forest Service, concerned with the rapid disappearance of the nation's wild lands, conducted a review of the extent of wilderness remaining in the National Forests. From this review came the first set of administrative regulations for the establishment of a system of "primitive" areas protected for their wilderness values. Between 1929 and 1939, as many as 76 primitive areas, totaling about 14 million acres, were set aside.

In 1939, Bob Marshall, an energetic wilderness enthusiast who headed up the Forest Service's Division of Recreation, placed into effect a new set of regulations to guide the protection of wilderness in the National Forests. In general, these new guidelines were more restrictive than the earlier primitive area designation. They called for the review of the existing primitive areas and their designation as wilderness or wild areas (the difference being primarily size). However, World War II disrupted the review and little had been accomplished as the 1950s dawned.

Immediately following World War II, two social developments with important implications for wilderness unfolded. First, the period of postwar prosperity created record demands for the goods and services proffered by the nation's public lands. A burgeoning population, coupled with the demand for "the good life," placed previously unknown pressures upon the nation's natural resources. Timber harvesting, mining, and other extractive industries grew at record levels. As they expanded, the remaining wild lands were further jeopardized.

Second, as the demands for material goods increased, so too did the demands for the nonconsumptive services of the public lands. The rapid growth rates were fed by four principal factors: population growth, rising incomes, improved transportation, and increased leisure time. Collectively, they contributed to annual growth rates of nearly 10% at federal and state parks. In response to such pressure, the Forest Service and National Park Service initiated programs in the mid-1950s to accelerate the level of capital investment in developmental programs. Access, interpretive facilities, and accommodations were expanded to deal with the rising tide of visitors. But with such steps came fears that wild country in forests and parks would be lost in the rush to accommodate more people. Although much of the interest in wilderness preservation focused on the protection of natural conditions, there was also interest in the value of such areas as places of recreation. In fact, the values of wilderness to the public were seen by some as the only basis for its protection. Moreover, given the relatively low use levels then present, the idea of controlling recreational use was not seen as needed; one commentator remarked, "the only limitation should be the natural one set up by the modes of travel possible" (Hendee et al., 1978). To people like Leopold and Marshall, wilderness represented a place where visitors could escape the omnipresent trappings of civilization. A key aspect of the wilderness image for both was its value as a setting where one could enjoy a sense of solitude.

Concern with the growing loss of wilderness led to the conviction on the part of conservationists that adequate wilderness protection was possible only through enactment of a law giving wilderness legal status. In 1956, a bill was introduced into Congress calling for the establishment of a National Wilderness Preservation System. Eight years later, such a system was created when the Wilderness Act (PL 88-577) was signed. In little more than a century, wilderness had progressed from a condition that society strove to overcome to one valued and protected by law. The conception of what wilderness was and the values it held similarly had evolved.

THE DILEMMA OF WILDERNESS MANAGEMENT

With passage of the Wilderness Act, the perceptual construct of wilderness became codified in law. The meaning and symbolism associated with wilderness obviously still remained—the feelings of awe, fear, and joy such areas evoke are beyond legal prescription. Yet there were now also legally prescribed qualities that imposed obligations upon those charged with its management. Two key attributes are embodied in the legal definition of wilderness. The first is naturalness; wilderness represents a setting where natural environmental forces are to operate beyond human control as much as possible, "where earth and its community of life are untrammeled by man," to use the words of the Act. Second, wilderness is to provide "outstanding opportunities for solitude or a primitive and unconfined type of recreation." Typically, this is interpreted to mean that in at least some portion of most wildernesses, visitors can expect relatively low levels of contact with others. Both of these qualities are consistent with historical perceptions and conceptions of wilderness as an area showing little direct or secondary evidence of human use.

But a dilemma faces wilderness managers today. Whereas the basic legal objective of wilderness is to preserve the qualities of naturalness and solitude, such areas are also for public use. The broad public interest in, and support of, wilderness that has given it a powerful political base has also resulted in growing use pressures that potentially jeopardize the very qualities such areas were designated to protect.

Recreational use of wilderness and undeveloped backcountry areas in forests and parks has grown steadily over the years. Although the reliability of use figures in wilderness is low, the pattern is clearly one in which use has grown; National Forest wilderness use has grown at an average annual rate of about 5% since 1965, although much of this growth appears related to the large expansion in the number of reporting areas during the period (from 88 areas in 1965 to 330 today).

In addition to measures of absolute use, the use density in individual areas varies widely; Table 1 shows a range of densities in selected wildernesses (a visitor day is defined as a 12-hour stay by one individual and is a standard

TABLE 1. Use Intensities in Selected National Forest Wildernesses, 1985

Area (State)	Visitor days per acre
Endicott River (AK)	.01
Galiuro (AZ)	.10
Citigo Creek (TN)	.50
Alpine Lakes (WA)	1.00
Sandia Mountains (NM)	1.35
Dolly Sods (WV)	2.28
Joyce Kilmer-Slickrock (NC-TN)	3.05
Desolation (CA)	3.51
Never Summer (CO)	4.25
Devil's Backbone (MO)	11.40
National average	.37

reporting measure). Although there are wide variations in the length of use seasons in these areas as well as in the proportion of area actually available for use (because of variations in topography and vegetation), there is nevertheless an enormous range in the density levels found in wilderness—over a 1,000-fold range between the Endicott Range in Alaska and the Devil's Backbone in Missouri. But both are wildernesses, managed under the same legal mandate, with the same apparent requirement to provide for "outstanding opportunities for solitude." Such conditions pose a difficult challenge to those responsible for wilderness management.

But high density is not the equivalent of crowding (Stokols, 1972). A variety of mediating variables influence the actual levels of contact that occur among recreationists. Moreover, solitude is only one appeal cited by visitors as a reason for visiting wilderness and frequently it is not the most important. Thus, managing wilderness to ensure "outstanding opportunities for solitude" is more than managing use densities or monitoring visitor satisfaction. It also involves more than the simple isolation of people from one another. To understand the role of solitude as a dimension of the wilderness recreation experience, we need to understand how people regulate access to themselves and the functions these different states of access provide.

A GENERALIZED MODEL OF PRIVACY AND CROWDING

The distinction between density and crowding has been extensively discussed (Altman, 1975; Stokols, 1972). Density involves an objective statement of the number of persons per unit space. Crowding is the negative evaluative judgment that a given density is excessive and that it somehow impairs an individual's satisfaction or performance.

What leads one to evaluate a condition as crowded? Altman (1975) offers a useful model to describe this process. He focuses on the interrelationships of four key concepts—privacy, personal space, territoriality, and crowding. *Privacy* is the cornerstone concept, defined as "a central regulatory process by which a person (or group) makes himself more or less accessible and open to others." An individual regulates interaction with others as part of an interpersonal boundary process; by altering the degree of openness to others, a hypothetical personal boundary is made more or less open to interaction with others. *Personal space* and *territoriality* are mechanisms to regulate access to the individual to achieve desired levels of privacy, and *crowding* describes the resultant condition when these privacy mechanisms do not function effectively.

This model involves a dynamic process in which the individual subjectively desires an ideal level of privacy or contact with others. This desired ideal state is influenced by a variety of antecedent and psychological variables. The desired state is situationally specific—the ideal privacy level will differ between that sought in an evening session drinking with friends and that sought on a family wilderness trip. This idealized state operates so as to provide the basis for the evaluation of actual, or achieved, levels of contact with others. If actual contact exceeds that desired, the potential for evaluating the condition as crowded exists (note the stress on potential: whether the situation is defined as crowded or not will depend upon the particular boundary-control mechanisms brought into play). However, if desired and actual levels of contact are coincident, then the boundary-regulation system is functioning properly.

Another important element of Altman's model is the availability of a variety of mechanisms to deal with imbalances between desired and achieved levels of privacy. These include verbal and nonverbal responses to restrict or encourage contact, territorial behaviors that help define the desired level of contact, and psychological adjustments that help the individual reduce the dissonance that would otherwise develop when uncontrolled intrusions occur.

Privacy is a broad, encompassing concept, yet only limited investigations of its form and function have been conducted. "Few values so fundamental to society as privacy have been left so undefined in social theory or have been the subject of such vague and confused writing by social scientists" (Westin, 1967). The conventional conception of privacy suggests withdrawal from social interaction. Increasingly, however, privacy is seen as a dialectical concept in which the individual controls the opening and closing of the self to others; the "individual is continually engaged in a personal adjustment process in which he balances the desire for privacy with the desire for disclosure and communications of himself to others, in light of the environmental conditions and social norms set by the society in which he lives" (Westin, 1967). Altman (1975) continues this theme of privacy as a dialectic process: "Privacy is profitably conceived of as an interplay of opposing forces . . . different balances of opening and closing the self to others."

Privacy has several dimensions. Westin (1967) identified four:

> *Solitude:* separation of the individual from the observations of others. It is the most complete state of privacy an individual can achieve.
> *Intimacy:* the individual acts as part of a small, selected group of others in a close, relaxed, and frank relationship.
> *Anonymity:* the individual attains freedom from identification, surveillance, and control in a public setting.
> *Reserve:* the individual establishes psychological barriers against unwanted intrusions and the need to limit personal communication is protected by the willing discretion of others.

An important companion concept to that of privacy is freedom of choice. Freedom of choice reflects the perceived ability to control both the information people must process and the behavior demanded of them by others (Hammitt, 1982). Proshansky, Ittelson, and Rivlin (1970) propose that privacy maximizes an individual's freedom of choice, thereby enhancing control over their activities. In particular, territoriality—the control over space—is a principal mechanism in determining what will and will not take place in a given space. Privacy represents a principal way in which people can control their environment and, therefore, the demands by others upon them. As Hammitt (1982,

p. 481) notes, "Privacy, therefore, serves to increase freedom of choice, since it gives humans control over the types of information they must process."

Privacy, along with the ideas of personal space, territoriality, and crowding, represent useful concepts for considering the issue of appropriate use in wilderness. Wilderness represents an environmental setting in which privacy—the ability to withdraw voluntarily from unwanted contact with others—is traditionally associated. How to establish some measure of appropriate use levels in order to ensure these desired levels of contact has long commanded the attention of managers and researchers. Although the basic model around which much of this attention focuses differs in some respects from that of Altman, it also shares many concepts. We now turn to a brief review of the efforts to identify and define wilderness carrying capacity.

THE RECREATIONAL CARRYING CAPACITY MODEL

There has long been concern about the impacts of excessive recreational use. As early as 1936, a National Park Service employee, Lowell Sumner, questioned "how large a crowd can be turned loose in a wilderness without destroying its essential qualities?" Such areas "cannot hope to accommodate unlimited numbers of people." Later he proposed that use of wilderness be kept "within the carrying capacity or 'recreational saturation point,'" defined as "the maximum degree of the highest type of recreational use which a wilderness can receive, consistent with its long-term preservation" (Hendee et al., 1978, p. 33).

As noted in the introduction, the period following World War II saw rapid growth in the recreational use of forests and parks. A robust economy set the stage for seemingly unlimited future expansion. A framework was needed within which decisions could be made as to how much use could occur before the very qualities sought by visitors were lost.

The concept of carrying capacity seemed well suited to filling this need. Resource managers were familiar with the concept; it is a central notion in fields such as range and wildlife management. Carrying capacity describes the limitation on use of an area set by natural factors of environmental resistance, such as food, shelter, or water. In the field of wildlife management, for instance, carrying capacity describes the number of animals of a particular species that can populate an area on a sustained basis, given available food, shelter, and water.

The apparent property of defining the amount of use a resource setting could tolerate made carrying capacity an attractive concept to recreation managers faced with burgeoning use levels. If it could be determined how many people could use a recreational setting before unacceptable impacts occurred, managers would have a clear standard for establishing use limits with an objective, biological basis for their rationale.

The carrying capacity concept was broadened to include social concerns.

However, the addition of a social component also implied that the determination of carrying capacity involved more than a straightforward technical assessment; setting such a limit implicitly invoked a sociopolitical process as well as a biophysical one (Burch, 1984). As the preface to an early investigation observed, "the study . . . was initiated with the view that the carrying capacity of recreation lands could be determined primarily in terms of ecology and the deterioration of areas. However, it soon became obvious that the resource-oriented point of view must be augmented by consideration of human values" (Wagar, 1964).

The interest in defining recreational carrying capacity spawned a large number of investigations beginning in the early 1960s. Although Wagar's seminal monograph *The Carrying Capacity of Wildlands for Recreation* (1964) was not data based, it nevertheless introduced some important considerations in the discussion of recreational carrying capacity. Wagar suggested that as the needs or motives underlying recreation participation changed, so too would the relationship between the amount of recreational use involved and the extent to which those needs were satisfied. Increasing levels of use would increase the level of satisfaction, or quality, for those experiences where companionship with others was sought. Conversely, similar use levels would detract from the quality of these experiences where solitude was sought. "The effects of crowding on the satisfaction derived from a specific activity can then be evaluated by considering the needs that commonly motivate it," Wagar concluded. His work provided early conceptual support for the dialectical nature of how people allow access to themselves, depending upon different motivational circumstances.

The recreational carrying capacity model has evolved considerably. In a review of the conceptual underpinnings of the research on crowding in recreational settings, Gramann (1982) discerned two distinctive theoretical themes. Crowding as "stimulus overload" occurs "when the level of social stimulation exceeds that desired and the individual is unable to reduce that stimulation through adaptive strategies." Crowding as "social interference" argues that "human behavior is often goal directed, and crowding attributions occur when the number, behavior, or proximity of other persons in a setting is incompatible with an important goal and thus interferes with its attainment" (pp. 111–112).

These respective conceptualizations of crowding share two common aspects with Altman's privacy regulation model. First, both suggest that people possess expectations about the level of social stimulation they seek and the kinds of experiential goals they desire. Crowding occurs when these desired social states are not achieved. Second, people possess an array of adaptive strategies they employ to achieve a desired social state. Again, crowding occurs when such mechanisms fail.

In order to understand crowding in wilderness settings, both models also direct attention to identifying the discrepancies between desired levels of interaction and the extent to which expectations about appropriate interaction are disrupted by the presence of others. Three broad classes of expectation regarding others can be identified: appropriate levels of others, appropriate behavior of others, and appropriate evidence of others. In each case, violations of what are considered to be desired levels of interaction produce feelings of crowdedness.

APPROPRIATE LEVELS OF OTHERS

There is substantial evidence that wilderness visitors are concerned about the numbers of others they encounter and that wilderness is a place in which relatively low levels of interaction are expected. Half of the respondents surveyed by Stankey (1973) reported that meeting others bothered them; only 20% found it enjoyable. Stankey (1980) also examined the differences in attitudes toward use levels in two areas, one heavily and the other lightly used. Despite a wide difference in density levels in the two areas, respondents subscribed to a strikingly similar norm expressing an expectation of limited interaction with others.

However, Stankey also reported that median satisfaction levels in the high-use area were consistently higher at increasing levels of contact than in the low-use area. Although there was a high degree of shared meaning in the generalized concept of appropriate levels of interaction between the two areas, the higher-use levels in the one area had resulted in a norm accommodating the typically higher levels of interaction one could expect to encounter. Such a phenomenon demonstrates Altman's (1975) assertion that shifting expectations constitute one reason people are able to reduce the discrepancy between desired and achieved levels of interaction. The actual interaction levels found in the high-use area, in effect, made that place a different kind of place, one in which differing expectations about appropriate interaction with others were called for.

Although previous research suggests that high densities do not necessarily constitute crowding, much attention has focused on such a bivariate conception. Statistically, such an approach has yielded little explanation. Absher and Lee (1981) found that density accounted for only 7% of the variance in the perception of crowding in the backcountry of Yosemite National Park, but when experience, visitor characteristics, and motives were considered, 26% of the variance could be explained. They conclude "it seems that the common-sense notion of crowding in recreation settings as a phenomenon dependent upon sheer numbers of other people must be reassessed in favor of more complex formulations that incorporate motivation and individual characteristics" (p. 244).

A variety of antecedent, situational, and psychological factors mediate the evaluation of a given level of interaction as crowded. Again, expectations greatly shape this evaluative process. Shelby (1980) found virtually no relationship between density and perceived crowding on the Colorado River but did when expectations for contact were included. Similarly, Womble and Studebaker (1981) found that density accounted for less than 10% of the variation in perceived crowding in Katmai National Monument, but the addition of expectations raised this to 20% and the addition of preferences, to 37%. However, when expectations are poorly formed or lacking, crowding concerns are absent. Among river runners on the Grand Canyon, 90% were on their first trip and there was little association between their expectations for interaction with others and reported crowding (Shelby, 1980).

For those to whom low levels of interaction are salient, we can expect different conceptions as to what level of interactions are defined as crowded and how crowding affects their experience. Lucas (1985) found that among visitors who rated solitude as an important dimension of their wilderness experience, both their evaluation of the numbers of others met each day and the satisfaction associated with those encounter levels differed significantly in the predicted direction from those who rated solitude of low importance. Similarly, McCool (1983) found that in a comparison of persons ranking in the upper and lower quartiles on a scale measuring the importance of solitude/stress release, those scoring high tended to react negatively more frequently to the same level of encounter than those who scored low.

If the generalized image of wilderness as a place of solitude is indeed subscribed to by visitors, the lack of association between perceived crowding and satisfaction is, on the face of it, puzzling. If people value low levels of interaction with others and report that achieved levels of interaction exceed those desired, thereby leading to the definition of the situation as crowded, one would intuitively assume that dissatisfaction would follow.

However, as Altman (1975) suggests, there is a wide range of adjustment mechanisms that people can employ to cope with discrepancies between desired and actual levels of interaction. Some of these mechanisms involve behavioral changes; people select different times or places to go to in order to avoid conditions that violate desired levels of interaction. Because such strategies can impose significant costs (time, money, planning), we might speculate that such steps are more likely to be taken by those for whom solitude is a salient motive. But many other motives underlie wilderness use and it is likely that others cope with excess interaction via more psychologically based strategies, such as redefining the nature of the place (and hence the expected levels of interaction) or by stressing nondensity-dependent aspects of the experience, such as being close to nature or family enjoyment.

APPROPRIATE BEHAVIOR OF OTHERS

The predominant social unit in recreation settings is the group, composed either of family members and/or acquaintances. Even in wilderness, small groups dominate, with typically fewer than 5% of groups comprising a single individual (Hendee et al., 1978).

This state of "being alone together" (Hammitt, 1982; Lee, 1977), far from being an internally contradictory condition, is common to most wilderness experiences. Although the importance of solitude ranks high for most wilderness visitors, the conception of what solitude means to visitors is something other than the stereotypical solitary figure. Instead, it is more in keeping with the concept of intimacy suggested by Westin (1967), with crowding occurring when the presence of others and their associated behavior threatens the functioning of the group.

Activities that conflict with the goal of intragroup social interaction represent a form of the social interference model of crowding suggested by Gramann (1982). Although the number of other users can lead to such interference, the behavior of others as well as their proximity can lead to a situation that conflicts with a salient psychological goal (Stankey & McCool, 1984). Behavioral effects, Gramann (1982) argues, often are more important than density (i.e., the numbers) of others. Moreover, such conflicts also potentially disrupt one or more of the functions that privacy fulfills. For example, when actual use levels exceed those desired, the extent to which the individual can realize a sense of independence or limited communication with others is reduced, with a consequent rise in the sense of crowding (Westin, 1967).

The intragroup focus of interaction in wilderness settings as opposed to a desire for individualistic solitude is further confirmed by the work of Twight, Smith, and Wissinger (1981) and Hammitt (1982). Following Westin's (1967) model of solitude dimensions, these investigators confirmed that the dimension of intimacy rather than solitude rated highest. Hammitt (1982) concludes "wilderness solitude is not so much individual isolation as it is a form of privacy in a specific environmental setting where individuals experience an acceptable degree of control and choice over the type and amount of information they must process." Manning (1985) agrees: "solitude in outdoor recreation may have more to do with interaction among group members free from disruption than with actual isolation . . . as long as contacts with other groups are not considered disturbing they do not engender feelings of crowding or dissatisfaction" (p. 81).

What behaviors are "disturbing and disruptive"? The affect of the numbers of others encountered was noted earlier, but as the above discussion suggests, conditions other than use numbers appear more important. A recurring finding in the carrying capacity literature is that the type of use encountered, as opposed to the amount, is often the critical variable in whether a situation is defined as crowded or not. West (1981) reported that although about one-third of the visitors to the Sylvania Recreation Area in Northern Michigan said that the presence of others decreased their enjoyment, only one-third of these indicated they were bothered by density-related issues, such as crowding. The remainder indicated they were bothered by the inappropriate behavior of others, such as playing radios, littering, and other violations of backcountry social norms. Clearly, the definition of appropriate interaction with others is founded upon more than expectations about the level of encounters. The nature of encounters is also important and interactions that violate situationally specific norms of appropriate behavior contribute to a sense of crowding.

Furthermore, differing perceptions of appropriate behavior can lead to sharply different conceptions of what use levels constitute crowding. In most wildernesses, travel is restricted to either foot or horseback, although mechanized use, primarily motor boats, is found in Minnesota's Boundary Waters Canoe Area Wilderness. There, Lucas (1964) reported that canoeists complained of crowding more than twice as often as any other group. Moreover, they sharply differentiated between other canoeists and those traveling by motor when asked how many other users they could meet in a day before there was "too much use." Although canoeists could accept up to five encounters daily with other canoeists before crowding was experienced, no contacts with motor boaters were considered acceptable. On the other hand, motor boaters said "no limit" to canoe encounters and as high as 100 other motor boats. Similar, albeit less striking, patterns have been reported in western wildernesses between backpackers and horseback riders (Stankey, 1973).

Two issues seem important here. First, the variable reaction to others obtained from the two groups reflects a sharp difference in salient motives. Motor boaters typically were motivated by fishing; canoeists, on the other hand, rated fishing low as an attraction and rated the area's wilderness qualities as most important. The very presence of mechanized equipment in an area called wilderness, where an essential quality is the absence of modern conveyances, likely represented a major source of conflict to canoeists. Such a situation constitutes a clear form of a behavioral crowding effect, defined by Gramann (1982) as a condition where the objectionable behavior interferes with the achievement of an important psychological goal, thereby reducing the tolerance of others.

A second issue focuses on what Lee (1977) has described as the concept of "likeness." He observes that in recreation settings, participants seek to find a "scheme of order with others similar enough to themselves to be able to take for granted many everyday normative constraints." The perception of shared "likeness" also means that the level of voluntary attention one must devote to the environment is reduced and, accordingly, the level of energy expended to maintain freedom of choice (Hammitt, 1982). Voluntary attention occurs when the stimuli around an individual require that person's active and constant involvement; it is therefore a cost. A consistently cited value of wilderness is its role as an environmental setting where the individual can escape the demands of voluntary attention and engage in its involuntary counterpart, defined as a passive and reflexive state imposing little, if any, cost. Thus, when the lack of shared norms raises the environmental demands upon an individual, as when the motor boater enters the wilderness world of the canoeist, the reflexive, aroused state provoked by the natural setting is disrupted, with a consequent interpretation of the situation as crowded (Hammitt, 1982).

The need to employ voluntary attention in order to maintain a state of congruency between desired and achieved interaction with others represents a major cost imposed upon visitors. In order to contend with crowding that would otherwise occur, persons are required to exert a considerable level of effort. Given the qualities of escape, respite, and quietude that wilderness visitors seek, violations of the expected nature of interaction with others must necessarily be countered with the implementation of a series of mechanisms with behavioral, psychological, and physiological costs. As these costs rise, visitors may be faced with balancing the benefits of achieving congruency between desired and achieved interaction, on the one hand, and the constraints imposed upon their behavior and freedom of choice in order to achieve that congruency, on the other.

The normative nature of crowding perception lies at the root of much of the conflict occurring between recreation groups. Shared notions of appropriateness result in the avoidance of those behaviors that interfere with others; when these norms are not known or shared, conflict often arises. Much of what is defined as crowding derives not from excessive contact with others but contact with others in a manner defined as inappropriate, such as in the case of mode of travel.

Altman's model also suggests that privacy regulations can be seen as a shifting set of expectations regarding desired privacy. The perceived character and function of a place can evoke different conceptions of appropriate interaction. Such expectations can apply at both a macro as well as micro scale. Shelby (1981) found that visitors to Oregon's Rogue River defined appropriate use levels significantly differently when asked to consider the river as a "wilderness" as opposed to a "primitive recreation area." Lucas (1985) and Stankey (1980) report that from two-thirds to three-fourths of visitors define a norm of campsites away from others, typically defined as "out of sight and sound." Other spatial units might exist in which well-defined norms of interparty interaction are found. Hendee, Clark, and Daily (1977) reported that members of fishing groups at backcountry lakes tended to keep close to one another but most remained 100 feet or more away from the members of other groups. Such "bubbles" of personal space that define appropriate distancing between one another are a common mechanism for controlling access to one's self (Burch, 1981).

The literature clearly suggests that wilderness visitors establish expectations regarding not only the levels of interaction they consider appropriate but the kinds of interactions as well. The behavior of others, more so than their numbers, governs much of the evaluation as to whether their presence is defined as crowded or not. It also appears that the ability of people to cope with violations of behaviorally-based expectations of appropriate interaction is limited in contrast to those that are restricted to appropriate levels of interaction. That is, whereas visitors have a wide range of options that appear reasonably successful in contending with higher than desired levels of interaction, they appear to have fewer options, and are less successful, in coping with violations of expectations regarding appropriate behavior.

CROWDING AS EVIDENCE OF OTHERS

Crowding can occur even when others are not present, such as when the evidence of others is appraised as inappropriate or as symbolic of non-normative behavior. It represents another form of a goal interference model of carrying capacity (Gramann, 1982), where the conditions related to use are perceived as limitations on the choices available to the individual (Stokols, Rall, Pinner, & Schopler, 1973).

This view of crowding has special importance in wilderness, where the naturalness of the environmental setting and the absence of human influence are critical attributes. When evidence of the previous presence of others is seen as excessive or inappropriate, crowding occurs. However, this aspect of wilderness crowding has received little attention, despite some evidence that it might be not only a major source of crowding perception among wilderness visitors but also an aspect of the wilderness setting subject to a relatively high degree of management control. For instance, Stankey (1973) found that evidence of litter and environmental impacts had a greater influence upon the perception of crowding than did contacts with other parties. Similarly, Vaske, Graefe, and Dempster (1982) reported that the perception of environmental disturbance was the strongest predictor of perceived crowding in Virginia's Dolly Sods Wilderness Area.

Hammitt (1983) has suggested that the effects of the evidence of others argues for an ecological approach to the treatment of crowding. In particular, determining the functional preferences of visitors would serve to approve the ability to assess how "affordances" (Gibson, 1977) (environmental aspects that have functional consequences, including social and behavioral significance), affect the perception of crowdedness. The presence of litter or environmental impact interferes with the function of the environment to provide experiences related to naturalness or the absence of the evidence of others, thereby leading to the perception of crowding.

The concept of crowding as a result of the evidence of others provides further support of the model of crowding presented by Altman (1975). Again, we see that wilderness visitors establish expectations about appropriate interactions; in this case, with regard to the visible evidence of past use. When conditions exceed these desired levels of interaction with the evidence of use, crowding results.

Three important points emerge from the preceding discussion. First, wilderness visitors do regulate access to themselves. Although the conventional terminology describes this desired state as one of solitude, it is more akin to the conception of intimacy as described by Westin (1967): a state in which the individual acts as a member of a small, closely knit group, holding shared meanings regarding their environmental circumstances. In such groups, "to enjoy nature," "to enjoy solitude," and "to enjoy socialization" can be mutually compatible and simultaneously sought by participants.

Second, wilderness participants establish expectations regarding the level and character of desired interaction with others. These expectations constitute the standard against which actual use conditions are tested; when actual conditions exceed those desired, the potential for crowding is present. However, visitors have at their disposal a wide range of mechanisms they can employ to reduce the discrepancy between desired and achieved levels of interaction. Such mechanisms vary in their acceptability, in their relative success, and in the costs they impose.

The desired levels of interaction also vary greatly in space, time, and social context. Even within an area, variable standards of desired levels of interaction can be found, shaped by expectations based upon such factors as previous experience.

Finally, a complex web of antecedent, psychological, and situational characteristics influences the extent to which a condition is perceived as crowded. Mediating influences, such as preferences and expectations, help explain how people cope with use conditions that would otherwise be defined as crowded (Schreyer & Roggenbuck, 1978; Shelby, Heberlein, Vaske, & Alfano, 1983). Such influences act to reduce the discrepancy between desired and achieved levels of interaction with others and therefore, the extent to which crowding occurs. Expectations are particularly important because they are typically derived from previous experience; however, when such expectations are formed from limited or inaccurate information, their predictive value is greatly reduced, as is their effectiveness in reducing the discrepancy between desired and achieved levels of interaction.

FUTURE DIRECTIONS FOR PRACTICE, POLICY, AND RESEARCH

Although people can employ a variety of mechanisms with which to deal with higher than desired use levels, there are also strategies that can be implemented by wilderness managers to prevent, or at least, to reduce the occurrence of crowding. However, the capacity to develop and implement effective management programs largely rests on an improved understanding of the attributes that give rise to crowding perceptions and the relative efficacy of the various strategies that are employed to deal with crowding. Such research has been initiated, but further work is needed:

MANAGING CROWDING IN WILDERNESS SETTINGS

There are a wide range of actions that managers might employ in response to wilderness crowding. They can be arrayed along a continuum, from those relying upon persuasion and information to those where control is externally applied and often accompanied by sanctions and formal procedures, such as permit systems (Hendee et al., 1978).

Research on visitor attitudes toward the various management alternatives is extensive and has been reviewed recently (Stankey & Schreyer, 1987). Several conclusions emerge from this research. First, most users express a willingness to accept use limitations. Lucas (1985) found that wilderness visitors over a ten-year period continued to show support for "restricting the number of visitors to an area if it is being used beyond capacity." Although no effort to define capacity was made, over three-fourths supported such controls.

However, interarea use differences provided varying attitudes toward control in three eastern wildernesses studied by Roggenbuck, Watson, and Stankey (1982). The major difference was when the need to impose controls might arise. In the Shining Rock, with one of the highest use densities in the country, nearly one-fourth thought controls to lower use were needed immediately, another 30% thought they were needed to hold use at current levels, and nearly 40% thought they would be needed in the future. In the Joyce Kilmer/Slickrock, on the other hand, a lightly used area by eastern standards, the majority of users felt controls would be needed, but only in the future and when overuse occurred. In all areas, there was little support for the idea that controls were not needed at present or in the future.

Such research suggests that most wilderness visitors value the state of privacy highly and are willing to accept externally imposed restraints in order to achieve and/or maintain a desired level of interaction. It also appears that visitors are able to evaluate threats to this desired state of privacy and are prepared to accept external controls when their personal repertoire of mechanisms (spatial or temporal adjustments, etc.) do not appear adequate to deal with the situation.

A second general conclusion about use control is that there is a strong preference for indirect forms of management. In particular, there is support for those actions emphasizing the use of information as a technique for changing use distributions (both spatially and temporally) and for improving visitor behavior. On reviewing the research on the use of information as a management tool, Brown, McCool, and Manfredo (1987) conclude that although information can be effective in redistributing use, it must be delivered at a point in the decision-making process where it is still capable of influencing the individual's choice. For example, some early studies where information was supplied to alter visitors' spatial behavior failed because the basic decision of where to go had been made prior to receipt of the information.

In addition to the timing of the delivery of information, it is important to recognize that the multiple motives underlying wilderness visitation mean that various kinds of information are needed to alter behavior. Information solely related to use intensity, for example, typically will have little effect on user behavior; one successful redistribution program relied upon a complex mix of information, including scenic opportunities, recreational activities, challenge, and the biophysical character of the environment in addition to likely use levels (Krumpe & Brown, 1982).

The third conclusion about use control concerns the implementation of direct actions, including fees, permits, and rationing systems. Although visitors show a decided preference for indirect measures, there is support for the more restrictive measures, with the criterion for acceptance the extent to which such actions are seen as necessary to protect wilderness conditions (Brown et al., 1987). Although the point at which people believe conditions are threatened is not obvious, there is nevertheless a rational basis underlying the decision to accept or reject controls over further use increases.

As the previous discussion of research points out, crowding occurs when the expectations of desired levels and types of interaction are violated. These expectations of access to the self are formed with regard to many factors other than level of encounters. Yet, with few exceptions, much of the management and research attention concerned with the control of crowding has been on the regulation of use levels.

Such a focus has the unfortunate effect of giving the appearance of responding to a problem while ignoring other, perhaps more useful, avenues. Controlling access to a resource is politically sensitive; controlling access to a resource whose very essence is the absence of control is particularly controversial. The very idea of wilderness management has been questioned as an internally contradictory concept. Yet the fact that wilderness, as a special kind of place and space, is a scarce and fragmented resource under considerable pressure means that the issue of its management is largely one of "how" rather than "whether" (Lucas, 1973).

Managing for solitude is complex. Managers can regulate use levels by controlling entry, but this has only a limited effect on actual levels of intergroup contact and even less effect on the perception of crowding (Shelby & Heberlein, 1986). To some extent, interparty contact can be influenced, although to do so requires the imposition of strict regulatory controls that jeopardize the nature of the desired experience. In the final analysis, the direct management of privacy, or "solitude," in wilderness settings can be only partially achieved, given the lack of uniformly agreed upon notions as to the specific dimensions and characteristics of wilderness solitude. But it is also apparent that the kind of programs instituted in wilderness can have a positive (or negative) influence upon the ability of visitors to achieve desired experiences.

FUTURE DIRECTIONS OF RESEARCH

The biologically based model of carrying capacity was adopted to grapple with questions of overuse in wilderness settings, at least in part, because of the apparent objectivity it brought to this complex issue. But the issues of determining the appropriate number of cattle on a range and resolving when crowding in wilderness settings occurs are fundamentally different; as a consequence, the carrying capacity metaphor is largely inappropriate. Yet its long association with the field of wildland recreation management means that it likely will remain a common part of the terminology. Consequently, it is important that the underlying processes and premises of managing for density-dependent experiences in wilderness be understood.

Establishing measures of appropriate use conditions in wilderness—including level, type, and behavior—is a judgmental matter. The conception of appropriate use varies widely and along a number of dimensions: between manager and visitor, between novices and experienced users, and so on. The plethora of views makes the task of formulating a logical basis for a judgment difficult. Nevertheless, there do seem to be logical and systematic ways in which it can be approached. For example, Shelby and Heberlein (1986) argue that to establish socially based capacity limits, there must be agreement both as to the relevant groups who will determine the kinds of experiences to be provided and appropriate levels of these experiences. In the case of wilderness, the basic objectives for which such areas are to be managed have been established through the political marketplace, but the determination of the specific dimensions of the experiences associated with such areas remains unresolved. Efforts to guide such decisions have been attempted; Stankey (1973), for example, argued that the views of visitors whose conception of wilderness most closely matched that described by the 1964 Wilderness Act should be given primary attention. Shelby (1981) has argued that although a wide variation of views exist among users, there may be more consensus than is often believed.

A fundamental research need, thus, would appear to be a clarification of the range and distribution among user populations as to the perceptions of appropriate use in wilderness settings.

The specific environmental and social conditions that give rise to the perception of crowding also vary. Although there is an implicit assumption that crowding is density dependent, we have seen that it is a more complex condition, occurring when the boundaries to regulate privacy are violated by not only excessive numbers of others, but their non-normative behavior or evidence of inappropriate behavior as well. Some forms of crowding are likely more easily addressed than others. Inappropriate behavior that contributes to environmental impact or to the increased awareness of others might be more susceptible to management influence, through education, than other forms of crowding. Such differences also entail implementation of different approaches to crowding management, as many impacts are density independent, such as littering. But underlying the opportunity to make progress there is the need for a better understanding of the conditions that give rise to the perception of crowding and the ways in which such perceptions are mitigated by the social and environmental attributes of the setting.

Although crowding is recognized by users and managers alike as a problem in wilderness settings, it is neither the most important issue for many visitors nor a condition that can be clearly and unequivocally associated with a loss of satisfaction. A wide array of adaptive and mitigative mechanisms are employed by visitors. Some are psychological in nature, permitting the individual a means to avoid dissonance and psychological discomfort. Both expectations and preferences have received much attention by researchers (Schreyer & Roggenbuck, 1978; Shelby et al., 1983). In general, the research suggests that expectations are most useful as predictors of how actual use conditions will be evaluated. Preferences are also important. They provide a measure of desired states of privacy and are therefore of particular value in helping establish the kinds of evaluative standards called for in newly formulated models for wildland management, which rest on a management-by-objectives basis. There is a need to profile the range and distribution of these expectations and preferences as well as to discover more about the processes through which they are formed and communicated.

Adaptive responses to crowding are not limited to the psychological. Behavioral mechanisms are also employed, ranging from the decision to avoid times and/or places known to be overused to staying home. However, because most knowledge about wilderness users is derived from one-time, cross-sectional surveys, conducted during peak-use times, it is easy to miss such behavior. This is potentially a serious omission, as use conditions that promote such behavior are of particular concern. The phenomenon of such spatial behavior has been labeled "succession-and-displacement" (Clark, Hendee, & Campbell, 1971), and although its magnitude is not clear (Nielsen & Endo, 1977), it remains an area of concern and needed investigation. Not only is an increased effort to investigate the substantive issues needed, but alternative methodological designs are required as well. In particular, longitudinal designs are needed to help follow cycles of wilderness behavior and the association between such changes and other shifts, including wilderness use levels, the introduction of intervening opportunities, and lifestyle changes. Such research designs would also reveal if norms of appropriate use are changing over time.

Judgments of appropriate use are embodied in norms and it is clear that reasonably well agreed-upon judgments do exist among wilderness users (Shelby, 1981). Such norms provide a sound basis for the prescription of standards to guide wilderness planning. What is not clear is how such norms evolve, are communicated, and reinforced. Nevertheless, they represent useful concepts that management can utilize; a greater understanding of the process underlying their development would be helpful.

Burch (1981) has argued that managerial intervention in wildland management, particularly in terms of regulating access to resources, reflects more of an ideological bias than it does a well-informed, rational decision. He contends that other primates as well as humans have evolved a variety of mechanisms to regulate and manage conflict and personal spacing behavior. His arguments rest on the idea that "natural" cycles of adjustment may be operating that largely obviate the need for managerial intervention. For example, changing structures in the sociodemographic character of society, such as the increasing proportion in older age classes, where participation rates are lower, mean that current use levels might soon decline.

A recent analysis of trends in wilderness and backcountry use lends support to Burch's proposition. Stankey and Lucas (1986) report that although total use of wilderness and backcountry areas has grown greatly since 1964, the growth is almost wholly a function of the increase in the number of areas reporting such use. When the growth in area is controlled, the figures show a decline in use since about 1980. Although the reasons for this decline are not clear, it is apparent that wilderness recreation use, like most spheres of human activity, is subject to cyclic changes. The research challenge is to help establish the linkages between such macro-level changes (e.g., changing age structure, changes in patterns of work in families) and the use of wilderness settings.

Finally, the literature strongly suggests that few experiences are solely density dependent; most are linked to other behavioral characteristics as well as to the relative salience of that experience domain to the visitor. Clarifying the linkage among density, behavioral characteristics, and experiences would enhance the ability of management to determine the impacts of changing densities and the relative values gained in altering or controlling other aspects of user behavior.

Wilderness is a fragile quality, both in terms of its physical–biological conditions and the experiences such conditions provide to society. Such areas are valued because they offer a kind of place where close interpersonal relationships can be enjoyed in the midst of natural, undisturbed surroundings. However, pressures on wilderness settings require that management programs be instituted to help ensure that the opportunity for such kinds of experiences be retained. Applying appropriate management actions requires a blend of a clearer understanding of the role and function of the wilderness experience for the individual along with a sensitivity to the limits of direct management intervention in creating a condition of privacy and solitude.

REFERENCES

Absher, J. D., & Lee, R. G. (1981). Density as an incomplete cause of crowding in backcountry settings. *Leisure Sciences,4,* 231–247.

Altman, I. (1975). *The environment and social behavior.* Monterey, California: Brooks/Cole.

Brown, P. J., McCool, S. F., & Manfredo, M. J. (1987). Evolving concepts and tools for recreation user management in wilderness: A state-of-knowledge review. In R. C. Lucas (Ed.), *Proceedings—National wilderness research conference: Issues, state-of-knowledge, future directions* (USDA Forest Service General Tech. Rep. No. INT-220, pp. 320–346). Odgen, UT: Intermountain Research Station.

Burch, W. R., Jr. (1981). The ecology of metaphor—spacing regularities for humans and other primates in urban and wildland habitats. *Leisure Sciences, 4,* 213–230.

Burch, W. R., Jr. (1984). Much ado about nothing—some reflections on the wider and wilder implications of social carrying capacity. *Leisure Sciences, 6,* 487–496.

Clark, R. N., Hendee, J. C., & Campbell, F. L. (1971). Values, behavior, and conflict in modern camping culture. *Journal of Leisure Research, 3,* 143–159.

Gibson, J. J. (1977). The theory of affordances. In R. E. Shaw & J. Bransford (Eds.), *Perceiving, acting, and knowing: Toward an ecological psychology* (pp. 67–82). Hillsdale, NJ: Erlbaum.

Gramann, J. H. (1982). Toward a behavioral theory of crowding in outdoor recreation: An evaluation and synthesis of research. *Leisure Sciences, 5,* 109–126.

Hammitt, W. E. (1982). Cognitive dimensions of wilderness solitude. *Environment and Behavior, 14,* 478–493.

Hammitt, W. E. (1983). Toward an ecological approach to perceived crowding in outdoor recreation. *Leisure Sciences, 5,* 309–320.

Hendee, J. C., Clark, R. N., & Daily, T. E. (1977). *Fishing and other recreation behavior at high-mountain lakes in Washington State.* (USDA Forest Service Research Note PNW-304). Portland, OR: Pacific Northwest Forest and Range Experiment Station.

Hendee, J. C., Stankey, G. H., & Lucas, R. C. (1978). *Wilderness management.* Washington, DC: U.S. Government Printing Office.

Krumpe, E. E., & Brown, P. J. (1982). Redistributing backcountry use through information related to recreation experiences. *Journal of Forestry, 80,* 360–362.

Lee, R. G. (1977). Alone with others: The paradox of privacy in wilderness. *Leisure Sciences, 1,* 3–19.

Lucas, R. C. (1964). Wilderness perception and use: The example of the Boundary Waters Canoe Area. *Natural Resources Journal, 3,* 394–411.

Lucas, R. C. (1973). Wilderness: A management framework. *Journal of Soil and Water Conservation, 28,* 150–154.

Lucas, R. C. (1985). *Visitor characteristics, attitudes, and use patterns in the Bob Marshall Wilderness Complex, 1970–82* (USDA Forest Service Research Paper No. INT-345). Ogden, UT: Intermountain Research Station.

Manning, R. E. (1985). Crowding norms in backcountry settings: A review and synthesis. *Journal of Leisure Research, 17,* 75–89.

McCool, S. F. (1983). Wilderness quality and wilderness solitude: Are they related? In S. McCool (Ed.), *The Bob Marshall Wilderness visitor study* (pp. 40–61). Missoula, MT: University of Montana.

Nash, R. (1982). *Wilderness and the American mind.* New Haven, CT: Yale University Press.

Nielsen, J. M., & Endo, R. (1977). Where have all the purists gone? An empirical examination of the displacement process hypothesis in wilderness recreation. *Western Sociological Review, 8,* 61–75.

Proshansky, H. M., Ittelson, W. H., & Rivlin, L. G. (1970). Freedom of choice and behavior in a physical setting. In H. M. Proshanksy, W. H. Ittelson, & L. G. Rivlin (Eds.), *Environmental psychology: Man and his physical setting* (pp. 173–182). New York: Holt, Rinehart & Winston.

Roggenbuck, J. W., Watson, A. E., & Stankey, G. H. (1982). Wilderness management in the southern Appalachians. *Southern Journal of Applied Forestry, 6,* 147–152.

Schreyer, R., & Roggenbuck, J. W. (1978). The influence of experience expectations on crowding perceptions and social-psychological carrying capacities. *Leisure Sciences, 1,* 373–394.

Shelby, B. (1980). Crowding models for backcountry recreation. *Land Economics, 56,* 43–55.

Shelby, B. (1981). Encounter norms in backcountry settings: Studies of three rivers. *Journal of Leisure Research, 6,* 433–451.

Shelby, B., & Heberlein, T. A. (1986). *Carrying capacity in recreational settings.* Corvallis, OR: Oregon State University Press.

Shelby, B., Heberlein, T. A., Vaske, J. J., & Alfano, G. (1983). Expectations, preferences, and feeling crowded in recreation activities. *Leisure Sciences, 6,* 1–14.

Stankey, G. H. (1973). *Visitor perception of wilderness recreation carrying capacity* (USDA Forest Service Research Paper No. INT-142). Ogden, UT: Intermountain Forest and Range Experiment Station.

Stankey, G. H. (1980). *A comparison of carrying capacity perceptions among visitors to two wildernesses* (USDA Forest Service Research Paper No. INT-242). Ogden, UT: Intermountain Forest and Range Experiment Station.

Stankey, G. H., & Lucas, R. C. (1986). *Shifting trends in backcountry and wilderness use.* Paper presented to the First National Symposium on Social Science and Resource Management, Corvallis, OR, June.

Stankey, G. H., & McCool, S. F. (1984). Carrying capacity in recreational settings: Evolution, appraisal, and application. *Leisure Sciences, 6,* 453–473.

Stankey, G. H., & Schreyer, R. (1987). Attitudes toward wilderness and factors affecting visitor behavior: A state-of-knowledge review. In R. C. Lucas (Ed.), *Proceedings—National wilderness research conference: Issues, state-of-knowledge, future directions* (USDA Forest Service General Tech. Rep. No. INT-220, pp. 246–293). Ogden, UT: Intermountain Research Station.

Stokols, D. (1972). On the distinction between density and crowding: Some implications for future research. *Psychological Review, 79,* 275–277.

Stokols, D., Rall, M., Pinner, B., & Schopler, J. (1973). Physical, social, and personal determinants on the perception of crowding. *Environment and Behavior, 5,* 87–115.

Twight, B. W., Smith, K. L., & Wissinger, G. H. (1981). Privacy and camping: Closeness to the self vs. closeness to others. *Leisure Sciences, 4,* 427–441.

Vaske, J. J., Graefe, A. R., & Dempster, A. (1982). Social and environmental influences on perceived crowding. In *Proceedings of the Wilderness Psychology Group Conference* (pp. 211–227). Morgantown, WV: West Virginia University.

Wagar, J. A. (1964). *The carrying capacity of wildlands for recreation* (Forest Science Monograph No. 7). Washington, DC: Society of American Foresters.

West, P. C. (1981). Perceived crowding and attitudes toward limiting use in backcountry recreation areas. *Leisure Sciences, 4*, 419–425.

Westin, A. F. (1967). *Privacy and freedom*. New York: Atheneum.

Womble, P., & Studebaker, S. (1981). Crowding in a national park campground. *Environment and Behavior, 13*, 557–573.

Index

Absher, J. D., 286
Accessibility of public spaces, 164
Adaptation
  in human ecosystem, 260
  in responses to crowding, 295–296
Adaptive Environments, Boston, 101
Adelmann, B. J. E., 237, 238
Adventure playgrounds
  activities in, 90–91
  adult participation in, 98
  manipulative settings in, 113–114
  play value of, 93–99
Affect, urban
  measures of, 37
  salient dimensions in, 39–40
Age, and participation in water-based recreation, 229, 241
Agee, J. K., 270
AIDS quilt, touring public spaces, 163
Alabama, farmers' markets in, 58, 65
Alaska
  Endicott Range wilderness area, 281, 282
  national parks in, 268
Alienation, 13
Alpine Lakes, Washington, 281
Altman, I., 1–4, 77, 123, 157, 159, 282, 283, 286, 287, 291
Amedeo, D., 225
American Association of Zoological Parks and Aquariums, 174
Andel, J. van, 90
Anderson, A., 26
Anderson, D. H., 232, 233, 237, 239, 240
Anderson, L. M., 47
Animal–environment research in zoological parks, 175–177

Animals in playgrounds, 112
Animators in playgrounds, 103–104
Appleton, J., 45, 226
Appleyard, D., 34, 35, 38, 47, 167
Aquatic environments. *See* Water-based recreation
Archer, R., 61
Architecture. *See* Buildings
Arctic landscape, reactions to, 230
Arendt, H., 8, 10, 15, 123
Arizona
  Galiuro wilderness area, 281
  Grand Canyon, 224, 257, 287
Arkansas, Buffalo River floaters in, 235
Arnstein, S., 158
Arousal, and evaluation of environment, 40, 41
Art parks, 197
Ashby, W., 268
Assumptions about public life, 7–8
  and management of parks as human ecosystems, 256–258
Attachment to public spaces, factors in, 155–156
Atwood, M., 142
Auditory environment
  in farmers' markets, 71–72
  and scene judgments, 38
Australia, playground accidents in, 87

Baker, N. J., 224
Bakos, M., 106
Baldassare, M., 156
Balling, J. D., 226, 233
Balmforth, N., 94
Barash, D. P., 256
Barker, J. F., 16

Barth, G., 125, 126
Becker, F., 86, 166
Beckman, T. N., 60, 66
Beer, V., 183
Bellah, R., 8, 10
Bengtsson, A., 94
Benjamin, J., 94
Benn, S. I., 123
Bennett, J. W., 260
Berk, S. F., 127
Berlyne, D. E., 41, 42, 44
Berman, M., 149, 165
Bernard, C., 129
Berry, W., 272
Beyer, W., 268
Birney, B., 176, 184, 186
Bishop, D. W., 229
Bitgood, S., 179, 180, 182, 183, 186
Björklid, P., 84, 86, 96, 103
Blacks, participation in water-based recreation, 230
Blackwell, C., 268
Block, R., 174
Blue, G. F., 112
Boating, crowding in, 237–238, 289
Boehm, E., 96
Bog environment, reactions to, 233
Boice, R., 175
Bormann, F., 271
Borum, M., 180
Bosselmann, P., 166
Boston
  Adaptive Environments in, 101
  community gardens in, 156
  Copley Square, 168
  farmers' markets in, 59, 168
  Franklin Park, 198–207
  interagency groups for public space policy, 154
  Italian community in North End, 26
  Kennedy Library, 166
  Lenox-Camden Playground, 92, 95
  Quincy Market, 25
Botanical gardens in cities, 196
Boulding, K., 91
Boundary Waters Canoe Area, Minnesota, 217, 232, 237, 289
Bowlby, S. R., 128
Boyce, W. T., 90
Boys, J., 122, 135
Brambilla, A., 9
Brennan, T., 181, 183
Brill, M., 8–28, 123, 149, 150

Brooker, J. R., 64
Brown, B., 157
Brown, D., 130, 135
Brown, P. J., 293
Bruhn, J. G., 258
Brunswik lens model as framework for environmental esthetics, 36
Brush, R. O., 225
Bruya, L., 83
Bryan, H., 232
Buffalo River, Arkansas, 235
Buhyoff, G. J., 229, 234
Buildings
  American and European, comparison of, 15–16
  design cues limiting access to, 23, 152, 154, 164
  recall of, factors affecting, 35
  as settings for life, 19
  symbolic meanings of styles in, 46–47
  zoning codes for, 21
Bunting, T. E., 231
Burch, W. R., Jr., 231, 256, 285, 290, 296
Burger, J. M., 156
Burke, P., 59, 60, 65, 66, 72, 74
Burks, M., 184
Business interests, compared to government policies, 24–25

California
  Berkeley Environmental Simulation Laboratory, 166
  building recall study in Orange, 35
  Central Park in Davis, 156
  community garden and park in Sacramento, 150, 160, 164
  Desolation wilderness area, 281
  Disneyland, 133
  employee gardens in, 160–161
  Environmental Yard in Berkeley, 91, 93, 99, 100
  farmers' markets in, 58, 64, 65, 68, 76, 168
  flooding of Hetch Hetchy Valley, 279
  historic landmarks in Los Angeles, 135–136
  homelessness in, 162
  Mt. Whitney overuse by climbers, 277
  playground in Davis, 166
  Power of Place, Los Angeles, 142
  San Diego Zoo, 185
  Village Homes study in, 86
  Yosemite National Park, 279, 286
  See also San Francisco

Index

Calip, T., 176
Campbell, S. D., 91
Canada
  public spaces in Toronto used by women, 135, 141
  use of public spaces in Montreal, 134–135
  waterfront park in Toronto, 196–197
  Women Plan Toronto, 135, 141
Canter, D., 44
Cape Hatteras National Seashore, 268
Carhart, A., 279
Carp, F., 33, 50
Carr, S., 121, 140, 152, 155, 156
Carrying capacity concept, and recreational use, 284–286
Catlin, G., 279
Catton, W. R., Jr., 237, 242, 243, 257, 258
Change, effects of. *See* Transformations of public life
Characteristics of public spaces, 131
Cheek, N. H., 178, 262, 263
Chesapeake Bay
  multiple jurisdictions in, 223
  waterfowl hunters in, 234
Chidister, M., 150, 155
Childcare by women, 127
  and use of public spaces, 135, 139, 141
Childhood experiences affecting recreational activities, 231
Children
  playgrounds for. *See* Playgrounds
  right to play, 85
  use of outdoors, 84–85
  visits to zoological parks, 177, 178, 179, 182, 184
China, panda protection in, 267
Chomsky, N., 256
Cichoki, M. K., 121, 127
Citigo Creek, Tennessee, 281
Civil liberties, erosion of, 23
Civility in public life, loss of, 10
Clark, R. N., 244, 296
Clements, F., 258
Clubhouses in playgrounds, 91, 95
Cobb, E., 101
Cockrell, D., 233, 235
Coe, J., 176
Cognition, urban, 32–36
  building recall in, 34–35
  imageability in, 34
  individual differences in, 34
Collins, A. J., 70, 71, 75

Colorado
  botanical gardens in Denver, 196
  Never Summer wilderness area, 281
  Trappers Lake, 279
Colorado River, density and crowding in, 286
Colton, C. W., 233, 238
Commerce-and-pleasure strand of public life, 11–12
Communication and information portion of public life, changes in, 11, 17–18
Community activism, in control of environment, 155–156
Community affairs, participation in, 10–11
Community gardens and parks, 150, 156, 160, 164
  control of, 167
  satisfaction with, 165
Compatibility, environmental cues for, 42
Complexity and order, in urban perception, 41–44
Conflicts
  in national parks and local populations, 265–267
  in urban design, resolution of, 165–166
  in water-based recreation, 222–223, 242
Connecticut, farmers' markets in, 65
Consortium of Aquariums, Universities, and Zoos, 174
Consumer Product Safety Commission, 87, 90
Content variables, in urban perception, 45–48
Control of public space, 133, 147–169
  accessibility in, 164
  conflicts in, 165–166
  definition and dimensions of, 158–159
  design and management opportunities in, 166–168
  as environmental concept, 154–156
  in gardening activities, 159–161
  in neighborhood parks, 167
  and ownership benefits, 164–165
  as participation concept, 157–158
  personalization in, 162–164, 167
  in plazas and downtown spaces, 167–168
  private interests versus public needs in, 161
  and problem of homeless people, 161–162
  as psychological concept, 156–157
  public interests in, 150–154

Control of public space (*Cont.*)
  recommendations for, 168–169
  safety issues in, 165
  and street design, 167
Conway, W. G., 184
Cooper, C., 95
Cooper Marcus, C., 84, 110, 114
Coughlin, R. E., 238, 239
Cowan, R., 124
Cowdin, N. P., 239
Craik, K. H., 36, 38, 44
Cranz, G., 26, 121, 155, 194
Crime, and fears of women, 128–129, 141
Cross, J., 65
Crowding
  adaptive responses to, 295–296
  and appropriate levels of others, 286–287
  and behavior of others, 287–290
  density compared to, 282, 286
  as evidence of others, 290–292
  and ideas of privacy, 282–284
  management in wilderness settings, 292–294
  in water-based recreation, 236–238
Cullen, G., 182
Cultural factors in water-based recreation, 230
Cultural programs in urban parks, 198

Daniel, T. C., 186, 226, 230
Dasmann, R., 266
Davidoff, L., 125
Davis, W. G., 79
Deardon, L., 233, 235
Dearinger, J. A., 224
DeBellevue, E., 268
Definition of public space, 123
Denali National Park, 268
Denmark
  adventure playgrounds in, 96
  play leadership and animation in, 104
Density, compared to crowding, 282, 286
Derickx, C., 86
Derwin, C., 176
Design of public spaces
  affecting use by women, 134–136, 140–142
  to discourage use, 23, 152, 154, 164
  and increased control, 166–168
  participation in, and user satisfaction, 157–158, 166–169
  suggested activities in, 26–28

Desolation wilderness area, California, 281
Devil's Backbone wilderness area, Missouri, 281, 282
Devlin, K., 33, 34, 44, 46
Diamond, S., 139
Diesing, P. R., 13
Dietrich, R., 66
Dinosaur National Monument, river recreationists in, 231
Disabilities in childhood, and playground activities, 101–102
Disneyland, control of space in, 133
Distribution of public lands, 1
District of Columbia
  farmers' markets in, 60
  Vietnam Veterans Memorial in, 163
  zoological park in, 197
Ditton, R. B., 232, 233, 236, 238
Diversity
  in playgrounds, 91–92, 95
  and segmentation of society, 26
  in urban parks, 196–197
Dolly Sods wilderness are, 281, 191
Domestic spaces, as private areas for women, 123
Doughtery, D., 156
Dowell, D. L., 234
Driver, B. L., 217, 218, 219, 231, 232, 237, 244, 245
Drug dealers using public space, 157
Dubois, E., 126
Dubos, R., 226, 257
Duncan, J., 101
Duncan, O. D., 258

Ecological variables, in urban perceptions, 45–48
Ecology, human
  in parks, 260–262
  perspective of, 258–260
  roots of, 258
Economic and social principles or organization, comparison of, 13
Educational efforts. *See* Interpretive programs
Elshtain, J. B.,124, 126
Employee gardens in California, 160–161
Endicott Range wilderness area, Alaska, 281, 282
Engels, F., 11–12
England. *See* United Kingdom
Enjeu, C., 122

Index

Entertainment in public streets, 18
Environment
   and community activism, 155–156
   simulations affecting development of, 166
Environmental Design Research
     Association, 213
Environmental Protection Agency, 223
Eriksen, A., 102
Esbensen, S. B., 85
Escape, in water-based recreation, 229–230
Esposito, C. V., 38
Esthetics, urban, 33, 36–48
   and affecting responses, 37
     salient dimensions in, 39–40
   auditory cues in, 38
   collative variables in, 41–45
   complexity and order in, 41–44
   ecological/content variables in, 45–48
   framework for, 36–38
   naturalness in, 45–46
   novelty and familiarity in, 44–45
   nuisances affecting, 47–48
   organizing variables in, 41–45
   perceptual/cognitive measures of, 36
     salient dimensions in, 38–39
   physical measures of, 36
   physical variables in, 41–46
   psychophysical measures of, 37
   public policy affecting, 51–52
   spatial behavior measures of, 37
   spatial variables in, 45
   and symbolic meanings of styles, 46–47
   visual cues in, 38
Ethnic groups
   contacts in farmers' markets, 67–68
   participation in water-based recreation, 230
Eubanks-Ahrens, B., 167
European cities, public and private space in, 16
Euro-Urbanists, 9, 14–15, 17, 25, 150
Evans, G., 34, 35
Everglades National Park, 268
Exclusionary actions
   in design of public spaces, 23, 152, 154, 164
   in segmentation of society, 26

Familiarity
   affecting environmental appraisals, 38
   and participation in water-based recreation, 233
   in urban perceptions, 44–45

Family life, changes in, 12–13
Faris, E. L., 258
Farmers' markets, 57–79, 149, 167–168
   benefits of, 61–69
   civic utility of, 61, 75–76
   consumer benefits in, 64–66
   customers for, 70–71
   in Europe and Third World, 79
   freshness and flavor of items in, 65, 75
   functional requirements for, 69–73
   future of, 74–76
   future directions of research in, 76–79
   gender roles in, 78
   history of, 59–61
   hours of operation for, 66, 79
   intergroup contacts in, 66–68, 77
   linkage to other open-space programs, 73–74
   openness of, and contact with nature, 68–69
   organization of, 72–73
   as outlet for small farmers, 64
   prices in, 65
   products in, 71–72
   reactions of local merchants to, 62, 79
   schedules for, 70
   sites for, 69
   social atmosphere in, 65–66, 75
   space assignments in, 77
   structures in, 69–70
   traditions in, 72
   typology of, 58–59
   in urban revitalization, 61–64
   vendors in, 71
Faust, C., 185
Fedler, A. J., 234
Festival markets, 11, 25, 58, 149
Field, D. R., 220, 229, 230, 241, 242
Finlay, T., 183, 186
Fire Island, beach erosion in, 257
Fischer, C., 149
Fisher, A. C., 236
Fjeld, C. R., 73
Flea markets, 58
Florida
   Everglades National Park, 268
   zoological park in Miami, 197
Florin, P., 166
Forrest, A., 123, 130, 131, 135
Foucault, M., 20
Fox, M. B., 121, 127
France, play leadership and animation in, 104

Francis, M., 26, 57, 86, 112, 121, 131, 134, 140, 147–169, 195
Franck, K. A., 121–142
Franklin Park, Boston, 198–207
  active recreation in, 204, 206
  image of, 203
  interpretive information in, 204–205
  passive recreation in, 203–204
  planning issues in, 201–202
  rationale for new master plan in, 199–201
  research results in, 203–205
    application for design process, 205–207
  research strategy for, 202–203
Frost, J. L., 83, 85, 102
Furniture, movable, in public spaces, 162, 167

Galiuro wilderness area, usage of, 281
Gardens
  community, 150, 156, 160, 164
  and public space use, 159–161
  satisfaction with, 165
  in playgrounds, 112
Gärling, T., 45
Garner, R., 173, 174, 175
Gaunt, L., 107
Gehl, J., 147, 155
Geller, D. M., 39
Gender roles. *See* Sex roles
Georgia, Civil War battle exhibits in Atlanta, 198
Germany, Hamburg Zoo in, 174
Gibson, J. J., 291
Gifford, R., 38
Gila National Forest, New Mexico, 279
Glacier Bay National Park, 268
Glacier National Park, 268
Glazer, N., 149, 150
Godbey, G., 195
Goffman, E., 69, 76, 129, 147
Gold, S., 57, 195
Goldstein, J., 73
Goodall, J., 176
Goodey, B., 167
Goddman, P., 9
Gordon, M. Y., 121, 128
Government
  in development of farmers' markets, 57–58
  policies compared to business interests, 24–25

Government (*Cont.*)
  in regulation of esthetics, 51–52
  role of agencies in public space policy, 153–154
  support for playgrounds, 106
Graefe, A. R., 236, 238
Gramann, J. H., 229, 237, 246, 285, 288, 289, 291
Grand Canyon
  density and crowding in, 287
  foreign visitors to, 257
  river floating in, 224
Gratzer, M. A., 220, 227
Green, M., 176
Griffin, S., 121, 137, 138
Griswold-Minois, R., 65
Groat, L., 35, 46, 51
Grocery stores as social centers, 60
Gröning, G., 106
Group affiliation, and participation in water-based recreation, 234–236, 246
Guiliano, G., 127
Gutman, R., 16, 26

Habitat theory of landscape esthetics, 225–226
Hack, G., 156
Hagenbeck, C., 174
Hale, L., 268
Hall, C., 268
Halprin, L., 196
Hamburg Zoo, 174
Hammitt, W. E., 233, 238, 245, 285, 287, 288, 289, 291
Hancocks, D., 173, 175, 176
Handicapped children in playground settings, 101–102
Hanssens, C., 65
Harassment of women, 129–130
Hardin, G., 222
Harrison, B., 279
Harrison, J. D., 34, 35
Hart, R., 100, 101, 106, 113, 156, 167
Hart, W. J., 261
Hartmann, H., 127
Hawaii, farmers' markets in, 58
Hawley, A. H., 258, 260
Hayden, D., 122, 135, 140, 141, 142
Hayward, D. C., 90, 91, 94, 95, 96, 167
Hayward, J., 193–214
Heberlein, T. A., 223, 236, 237
Hecock, R. D., 229

Index

Heft, H., 34
Heidiger, H., 176
Hendee, J. C., 231, 277–278, 280, 284, 287, 290, 292
Henderson, P. L., 64, 74
Henley, N., 127, 138
Hershberger, R. G., 33, 38
Hershey chocolate factory, 198
Herzog, T. R., 44, 224, 227
Hess, J. L., 62
Hesselgren, S., 45
Hester, R., 57, 156, 158, 195
Hetch Hetchy Valley, flooding of, 279
Heusser, C. P., 109
Heywood, J. L., 214, 235
Higgins, K., 66
Hightower, J., 64
Hilker, K., 182
Hill, C., 178
Hirschon, R., 124
Hiss, T., 31, 147
Historical aspects
  of farmers' markets, 59–61
  of public life, 14–20
  of wilderness concept, 278–280
  of women's use of public spaces, 122–126
  of zoological parks, 173–174
Hodges, S., 180
Hodgson, R. W., 225, 234
Holland, playgrounds in Rotterdam, 86, 99
Holme, A., 86
Home-based work, issues in, 21
Homelessness, and use of public space, 161–162
Hood, M., 177, 178
Hood River in Oregon, windsurfing in, 224, 246
Hoots, T. A., 230
Horayangkura, V., 33, 39, 45
Household work by women, 127
Hubbard Brook studies, 271

Iacofano, D., 101, 155, 158, 166
Illinois
  botanical gardens in Chicago, 196
  Brookfield Zoo, 183
  Chicago as social laboratory, 258
  farmers' markets in, 58, 61, 64
Illusion and nostalgia for public life, 25–26
Im, S. B., 152

Imageability, urban, 34
  and perceived quality, 35–36
Indiana
  farmers' market in Terre Haute, 69
  zoological park in Indianapolis, 197
Information and communication portion of public life, changes in, 11, 17–18
Interpretive programs
  in aquatic environments, 233–234
  in Lowell historical park, 211–212
  in urban parks, 197–198, 204–205
  in zoological parks, 181–182
Involvement in environment, and urban perceptions, 41–42
Isle Royale, 268
Isogai, H., 65
Isolation and visibility in public, 10
Ittelson, W. H., 218

Jackson, E. L., 237
Jackson, J. B., 16, 27, 57, 154
Jackson, K. T., 125
Jambor, T., 105
Japan, play leadership and animation in, 104
Johnson, D. R., 195
Johnston, G. A., 222, 223
Joslin, P., 177, 178
Jumper, S. R., 65, 72

Kansas, prairie national park in, 268
Kaplan, R., 159, 160, 165, 182, 186, 187, 195, 203, 226, 227, 229
Kaplan, S., 35, 41, 42, 45, 186, 187, 227
Karim, M. B., 79
Katmai National Monument, density and crowding in, 286
Kelly, J. R., 229
Kessel, S., 268
Keuls, E. C., 124
Kimber, C. T., 159
Kingsley, C., 12
Kinkowski, W. S., 161
Kirkby, M. A., 111
Kirp, D. L., 139
Knopf, R. C., 229, 231, 232, 233, 234, 235, 244, 245, 247
Knopp, T. B., 229
Knowles, E. S., 77
Kornblum, W., 135, 136, 195
Korosec-Serfaty, P., 26
Kowinski, W. S., 61
Krumpe, E. E., 293
Krutilla, J. V., 221

Lambert, J., 94
Land occupied by urban areas, 32
Landmarks, importance in cognitive learning, 34
Langdon, P., 47
Langer, E., 156
Langley, J. D., 90
Lansing, J. B., 33, 45, 47
Laslett, B., 125
Leavitt, J., 140
Lee, R. G., 263, 287, 289
Leedy, D. L., 112
Lefcourt, H., 156
Lennard, S. H., 148
Lens model as framework for environmental esthetics, 36
Leopold, A., 279, 280
Lerner, G., 124
Leveen, E. P., 74
Levine, C., 147
Levitas, G., 9
Liebhardt, F., 174
Lime, D. W., 217, 229, 230, 234, 239, 240, 241
Lindbloom, C. E., 262
Litton, R. B., Jr., 217, 220, 224
Locasso, R., 38
Location of public spaces, and use by women, 134
Lockeretz, W., 74
Lofland, L., 122, 136, 148, 149
London
  playground use in, 86
  Zoological Society, 174
Lorenz, K. Z., 226
Louisiana, farmers' markets in, 58, 64, 71
Lowell historical park in Massachusetts, 207–213
  interpretive projects in, 211–212
  need for research in, 207–208
  research results in, 210–212
    application to planning and management, 212–213
  research strategy in, 209–210
  users of, 210–211
Lowenthal, D., 42
Lozano, E., 48
Lozar, C. C., 65, 66
Lucas, R. C., 229, 237, 238, 277, 287, 289, 290, 292, 294
Lynch, K., 32, 33, 34, 35, 148, 156, 158, 164
Lynes, R., 46, 50
Lyons, E., 51

Machlis, G. E., 255–273
Macia, A., 231
Malls. *See* Shopping malls
Management
  and increased control of public space, 166–168. *See also* Control of public space
  of parks as human ecosystems, 255–273
    assumptions in, 256–258
    future directions in research of, 271–272
    variables affecting, 260–262
  of playgrounds, risk prevention in, 105
  of water-based recreation, 239–240
  of wilderness areas, 277–297
Managers and owners of spaces, 152
Mandler, G., 44
Manning, R. E., 229, 235, 236, 239, 288
Maple, T., 176
Markin, R. J., 60, 65
Markowitz, H., 176
Marshall, R., 279, 280
Martin, J., 173–188
Marx, K., 13
Maryland
  Harborplace in Baltimore, 25
  waterfront park in Baltimore, 196–197
Mason, G., 86
Mason, J., 111
Massachusetts
  farmers' markets in, 57, 74
  Lowell historical park, 207–213
  Old Sturbridge Village, 198
  See also Boston
McAvoy, L., 239
McCamant, K., 141
McCool, S. F., 287
McDonough, M. H., 229
McKechnie, G. E., 231
McKenzie, R. D., 258
Meisner, F., 61, 72, 76
Melton, A., 179
Menageries, European, 174
Michelmore, A. P. G., 176
Michelson, W., 51, 127, 128
Michigan
  community gardens in Ann Arbor, 159
  Isle Royale, 268
  Sylvania Recreation Area, 288
Micklin, M., 259
Milburn, T., 77
Miller, J., 103, 127, 268
Minnesota, Boundary Waters Canoe Area in, 218, 232, 237, 289

Index

Mintz, N. L., 38
Missouri
  Devil's Backbone wilderness area, 281, 282
  farmers' markets in, 70, 75
  Soulard Market in St. Louis, 69
Mitchell, G., 177
Mobility of women, restrictions in, 130
Monchaux, S. de, 106
Montana, Glacier National Park in, 268
Montreal, use of public spaces in, 134–135
Moore, G. T., 34, 85, 90, 94, 96, 101, 102, 114
Moore, R. C., 83–114
More, T. A., 213, 234
Moreland, G., 105
Moser, G., 238, 239
Motivations
  for river floating, 232, 233
  for wilderness visitation, 293
  for zoological park visits, 178
Moulton, C. J., 64
Movement, and urban perceptions, 49
Mugangu-Trinto, E., 266
Muir, J., 279
Mumford, L., 140
Myers, D. G., 178
Mystery
  in aquatic environments, 227
  in design, effects of, 182
  as spatial variable, 45

Nager, A. R., 129, 164
Nasar, J. L., 31–53, 167
Nash, R., 223, 277, 278
National Environmental Policy Act of 1969, 51
National Forests, wilderness in, 279
National Gardening Association, 159
National Historical Park in Lowell, Massachusetts, 210
National parks
  as human ecosystems, 255–273
  modeling of, 267–271
  and local community needs, 265–267
  visitor studies in, 263–265
National River Recreation Survey of 1979, 235
National Safety Council, 85, 87
Naturalness, esthetic value of, 45–46
Neighborhood life
  changes in, 12–13
  compared to public life, 25

Never Summer wilderness area, Colorado, 281
New Jersey, farmers' markets in, 67
New Mexico
  Gila National Forest, 279
  Sandia Mountain wilderness area, 281
New York City
  Bryant Park studies, 136, 154, 164
  Citicorp atrium, 135, 196
  community gardens in, 156, 160
  design cues limiting access to public spaces, 23, 152, 154, 164
  environmental simulations in, 166
  Exxon Mini Park, 137, 157
  Federal Plaza, 152
  Grace Plaza, 152
  Grand Central Station, 135
  Greenmarkets, 68
  homelessness in, 162
  interagency Open Space Task Force, 154
  Jefferson Market Garden, 151
  North Park in Battery Park City, 156
  Playgrounds for All Children, 101
  Seagram Building, 196
  solar access issues in, 161
  use of public spaces in, 134, 135, 136–137
  zoning ordinance of 1961, 25
New York State
  Bronx Zoo, 184
  erosion of Niagara Falls, 234
  farmers' markets in, 61, 64, 73
  Fire Island beach erosion, 257
  playground use in, 86
  reactions to coastal scenes in, 233
New York Zoological Society, 174
New Zealand, playground accidents in, 90
Newspapers, localized editions of, 17–18
Niagara Falls, erosion of, 234
Nicholson, M., 265
Nicholson, S., 114, 167
Nielsen, J. M., 296
Nieman, T. J., 233
Nonuse of public spaces, 57, 152
Nordhaus, R. S., 108
Nordin, C., 79
North Carolina
  Cape Hatteras National Seashore, 268
  Joyce Kilmer/Slickrock area, 281, 293
  waterfront boardwalk in Manteo, 156
Nostalgia and illusions of public life, 25–26
Novelty and familiarity, in urban perceptions, 44–45

Nuisances, and perception of
    environmental quality, 47–48

Odeum, E. P., 226
Odum, H., 268
Ohio, economic areas of Columbus, 259
Oliver, S. S., 234
Olmsted, F. L., 196, 198, 199
Olweg, K. R., 100
Oostendorp, A., 33, 36, 38, 39, 40, 41, 42
Openness
    in farmers' market sites, and contact with nature, 68–69
    as spatial variable, 45
Order and complexity, in urban perception, 41–44
Oregon
    farmers' markets in, 62–64
    plaza in Portland, 163, 198
    Portland Women's Night Watch, 138
    Rogue River, 290
    windsurfing on Hood River, 224, 246
O'Reilly, J., 173–188
Orlick, T., 110
Osgood, C. E., 40
Ostroff, E., 102
Outdoors, children's use of, 84–85. *See also* Playgrounds
Ownership of space, 152
    and public access to aquatic environments, 222
    real, 164–165, 167
    symbolic, 165, 167

Palmer, J., 195, 224, 225
Panda protection in China, 267
Parks as human ecosystems, 255–273
Parks in urban areas, 193–214
    active recreation in, 195, 204
    behavior-based trends in planning of, 195–198
    changing concepts of, 194–195
    cultural programs in, 198
    diversification in, 196–197
    factors affecting use of, 194–195
    Franklin Park, Boston, 198–207
    future directions for design of, 213–215
    history of, 15
    interpretive projects in, 197–198, 204–205
    Lowell historical park, Massachusetts, 207–213
    passive experiences in, 195, 203–204

Participation in design, and user satisfaction, 157–158, 166–169
Parton, W., 268
Pateman, C., 139, 158
Paths
    importance in cognitive learning, 34
    in playgrounds, 108
Paxson, L., 121–142
Pearlman, K. T., 51
Pease, R. L., 64
Pederson, A., 64, 71
Peiss, K., 121
Pelsue, N. H., 74
Pennsylvania
    Civil War battle exhibits in Gettysburg, 198
    farmers' markets in, 58, 59, 65
    Hershey chocolate factory, 198
Personality, and recreation behavior, 231
Personalization of public spaces, 162–164
    movable furniture in, 162, 167
Peskin, S. M., 207
Petersen, J., 94, 96
Pickup, L., 127
Piercy, M., 142
Pitkin, H. F., 123, 124
Pitt, D. G., 217–247
Place, concepts of, 2
Plattner, S., 58, 65
Play for All program, 102
Playgrounds, 83–114
    adventure
        activities in, 90–91
        adult participation in, 98
        manipulative settings in, 113–114
        play value of, 93–999
    animals in, 112
    children with disabilities in, 101–102
    clubhouses in, 91, 95
    contemporary, activities in, 90
    criticism of, 83
    designer involvement in, 106
    diversity in, 91–92, 95
    entrance/exit settings in, 107
    equipment and structures in, 109–110
    fences, enclosures, and barriers in, 109
    fieldhouse and storage settings in, 114
    gardening in, 112
    gathering places in, 114
    groundcovers and safety surfaces in, 110–111
    information exchange on, 105–106
    landforms/topography in, 111

Index

Playgrounds (Cont.)
  leadership and animation needs in, 103–105
  and mobile play programs, 104
  multipurpose games in, 110
  national action program for, 102–103
  natural settings in, 100–101
  pathways in, 108
  patterns of play in, 92–93
  preventive risk management in, 105
  public/private partnership in, 106
  recommendations for, 102–114
  research findings in, 85–102
  safety of, 83–84, 87–90
  sand, dirt, and soil in, 113
  signage and display settings in, 108
  social integration in, 99–102
  stage settings in, 114
  and studies of play settings, 90–91
  traditional, activities in, 91
  trees and vegetation in, 111
  use of, 86–87
  water in, 112–113
Plazas
  control of space in, 167–168
  design for public use, 196
Pliskin, J., 180
Polanyi, K., 79
Pollution, affecting water-based recreation, 239
Population density
  in urban areas, 32
  various countries compared, 17
Portland Women's Night Watch, 138
Power of Place, Los Angeles, 142
Prairie national park in Kansas, 268
Privacy, and perception of crowding, 282–284
Private enterprises, compared to public services, 24
Private property
  buildings with open spaces, 154
  and public access to aquatic environments, 222
Private realm
  compared to public life, 20
  intrusions into public one, 22–23
  intrusions of public into, 20–21
  definition of, 123
Privatization of public spaces and society, 13, 149, 161
Produce markets, 58
Project for Public Space, 74, 136–137, 155, 157

Property rights, and public access to aquatic environments, 222
Proshansky, H. M., 283
Prus, R., 149
Psychological aspects
  in aquatic environment preference, 227
  in control of public space, 156–157
  in water-based recreation, 231, 232–234, 245
Public interests in public space, 150–154
Public life
  compared to neighborhood life, 25
  compared to private realm, 20
  historical aspects of, 14–20
  images of, 8–10
  intrusions into private realm, 20–21
  nostalgia and illusions of, 25–26
  relation to public environment, 7–8
Public services, compared to private enterprise, 24
Puerto Rico, gardens in, 159
Purcell, A. T., 33, 44
Pyle, J., 58, 72, 76

Rabb, G., 174, 178, 180
Radio, public expression in, 18
Rainwater, C., 102
Rape, and fears of women, 128–129, 141
Rapoport, A., 19, 46, 50, 155
Recommendations for future design and research, 26–28, 48–53
  in control of public spaces, 168–169
  for farmers' markets, 76–79
  for managing parks as human ecosystems, 271–272
  for playgrounds, 102–114
  for urban parks, 213–215
  for water-based recreation, 242–247
  for wilderness management, 294–297
  for women's use of public spaces, 137–142
  for zoological parks, 185–188
Recreation
  in playgrounds, 83–114
  in shopping activities, 149
  water-based, 217–247
Redfield, R., 257
Reed, T., 177
Refuge, as spatial variable, 45, 226
Reinhardt, H., 177
Reiter, R., 124
Rhoads, D., 184
Ricklefs, R. E., 260

Riger, S., 128
Rijnen, J., 99
Riley, R. B., 27
River floating
　crowding affecting, 236, 237, 238
　group affiliation in, 235
　motivations for, 232, 233
Rivlin, L., 134
Robertson, I., 257
Robinette, G., 108
Robinson, E., 180
Rodale, R., 73
Rogers, H. T., 76
Roggenbuck, J. W., 234, 238, 240, 293
Rogue River, Oregon, 290
Romesburg, H., 268
Roper, J., 180
Rosa, E. A., 260
Rosaldo, M. Z., 123
Rosenfeld, S., 178, 179, 181, 183
Rothman, S. M., 126
Rouse Company, 11
Rowe, C., 22
Roy, E. P., 64, 71
Rudofsky, B., 9
Rural areas, contact with city dwellers in farmers' markets, 67
Russell, J. A., 33, 36, 39, 40
Rutherford, G., 90

Saegert, S., 125, 127, 140, 156
Safety
　and perceptions of women, 128–129, 141
　of playgrounds, 83–84, 87–90
　and use of public space, 165
Sagoff, M., 221
San Francisco
　children's use of outdoors in, 84, 86
　environmental simulations in, 166
　farmers' market in, 67, 74
　interagency groups for public space policy, 154
　solar access issues in, 161
San Francisco Zoo, 184
Sand, as play material, 113
Sandia Mountains, New Mexico, 281
Sanoff, H., 106
Savanna landscapes, reactions to, 226
Scheppele, K. L., 128
Schicker, L., 112
Schneekloth, L., 101
Schooler, C., 127

Schools Council, 83
Schreyer, R., 231, 232, 242, 244, 292, 295
Schroeder, H., 160, 165
Scott, J. W., 124
Screven, C., 179
Seamon, D., 70, 149
Sebba, R., 83
Segal, J. L., 175
Segmentation of society, exclusionary actions in, 26
Sennett, R., 8, 10, 15, 149
Serra, R., 152
Serrell, B., 180, 181
Sex roles
　in farmers' markets, 78
　and segregation in public spaces, 124, 135
　and separation of spheres in 19th century, 124–125
　See also Women's activities
Sexual assault, and fears of women, 128–129, 141
Shafer, E. L., Jr., 220, 226, 227
Sharistanian, J., 124
Sharpe, G., 197
Shaw, L. G., 101
Shelby, B., 236, 244, 246, 286, 287, 289, 292, 294, 295, 296
Shenandoah National Park, visitor studies in, 264, 266
Shepherd, P., Jr., 225
Sherif, M., 77
Shettel-Neuber, J., 176, 179, 183, 185, 186
Shier, H., 94
Shining Rock area, crowding in, 293
Shopping
　in farmers' markets. See Farmers' markets
　and grocery stores as social centers, 60
　recreational, 149
　and women's use of public space, 128, 134–135
Shopping malls
　affecting street life, 22
　communal role of, 18–19
Silverstein, M., 65, 66
Simonton, D. K., 50
Simulations, environmental, affecting design, 166
Sitte, C., 8, 16, 225
Skyway systems, affecting street life, 22
Smith, G. F., 44
Smith-Rosenberg, C., 126

Index

Smithson, P., 15
Social and economic principles of organization, comparison of, 13
Socialization
  in playgrounds, 99–102
  by women, 127
Socioeconomic factors, in participation in water-based recreation, 228–230
Sociophysical factors in urban perceptions, 50–51
Solar access, as issue in public spaces, 161
Solitude in wilderness areas, 277–297
Sommer, R., 57–79, 162, 167, 181, 184
Sonnenfeld, J., 230, 231, 233
Space, concepts of, 2
Spatial variables in urban perceptions, 45
Sports parks, 197
Stainbrook, E., 225
Stankey, G. H., 237, 243, 277–297
Stansell, C., 121, 124, 125, 126
Steele, L., 139
Stevenage New Town study of playground use, 86
Stewart, J., 165
Stokols, D., 282, 291
Storr, R., 152
Street life
  loss of, 21–22
  as urban pathology, 15, 21
Streets
  American interest in, 16
  and character of urban areas, 32
  control and design of, 167
  realities of scenes in, 11–12
Style, architectural, symbolic meanings of, 46–47
Suburbs and small towns, public life in, 16
Sullivan, J. W., 69
Sumner, L., 284
Supermarkets, 58, 60
  compared to farmers' markets, 65–66
Susquehanna River inflow to Chesapeake Bay, 223
Sutherland, A. T., 94
Sutton-Smith, B., 107
Sweden
  Main Square in Malmoe, 26
  play leadership and animation in, 104
  playgrounds adjacent to Tanto Estate blocks, 86
  study of Stockholm housing estates, 103
Sweeney, T., 84, 87
Sweet, M. L., 59

Tabibian, J., 27
Talbot, J. F., 195, 196
Taylor, S., 65
Technology levels, in water-based recreation, 223–224, 236–237
Television, public expression in, 18
Tennessee
  Citigo Creek wilderness area, 281
  farmers' markets in, 65
  imageable elements in Chattanooga and Knoxville, 36
  Joyce Kilmer/Slickrock area, 281, 293
Territoriality
  characteristics of, 157
  and concepts of privacy, 283
Texas
  farmers' markets in, 58, 64
  waterfront park in San Antonio, 196–197
Theatre groups, public performances of, 18
Theme markets. *See* Festival markets
Thomsen, C. H., 106
Thoreau, H. D., 278
Time of day, and women's use of public space, 137
Timson, R., 176
Titre, J., 237, 238
Toronto
  public spaces used by women, 135, 141
  waterfront park in, 196–197
Transformations of public life, 7–28
  and changes in esthetic values, 49–50
  in commerce and pleasure, 11–12
  in community affairs, 10–11
  in family and neighborhood life, 12–13
  historical aspects of, 14–20
  images and illusions in, 8–10
  in types of public spaces, 150
Transportation modes used by women, 127–128
Travel by women, 127–128
Tuan, Y. F., 233
Tuolumne River, dam in, 279
Turnage, J., 185
Tuttle, P., 47
Twight, B. W., 245, 288
Tyburczy, J., 61, 79
Tyler, T. R., 156
Tyrwhitt, J., 9

Udd, E., 239
Ulrich, R., 38, 46, 156, 160, 165, 182, 183, 187, 224, 225, 227

United Kingdom
  Department of Environment, 84
  Handicapped Adventure Playground Association in England, 101
  play leadership and animation in, 104
  playground use in London, 86
  Zoological Society in London, 174
Urban areas
  cognition in, 32–36
  control of public space in, 147–169
  elements in identity of, 34
  esthetics in, 33, 36–48
  evaluation of public places in, 31–53
  farmers' markets in, 57–79
    contact with rural residents in, 67
  land occupied by, 32
  parks in, 193–215
  playgrounds in, 83–114
  population density in, 32
  realities of street scenes in, 11–12
  selection as setting for life, 19
  streets defining character of, 32
  women's activities in, 121–142
Use of public spaces, 136–137, 149
  factors affecting, 136–137
  needs of users in, 152
User control of public spaces, 147–169
Utah, river recreation in, 231

Van Vliet, W., 84, 164
Vanek, J., 128
Vaske, J. J., 232, 233, 235, 237, 238, 291
Vayda, A. P., 259
Vegetation
  in playgrounds, 111
  reactions to, 165
Venezuela, study of building recall in Ciudad, 35
Verderber, S., 178
Verkerk, J., 91
Vermont, farmers' markets in, 74
Vernez-Moudon, A., 150
Vidler, A., 26
Virginia
  Colonial Williamsburg, 198
  Shenandoah National Park visitor studies, 264, 266
Virunga National Park in Zaire, 266–267
Visibility and isolation in public, 10
Visual access, and use of public space, 164

Visual qualities
  in aquatic landscapes, 227–228
  in scene judgments, 38
Von Bertalanffy, L., 267–268

Wagar, J. A., 285
Wakeman, B. N., 182
Wandersman, A., 157
Wann, J. L., 78
Warner, M., 136
Warner, S. B., 23, 156
Washington
  Alpine Lakes wilderness area, 281
  Cascades National Park, 263
  Mt. St. Helen eruption, 257
  Pike Place Market, Seattle, 65, 71, 74
Water
  in playgrounds, 112–113
  in zoological parks, 183
Water-based recreation, 217–247
  age factors in, 229, 241
  attraction of, 224–228
    dimensions of, 225–228
  boundary issues in, 223
  characteristics of participants in, 228–231
    childhood experiences, 231
    culture and ethnicity, 230
    psychological aspects, 231
    socioeconomic, 228–230
  common property and public trust in, 222–223
  conflicts in, 242
  encounters with others in, 236–238
  experience level in, 232–233, 241, 245
  familiarity affecting, 233
  geographic scale in, 220
  group behavior in, 234–236, 246
  individual differences in, 244–245
  information programs in, 233–234
  institutional characteristics of, 221–223
  management strategies in, 239–240
  motivations in, 232, 245
  multiple jurisdictions in, 223
  negative externalities in, 220–221
  perception of water quality affecting, 238–239
  perceptual clues in, 219–220
  physical characteristics of, 219–221
  physical setting affecting, 238–239, 243–244
  preservation values in, 221

Index

Water-based recreation (*Cont.*)
  psychological aspects of, 231, 232–234, 245
  research needs in, 242–247
  satisfaction measures in, 243
  scenic value of, 224–225
  social context of, 234–238
  technological adaptations in, 223–224, 236–237, 241–242, 246
  transaction of people and environment in, 218–219
  trends in, 240–242
Waterfowl hunting
  crowding affecting, 236
  motivations in, 232
Waterfront park developments, 197
Weinberg, G. M., 268
Wekerle, G. R., 122, 134, 135, 140, 141
Wellman, J. D., 229, 230, 233
Welter, B., 124
Wendling, R. C., 230
West, P. C., 288
West Virginia
  Dolly Sods wilderness area in, 281, 291
  farmers' markets in, 57
Westin, A. F., 283, 288, 291
Westland, C., 104, 112
Wheeler, L., 177, 178
White, J., 181
White, L., Jr., 257
White, M., 12
White, R. W., 156
Whitehead, A. N., 85
Whyte, W. H., 52, 74, 121, 134, 137, 140, 148, 152, 155, 167, 195
Wiedermann, D., 164, 165
Wilderness Act of 1964, 277, 280, 295
Wilderness areas, 277–297
  appropriate levels of others in, 286–287
  behavior of others in, 287–290
  carrying capacity model of, 284–286
  and crowding as evidence of others, 290–292
  dilemma of management in, 280–282
  future directions of research in, 294–297
  historical aspects of, 278–280
  increased usage of, 281–282
  management of crowding in, 292–294
  and model of privacy and crowding, 282–284
Wiley, W., 68
Wilkinson, P. F., 85, 106

Williams, D. R., 244
Williams, M. L., 235
Winkel, G., 47
Wisconsin, farmers' markets in, 58
Wohlwill, J. F., 36, 37, 39, 42, 44, 46, 48, 50, 52
Wolf, P., 27
Wolf, R., 178, 180, 181, 183
Womble, P., 237, 238, 286
Women's activities, 121–142
  and characteristics of public spaces, 131–137
    control and roles of entry, 131–134
    diversity of users, 136–137
    location, 134
    physical design, 134–136
    portrayal of women, 135–136, 139
  conceptual framework for studies, 130–131
  employment in, 125–126
  in farmers' markets, 78
  fear of crime in, 128–129, 141
  harassment in, 129–130
  historical aspects of, 122–126
  household work in, 123–125, 127
  participation in public sphere
    in contemporary context, 126–142
    in 19th century, 125–126
  recommendations for, 137–142
    design, 140–142
    education, 138
    policy directions, 139–140
  restricted mobility, in 130
  safety issues in, 165
  and separation of sexes and spaces, 123–124
  in 19th century, 124–125
  socialization in, 127
  travel in, 127–128
Wood, D., 83, 113
Woodcock, D. M., 45
Woodmansee, R., 270
Wortman, C., 156
Wright, R. G., 268, 269

Yampa River, Utah, 231
Yellowstone National Park
  establishment of, 279
  visitor studies in, 264, 265
Yoesting, D. R., 231
Yosemite National Park, 279
  density and crowding in, 286
Young, G. L., 260

Zaire, Virunga National Park in, 266–267
Zimring, C., 105
Zoning codes
　effects of, 15–16, 21
　incentive formulas in, 22–23
Zoological parks, 173–188, 197
　animal–environment research in, 175–177
　contemporary context of, 174–175
　future directions of research in, 185–188
　historical aspects of, 173–174
　staff–environment research in, 185
　visitor–environment research in, 177–185
　　circulation in, 179

Zoological parks (*Cont.*)
　visitor–environment research in (*Cont.*)
　　demographics in, 177–178
　　educational efforts in, 181–182
　　exhibit behavior in, 182–184
　　graphics in, 179–181
　　motivation in, 178
　　orientation in, 178–179
　　visit outcomes in, 184–185
Zoological Society of London, 174
Zube, E. H., 1–4, 16, 27, 38, 50, 51, 150, 152, 155, 183, 186, 226, 229, 230, 231, 234, 244